AF166744

THE LAW OF STRANGERS

From the Nuremberg Trials to contemporary human rights, Jews have long played prominent roles in the making of international law. But the actual ties between Jewish heritage and legal thought remain a subject of mystery and conjecture even among specialists. This volume of biographical studies takes a unique interdisciplinary approach, pairing historians and legal scholars to explore how Jewish identities and experiences shaped modern legal thought and activism. Using newly discovered sources and sophisticated interpretative methods, this book offers an alternative history of the twentieth-century international legal profession – and a new model to the emerging field of international legal biography.

James Loeffler is Jay Berkowitz Professor of Jewish History at the University of Virginia and former Dean's Visiting Scholar at the Georgetown University Law Center. He is the author of *Rooted Cosmopolitans: Jews and Human Rights in the Twentieth Century*.

Moria Paz is a Fellow at the Center for National Security and the Law at the Georgetown University Law Center and a Fellow at the Stanford Law School, and the author of the forthcoming book, *Network or State? International Law and the History of Jewish Self-Determination*.

The Law of Strangers

JEWISH LAWYERS AND INTERNATIONAL LAW IN THE TWENTIETH CENTURY

Edited by

JAMES LOEFFLER
University of Virginia

MORIA PAZ
Georgetown University and Stanford University

CAMBRIDGE
UNIVERSITY PRESS

University Printing House, Cambridge CB2 8BS, United Kingdom

One Liberty Plaza, 20th Floor, New York, NY 10006, USA

477 Williamstown Road, Port Melbourne, VIC 3207, Australia

314-321, 3rd Floor, Plot 3, Splendor Forum, Jasola District Centre, New Delhi - 110025, India

103 Penang Road, #05-06/07, Visioncrest Commercial, Singapore 238467

Cambridge University Press is part of the University of Cambridge.

It furthers the University's mission by disseminating knowledge in the pursuit of education, learning and research at the highest international levels of excellence.

www.cambridge.org
Information on this title: www.cambridge.org/9781316506028
DOI: 10.1017/9781316492826

© Cambridge University Press 2019

This publication is in copyright. Subject to statutory exception and to the provisions of relevant collective licensing agreements, no reproduction of any part may take place without the written permission of Cambridge University Press.

First published 2019
First paperback edition 2022

A catalogue record for this publication is available from the British Library

Library of Congress Cataloging in Publication data
NAMES: Loeffler, James Benjamin, editor. | Paz, Moria, editor.
TITLE: The law of strangers : Jewish Lawyers and International Law in the Twentieth Century / edited by James Loeffler, Moria Paz.
DESCRIPTION: New York : Cambridge University Press, 2019. | Includes bibliographical references and index.
IDENTIFIERS: LCCN 2019008805 | ISBN 9781107140417 (hardback)
SUBJECTS: LCSH: International law – History – 20th century – Biography. | Jewish lawyers – History – 20th century – Biography. | International law – Religious aspects – Judaism.
CLASSIFICATION: LCC KB259 .L39 2019 | DDC 341.092/3924–dc23
LC record available at https://lccn.loc.gov/2019008805

ISBN 978-1-107-14041-7 Hardback
ISBN 978-1-316-50602-8 Paperback

Cambridge University Press has no responsibility for the persistence or accuracy of URLs for external or third-party internet websites referred to in this publication, and does not guarantee that any content on such websites is, or will remain, accurate or appropriate.

לאיליי, אביגיל ואלכסנדר אהובי נפשי.
  – M.P.

For my parents.
  – J.L.

Contents

Acknowledgments   *page* ix

About the Contributors   xi

Introduction   1
James Loeffler and Moria Paz

PART I HERSCH ZVI LAUTERPACHT   21

1   The "Natural Right of the Jewish People": Zionism,
    International Law, and the Paradox of Hersch Zvi Lauterpacht   23
    James Loeffler

2   A Closet Positivist: Lauterpacht between Law and Diplomacy   43
    Martti Koskenniemi

PART II HANS KELSEN   49

3   Assimilation through Law: Hans Kelsen and the Jewish
    Experience   51
    Eliav Lieblich

4   Philosophy beyond Historicism: Reflections on Hans Kelsen
    and the Jewish Experience   82
    Leora Batnitzky

PART III LOUIS HENKIN   91

5   Louis Henkin, Human Rights, and American
    Jewish Constitutional Patriotism   93
    Samuel Moyn

6   Constitutionalism, Human Rights, and the Genealogy
    of Jewish American Liberalism   118
    William E. Forbath

    PART IV EGON SCHWELB   141

7   The *Via Media*: Egon Schwelb's Mid-century Stoic Legalism
    and the Birth of Human Rights Law   143
    Mira Siegelberg

8   "Emotional Restraint" as Legalist Internationalism: Egon
    Schwelb's Liberalism after the Fall   167
    Umut Özsu

    PART V RENÉ CASSIN   175

9   A Most Inglorious Right: René Cassin, Freedom
    of Movement, Jews, and Palestinians   177
    Moria Paz

10 There's No Place Like Home: Domicile, René Cassin,
    and the Aporias of Modern International Law   204
    Nathaniel Berman

    PART VI SHABTAI ROSENNE   219

11 Shabtai Rosenne: The Transformation of Sefton Rowson   221
    Rotem Giladi

12 Shabtai Rosenne: A Personal Aspect   249
    Philippe Sands

    PART VII: JULIUS STONE   255

13 Enabling and Constraining: Julius Stone and the
    Contradictions of the Sociological Path
    to International Law   257
    Jacqueline Mowbray

14 An Axionormative Dissenter: Reflections on Julius Stone   284
    David N. Myers

Index   296

Acknowledgments

This book grew out of a conversation between the editors that began at an Association for Jewish Studies conference panel in Boston many years ago. We pondered what insights might emerge from exploring international legal history from the particular perspective of the Jewishness of some of its most prominent makers in the century spanning the 1870s to the 1970s. We wondered as well where a deliberate interdisciplinary pairing of historians and legal scholars in self-conscious dialogue might lead. This original conversation turned into a long-running inquiry. Subsequent conference sessions at the Law and Society Association, Brandeis University, and the Fritz Thyssen Stiftung further refined the book's conception.

Along the way, we have incurred a variety of debts to individuals and institutions. We thank first and foremost our contributors for their extreme forbearance and flexibility in undertaking this decentralized, collective endeavor. Without benefit of ever having all met in one place at one time, they have responded with enthusiasm and understanding to the logistical demands of our book-development process. Though outside the formal process, David Luban served as a wonderful interlocutor, while Leora Bilsky, A. Dirk Moses, and Annette Weinke shared key thoughts about the problem of writing Jewish international legal history. We also benefited from the work of other scholars who first imagined what Jewish international legal history might look like, including, among others, Martti Koskenniemi, Pnina Lahav, Reut Paz, and Phillipe Sands.

We are grateful to the University of Virginia Graduate School of Arts and Sciences for financial support and Stanford University Law School. We are especially thankful to Dani Bernstein for her expert editorial assistance in the early stages of the project. At Cambridge University Press, we thank John

Berger and Joshua Penney, as well as Puviarassy Kalieperumal and Silvia Glick.

The cover photograph comes from the Soviet Jewish photographer Evgeny Khaldei, who chronicled the Nuremberg Trials. The image of a prosecutor's desk, showing the physical traces of justice in progress, absent the individuals who perform that work, testifies to the elusive character of biography in international law's past. For permission to use the cover image by Evgeny Khaldei, we thank his daughter, Anna Khaldei, and Claartje van Dijk and the International Center for Photography.

We kindly acknowledge Oxford University Press for permission to reprint materials in chapter eleven.

Finally, we would like to thank our families, who have lived with the making of this book. They were a constant reminder of how much our world of ideas is ultimately inseparable from the lives we live together with the people we love most.

About the Contributors

Leora Batnitzky is Ronald O. Perelman Professor of Jewish Studies and a Professor of Religion at Princeton University.

Nathaniel Berman is Rahel Varnhagen Professor of International Affairs, Law, and Modern Culture at Brown University.

William E. Forbath is Lloyd M. Bentsen Chair in Law and Associate Dean for Research at the University of Texas at Austin Law School.

Rotem Giladi is Research Associate at the Simon Dubnow Institute in Leipzig, a Docent in International Law at the Erik Castrén Institute of International Law and Human Rights at the University of Helsinki, and an adjunct professor of Law at the Hebrew University in Jerusalem.

Martti Koskenniemi is Professor of International Law and Director of the Erik Castrén Institute of International Law and Human Rights at the University of Helsinki.

Eliav Lieblich is Associate Professor in Law at the Buchmann Faculty of Law of Tel Aviv University.

James Loeffler is Jay Berkowitz Professor of Jewish History at the University of Virginia.

Jacqueline Mowbray is an associate professor at the University of Sydney Law School.

Samuel Moyn is Henry R. Luce Professor of Jurisprudence at Yale Law School and Professor of History at Yale University.

David N. Myers is Sady and Ludwig Kahn Professor of Jewish History at the University of California at Los Angeles.

Umut Özsu is Assistant Professor of Law and Legal Studies at Carleton University.

Moria Paz is a Fellow of the Georgetown Center on National Security and the Law, Georgetown University Law Center and a Fellow of Stanford Law School.

Philippe Sands is Professor of Law at University College London.

Mira Siegelberg is Lecturer in History and Law at Queen Mary University of London.

Introduction

James Loeffler and Moria Paz

We think of international lawyers as "a society of Brahmins," Justice Robert Jackson told the American Society of International Law in an April 1945 lecture, "but it would be nearer the truth to say that it is a collection of pariahs." Jackson's suggestive comment came at a key juncture in the history of international law. Two weeks later, the United Nations Conference on International Organization opened in San Francisco, where the nations of the world gathered to negotiate a legal charter for a new post-war era of global community. The following month Jackson stepped down from his position on the U.S. Supreme Court to begin his tenure as the chief American prosecutor of the Nuremberg trials. Both events combined to form what he called "one of those infrequent occasions in history when convulsions have uprooted habit and tradition in a large part of the world and there exists not only opportunity, but necessity as well, to reshape ... international law."[1]

This kind of change did not come easy. Many obstacles stood in its way. The task of transforming international law, Jackson argued, began with diversifying the profiles of its practitioners. The cozy, insular nature of the profession had long prevented its message from taking root more broadly in society. A generation earlier, he reminded his audience, President Woodrow Wilson had told a meeting of the International Law Society at Paris in 1919 that international law had become the province of an elite sect, "handled too exclusively by the lawyers." In fact, Jackson now explained, the problem ran deeper. It was not merely lawyers, but "a too exclusive group of lawyers," divorced from the rest of society, who had failed to "bring international law out of the closet where President Wilson found it and impress it upon the consciousness of our people."[2] It was the very cloistered elitism of

---

[1] Robert H. Jackson, *The Rule of Law Among Nations, Address Delivered at the American Society of International Law* (April 13, 1945), 10 AM. SOC. INT'L L. PROC., 10, 13 (1945).
[2] *Id.* at 13.

international lawyers that had led to their progressive marginalization. The Brahmins had become pariahs.

In truth, Jackson's remarks belied his own power as well as that of his fellow members of the American Society for International Law. They were much more insiders than outsiders. Jackson himself represented the highest legal authority of the most powerful government in the world at the time. In authoring the International Military Charter, he literally wrote the Nuremberg trials into existence. But in another sense Jackson's 1945 reflections about law and identity do point to a number of perennial questions that scholars regularly grapple with today: Who writes international law? And when and why do they choose to do so? Is international law a product first and foremost of strong, powerful states and their political elites, who selectively consent to constraints on their power or that of their opponents? Or does it emerge from the ranks of the weak and the marginal, state and non-state actors, who seek to realize ideals of justice and community above and beyond the realm of state sovereignty? Is the story of modern international law, in other words, one written by pariahs or by Brahmins?

In the twentieth century, it was above all the Jews who came to embody these questions. In the spring of 1945, when Jackson delivered his remarks, the Allied forces had only just begun to liberate the death camps of Europe. The problem of justice took on a terrible new meaning in light of the Holocaust. After Auschwitz, it was hard not to look at Jews as the ultimate example of a people failed by international law. Their suffering elevated them into the consummate symbol of the universal victim, the quintessential pariah.[3]

Yet the twentieth century was undeniably also an age of distinguished individual Jewish legal achievement. Across Europe, the United States, and beyond, Jewish lawyers made dramatically outsized contributions to international law in the fields of human rights and humanitarian law, genocide and atrocity law, and legal philosophy. Some of these individuals are well known today, including many recognized titans in the annals of international law, such as Thomas Buergenthal, Louis Henkin, Rosalyn Higgins, Hans Kelsen, Hersch Zvi Lauterpacht, and Lassa Oppenheim. Other figures continue to command a select measure of public attention and even heroic acclaim, such as René Cassin and Raphael Lemkin. Behind them stand a long line of other

---

[3] Hannah Arendt, *The Jew as Pariah: A Hidden Tradition*, 6 JEWISH SOCIAL STUDIES Feb. 1944, at 99.

distinguished Jewish international lawyers, who left deep imprints in the history of law and legal thought even as their names grew obscure over time.[4]

It is easy to chart this pattern of individual Jewish achievement in the realm of international law, but much harder to reconcile this visible success with the image of collective Jewish marginality.[5] A case in point is Nuremberg. Recent years have brought dramatic attention to the impact of a small cluster of European-born Jewish international lawyers on the formulation of international criminal law at the close of World War II. Many commentators explain that their very powerlessness and suffering as victims of war, genocide, and antisemitism impelled these individual Jews to seek remedies in the realm of international justice. As scholars have now documented, figures like Lemkin, Lauterpacht, Sheldon Glueck, and Jacob Robinson operated behind the scenes to draft legal briefs and prosecutorial statements, provide crucial material evidence, and forge the very concepts of "crimes against humanity," the "crime of aggression," and "genocide."[6] They could not have achieved any of this impact were they not granted unprecedented access to the centers of global legal power at the time. Yet in other ways these individuals were also deliberately excluded by the American and British governments on account of their Jewishness. In some cases this discrimination rose to the level of blatant antisemitism that closed off professional pathways and public opportunities.

Hence when surveying the story of Jews and Nuremberg, it is clear that both images are accurate. These Jewish international lawyers were both minority outsiders and individual legal insiders, present and absent at the same time. In

---

4 Among others, these include the likes of Tobias Asser, Norman Bentwich, Yoram Dinstein, Nathan Feinberg, Ernest Frankenstein, Wolfgang Friedmann, Sheldon Glueck, Paul Guggenheim, Georg Jellinek, Erich Kauffmann, Manfred Lachs, Ruth Lapidoth, Max Laserson, Charles-Léon Lyon-Caen, Theodor Meron, Boris Mirkin-Guetzévitch, Marion Mushkat, Emil Stanisław Rappaport, Charles Salomon, Jerzy Sawicki, Stephen Schwebel, Judith Shklar, Louis Sohn, Aron Trainin, and Mark Vishniak.

5 Dietrich Beyrau, *Disasters and Social Advancement. Jews and Non-Jews in Eastern Europe*, OSTEUROPA, 2008, at 25.

6 Michael Marrus, *Three Jewish Émigrés at Nuremberg: Jacob Robinson, Hersch Lauterpacht, and Raphael Lemkin in* AGAINST THE GRAIN: JEWISH INTELLECTUALS IN HARD TIMES, 240 (Ezra Mendelsohn, Stefani Hoffman, and Richard I. Cohen, eds., 2013); Martti Koskenniemi, *Hersch Lauterpacht and the Development of International Criminal Law*, 2 J. INT'L. CRIM. JUST., 810 (2004). See also the recent work of PHILIPPE SANDS, EAST WEST STREET: ON THE ORIGINS OF 'GENOCIDE' AND 'CRIMES AGAINST HUMANITY' (2016) and JAMES LOEFFLER, ROOTED COSMOPOLITANS: JEWS AND HUMAN RIGHTS IN THE TWENTIETH CENTURY (2018).

truth, that tension between exclusion and accomplishment runs through the larger modern story of Jews and modern international law. It is possible to be at once both Brahmin and pariah.[7]

Making sense of those diverse, shifting, and often contradictory Jewish roles in the international legal profession – and the intertwining of personal and professional identities in the creation of international law – are the twin goals of this book. We wish to explore the undeniable interaction between Jewish minority experience and international legal activism. Yet we also seek to avoid reducing our inquiry to facile clichés or interpretative overreach in pursuit of biographical uniformity for the sake of coherence. In fact, we believe that close examination of the Jewish case invites a larger reconsideration of the intertwined fates of insiders and outsiders, Brahmins and pariahs, lawyers and law in the domain of modern legal history.

That re-evaluation begins with a core set of questions: Does personal biography drive legal thought? Do individual and collective historical experiences leave their marks on the shape of modern law? What constitutes the Jewish "contribution" – a loaded word with its own genealogy – to international law?[8] Is it the sum total of novel legal ideas by individual Jews? The large-scale passage of Jews into specific sectors of the legal profession? Or a narrower subset of legal concepts with discernible Jewish cultural or religious paternities? And who decides? In what follows, we offer a brief

---

[7] A parallel story might be told of Jewish involvement in the Soviet prosecution at Nuremberg. See Francine Hirsch, *The Soviets at Nuremberg: International Law, Propaganda, and the Making of the Postwar Order*, 113 AM. HIST. REV., 701 (2008), and Michelle Jean Penn, The Extermination of Peaceful Soviet Citizens: Aron Trainin and International Law (2017) (unpublished Ph.D. dissertation, Univ. of Colorado at Boulder). On the related story for Communist Poland, see TADEUSZ CYPRIAN AND JERZY SAWICKI, PRAWO NORYMBERSKIE (1948), JERZY SAWICKI, LUDOBÓJSTWO: OD POJECIA DO KONWENCJI, 1933–1948 (1949), MARION MUSHKAT, POLISH CHARGES AGAINST GERMAN WAR CRIMINALS SUBMITTED TO THE UN WAR CRIMES COMMISSION (1948), and MARION MUSHKAT, THE PROTECTION OF HUMAN RIGHTS (1948).

[8] *See* THE JEWISH CONTRIBUTION TO CIVILIZATION: REASSESSING AN IDEA (Jeremy Cohen & Richard Cohen, eds., 2008). Jeffrey Shandler describes the Jewish practice of "inventorying" as a "hallmark of modern Jewish culture, which also engages the modern practice of celebrity, [and] involves listing renowned or accomplished Jews: great theologians, writers, military heroes, scholars, politicians, artists, athletes. This is a totemic practice, providing Jews with rosters of worthy members of their people parallel to emblematic lists of other peoples." Jeffrey Shandler, Keepers of Accounts: The Practice of Inventory in Modern Jewish Life, Address before University of Michigan for David W. Belin Lecture in American Jewish Affairs (Mar. 11, 2010) (transcript available at the Jean & Samuel Frankel Center for Judaic Studies), http://hdl .handle.net/2027/spo.13469761.0017.001.

survey of prior key attempts to answer these questions, before proceeding to discuss the organization and main conclusions of this book.

***

Any discussion of Jews and international law must begin by confronting a basic paradox of Jewish history. Modern Jews hailed from an ancient religious civilization suffused by law and legal consciousness. From Abraham's famous arguments with God through the legal contractual structure of Biblical theology to the sanctification of law itself in Rabbinic Judaism, Jews imagined the world in terms of a comprehensive legal humanism. Furthermore, from antiquity onward Jews found themselves deeply engaged with world events and global empires, whether in their ancient homeland or in centuries of diasporic exile. Yet at the same time the immense written record of Jewish thought displays virtually no interest in the concept or practice of international law. Even in more recent times, when Jews found themselves in the heart of an early modern Christian Europe beginning to create the Law of Nations, the rabbis scarcely acknowledged the development. The same held true well into the nineteenth century, as questions of Jewish religious jurisprudence and European civil law acquired urgent political significance. There too neither rabbis nor secular Jewish intellectuals took up the subject of international law. Even as Jews began flocking to the European legal profession in massive numbers in the late nineteenth century, they hardly exhibited conspicuous collective interest in international law. Why, then, did some Jewish attitudes begin to change in the early twentieth century? How do we explain the dramatic boom in international Jewish lawyers that dates from that time and continues up until the present?[9] In what follows, we survey four key approaches to answering these questions: (a) primordialist; (b) modernist; (c) antiquarian; and (d) biographical.

The first author to parse the meaning of this modern pattern of Jewish international lawyering was himself a symbol of it. During World War I, New York international lawyer Arthur Kuhn (1876–1954), one of the founders of the American Society for International Law, set out to investigate the link between Jews and international law. In his 1917 article, "Jewish International Lawyers," published in the leading American Jewish intellectual organ of his day, the *Menorah Journal*, he eagerly catalogued the large number of Jews involved in the international legal profession. Kuhn attributed this

---

[9]   James Loeffler, *"A long Jewish tradition?": The Promise and Peril of Jewish Legal Biography*, to appear in Annette Weinke and Leora Bilsky, eds., ÉMIGRÉ LAWYERS AND INTERNATIONAL LAW, in preparation.

phenomenon to an ingrained "aptitude for controversial reasoning and a keen sense of ethical issues," along with the Jewish outsider mentality, since in international law "there is an especial need for detachment from local viewpoints and the ability to escape in thought from purely national environment."[10]

To explain the disjuncture between the preponderance of modern Jewish lawyering and the evident lack of Jewish participation in the development of Western international legal thought, Kuhn resorted to a rhetorical strategy of historical esotericism. He ascribed a hidden Jewish genealogy to modern international law. Judaic heritage filtered through sixteenth- and seventeenth-century Christian Hebraism had actually produced the key ideas of modern sovereignty and international law. Operating in a period in Western history "in which Christian dogma and formalistic theology ruled upon a narrow and bigoted plane," he explained, the Dutch Christian Hugo Grotius turned to the "ancient Mosaic law," with help from contemporary European rabbis, to find inspiration for his conception of the Law of Nations. The same held true in the other canonical works of Jean Bodin and John Selden. By virtue of their extensive reliance on Jewish religious sources, these Christian legal thinkers "may fairly be referred to as 'Jewish' in the objective rather than the subjective sense."[11] Thus, even if Jews did not directly perform intellectual labor in the workshops of Western legal thought, then, their ideas and their figural presence catalyzed the Western international legal imagination.[12]

In spite of its empirical limitations and apologetic character, Kuhn's idea of a hidden Jewish genealogy to international law has remained an attractive if contentious theme across the twentieth century.[13] The English-born Israeli international lawyer Shabtai Rosenne, the subject of a chapter and commentary in the present volume by Rotem Giladi and Philippe Sands, respectively, pondered the same question repeatedly from the 1950s to the 2000s. Like Kuhn, he gestured, albeit somewhat vaguely, to the Jewish contribution to the late medieval and early modern Christian Protestant formulation of international law as part of "the threefold heritage of the ancient Mediterranean world, the heritage of Rome, Athens, and Jerusalem." Proud as he was of this claim to

---

[10] Arthur Kuhn, *Jewish International Lawyers*, 3 THE MENORAH JOURNAL 274 (1917).

[11] *Id.* at 275.

[12] Besides his amateur legal historical scholarship, Kuhn also joined in one of the first efforts to mobilize international law to combat European antisemitism. *See* ARTHUR KUHN, INTERNATIONAL LAW AND THE DISCRIMINATIONS PRACTICED BY RUSSIA UNDER THE TREATY OF 1832 (1911).

[13] See, for instance, Nathan Isaacs, *The Influence of Judaism on Western Law, in* THE LEGACY OF ISRAEL, 385 (E. Bevan & C. Singers, eds., 1927).

influence, Rosenne acknowledged the paucity of rabbinic discourse on international law. In search of an exception, he pointed to the figure of Benedict (Baruch) Spinoza. This was an odd choice, he conceded, because Spinoza held a reputation as both a renegade Jewish apostate and the author of a "pessimistic," Hobbesian view of international law. Yet Rosenne held out hope that "more thorough research into Spinoza's influence on the development of the philosophy of law and international relations" might yield an image of "these concepts more closely to the relevant Jewish teachings" and certify Spinoza as a proponent of "the international Messianism which has appeared through Jewish thought from the days of the Prophet Isaiah onwards."[14]

In his desire to locate primordial Jewish roots for legal universalism in some esoteric tradition, Rosenne stepped beyond the bounds of available historical evidence. Nevertheless, his genealogical impulse has continued to resonate down to the present. In recent years, political scientists and historians working in the nascent field of Hebraic political studies have revived the search for overlooked Jewish antecedents. Through close rereadings of early modern Christian thinkers, these scholars argue that Western legal thought emerged from a deep European engagement with images and texts drawn from classical Judaism.[15] Meanwhile, working from the other direction, an even newer strain of scholarship has sought to retrace how traditional rabbinic authorities actually approached questions of international law.[16]

---

[14] Shabtai Rosenne, *The Influence of Judaism on the Development of International* Law: *An Assessment, in* RELIGION AND INTERNATIONAL LAW, 71 (Mark Janis & Carolyn Evans, eds., 1999). Rosenne's essay was a revised version of a study he first published four decades earlier as *Hashpa'at ha-yahadut al ha-din ha-beinle'umi*, 3 HA-PRAKLIT, 1957, at 3, and Rosenne, *The Influence of Judaism on the Development of International Law*, 5 NEDERLANDS TIJDSCHRIFT VOOR INTERNATIONAL RECHT 119 (1958). *See also* S. Rosenne, AN INTL. L. MISCELLANY, 509 (1993). For other similar genealogical approaches, *see* Cyril Picciotto, *International Law in Its Bearing upon the Jewish Question*, THE SENTINEL, May 1912, at 9 and Prosper Weil, *Le Judaïsme et le Développement du Droit International*, 151 RECUEIL DES COURS, 252 (1976).

[15] POLITICAL HEBRAISM: JUDAIC SOURCES IN EARLY MODERN POLITICAL THOUGHT (Gordon Schochet, Fania Oz-Salzberger, & Meirav Jones, eds., 2008); ERIC NELSON, THE HEBREW REPUBLIC: JEWISH SOURCES AND THE TRANSFORMATION OF EUROPEAN POLITICAL THOUGHT (2011). All the same, other scholars have argued that the deep pattern of Christian theological antipathy toward Judaism left its traces in early international law. *See* David Kennedy, *Images of Religion in International Legal Theory, in* THE INFLUENCE OF RELIGION ON THE DEVELOPMENT OF INTERNATIONAL LAW, 151 (Mark Janis, ed., 1991).

[16] Amos Yisrael-Flishauer, Ya̲ḥas he-halakhah li-mishpat ha-beinle'umi: nitua̲ḥ ha-pesikah u-netua̲ḥ tehelikhi (2011) (unpublished Ph.D. dissertation, Tel Aviv University); Michael Broyde, *Public and Private International Law from the Perspective of Jewish Law, in* OXFORD HANDBOOK OF JUDAISM AND ECONOMICS, 365 (Aaron Levine, ed., 2010); Ilan Fuchs and Aviad Yehiel Hollander, *National Movements and International Law: Rabbi Shlomo Goren's Understanding of International Law*, 2 J. L. & REL. 29, 301 (2014); Alexander Kaye, THE LEGAL

Rather than define some sort of primordial genealogical relationship between international law and Judaism, another line of inquiry has taken a modernist approach. These scholars have focused on the political and sociological conditions obtaining in nineteenth-century Europe and thereafter as the primary inspiration for the Jewish gravitation to international law as career and cause. Legal historian Pnina Lahav, as one example, has proposed a modernist counter-genealogy to primordialists hunting in the European past in search of forgotten Judaic roots. She suggests that nineteenth- and twentieth-century European Jews turned to international law as a vision for concrete legal protection against state violence and official discrimination on the one hand and a post-traditional utopian re-envisioning of international community on the other:

> My admittedly broad hypothesis is that in the "age of reason," the promise of international law touched a deep chord in the heart of Jewish scholars. The ideal of a law of nations, a government of nations, external and superior to the nation-state, had a very powerful appeal to the recently emancipated Jews. For if a legal system superior to positive municipal law could be constructed, then Jews would find relief from the prejudices and discrimination embedded in that municipal law. Further, the universalist and somewhat Utopian idea of a law of nations and a government of nations invoked the prophetic Jewish yearning for a Messianic age of peace and harmony. I suggest that it was this combination – the relief from prejudicial chauvinism on the one hand, and the yearning for a New World Order on the other – that attracted Jewish students to international law.[17]

Lahav's explanation tracks closely against a larger conventional narrative of international law as an alternative political vision of a supranational authority that would substitute transnational governance for traditional state sovereignty. There is an intuitive logic to this account. Living as a stateless minority in historical diaspora, European Jews were particularly sensitized to issues of modern state power and territorial sovereignty. The more Jews confronted the dramatic expansion of state-driven violence and the perils of statelessness in the twentieth century, the more they imagined international law to be a compelling realm of transnational human community and avenue for global justice. Still, any empirical test of this hypothesis requires grappling with the evident diversity in how Jews actually conceptualized, practiced, and

PHILOSOPHIES OF RELIGIOUS ZIONISM, 1937–1967 (2012) (unpublished Ph.D. dissertation, Columbia University).

[17] Pnina Lahav, *The Jewish Perspective in International Law*, 87 AM. SOC. INT'L L. PROC. 331, 332 (1993).

interpreted international law. In reality, some Jewish lawyers reified sovereignty while others critiqued it – and sometimes the same person did both. Indeed, the familiar image of Jewish legal internationalism must be balanced against the substantial roster of prominent Jewish figures who struck decidedly arch-positivist and sovereigntist positions regarding international law.[18]

Another complicating factor is the that most modern European and American Jews framed their pursuit of political equality *not* in terms of transnational rights but national citizenship. Jewish appeals to the Law of Nations and the Rights of Man came rarely in the long nineteenth century; applications for the Rights of Citizen proved the norm. Even when late nineteenth-century and early twentieth-century Jewish elites in Western Europe and the United States sought to combat persecution of fellow Jews in Eastern Europe and the Middle East, they typically used the power of their own citizenship as the basis for their calls for diplomatic intervention based on bilateral treaties or imperial politics.[19] None of this invalidates the possibility of a sociological basis for the Jewish predilection for international law. On the contrary, it only deepens the need for systematic historical studies of the profession of Jewish international lawyering.

The clash between primordialist and modernist narratives continues to inform much present-day scholarship. At the same time, a third cohort of scholars has adopted a minimalist approach to parsing the meaning of Jewish international lawyering. Rejecting both primordialist and modernist narratives, they dismiss the possibility of explaining the Jewish historic affinity for international law in terms of any shared Jewish values, identities, or interests.[20] They treat Jewish international lawyering as an accident of circumstance best chronicled in

---

[18] Thus, for instance, the internationalist efforts of Lauterpacht in the 1940s and Lemkin in the 1950s were vigorously opposed by the Jewish dean of Yale Law School, Edwin Borchard, one of the leading American international law scholars of his day and a highly vocal isolationist. *See* Elihu Lauterpacht, The Life of Hersch Lauterpacht 188 (2010) and Mira Siegelberg, *Unofficial Men, Efficient Civil Servants: Raphael Lemkin in the History of International Law*, 15 J. Genocide Res. 297, 307 (2013).

[19] Read in this light, the Zionist drive for sovereignty in a Jewish nation-state can be seen not as a rejection of the liberal model but as an attempt to create a political framework in which Jews could realize citizenship precisely along the Western model. *See* Orit Rozin, A Home for All Jews. Citizenship, Rights, and National Identity in the New Israeli State (2016). On Israeli lawyers and international law, *see* Rotem Giladi, A *"Historical Commitment"? Identity and Ideology in Israel's Attitude to the Refugee Convention 1951–4*, 37 Int'l Hist. Rev., 745 (2014).

[20] In the first instance, this is manifested in the decision by some scholars simply to pass over in silence the Jewish identities of some legal luminaries. See, for instance, the absence of Jewishness as a category of analysis in the specific treatment of figures Lassa Oppenheim, Hans Kelsen, and Hersch Lauterpacht in the Oxford Handbook of the History of International Law (Bardo Fassbender & Anne Peters, eds., 2012).

antiquarian fashion without ascribing it larger historical meaning. In his 1999 study of German Jewish international lawyers, Kurt Siehr refuses to speculate "about the Jewishness of private international law and comparative law," on the grounds that doing so would constitute a false concession to "nationalism or racialism in law and justice."[21] Likewise, in their 866-page anthology, *Jurists Uprooted: German-Speaking Émigré Lawyers in Twentieth-century Britain* (2004), the most comprehensive biographical lexicon of Jewish lawyers to appear to date, editors Jack Beatson and Reinhard Zimmermann deliberately reject any link between these lawyers and their Jewish identities. They write: "Jewishness can unambiguously only be defined as a matter of religion. The concept of 'a' Jewish culture ... is an artificial fabrication of anti-Semitic (as well as Zionist) ideology."[22] Zimmermann and Beatson evince anxiety that the sociological study of Jews as an ethnic group shaped by historical experience, cultural traits, or political ideologies equates automatically with racial essentialism. They assert that a fundamental danger inheres in any such investigations. Ironically, however, the solution they offer is to advance the alternative idea that religion is a more stable and less politically dangerous category of analysis and ascription than shared culture.[23] This ignores the fact that religion and culture can hardly be separated by a clear line in Jewish historical experience. Any attempt to do so is itself a product of the post-Enlightenment Western liberal framework, which insisted on stripping Jews of their collective identities as part of a premodern ethnoreligious community in order to integrate them as individual citizens into the modern nation-state. Nor does it do justice to the generations of Jews who have consciously defined themselves as an ethnic group, a secular culture, or a nation.[24]

---

[21] Kurt Siehr, *German Jewish Scholars of Private International Law and Comparative Law – Especially Ernst Frankenstein and His Research*, in MÉLANGES FRITZ STURM: OFFERTS PAR SES COLLÈGES ET SES AMIS À L'OCCASION DE SON SOIXANTE-DIXIÈME ANNIVERSAIRE 1673 (Fritz Sturm & Jean-François Gerkens, eds., 2d. vol., 1999).

[22] UPROOTED: GERMAN-SPEAKING ÉMIGRÉ LAWYERS IN TWENTIETH-CENTURY BRITAIN (Jack Beatson & Reinhard Zimmermann, eds., 2004). A parallel effort in the American context is ERNST C. STIEFEL AND FRANK MECKLENBURG, DEUTSCHE JURISTEN IM AMERIKANISCHEN EXIL (1933–1950) (1991). On the issues of reconstructing the Jewish presence in the German legal profession, see Konrad Jarausch, *Jewish Lawyers in Germany, 1848–1938. The Disintegration of a Profession*, 36 LEO BAECK INST. Y.B., 171 (1991).

[23] As Zimmermann writes elsewhere, "The Jews are the people of the Law. Belief in, and devotion to, justice and scholarship belong to the constituent elements of Jewish identity. Thus, even within a predominantly gentile environment, a strong Jewish community can be expected to render, or to have rendered, a significant contribution to legal scholarship." Reinhard Zimmermann, *The Contribution of Jewish Lawyers to the Administration of Justice in South Africa*, 29 ISR. L. REV. 250 (1995).

[24] On the historiography of Jewish identity, particularly in modern Central Europe, and the methodological challenges involved in its study, *see* PAUL MENDES-FLOHR, GERMAN JEWS:

Ultimately, these attempts at antiquarian anti-essentialism fall back on another potentially more insidious form of soft essentialism.[25] In their case, Beatson and Zimmermann wish to ascribe Jewish lawyers a shared status beyond their mere belonging to the category of Nazi victims. In place of Jewish ethnicity, religion, or nationhood, then, they instead subsume the entire European Jewish experience under the *German* national paradigm. Hence a figure such as Hersch Lauterpacht, whose first three languages were Polish, Yiddish, and Hebrew, whose career in German-speaking legal academia was limited to two years at the University of Vienna (preceded by a Polish legal education and followed by an English law degree), and who left continental Europe two decades before the Holocaust, is treated in their volume as a chapter in transnational German émigré legal history. This raises the disturbing prospect that the very act of retracing the lives of Jewish lawyers requires making them first into Germans, risking the reification of the very nationalism the editors wish to critique.[26]

It seems unlikely that Beatson and Zimmermann consciously aim to perpetuate German nationalism in their biographical catalogue of Jewish lawyers.[27] Yet their ambivalence about Jewishness as a category of analysis suggests deeply rooted, ongoing concerns about Holocaust memory, antisemitism, and the politics of the past.[28] As is well known, Nazi legal theoreticians sought

---

A DUAL IDENTITY (1999); Samuel Moyn, *German Jewry and the Question of Identity: Historiography and Theory*, 41 LEO BAECK INST. Y.B. 291 (1996); and DAVID N. MYERS, RESISTING HISTORY: HISTORICISM AND ITS DISCONTENTS IN GERMAN-JEWISH THOUGHT (2003).

[25] Jack Beatson and Reinhard Zimmerman, *Preface* of BEATSON AND ZIMMERMAN, *supra* note 22, at 2.

[26] Michael Steinberg has noted the problem of an uncritical elision of the distinction "between German culture and German national culture" deriving from the unification of Germany in 1871. "The historiography that does not differentiate historically or critically between Germanness and German nationalism," Steinberg cautions, "takes on a normative investment that finds both Jewish legitimacy and Jewish pleasure in the importance, self-importance, and legitimacy of the German national project." MICHAEL P. STEINBERG, JUDAISM MUSICAL AND UNMUSICAL 188 (2007).

[27] For a discussion of these issues, see Vivian Grosswald Curran, *Voices Saved from Vanishing*, Pitt Law, Legal Studies Research Paper Series Working Paper No. 2009–18, 461 (2009).

[28] Zimmermann writes that, after being mistaken for a Jew in 1980s South Africa on account of his German last name, he "suddenly realized how, for obvious historical reasons, our attitude towards national, racial and religious identity, and towards Jewish identity in particular, has been warped and to what extent we, as Germans, have lost any sense of unselfconscious innocence in these matters." Zimmermann, *supra* note 23, at 250. For the intrusion of these issues directly into Beatson's experience in a different way, see Adrian Cohen, *Top Lawyers Face Scandalous Attacks on Integrity*, THE JEWISH CHRONICLE, Aug. 18, 2016, www.thejc.com/comment/analysis/top-lawyers-face-scandalous-attacks-on-integrity-1.62750; and

to delegitimize law itself by crafting a myth of nefarious Jewish influence in modern German and international law.[29] Hence these contemporary authors struggle with the fine line between highlighting the number of Jews involved in the legal profession and ascribing a fixed meaning or larger Jewish ethos to that dramatic quotient. Counting Jews remains a fraught exercise for scholars.

Truth be told, when it comes to law, all description contains an element of prescription. The primordialist school typified by Kuhn and Rosenne ascribes a Jewish genealogy to international law for obvious reasons of Jewish apologetics and cultural pride. It fits a pattern of Jewish intellectuals seeking to burnish the reputation of Judaism's contemporary relevance and benign influence in moments of crisis and change, such as the aftermath of global war and the dramatic Jewish political events in the Middle East in 1917 and 1948. Lahav's modernist historicist approach might be similarly viewed as reflecting another key moment of change in the post-Cold War era of the early 1990s. As liberal internationalism sought its own deeper origin story in the nineteenth-century march of progress, Jewish international lawyers made for a particularly attractive example of legal idealism personified.

Seeking ways out of these conceptual and methodological cul-de-sacs, a fourth cohort of scholars have turned to the genre of legal biography to isolate the meaning of Jewishness among individual international lawyers. Rather than insist on a single geographical or political context as the determining factor in the shaping Jewish approaches to international law and lawyering, this new biographical approach seeks to recover historically rooted intellectual affinities and subjective understandings without falling into the trap of essentialism. In place of large-scale sociological explanations, it seeks answers in the subtler interplay between critical thought and personal experience. Chief among these efforts is the magisterial legal history of Martti Koskenniemi in his 2004 classic, *The Gentle Civilizer of Nations. The Rise and Fall of International Law 1870–1960*. There, he offers highly textured biographical portraits of a number of pivotal European Jewish thinkers in the twentieth-century international legal field. Building on this work, Reut Paz has provided a granular reading of the identities and ideas of four leading figures in her pathbreaking 2010 study, *A Gateway between a Distant God and a Cruel World: The Contribution of Jewish German-Speaking Scholars to*

Hard-Left Activists Target Judge with "Zionist" Slurs, THE JEWISH CHRONICLE, Aug. 18, 2016, www.thejc.com/news/uk-news/hard-left-activists-target-judge-with-zionist-slurs-1.62752.

[29] RAPHAEL GROSS, CARL SCHMITT AND THE JEWS. THE 'JEWISH QUESTION,' THE HOLOCAUST, AND GERMAN LEGAL THEORY (2007). *See also* DAN DINER, BEYOND THE CONCEIVABLE: STUDIES ON GERMANY, NAZISM, AND THE HOLOCAUST 49 (2000).

International Law.[30] These and other related studies by many of the contributors to the present volume retrace the lives of individual figures both famous and obscure in search of patterns that may explain the emergence of legal cosmopolitanism as a whole and the specific Jewish presence within it. They suggest the possibility of a productive continuum between the two extremes of flattening individual lives into an overly simplified pattern or denying any coherent and unified historical meaning to Jewish collective behavior.

Our approach to Jewish legal history in this volume takes the new legal biography as our point of departure. Yet we seek to extend its conceptual reach by embracing an explicitly multidisciplinary approach. For the turn to biography for international legal history ultimately requires a reckoning with the core theoretical and methodological questions of modern Jewish historiography. Chief among these is the matter of how to relate the whole to the part in terms of representations of the Jewish past. Where precisely does the border lie between an exceptional Jewish life and a Jewish story that can stand in for the larger Jewish experience? How much do the dark shadows of the Holocaust and the enduring Israeli-Palestinian conflict shape our conceptions of Jews and Jewishness in the past? How do we define an idea as "Jewish" or even derived from Jewish experience given the extremely fluid and contingent nature of Jewish identity in the post-Enlightenment period? Legal scholars are of course familiar with these sorts of questions. Yet each academic discipline typically offers different sorts of answers based on its own analytical instruments and methodological assumptions. Hence our dual aim in inviting a roster of colleagues to undertake this book project: to produce a critical group portrait of international Jewish lawyering and to engender an intellectual conversation about how best to write the Jewish legal past.[31]

***

The protagonists of this book are seven individuals who have all came of age between the two World Wars and worked through the heart of the twentieth century: René Cassin, Louis Henkin, Hans Kelsen, Hersch Zvi Lauterpacht, Shabtai Rosenne, Egon Schwelb, and Julius Stone. We choose these men because they share at least three characteristics. First, they were all Jews, both by birth and by self-identification. Their awareness of their own religion and

---

[30] REUT PAZ, A GATEWAY BETWEEN A DISTANT GOD AND A CRUEL WORLD: THE CONTRIBUTION OF JEWISH GERMAN-SPEAKING SCHOLARS TO INTERNATIONAL LAW (2011).

[31] MOSHE ROSMAN, HOW JEWISH IS JEWISH HISTORY? (2007); Jacques Picard, Jacques Revel, Michael P. Steinberg, Idith Zertal, *Introduction: Thinking Jewish Modernity, in* J. Picard et al., eds., MAKERS OF JEWISH MODERNITY: THINKERS, ARTISTS, LEADERS AND THE WORLD THEY MADE (2016), 1–15.

ethnicity, however, varied considerably. Kelsen, for example, converted to Christianity not once but twice in his life, yet asserted that he retained a strong tie to his Jewishness. By contrast, Henkin openly practiced Orthodox Judaism all his life, but insisted that Jewish religion had little bearing on his professional life, including his ideas of international law and human rights.

Second, these individuals are well known today for their dramatic contributions to the development of modern international law. Cassin, Lauterpacht, and Henkin are widely synonymous with the birth and development of international human rights law, while Kelsen is renowned as one of *the* founding fathers of modern legal philosophy. The reputations of Stone, Schwelb, and Rosenne may have diminished over time by comparison, yet they remain remembered in specialist circles as deeply significant figures.

The third characteristic is a by-product of the first two. It involves a selection bias: all the subjects in our book, the earliest generation of Jewish international lawyers, are men. This gendered dimension of Jewish international lawyering may not be surprising. For the international legal profession between the two World Wars was heavily male.[32] But this masculinist culture enveloping international law may also reflect the deeper gendered dynamics of the Jewish pathways into European society.[33]

Starting from these common characteristics, we seek to determine how relevant Jewishness is to an understanding of the roles of these seven legal giants in the making of modern international law. In other words, should these men be recalled today as grand statesmen or academics who transcended their Jewish origins and attachments in their international legal work and public behavior (as in the nineteenth-century maxim to be "a man in the street and a Jew at home")[34], or should their legal achievements be read against individual Jewish biographies, the latter affecting the former?

---

[32]   There is much literature on the gendered aspect of international law., One example: Fareda Banda and Catharine A. MacKinnon, *Sex, Gender and International Law*, 100 Am. Soc. Int'l L. Proc. 243 (2006).

[33]   Reut Paz, *Forgotten Kelsenian? The Story of Helen Silving-Ryu (1906–1993)* 25 Eur. J. Int'l. L. 1123 (2014). See also Sara L. Kimble & Marion Röwekamp, eds., New Perspectives on European Women's Legal History (2017), and Jane Mossman, The First Women Lawyers: A Comparative Study of Gender, Law and the Legal Professions (2006).

[34]   This phrase became the central motif in nineteenth-century European Jewish liberalism, particularly in Russia. As historian Michael Stanislawski points out, however, the original meaning of this phrase was not to partition Jewish particularism and European universalism into private and public, but to argue for an integration of Jews into broader civil society and culture. Hence the very bastardization of the phrase reflects the same process of blanket application of Western liberal categories onto the

Our shared intuition lays with the latter proposition, namely the Jewish identity of our protagonists mattered a great deal in the evolution of their careers and legal ideas. But to test that assumption in a critical manner, we have formulated it in the form of two overarching questions. The first question regards the influence of Jewishness on their personal choice of law and professional practice: Can the legal activity of all of these men be traced back in some finite way to their Jewishness? Is there, in other words, a common Jewish motivation lurking behind the attraction of Cassin, Kelsen, Henkin, Lauterpacht, Rosenne, Schwelb, and Stone to certain international legal doctrines, but not others, leading them to different interpretations of the law, and not to alternative meanings? If yes, does this attraction reflect a generic preoccupation with the fate of the Jews as a people in the broadest sense of the term? Or is it something much narrower, focused on their own particular male lives lived in a specific fifty-year period stretching between the horrors of World War I through World War II and the Holocaust in Europe to the post-war rise of American Jews and the State of Israel?

The second question shifts our focus from causal origins to doctrinal impact: Did the legal activity of these men leave a particularly Jewish footprint on international law? Here, there are at least four alternative answers, each of which in turn generates still further questions:

Yes, by virtue of their Jewishness, Jews altered international law. In light of the extraordinary predominance of these men in the profession during the twentieth century, we might reasonably posit that the international legal order bears the direct stamp of their experience. As such, doctrines that corrected for harms that impacted Jews came to be foregrounded in international law, while other types of harm less immediately relevant to Jewish life, were minimized or maybe even passed over altogether. Hersch Lauterpacht, whom James Loeffler and Martti Koskenniemi analyze in their contributions, offers one possible example of this thesis. Lauterpacht famously crafted Article 6 of the Nuremburg Charter, making crimes against humanity, war crimes, and the crime of aggression formally subject to modern international law. Was it the fact that wartime atrocities were a particularly relevant legal problem for Jewish victims of the Holocaust, including Lauterpacht's very own family, that made atrocity law more salient to him, such that Article 6 was written in a way that responds to needs and experiences that were associated with Jews at that

Jewish historical experience in ways that marginalized Jewishness in the process. See Michael Stanislawski, Yehudah Leib Gordon, www.yivoencyclopedia.org/article .aspx/Gordon_Yehudah_Leib, and MICHAEL STANISLAWSKI, FOR WHOM DO I TOIL?: JUDAH LEIB GORDON AND THE CRISIS OF RUSSIAN JEWRY 50 (1988).

moment? If so, did the widespread international attention given to Article 6, as it exists today, mean that other possible types of harm, such as gender-based violence or economic destruction, were left unattended in the body of the law? Finally, how did Lauterpacht himself conceive of the relationship between the universality of Article 6 and the particularity of Jewish persecution during the Holocaust?[35]

No, their Jewishness did not decisively shape their international legal work. Under this alternative paradigm, the participation of these men in the construction of international law from roughly 1920 to 1980, as dramatic as it was, left behind no significant impact that can be traced back to their shared historical experience, or religious, cultural, or national identity. James Crawford has already identified a fundamental problem with "assigning and measuring influence in international law." The evolution of international law, he argues, ultimately derives from much broader and longer-term processes than can be mapped against any one individual life. Given the "collective character of so much of the work," international legal history is better understood as the product of a large-scale "pattern of practice and language rooted in a long history" than a tale of biographically driven breakthroughs.[36]

René Cassin, as discussed below by Moria Paz and Nathaniel Berman, and Louis Henkin, as explored by Samuel Moyn and William Forbath, are interesting in this respect. Both men were Jewish, and were both publicly linked with Jewish political life. At the same time, both were widely credited with the birth, development, and systemization of human rights law. But were the two causally connected? Are not international human rights doctrines simply too big and complex to be traceable back to the biography of either man? In the case of Henkin, moreover, he explicitly denied any link between his traditional religious Judaism and his ideas of international human rights. As such it seems plausible to explain his legal thought more by reference to his status as a proud American immigrant than his Jewish background and his deep knowledge of the corpus of rabbinical law. Was his Jewishness really relevant to his legal thought? Cassin, meanwhile, often foregrounded his Jewishness in his discussions of human rights. Indeed, as Paz and Berman explain, his vocal

---

[35] Something of this tension is captured in the argument of Nathan Feinberg that the legal concept of "genocide" should not necessarily be seen as a Jewish contribution to international law: "Although the extermination of millions of Jews by the Nazis was undoubtedly one of the factors which prompted the Polish-Jewish jurist Raphael Lemkin, at the height of the Second World War, to create the term 'genocide,' the term cannot be counted among those originating in the Jewish question, as there were many earlier precedents in history." Nathan Feinberg, *New Terms Created in Public International Law by the Jewish Question*, 8 IN THE DISPERSION (1968), at 73.

[36] James Crawford, *Public International Law in Twentieth Century England*, in BEATSON AND ZIMMERMAN, *supra* note 22, at 700.

positions on antisemitism and Zionism colored many of his later public legal engagements. Yet he came to his Jewish political identification only in the second half of his life, without the benefit of significant prior exposure to traditional Jewish religion and culture, and belatedly ascribed Jewish significance to his human rights work decades after it began. Thus despite his own claims to the contrary, Cassin's ideas may owe more to his French Republicanism and World War I military experience than his ancient Provençal Jewish roots or Dreyfus-era experience of antisemitism.

Indeed, if we take Crawford to his ultimate conclusion, the individual biographies of both Henkin and Cassin, whether that of a Jew or an immigrant, a Zionist or a French liberal, might be of little importance. Ultimately, states sign laws that reflect their needs and interests. In that sense, the individual preferences of the woman (or man) holding the drafting pen remain circumscribed by the larger government which they represent.

No, their Jewishness did not affect their international lawyering, but instead their legal work shaped their approaches to Jewish politics and communal life. We are accustomed to seek evidence of how individual agency reshapes legal doctrine. But in the Jewish case, it might be just as possible to speak of the opposite effect: how international law structures the practices and ideas of Jewish selfhood and society. Thus, for instance, wherever these men began on the continuum of their Jewishness, ultimately all, with one exception, Kelsen, as detailed by Eliav Lieblich and Leora Batnitzky, came to embrace Zionism or Jewish territorial nationalism, as one if not the only paradigmatic form of viable Jewish political identity. Moreover, all, again with Kelsen as an outlier, became active in supporting the Zionist endeavor to varying degrees. Was their political nationalism a product of their legal internationalism? In other words, did the very territoriality of modern international law – a system firmly entrenched in state-based territorial exclusivity as a criterion for a legitimate political action – affect their embrace of the (territorial) sovereign form as the ultimate mode for organizing Jewish politics?[37] As for Kelsen, and even arguably others discussed in this volume, moreover, we might posit that the lived experience of participation in the socio-professional fraternity of international lawyers led to a conscious detachment from various forms of political and religious group identification, Jewish and otherwise. In this reading, it was not Jews that lent international law its cosmopolitan flavor as much as international law that made certain Jews into cosmopolitans.

---

[37] On this, *see* MORIA PAZ, NETWORK OR STATE? INTERNATIONAL LAW AND THE HISTORY OF JEWISH SELF-DETERMINATION (forthcoming).

Yes and no, these three alternatives are not mutually exclusive. All of the preceding possibilities may be true to some extent for the seven men portrayed here. Or their shared Jewishness may not be isolatable as a discrete combination of traits and factors. Perhaps, we are dealing here not with a shared Jewish element but rather only with an overlapping "family resemblance," to use Ludwig Wittgenstein's formulation. No one factor applies to every international lawyer who is Jewish, yet still enough overlapping and criss-crossing features are distributed in their collective biography to permit a coherent description of them as Jewish international lawyers. "In spinning a thread we twist fibre on fibre," writes Wittgenstein, and "the strength of the thread does not reside in the fact that some one fibre runs through its whole length, but in the overlapping of many fibres."[38]

In foregrounding the Jewishness of our seven protagonists and reading their legal work against their biographies, this book tackles these questions head on. But it does not provide definitive answers regarding the fibers linking Jewish international lawyers to the law. Instead we offer insights on these questions in relationship to each individual. The larger meaning of these insights, crucially, we choose to leave deliberately open-ended. Rather than searching for conclusive, definitive answers, we hope to generate a framework for thinking about how to chart the historical intersections and intellectual transactions between Jews and international law. This framework, we hope, might profitably be used as a prospective model for further inquiries about culture and legal biography involving different collectivities such as minorities, religious diasporas, and corporations.

The methodological framework we adopt for our inquiry is an interdisciplinary dialogue among a carefully selected slate of international lawyers and historians. These contributors are divided into two groups. Members of the first cohort have been tasked with preparing a case study on one of these legal subjects: Moria Paz on René Cassin, Eliav Lieblich on Hans Kelsen, Samuel Moyn on Louis Henkin, James Loeffler on Hersch Lauterpacht, Rotem Giladi on Shabtai Rosenne, Mira Siegelberg on Egon Schwelb, and Jacqueline Mowbray on Julius Stone.

Each of these authors had freedom to choose the particular substance of her or his paper. Some begin from the protagonist. Others from the law. Some authors, moreover, focus on a specific doctrine. Others explore the entire body of law that is associated with the protagonist of their chapter. But they all put the individual's background and law in a dialectical relationship: They probe the biographical context of these Jewish men, and the professional and

---

[38] Ludwig Wittgenstein, *Philosophical Investigations* (1974), #67.

political projects that each tried to advance through his practice. They map out why each of these men came to endorse a particular legal position or argument at a distinct period or place and query how, if at all, this is connected to his Jewish identity, however defined.

In researching and writing their pieces, we invited the authors to engage with a set of questions: How and why did these Jewish men gravitate to international law as a profession and political ideal? What was the political and biographical context in which they worked? How did their identities – ethnic, cultural, gender, sexual, linguistic, national, religious, political, economic – shape their imagination of the modern international legal regime? How did international law impact their personal lives, gendered identities, and larger political projects? How did they view the risks and rewards of their turn to the law, both in their own personal life and career goals, and, more generally, in light of what they set out to achieve?

Importantly, at the same time that we encouraged the authors to place each protagonist within the context of his Jewishness, we also asked them to be mindful of reductionism. Our interest is in the ways in which Jewish lawyers are similar and, equally, in the ways they are not – those instances where their engagement with the law was idiosyncratic and reflected more their own particular dispositions, career possibilities and choices, and their personalities, rather than a common Jewishness.

Members of the second group, in turn, have been asked to complement the essays written by the first cohort with specially prepared commentaries. The slate here includes Nathaniel Berman on Paz, Leora Batnitzky on Lieblich, William Forbath on Moyn, Martti Koskenniemi on Loeffler, Philippe Sands on Giladi, Umut Özsu on Siegelberg, and David Myers on Mowbray. Much as with the first cohort, each commentator was too invited to choose his or her own entry point into the scholarly discussion. But, again similar to the authors of the different chapters, we have also asked our commentators to dialectically engage with the link between legal agency and particular influence on the law. Their results reflect a similarly diverse set of approaches, concerns, and attitudes toward the topics at hand.

In constructing this list of authors and commentators, we have deliberately matched a lawyer with an historian. Thus our biographical subjects are all examined from the methodological vantage points of both law and history. To enhance further the interdisciplinary value of this blended model of legal history, we have specifically asked the commentators not only to address the substance of each intellectual portrait, but also the aesthetics and methods of the discipline. Hence, our volume opens outward to the larger question of what is gained and what is lost by applying historical or legal lenses to the past.

In addition, we have also matched scholars spanning different states and at various stages of their academic careers. The authors in the book represent a range of different ethnic and religious backgrounds. This blend across countries, cultures, and seniority, we hope, will spark conversations on international law that are truly transnational and transcultural in nature.

Ultimately, this book is an attempt to discern some of the sources of modern international legal creativity. Our method will have been successful in so far as we lead the reader to understand the legal work and position of René Cassin, Hans Kelsen, Louis Henkin, Hersch Lauterpacht, Shabtai Rosenne, Egon Schwelb, and Julius Stone by grounding it in their real life and in reference to the contextual background from which their work arose. By this, we mean those moments when each of these legal giants participated in a larger trend of Jewish contributions to the law, *and* also those instances when each individual made his own decisive break with his peers or other legal community and struck out in pursuit of fresh ideas about international law. For the story we narrate is both one of deep continuities and profound ruptures, possibilities and structural limitations, sameness and difference, individual initiative and large-scale social forces. Like international law itself, the lawmaking contributions of these titans – much like our own efforts to contextualize their work today – are both reflections of humanity and conscious attempts to change it.

PART I

HERSCH ZVI LAUTERPACHT

1

The "Natural Right of the Jewish People"

Zionism, International Law, and the Paradox of Hersch Zvi Lauterpacht

James Loeffler

INTRODUCTION

In July 1948, while on a lecture tour in Colorado, Hersch Zvi Lauterpacht, the Whewell Chair of International Law at the University of Cambridge, received two urgent letters. The first was from the fledgling State of Israel, locked in a bitter war of independence against its Arab neighbors. The Israeli government now faced a new legal challenge. The Syrians had sought a ruling from the International Court of Justice invalidating the legal basis for the Jewish State's Declaration of Independence. The Israelis turned to Lauterpacht to ask what they should do.[1] Almost to the day this request for help arrived, Lauterpacht received a similar entreaty from the tiny Indian Principality of Hyderabad. This princely kingdom had the misfortune of being located physically in the heart of the new Union of India. With a population that was 85 percent Hindu and a Muslim ruler reputed to be the richest man in the world, Hyderabad had attempted to maintain its independence, declining to join either Pakistan or India. Now, as it faced the threat of Indian armies massing on its borders, its legal team contemplated a last-ditch effort to seek a legal injunction from the International Court of Justice or the UN Security Council securing its recognition as an independent state.[2]

From his hotel room, Lauterpacht hastily dispensed legal advice in the form of a memo for each case. To Hyderabad's attorneys, he advised that prospects for full political independence were unlikely. But he endorsed the idea of

---

[1] Letter from Jacob Robinson to Hersch Zvi Lauterpacht (July 16, 1948) (Lauterpacht Family Archive, Cambridge, England). Hereinafter, LFA.

[2] On the dilemmas of Hyderabad's claims to independence and the changing meaning of state sovereignty in the decolonizing moment, *see* Eric Lewis Beverly, Hyderabad, British India, and the World: Muslims Networks and Minor Sovereignty, c. 1850–1950, 50–74, 86–93 (2015).

securing a legal injunction against forcible conquest. Above all, he concluded, such a legal maneuver might help in the crucial larger arena of "international opinion."[3] To the Israelis, Lauterpacht gave the opposite advice. He recommended that they avoid the International Court if at all possible, telling them, "There is little doubt that the real purpose of the Syrian proposal ... is an attempt to challenge the entire jurisdiction of the United Nations on the issue of Palestine ... It is an attempt to overthrow a political and legislative decision of the General Assembly." Even though "there are good reasons for increasing the activity of the Court wherever opportunity offers," he wrote, neither the Court's "authority" and "reputation," nor that of the United Nations, as well as the cause of Jewish statehood, would be well served by its intervention in the Arab–Israeli dispute, a matter "which lies so conspicuously on the borderline of law and a most intractable problem of politics." Most important, Lauterpacht stressed, the Israelis should *appear* publicly willing to use the Court and project confidence about their chances in the event that their Arab opponents succeeded in bringing the case. In the realm of international politics, appearances were everything.[4]

On the face of it, it is not hard to reconcile these divergent responses by Lauterpacht. Both countries possessed strong claims to independence. Hyderabad had been its own state for over 200 years, after all. Israel had the UN Partition Resolution. Yet each faced very different geopolitical realities. The British government had turned down Hyderabad's request for diplomatic assistance. The princedom was largely left on its own. Israel had already secured recognition from the United States (de facto) and the Soviet Union (de jure). In each case, Lauterpacht acknowledged the justness of law and simply conceded the presence of politics in determining legal strategy.

Yet from another angle, Lauterpacht's divergent 1948 opinions also prove quite perplexing, even paradoxical. So too are his comments therein about law and politics. This was, after all, the renowned legal authority – named by many as "the greatest international lawyer of the 20th century" – who had spent decades arguing that international affairs could not be divided into separate political and legal precincts.[5] He had staked his entire career, in fact, on the

[3] My account of the Hyderabad case is based on the documents presented in ELIHU LAUTERPACHT, THE LIFE OF SIR HERSCH LAUTERPACHT 312–23 (2010).

[4] Hersch Lauterpacht, *Memo to the Provisional Government of Israel*, July 1948, LFA. See the reply in Letter from Jacob Robinson to Hersch Lauterpacht, July 21, 1948 (Israel State Archives, HL 00071706.81.D4.E4.CF).

[5] Philippe Sands, *The Memory of Justice: The Unexpected Place of Lviv in International Law – A Personal History*, 43 Case W. Res. J. Int'l. L., 739 (2010–2011). *See also* Philippe Sands, *My Legal Hero: Hersch Lauterpacht*, THE GUARDIAN, Nov. 10, 2010, www.theguardian.com/law/

proposition that, as he wrote in 1933, "all international disputes are, irrespective of their gravity, disputes of a legal character . . . capable of an answer by the application of legal rules."[6] Further, in 1947 he had written a whole book about the recognition of new states in international law. There he argued that the existing community of nations had an automatic positive obligation to recognize newly declared states, regardless of politics.[7] Now, he essentially dismissed Hyderabad's claim to independence. Meanwhile, the Zionist cause he deemed more just – but better left outside the judicial realm as too political. To top things off, he insisted that his involvement in the legal work for the Israelis remain strictly confidential.

How do we explain these contradictions between theory and reality, law and politics, for Lauterpacht? In this chapter, I address this question and at the same time ask us to reconsider the larger intertwined histories of Zionism and international law through the prism of legal biography. More specifically, I argue that a closer look at Lauterpacht's unpublished writings reveals three points all but forgotten today in the writing of international legal history:

1. The large-scale gravitation of Jews to international law in the twentieth century may seem in retrospect like a familiar story of Jews and cosmopolitan liberalism. But it can be equally, and perhaps better, understood as a forgotten chapter in the history of Jewish nationalism.

2. The common assumption that Zionists turned to legal sovereignty as a particularistic response to the failure of international law to protect Jews in the global arena is inaccurate. Instead, we do better to see Zionism and international law as co-constitutive historical phenomena, emerging out of the same moment of *fin de siècle* legal modernism.

3. When we seek to find the ideational sources for the revolution in twentieth-century international legal thought, including the revival of natural law and the rejection of legal positivism, we must take seriously the fact that one key locus for the birth of legal idealism lay precisely in the Zionist political imagination.

2010/nov/10/my-legal-hero-hersch-lauterpacht. Stephen Schwebel uses similar language in his book jacket blurb for LAUTERPACHT, THE LIFE OF SIR HERSCH LAUTERPACHT: "Hersch Lauterpacht was widely and rightly regarded as the greatest international legal scholar of the 20th century."

6　HERSCH LAUTERPACHT, THE FUNCTION OF LAW IN THE INTERNATIONAL COMMUNITY 158 (1933).

7　HERSCH LAUTERPACHT, RECOGNITION IN INTERNATIONAL LAW (1947).

EVERYWHERE A STRANGER?

The story of Jewish legal internationalism is often told as a classic example of a strategy by a persecuted, stateless minority group attempting to restrain the power of the modern state. Again and again, we read of how European-born Jewish lawyers wished to break the sovereign mold and introduce a new model of international law. Victims of anti-Semitism, statehood, and nationalism *in extremis*, they rejected both nation and state along with conventional sovereignty.

The many recent accounts of Lauterpacht's life and career exemplify this narrative of Jewish legal cosmopolitanism. Born in Habsburg Galicia in 1897, he studied law in Lemberg, took his doctorate in Vienna under Hans Kelsen, and then pursued further academic training in London. Thereafter, Lauterpacht rose quickly in British academia and international legal circles. He became one of the premier exponents and defenders of international law in the 1930s, advised the Americans and the British on the legality of the Lend-Lease Act, overturned the Defense of Superior Orders in British military law, conceived the legal concept of Crimes against Humanity for the Nuremberg Trials, and published one of the first proposals of what became the International Bill of Human Rights. Overall, he was singularly responsible for piercing the veil of state sovereignty, which allowed the entire field of public international law to develop in its modern form. He finished his career as a judge on the International Court of Justice in The Hague, before his premature death in 1960.

Lauterpacht's chroniclers emphasize that his intellectual move away from positivism to an idealist legal liberalism can be explained in large part as owing to his Jewishness. Having come face-to-face with the merciless forces of East Central European nationalist politics and violence in a crumbling multinational empire, he preached the gospel of international law as a necessary constraint on state power. A man who lost much of his family in the Holocaust, he charted new territory in terms of human rights, international law, and transnational criminal justice. Hence throughout his book-length meditation on the parallel lives of Lauterpacht and Raphael Lemkin, Philippe Sands stresses the experience of Jewish victimhood as the determining factor in the attraction of Jews to international law.[8] A similar interpretation surfaces in Oona Hathaway and Scott Shapiro's large-scale study of interwar legal internationalism, in which they introduce Lauterpacht, whom they laud as

---

[8] *See* PHILIPPE SANDS, EAST WEST STREET: ON THE ORIGINS OF 'GENOCIDE' AND 'CRIMES AGAINST HUMANITY' 19–20, 71 (2016).

the founder of the "New World Order," by way of a simple shorthand as "a Jew whose family was murdered in the Holocaust."[9] In his magisterial survey of the history of international law, Martti Koskenniemi reads Lauterpacht's embrace of a utopian, idealistic vision of "legal cosmopolitanism" as a strategy for "assimilation" into British society and a product of the "traditional Jewish association with liberal rationalism and individualist – hence cosmopolitan – ethics."[10] Owing to his "inter-European" status, we read in Yasuo Kita's dissertation, Lauterpacht represents "a proto-type of post-war modern international legal thought." "Jewishness implied European internationalism at that time," Kita adds, and hence Lauterpacht "tried to sublimate his Jewishness to [sic] the universal value."[11] In Michael Ignatieff's influential account, Lauterpacht and Lemkin were both men without countries who in the absence of nationhood lived out their lives in the bosom of international law: "[B]oth these men found a home in the law, and their passionate attachment to international law was a consequence of their homelessness anywhere else."[12]

There are certainly ways in which we could map these cosmopolitan readings on to Lauterpacht's legal internationalism. Indeed, read from one angle, his entire life's work was an extended argument for the reality of international law against the critiques of political realists and legal positivists. In his 1945 classic, the *International Bill of the Rights of Man*, he explains that the revival of natural law in the early twentieth century came as a direct response to the expansion of state power and the resurgence of "pagan absolutism as perfected in the German state."[13] He goes on to say that the purpose of law is to address "the ultimate unit of all law," which is the individual: "The law of nations and, we may say, the law of nature, by denying, as they needs must do, the absolute sovereignty of State, give their imprimatur to the indestructible sovereignty of

---

9   OONA A. HATHAWAY AND SCOTT J. SHAPIRO, THE INTERNATIONALISTS: HOW A RADICAL
      PLAN TO OUTLAW WAR REMADE THE WORLD XXI (2017).
10   MARTTI KOSKENNIEMI, THE GENTLE CIVILIZER OF NATIONS: THE RISE AND FALL OF
      INTERNATIONAL LAW 1870–1960 371 (2001).
11   Yasuo Kita, Sir Hersch Lauterpacht as a Prototype of Post-War Modern International Legal
      Thought: Analysis of International Legalism in the Universalization Process of the European
      Law of Nations 30 (2003) (Unpublished D.Phil. thesis, Law Department, University of
      Durham).
12   Michael Ignatieff, *Lemkin's Word*, THE NEW REPUBLIC, Feb. 26, 2001, at 26. For a similar
      treatment of Lemkin and Lauterpacht, *see* ANA FILIPA Vrdoljak, *Human Rights and
      Genocide: The Work of Lauterpacht and Lemkin in Modern International Law*, 4 EUR.
      J. INT'L. L., 1163 (2009).
13   HERSCH LAUTERPACHT, AN INTERNATIONAL BILL OF RIGHTS 40 (1945).

'man.'"[14] This humanistic defense of the individual against statist ideologies and realpolitik charts closely with Western liberalism. And in contrast to this focus on the individual's place in international law, Lauterpacht actually says relatively little about the "national" component of the modern state or collectivist identities.

It is therefore easy to assume that Lauterpacht was uninterested in, if not hostile to, nationalism. And yet there is the inconvenient fact of Lauterpacht's Zionism. As a young man during and immediately after World War I he founded several Zionist youth organizations. He contemplated aliyah (immigration to the Land of Israel) seriously enough to volunteer himself directly to the Zionist Executive for that purpose in 1920.[15] Even as he ultimately chose to remain in England and embarked on his rise in the ranks of legal academia, he continued to serve as a London correspondent for the Polish Zionist daily newspaper, *Nowy Dziennik*. Over the course of nearly fifteen years, he contributed hundreds of articles and feuilletons about the state of British and Jewish politics. He founded the World Union of Jewish Students in 1924 and led it through the next decade. In that capacity, he escorted an international delegation of 200 Jewish students to Palestine in 1925 to attend the opening of the Hebrew University of Jerusalem. While there, he joined Alfred Einstein, Haim Nachman Bialik, and other Zionist luminaries in laying the groundwork for the college's first Jewish residential dormitory, the "House of the Jewish Student."[16] From the 1930s through the 1940s, he consistently advised the Jewish Agency and the World Jewish Congress on legal matters involving partition and statehood. In 1948, he authored an important draft of the Israeli Declaration of Independence. He maintained close personal relations with several leading Zionist figures, visited Israel regularly, and contemplated retirement there.

Of course, one could easily overstate a causal linkage between Lauterpacht's Zionism and his vision of legal internationalism. Indeed, one way to look at Lauterpacht is to say that there no such connection exists. Zionism, according to that reading, simply represents a relic of his earlier past or an emotionalist concession to his social justice concerns and the impact of the Holocaust on him. This is the tack taken by his son Elihu Lauterpacht in his biography of his father. There, Lauterpacht's Zionism appears as little more than a matter of vestigial ethnic pride, an essentially private matter unconnected to his ostensibly apolitical career. Evidently concerned about current trends in Israeli

[14] *Id.* at 6, 49.
[15] Letter from Hersch Lauterpacht to the Zionist Executive (June 10, 1920) (LFA).
[16] Letter from Hersch Lauterpacht to Leon Lauterbach (Jan. 21, 1926) (LFA).

politics, Elihu takes pains to emphasize how his father's Zionism was driven by selfless ideals of social justice.[17] Sands, too, suggests that from his youth onward Lauterpacht "feared nationalism" and sympathized with his fellow Jews who opposed "Zionism as a form of abhorrent nationalism ... [He believed] a Jewish state in Palestine would inevitably oppress Arab inhabitants."[18] Meanwhile, Reut Paz, in her major study on key Jewish figures in international law, presses hard on the Jewish cultural and theological dimensions of Lauterpacht's legal thought, only to conclude that:

> The Jewish assimilation, as experience by Hersch Lauterpacht, was a more modern version of a Maskil's type: a Jew at home and a cosmopolitan outside in the world. Although Jewish nationalism (i.e. Zionism) was, figuratively speaking, in his blood, it too remained, most of the time, within the boundaries of the home.[19]

Thus Lauterpacht's biographers assume this active Zionist commitment simply vanished from his life and thought. Even Koskenniemi, who offers the most sustained engagement with Lauterpacht's Zionism, nevertheless positions it in opposition to his liberal cosmopolitanism. He terms Lauterpacht's Zionism an "essentially reactive" form of self-defense against "German and Austrian anti-Semitism." Strikingly, Koskenniemi concedes the strangeness of this narrative:

> It might seem curious that an active Zionist during the second decade of the 20th century was transformed into a cosmopolitan individualist during the third. However (at least part of) Jewish nationalism had been essentially reactive and had arisen to combat German and Austrian antisemitism. What Viennese Zionists such as Theodor Herzl – or Lauterpacht – wished to create was a secular, liberal democratic State; in this they were opposed by the rabbis and the religious right. When the protective need for a national Jewish State no longer seemed pressing – after Lauterpacht came to Britain – Zionism could transform back into a cosmopolitan ethos that was the natural home of the Jewish enlightenment. It was not until the oppression of German Jewry began that an extreme protective need arose anew.[20]

---

[17] Lauterpacht *supra* note 3, at 428: "Once he left Poland, where he had been politically active in the sense of pursuing his Zionist interests and organizing his contemporaries to resist local anti-Semitism, Hersch had little time for politics."

[18] SANDS, *supra* note 8, at 70.

[19] REUT PAZ, A GATEWAY BETWEEN A DISTANT GOD AND A CRUEL WORLD: THE CONTRIBUTION OF JEWISH GERMAN-SPEAKING SCHOLARS TO INTERNATIONAL LAW 198 (2012).

[20] KOSKENNIEMI, *supra* note 10, at 406.

The problem with this explanation is that we know too much about the history of Zionism to see it merely as a reactionary defense against anti-Semitism. Historians of Jewish politics have of late traced a much tighter, even symbiotic relationship between European liberalism and Jewish nationalism.[21] As a result, we cannot casually situate Zionism on one end of a static dichotomy between universalism and particularism.[22] Nor, for that matter, can the Jewish Enlightenment be understood as a pure expression of individualistic rationalism devoid of strong Romantic notions of peoplehood.[23] Painting Lauterpacht as an arch-cosmopolitan errs by virtue of projecting contemporary assumptions and anxieties about Zionism and international law back into a much earlier period. It further ignores the fuller history of Lauterpacht's Zionist legal thought – and falls prey to his own concerted efforts to conceal this part of his professional life. Dismissing or glossing over Lauterpacht's Zionism, we do more than ignore an interesting political wrinkle. We also risk missing the distinctive character of his Jewish legal internationalism. In Lauterpacht's mind, the twin projects of Jewish state-building and modern international law not only coincided temporally; they also informed one another directly.

Part and parcel of Koskenniemi's explanation of Lauterpacht is that he remained, in the final analysis, a nineteenth-century "rational man," inspired by a Victorian British ideal of law as a civilizing process and the British empire as an agent of historical progress. The British model of political empire was transmuted into an empire of global law. I agree that Lauterpacht idealized the nineteenth-century British Empire (and the Austrian *rechstaat* to a lesser extent) as a model for international society.[24] Yet the man who in the 1940s appeared to Isaiah Berlin as a quintessentially "dull" Cambridge scholar concealed a rich parallel life as a passionate, charismatic Jewish political

---

[21] MICHAEL STANISLAWSKI, ZIONISM AND THE FIN DE SIÈCLE: COSMOPOLITANISM AND NATIONALISM FROM NORDAU TO JABOTINSKY (2001); ARIE DUBNOV, ISAIAH BERLIN. THE JOURNEY OF A JEWISH LIBERAL (2012); and NOAM Pianko, *Cosmopolitan Wanderer or Zionist Activist? Sir Alfred Zimmern's Ambivalent Jewishness and the Legacy of British Internationalism*, 4 AB IMPERIO, 211 (2009).

[22] KENNETH MOSS, JEWISH RENAISSANCE IN THE RUSSIAN REVOLUTION (2009); DAVID N. MYERS, BETWEEN JEW AND ARAB: THE LOST VOICE OF SIMON RAWIDOWICZ (2008); NOAM PIANKO, ZIONISM AND THE ROADS NOT TAKEN. RAWIDOWICZ, KAPLAN, KOHN (2009); MICHAEL L. Miller and SCOTT Ury, *Cosmopolitanism: the end of Jewishness?* 3 EUR. REV. HIST.: REVUE EUROPEENNE D'HISTOIRE, 337 (2010).

[23] OLGA LITVAK, HASKALAH: THE ROMANTIC MOVEMENT IN JUDAISM (2012).

[24] For a useful discussion of other possible intellectual influences on Lauterpacht, *see* ROMAN Kwiecień, *Sir Hersch Lauterpacht's Idea of State Sovereignty – Is It Still Alive?* 13 INT'L. COMMUNITY L. REV., 25 (2011).

leader.[25] The evidence for the ongoing, extensive interplay between those two sides of Lauterpacht is considerable enough that we cannot simply treat them as chronologically distinct periods in his life or as separate personal and professional spheres. Hence, in the present chapter, I want to present, as it were, a unified model of Lauterpacht. My approach begins with an alternative locus for the source of Lauterpacht's internationalist imagination, one that speaks to emotionalism and romanticism as much as Austrian rationalism and British moralism. That missing piece of the puzzle of Lauterpacht's legal imagination is his Polish Zionism.

A POLITICAL LIFE

There is no question that, as Elihu Lauterpacht's biography makes plain, his father led an active career in Zionist youth politics in Austrian Poland during World War I and its immediate aftermath. Beginning in 1915, he assumed leadership roles in a number of Socialist Zionist groups in Lemberg. The national revival of the Hebrew language, Jewish minority rights in the emerging post-imperial states of Eastern Europe, and a future national homeland in the historic territory of Palestine were central planks in this Zionist platform. Lauterpacht's private correspondence, a large portion of which is also included in the biography's capacious array of primary sources, already testifies to his deep attraction to *eretz-yisrael*, the historic Land of Israel.[26] Many scholars have assumed that his settlement in England in 1923 marked the beginning of the end of his Zionist politics. From then on, Koskenniemi writes, in concurring with Elihu's biography, Lauterpacht "assimilated with post-war liberal internationalism, letting his Jewish background resurface only incidentally."[27]

Still, if we peer a bit more deeply into his remaining unpublished correspondence and other archived papers, we find plenty of evidence to suggest that Lauterpacht's Zionism did not wane. In 1923, he wrote to his future in-laws of his strong desire to settle in Israel, "whose future is the future of all of us."[28] He hoped to find a job in the British Mandatory administration or else embark on a career as an independent lawyer.[29] While a student at University

---

[25] Letter from Isaiah Berlin to his parents (Oct. 17, 1942), *in* ISAIAH BERLIN. LETTERS, 1928–46, 411 (Henry Hardy, ed., vol. 1, 2004).
[26] *See, for instance,* the Hebrew- and Yiddish-language letters between Lauterpacht and his wife from the 1920s, in the LFA.
[27] KOSKENNIEMI, *supra* note 10, at 371.
[28] Letter from Hersch Lauterpacht to Mikhl and Gitl Steinberg (Feb. 7, 1923) (LFA).
[29] *Id.*

College of London, he served as President of the Zionist Section of the Jewish Student Union and in the leadership of the all-England University Zionist Federation.[30] In the spring of 1924, Lauterpacht addressed 2,000 people at the opening congress of the World Union of Jewish Students in Antwerp. Speaking in a combination of Hebrew, Yiddish, and French, he called for "cultural and national co-operation between all the Jewish students throughout the world," a "Hebrew University" and Jewish national library in Jerusalem, and a "Jewish University in Europe."[31] He took pains to dispel the impression held by some at the time that "the only objective of the Congress was a demonstration against University anti-Semitism."[32] The larger aim of this student movement, he announced, was to pursue "political and legal action as can be based on public law and international treaties, and by appealing to public opinion" to ensure the "adequate protection of the rights of Jewish students at the Universities."[33]

Beyond these goals, Lauterpacht made one other controversial statement at the Antwerp gathering. "You, Zionists" in the audience, he declared, "must ensure that the World Union is created and remains apolitical, because this is a Zionist task: to organize the Jewish people and to unite them in the struggle for a better future." Lauterpacht's exhortation signaled an expansive notion of what Jewish internationalism meant to him in the mid-1920s. All Jews, led by the vanguard of enlightened Zionists, would look beyond anti-Semitism and party politics to a cosmopolitan notion of Jewish nationalism. Yet the socialist groups at the Congress seized on these very words as proof positive that the whole effort was a plot by their Zionist rivals to nationalize Jewish youth. A heated debate ensued. Despite the best efforts of Lauterpacht to convince his socialist peers that he intended the organization to be agnostic on intra-Jewish political conflicts, critics denounced the "Bourgeois, nationalist-chauvinist Congress."[34]

Undeterred, back in England Lauterpacht continued his pursuit of a Zionist internationalism that would unite all Jews into a single global framework. A few months later, he addressed the Inter-University Federation

---

[30]   University Zionist Federation, Report of First Executive Meeting, Jewish Student Union (March 1924) (LFA).

[31]   *Jewish Students' World Congress*, JEWISH CHRONICLE, May 2, 1924, at 17; *Jewish Students' World Congress*, JEWISH CHRONICLE, May 9, 1924, at 17.

[32]   Hersch Lauterpacht, The World Union of Jewish Students (unpublished manuscript) (LFA).

[33]   *Jewish Students' World Congress*, JEWISH CHRONICLE, May 9, 1924, at 17. For further details on the events, *see Der Weltkongress juedischer Studenten*, JUEDISCHE RUNDSCHAU, May 9, 1924, at 268.

[34]   Aryeh Tseytlin, *1-er alveltel. idish. studenten-kongres*, HAYNT, May 13, 1924, at 2.

of Jewish Students of Britain and Ireland during a summer retreat.[35] Urging the audience not to succumb to "British insularity" when contemplating their own Jewish identities, he declared, "By listening to the lecture you have stated implicitly that matters of Jewish interest do not end at the frontiers of this country, that for you the Jewish international unity is a living thing." This "Jewish unity," he stressed, was far different than mere "philanthropic or humanitarian aid when necessary for the Jewish co-religionists" around the world. Further, it could not be argued by logic, since this unity is "a matter of feeling and sentiment stronger than ourselves."[36] When he is honest with himself, he continued:

> The young Jew recognizes that he . . . is a member of two communities. He is bound to one with the memories of his life, with language, custom, education, with the ties of state and citizenship, he is bound with the other with memory of his past, with the elements of his blood, with the indestructible use of his most inward mental – and some say – physical structure. He cannot, if he is true with himself, disregard this second, Jewish, community. Call this community 'nation,' call it 'people,' call it 'race,' 'religion,' call it simply 'community,' call it as you like. Strive to realize the ideals of this community through the medium of a political State of your own as the Zionists do, strive to fulfill its commandments as Children of Israel taking in dispersion God's word as other Jews do – the World Union does not deride it . . . The World Union of Jewish Students is neither a religious, nor a national, nor a racial body – it is Jewish.[37]

With these impassioned words, he dismissed worries about dual loyalty and allegations of a narrow "nationalistic" agenda. But his pluralism had its limit. The greatest danger to Jews and Jewish honor, he told his fellow students, lay in the form of two specific groups: the "assimilationists" and the Marxist "Bundists." Each denied that a global Jewish nation existed. Each violated the principle of internationalism. The whole point of the World Union, by contrast, was to secure the "living foundation of world-embracing Jewish-community."[38]

Behind Lauterpacht's awkward locution lay a distinct vision of international Jewish collectivity. By disclaiming a partisan position and asserting what he

---

[35] A *Leamington Diary*, 1 BULLETIN OF THE INTER-UNIVERSITY FEDERATION OF JEWISH UNIVERSITY STUDENTS OF BRITAIN AND IRELAND, Nov. 1924, at 19.

[36] LAUTERPACHT, *supra* note 32.

[37] *Id.*

[38] Lauterpacht's conflict with Bundists grew out of a large controversy at the Antwerp conference, when Bundist representatives challenged the leadership over both its Zionist objectives and its decision to sing the political anthem "Hatikvah." *See Der Weltkongress juedischer Studenten*, JUEDISCHE RUNDSCHAU, May 9, 1924, at 268.

claimed was a neutral category of Jewishness itself, he advanced an argument for the reality of Jewish nationhood. To fill the yawning Jewish gap in the family of nations, Jews must assert their legal personality in the international order. Just as the liberal lawyer must defend the reality of the Rights of Man or the Law of Nations from those extreme positivists who would deny their existence, so too must Jews defend their very existence as a nation from its opponents without and within.

Lauterpacht shared this transnational vision of Zionism with a whole generation of predominantly East European Jewish lawyers who came of age during World War I. These Zionist internationalists held a dualist view of Jewish nationhood, in which national minority rights in the diaspora and territorial nationhood in Palestine would combine to normalize Jewish legal status and harmoniously order the post-imperial world.[39] In their estimation, Zionism gave Jews a much-needed international legal personality in an emerging community of post-imperial nations. Likewise, many of these Zionist internationalists did not limit their visions of Jewish territorial nationhood in Palestine to a conventional nation-state, but instead entertained various ideas of multinational or federal states. Jewish collectivity would then receive its own independent status in public international law as a legal personality separate from nation-statehood.[40] In truth, this distinctive current of political thought should not surprise us. It reflected the minority experience of Jewish nationalist politics in a multi-ethnic region of Europe. Particularly in Lauterpacht's Galician region of Poland, Zionist leaders from the outset insisted on legal recognition of Jews as a nation as a *conditio sine qua non* in their political program – despite constant resistance from both the Habsburgs and the Poles. They also looked to international law to secure their national rights and status in Poland and Palestine alike.[41] This cosmopolitan legalism did not preclude an allegiance to Jewish nationhood; it grew out of a struggle to realize that very nationhood in a rapidly shifting post-imperial world of nations and states. Hence it would be best to term Lauterpacht and many of his Jewish legal peers not as individual cosmopolitans but rather as cosmopolitan nationalists.

Contrary to popular perceptions, Lauterpacht's Zionist work did not cease in the early 1920s. He continued in the leadership of the World Union of

---

[39] James Loeffler, *"The Famous Trinity of 1917": Zionist Internationalism in Historical Perspective*, 15 Simon Dubnow Inst. Y.B. 211 (2016).

[40] Dmitry Shumsky, Beyond the Nation-State: the Zionist Political Imagination from Pinsker to Ben-Gurion (2018).

[41] *Id.* at 94.

Jewish Students into the early 1930s.[42] So too he practiced a decidedly *engagé* journalism and provided legal counsel to the World Jewish Congress, the Jewish Agency, and various other Zionist groups from the 1920s through the 1940s. All of these efforts were connected either specifically to issues of state-building, Jewish representation at the League of Nations, or combatting the direct threats of anti-Semitism. What did change during this period, however, was Lauterpacht's view of the relationship between nationhood and international law. For though he did not waver in his faith in the internationalist promise of Zionism, Lauterpacht began to reckon with the realities of an international order fast converging on a narrower model of nationhood concentrated within territorial nation-states. The first place Lauterpacht directly confronted this problem was in his international work against antisemitism.

Back in November 1918, Lauterpacht responded to the infamous Lemberg pogrom by asserting the need for Jewish minority rights. Justice demanded that international law recognize Jewish national autonomy as a minority group in Poland with linguistic and cultural rights even as it granted a homeland for Jews in Palestine.[43] Across the 1920s, however, he began to see just how limited the space for national minorities was in the interwar international legal order. Throughout that decade, he led the World Union of Jewish Students in an effort to oppose the antisemitic *numerus clausus* policies affecting many Jewish students in central and east European universities. Together with his friend Julius Stone, Lauterpacht tried unsuccessfully to pursue legal action through the League of Nations.[44] The stumbling block proved to be the Jewish legal status. Absent a kin-state, Jewish organizations had no sovereign legal personality with which to bring claims at the League. Jews were forced to rely on other states to advance their petitions through the state-based legal system of the League. For all of its progressive evolution, the interwar international legal system continued to resist providing a ready legal space for cultural groups between the categories of individuals and states.

Lauterpacht first learned that lesson in the fall of 1924, when he served as the Jewish delegate to the Warsaw Congress on International Education sponsored by the International Confederation of Students. He described his

---

[42] At least as late as 1933, for instance, he remained on the executive of the World Union of Jewish Students. *See World Union of Jewish Students*, JEWISH CHRONICLE, July 14, 1933, at 29.

[43] LAUTERPACHT, *supra* note 3, at 21; *Ha-veidah ha-mukdemet*, HA-TSEFIRAH, Jan. 9, 1919, at 3; JAMES LOEFFLER, ROOTED COSMOPOLITANS: JEWS AND HUMAN RIGHTS IN THE TWENTIETH CENTURY 8 (2018).

[44] Letter from Julius Stone to F. M. Rich (Nov. 16, 1926) (London Metropolitan Archive, Papers of the British Board of Jewish Deputies, ACC 3121 B4/I/10); Letter from Julius Stone to Hersch Lauterpacht (Aug. 23, 1927) (LFA).

delegation's aims as two-fold: "to obtain admission to the Conference as a [Jewish] Union with equal rights as other affiliated [national] Unions," and to raise the subject of *numerus clausus* policies. His efforts failed, he observed, because the organizing body insisted on admitting to its ranks "only such organizations as are constituted on a State basis." Poland might join representing the ethnically Polish students of Poland (though not necessarily the Jewish or Lithuanian Poles), but other diasporic national groups could not achieve recognition outside the state framework. Ironically, this put Lauterpacht in the same boat as the German National Union of Students, a nationalist group that sought to join as a transnational federation of German students across Europe. He recalled:

> The World Union was offered the position of an associate member with the character of an international organization and without the right to vote. This offer was rejected by the Jewish delegation, who regarded it as contrary to the dignity of Jewish students to consent to their union being called and admitted as an international organization.

In other words, what Lauterpacht sought was a *national* recognition of Jews. Merely being a transnational ethnic group was not sufficient to pass the entrance bar into the club of nations. He blamed this on "political tendencies" within the Congress on International Education.[45] The interwar legal order may have promised new forms of transnational international organization, but a logic of statism still prevailed.[46]

Lauterpacht carried this lesson about the reality of territorial states into his vision of Jewish nationhood. He never abandoned his willingness to contemplate a world in which international law might recognize new entities such as non-state actors.[47] But he recognized that modern international law was still premised on a world of territorial sovereignties. Hence, realistically, statehood was an imperative for achieving Jewish parity and legal personality among the family of nations. The lesson for Zionism was clear. Zionist leaders must cease our preoccupation with "the old questions of Jewish destiny, the clash between idea and organization, between community and society," he wrote in 1926, and focus instead on state-building in Palestine.[48]

---

[45]   Zwi LAUTERPACHT, *Relief Work*, 1 BULLETIN OF THE INTER-UNIVERSITY FEDERATION OF JEWISH UNIVERSITY STUDENTS OF BRITAIN AND IRELAND, November 1924, at 19.

[46]   See also L[auterpacht], *Nowy plan kadłubowego paktu gwarancyjnego a Polska*, NOWY DZIENNIK, Feb. 14, 1925, at 3.

[47]   NATAN Lerner, *Minority Rights and New Political Entities, in* NEW POLITICAL ENTITIES IN PUBLIC AND PRIVATE INTERNATIONAL LAW, WITH SPECIAL REFERENCE TO THE PALESTINIAN ENTITY, 247, 260 (Amos Shapira & Maia Tabory, eds., 1999).

[48]   Zwi Lauterpacht, *Ofenzywa z 77 Great Russell Street*, NOWY DZIENNIK, Apr. 8, 1926, at 2.

Heeding his own advice, Lauterpacht increasingly directed his personal Zionist activism in the late 1930s and 1940s toward providing legal counsel regarding the path to statehood. The clearest evidence of this role comes in a number of secret briefs he wrote in the 1940s about how to achieve recognition and Jewish membership in the United Nations.[49] Finally, in 1948 he was asked by Abba Eban to prepare a draft of the Israeli Declaration of Independence. The document was not adopted, for various reasons, though it did exert some influence on the drafting process.[50] For our purposes, it is instructive to quote briefly from his draft, which is preserved in unpublished form in the private archive of the Lauterpacht family. In this draft, he writes the following:

> [The] natural right of the Jewish people to national existence has received repeated recognition on the part of the nations of the world ... Justice requires that the Jewish people should be enabled, through an independent State in its ancient home, to preserve the life and the culture of the Jewish race, to carry on the torch of its contribution to the spiritual values and to the welfare of mankind, and to provide for the survival and the happiness of the anguished remnants of the most cruel massacre in history.[51]

Jews deserved a state as a matter of natural right. History had already issued its verdict, confirming this right through the recognition offered by the United Nations resolution. Lauterpacht went on to double down on this point:

> The inherent right of the Jewish people to national self-determination through statehood is independent of any express confirmation by an outside authority ... The Resolution of the General Assembly is and will remain a great and beneficent act of international distributive justice. The basic legal and moral features which underlie it cannot be affected or altered by changes to the political constellation in the relations of states ... [The Jewish people possess the] supreme right of self-defense and self-preservation.[52]

What is striking about this 1948 text is its departure from Lauterpacht's own theory of the nature of sovereignty and liberal positivist approach to state

---

49 *See*, for instance, Hersch Zvi Lauterpacht, *Memorandum to Jewish Agency*, 1947 (Israel State Archives, 93.3/3/70).

50 For careful scrutiny and varying interpretations of this document's genesis and reception, *see* YORAM Shachar, *Jefferson Goes East: The American Origins of the Israeli Declaration of Independence*, 2 THEOR. INQUIRIES L., 589 (2009); ELIAV Lieblich and YORAM Shachar, *Cosmopolitanism at a Crossroads: Hersch Lauterpacht and the Israeli Declaration of Independence*, 84 BRIT. Y.B. INT'L. L., 1 (2014); and Reut Paz, *Between the "Public" and the "Private,"* 22 EUR. J. INT'L. L., 863 (2011).

51 Hersch Zvi Lauterpacht, *The Act of Independence* (LFA).

52 *Id.*

recognition in international law. We recall that state recognition, per Lauterpacht, derived from positive state obligations based on absolute objective criteria such as effective control rather than subjective factors. As he writes in *Recognition*, "[L]egal personality is a creation of law, not of nature."[53] Why, then, did he assert Jewish natural right in his draft of the 1948 Israeli Declaration of Independence? It is of course possible to dismiss this text as a form of individual hypocrisy in which personal emotions temporarily clouded his capacity for legal reasoning. But it makes more sense to see it as a moment in which the complex interplay between idealism and positivism in Lauterpacht's legal thought reveals itself. For Zionism and international law were deeply intertwined in Lauterpacht's imagination. As this chapter's title suggests, they both derived from a paradox at the core of his legal model. That paradox is not his simultaneous affirmation and critique of sovereignty, but rather his liberal model of law that lacks any metaphysical underpinnings.

As Koskenniemi has noted, throughout his writings, Lauterpacht consistently appeals to a universal system predicated on common-sense notions of moral impulses. But he does not argue for the reality of this system from the standpoint of either philosophy or theology. Instead, he adopts an historical method to prove the eternal, hence universal character of the Law of Nature. This higher, natural law gives rise to the Rights of Man (in modern form human rights) and the Law of Nations (modern international law). All three interrelated ideas reinforce one another in a complicated circular turn.[54] What ultimately provides the authority for this moral system? Classical natural rights theory relied on a theological basis of the divine origins of morality and law. Modern logic relied on rationalist Kantian principles. Yet neither of those sources of authority fit Lauterpacht's model.[55] If rights were simply grounded in finite logic, then the law would not be able to evolve as needed for liberal progress. Natural rights, meanwhile, made no sense without a divine lawgiver. Lauterpacht's great hero, Hugo Grotius, the early modern progenitor of the Law of Nations, was a Christian humanist, who based his worldview on theological claims. But for Lauterpacht the answer came through pointing to history as an objective confirmation of a subjective, anti-essentialist legal nominalism. To borrow from Koskenniemi, Lauterpacht imagined an international legal order into existence by pretending it already existed.

---

53   LAUTERPACHT, *supra* note 7, at 49. See the discussion in Patrick Capps, *Lauterpacht's Method*, 82 BRIT. Y.B. INT'L. L. 248 (2012).
54   LAUTERPACHT, *supra* note 13, at 49.
55   On the trouble with classifying Lauterpacht in terms of conventional categories of legal thought, *see* Natan Feinberg, MASOT BI-SHE'ELOT HA-ZEMAN 230 (1980).

History did not merely validate law as real and inherent in human experience. It also offered the affective dimension that was crucial to human thought. In 1924, Lauterpacht told his fellow British Jewish students that national belonging was not merely a rational knowledge but "a matter of feeling and sentiment stronger than ourselves." In 1946 he wrote in *Commentary* magazine in similar terms that international law derives its "strength and vitality" from a "common faith in its reality."[56] It could not be proved, it simply had to be believed to become real. And it had to be felt. A collective, constructivist leap of faith was the starting point from which law took shape. Imagining Jewish nationhood and international law together, Lauterpacht willed into being a modern international legal order with a place in it for Jews. Zionism was the hidden immanent force in his mental picture of a law-filled modern world.

In truth, such a reading of Lauterpacht should not come as a surprise to historians. After all, we have long known that modern international law is as much a product of ethnic nationalism as statist internationalism.[57] Or more precisely, the new international law that arose during World War I grew out of an attempt to accommodate the reality of a world of post-imperial sovereign states with the surging forces of national consciousness. Even before fascism and communism challenged liberal internationalism in the interwar period, legal positivism crumbled from within during the course of the 1910s. The new legal modernism sought to balance idealist imperatives with the reality of an international system still clearly organized around state sovereignty. In Lauterpacht's Zionist legal imagination, the new law and the new Jewish nationhood were co-constitutive of one another. The Jewish nation was one necessary building block in the emerging modern international legal order.

If Zionism lay at the heart of Lauterpacht's legal thought, that only exacerbates the problem of understanding how he reacted as he did in the fateful year of 1948, when confronted with the parallel dilemmas of two post-imperial situations involving India/Pakistan/Hyderabad and Israel/Palestine. Given his Zionist commitments, it is perhaps not surprising that Lauterpacht proved more sympathetic to Israel's independence claim than that of Hyderabad.[58] But beyond hypocrisy, one detects another deciding element in his replies to the

---

[56] Hersch Lauterpacht, *International Bill of Rights: Second Phase*, 2 COMMENTARY 256 (1946).

[57] NATHANIEL BERMAN, PASSION AND AMBIVALENCE: COLONIALISM, NATIONALISM, AND INTERNATIONAL LAW (2012).

[58] It might be noted, however, that there was a complicated geopolitical context in play. The Nizam of Hyderabad was an overt supporter of the Palestinian Arab nationalist cause. *See* NICOLAS BLAREL, THE EVOLUTION OF INDIA'S ISRAEL POLICY: CONTINUITY, CHANGE, AND COMPROMISE SINCE 1922, 101 (2012).

questions on recognition: historical inevitability. In both cases, history had spoken. The Jewish drive for statehood, long in gestation, was well etched in the modern imagination as a possible outcome via the partition of Palestine. By contrast, the logic of state-building in India suggested one great partition to be accompanied by a consolidation of central rule. This left independent sovereignty for a small, landlocked principality like Hyderabad a very remote possibility. Historical progress dictated that Hindu India and Muslim Pakistan become independent, unified nations. Jewish Israel and Arab Palestine should as well. Princely territorial enclaves were relics of a feudal past that could not withstand the arc of modern history based on the ascendant logic of the nation-state.

There remains one other detail of Lauterpacht's simultaneous engagement with international law and Jewish nationhood in 1948 that deserves further explanation. As noted at the outset, in his dealings with the new Israeli government, Lauterpacht insisted on secrecy regarding his role as outside legal advisor. Why was such a step necessary? It is tempting today to perceive 1948 as a moment of final reckoning between Lauterpacht's Zionism and his larger legal internationalism. Indeed, this is the tack taken by many other astute recent chroniclers. To Paz, the Declaration of Independence episode presents evidence of Lauterpacht's public and private selves awkwardly intermingling despite his efforts – and those of his son and biographer – to draw a neat partition through his life. For Eliav Lieblich and Yoram Shachar, the episode bespeaks a painful clash between nationalism and democracy, or universalism and particularism. "[B]y participating in a national project," they conclude, "Lauterpacht's cosmopolitanism was compromised."[59] But one wonders whether the divergence of 1948, in the final analysis, represented as much of a "crossroads" as we assume it does today. After all, Lauterpacht made no secret of his affection for Israel or his pride in its achievements in the post-1948 period. His insistence on discretion was a strategic calculation, not an ideological one. He was less an anguished lawyer caught between conflicting loyalties as much as careful international jurist mindful of judicial proprieties and global politics. After 1948 Lauterpacht feared overidentification with the new Jewish state would jeopardize his own role as a protagonist in the new chapter of work in the field of international law. It was one thing to dispense advice in a semi-clandestine fashion to a Jewish political movement before 1948, quite another to enter into service for its legal diplomacy at the same moment as he aspired

[59]   Lieblich and Shachar, *supra* note 50, at 1.

to move higher in British governmental circles.[60] This dilemma grew still more acute when he joined the International Court in 1955. As a judge of the world's highest international tribunal, he now found that his particular Jewish identity had become politicized in a new way on account of the unresolved Arab–Israeli conflict.

Taken on net, Lauterpacht's dual careers in law and politics testify not to an unbridgeable gap between Zionism and international law but to their symbiotic historical development. A final expression of this sentiment comes from his 1949 correspondence. On the occasion of the opening of the Hebrew University's Law Faculty, Lauterpacht donated a full set of the *Revue Générale de Droit International et de Législation Comparée* to the school's new library. The volumes had once belonged to the great British international lawyer John Westlake. Now, he presented them as a special gift to his old Zionist comrade Natan Feinberg, the first dean of the Hebrew University Law School. The note that accompanied the gift is apparently lost. But four decades later, Feinberg quoted briefly from it in a letter to Judge Stephen Schwebel, an American Jew serving on the International Court of Justice, who at the time was contemplating his own biography of Lauterpacht. "It would have pleased John Westlake to know," wrote Lauterpacht to Feinberg, "that the set will now be housed in the city of the Prophets."[61] Ancient Israel had introduced both nationhood and universal law to the world of antiquity. Now both came home in their respective modern forms. It was this conviction that inspired Lauterpacht's audacious quest to renew the Law of Nations and the Jewish nation together. What Lauterpacht did not foresee was a situation in which the very city in question, Jerusalem, would come to symbolize the limits of international law to bring satisfactory justice to the two nations that claim it alike.

ACKNOWLEDGMENTS

I am grateful to Elihu Lauterpacht for providing unfettered access to the rich private archive of his father's Nachlass. For comments and criticisms of various drafts of this paper, I thank Abigail Green, Alexander Kaye, Moria Paz, Samuel Moyn, Rotem Giladi, Philippe Sands, David Luban, and Gil Rubin. I am particularly grateful to Martti Koskenniemi, from whom I have learned so much about Hersch Zvi Lauterpacht, for agreeing to comment on

---

[60] See BRIAN Simpson, *Hersch Lauterpacht and the Genesis of the Age of Human Rights*, 120 LAW QUAR. REV., 49 (2004).

[61] Letter from Natan Feinberg to Stephen Schwebel (Feb. 18, 1983) (Central Zionist Archives, A306, F144, "Zvi Hersch and Rachel Lauterpacht").

this chapter. For research assistance, I kindly thank Maryam Ismail, Jessica Kirzane, Nathan Kurz, Ewelina Malik, Matthew Stefanski, and Anat Vaturi. I also thank the staffs of the American Jewish Committee Archives, the British National Archives, the British National Library, the Center for Jewish History, the International Labor Organization Archives, the Israel State Archives, the Jagiellonian University Digital Library, the Johns Hopkins University Library Special Collections Division, the London Metropolitan Archive, and the YIVO Institute for Jewish Research.

2

A Closet Positivist

Lauterpacht between Law and Diplomacy

Martti Koskenniemi

The evidence from Hersch Lauterpacht's private correspondence that he sought "to renew the Law of Nations and the Jewish nation together"[1] is quite persuasive. Like many other Jewish professionals of the early twentieth century, Lauterpacht is likely to have felt no conflict whatsoever between his Jewish nationalism and his cosmopolitanism. Each had a moral-historical content; each informed the other. Like international law, Zionism was fed by impulses that were in part idealist, in part realist. This is no surprise. As I have explained elsewhere, any political-legal theory *needs* both elements so as to seem persuasive.[2] Jurists have long ago learned to respond to the interminable critiques that international law is just a moral utopia by demonstrating that its very foundation lies in state will, diplomacy, and the division of the world into territorial states. How could something so firmly anchored in the very structure of political power possibly appear as an offshoot of excess idealism? On the other hand, when they seem to veer too much into the direction of supporting of sovereign egoism, international lawyers routinely cite the lofty principles of the UN Charter, cases from international tribunals, or a human rights treaty that will invariably embrace whatever the position is that they intended to support. Sovereign statehood, as a whole juristic tradition from the post-glossators onward has stressed, is a creation of the law; the king is both a father and a son of justice.[3] Or to abstract from this into a final thesis:

---

[1] This and other quotes, unless specified, refer to James Loeffler, The *"Natural Right of the Jewish People"*: Zionism, International Law, and the Paradox of Hersch Zvi Lauterpacht, Chapter 1 in this volume.

[2] Martti Koskenniemi, From Apology to Utopia: The Structure of International Legal Argument (reprint 2005) (1989).

[3] See especially Ernst Kantorowicz, The King's Two Bodies: A Study in Medieval Political Theology 97–107 (1997). For the role of *jus gentium* as the foundation for statehood in late medieval legal theory, see Joseph Canning, A History of Medieval Political Thought: 300–1450, 162–72 (reprint 2009) (1996).

the "real" and the "ideal" are not so much antagonists as collaborators, coming to each other's rescue just before collapse.

That nationhood and the cosmopolitan order are, rightly understood, compatible with each other is a very common, perhaps even the ruling sentiment among international legal professionals. In the many records we have of legal advisors of states reflecting on their careers, absent is the narrative where somebody would report a tragic conflict between loyalty to one's nation and embrace of higher purpose. The two seem always, miraculously, to contain each other. The national interest is always in the long-term best interests of the world as well; and the cosmopolitan purpose never fails to coincide with the enlightened interest of one's nation. This not because of bad faith or cynicism on anybody's part. The pressure on legal professionals to live in a world with ultimate harmony is great, as E. H. Carr long ago instructed us, having his Cambridge colleague Lauterpacht specifically in mind.[4] In the opposite case, international law would appear immediately and embarrassingly "political" in the sense of excluding some interest, perspective, or position from its compass a priori, unable to give any kind of articulation to it, its "enemy."[5]

So, I agree with James Loeffler – Lauterpacht's legal cosmopolitanism and his Zionism "informed one another directly." But I do not see – as he does – this as the "distinctive character of his Jewish internationalism." It is the character of all internationalism that operates in the world, seeks allies, and tries to confront adversaries. Any nationalism needs a position outside itself, a theory in the light of which it can explain itself as defensible or perhaps even a necessary aspect of some larger frame of understanding. This may be a historical generalization, a theory of race or ethnicity, or a religious or linguistic principle. The history of nationalism is full of criteria allowing nations to point to their specificity among other nations. In this sense, the particular and the universal are not antagonists but co-constitutive elements in a single block of ideas, wholly dependent on each other.

I also agree with Loeffler that Lauterpacht is not at his strongest whenever he tries to articulate that larger principle or theory that would form the "idealist" face of his Zionism. His path-breaking *Human Rights and International Law* (1950), for example, never quite succeeds in laying out a "theory of human rights," even less a philosophy of rights but remains a somewhat nostalgic celebration of the English liberal rights tradition. His

---

[4] E. H. CARR, THE TWENTY-YEARS' CRISIS, 1919–1939, *e.g.*, 195 note 1 passim (2d ed., 1946).
[5] This would be the situation of Lyotard's famous *différend* – the case where a conflict-solution takes place in the idiom of one of the contestants, while the violation (or interest) felt by the other is not signified in it at all. For the side whose interest receives no recognition, the very system of conflict-solution can then only seem as a (political) imposition. *See* JEAN-FRANÇOIS LYOTARD, LE DIFFÉREND 24–25 (1983).

famous essay, "The Grotian Tradition in International Law" (1946) – which Lauterpacht himself thought best expressed his credo – looks toward, as Loeffler puts it, "common-sense notions of moral impulses." Lauterpacht chooses Grotius as his hero because he shares the bourgeois of the Dutchman – the "law of love, the law of charity, of Christian duty, of honor, and of goodness."[6] This is neither philosophy nor theory but, as I have tried to present it in my book *The Gentle Civilizer of Nations*, a "sensibility" that is eminently pragmatic and conservative, that believes the world's problems are either about misunderstandings or the work of evil. Radical otherness and incommensurate preferences make no appearance in this world. Reason will prevail once everybody has received a fair hearing. What is not finally included must be excluded, unmentioned. Silence reigns over Grotius as a legitimizer of Dutch colonial expansion.

Loeffler tries valiantly to salvage Lauterpacht as an intellectual by suggesting that a historical view underlay his Zionism, giving "objective confirmation" to his "subjective anti-essentialist legal nominalism." I find this slightly unpersuasive. Lauterpacht did not have much of an interest in history, as his son Eli once confirmed to me as I asked about the sparseness of historical references in his oeuvre. Of course, to some extent all good doctrinal work in international law is historical, and Lauterpacht's is certainly very good doctrinal work. One goes back to treaties, cases, events, and precedents to construct the path to one's normative conclusion. The very argument in both *Private Law Analogies* and *Function of Law in the International Community* required extensive research in both domestic and international legal history, not the history of legal thought but of legal rules and doctrinal positions. Moreover, the suggestion in those works as well as in many of his interwar articles – for instance "The So-Called Anglo-American and Continental Schools of International Law" (1931) – highlights the unity of law and of legal history. From the different national narratives, the same kinds of principles and legal institutions emerge. There is a strongly teleological feel in his principal works that associates with his faith in reason. It would, nevertheless, be wrong to sketch Lauterpacht as a "historical" thinker, for example by connecting his belief in progress with Immanuel Kant's cosmopolitan teleology. Lauterpacht was no philosopher; his generalizations simply reflected the educated common sense among liberals around him. Even his brief engagement with Baruch Spinoza did not occupy a philosophical so much as

---

[6] Hersch Lauterpacht, *The Grotian Tradition in International Law*, 23 Brit. Y.B. Int'l. L. 334 (1946).

a political plane, he was uneasy with the moral consequences of the philosopher's realism. Paradoxically, what Loeffler suggests is evidence of Lauterpacht's historical vision I see as part of what could perhaps be called his closet positivism.

Lauterpacht is, of course, regarded as a natural lawyer. I do not dispute this characterization. It was shared by his contemporaries (such as James Brierly for instance) and he himself flagged it expressly in the article on the Grotian tradition. But naturalism is not so far away from positivism as first-year law students have been instructed to think. The relationship between the two is analogous to what I wrote earlier about "idealism" and "realism." In order to appear persuasive to a professional audience natural law needs to demonstrate its content and applicability by reference to something factual and tangible, by some "positive" evidence from (historical) practice. Lauterpacht's legal-doctrinal work is full of such evidence: think for example of the principal argument in *Function of Law in the International Community*. Through painstaking analysis of a huge number of cases from courts and tribunals across the world, Lauterpacht derives the conclusion that law abhors a vacuum, that there is no evidence at all that courts would pronounce *non liquet* in case they were unable to find a treaty or a custom that applies to a case. This conclusion is then used to attack the ideology of sovereignty that suggests that states may be bound only when they have so consented. The power of Lauterpacht's main work lies in his occupying the very plane on which his adversary stands: positive evidence of state practice. But where his adversaries interpret that practice from the perspective of the "sovereignty" that they believe central to international law, and unsurprisingly find that it supports a wide domestic jurisdiction, Lauterpacht interprets it from the perspective of the idea of the unity of the legal system that is reconstructed on a daily basis by the pragmatic activity of international judges – and finds that indeed it does support this unity. At issue in the debate (of course there was very little of any express debate) is then not an opposition between "positivism" and "naturalism" – both sides occupy both positions – but a more obviously political and strategic question about international governance. To put it provocatively: Should the world be governed by diplomats or lawyers? If I call Lauterpacht "closet positivist" I mean that like most jurists, he was convinced that in order to persuade the audiences he was writing for, he needed to produce an impressive array of treaty law, cases, and precedents, the sort of arguments that "positivist" lawyers have been taught to appreciate. And as everyone knows, he did this quite successfully.

One final question remains, however. If it is true that, like so many others, Lauterpacht combined his nationalism with his cosmopolitanism, his positivism with his naturalism, why then did an attack on "sovereignty" constitute such a strong and remarkably coherent strand of all his work? The previous analysis suggests that locutions such as "international community" and "sovereignty" should both have been equal members of his argumentative arsenal. But they were not. An attack on "the sovereign state" or sometimes "sovereignty" is at the heart of all of his works, from *Private Law Analogies* to *Function of Law*, from *Recognition in International Law* to *International Law and Human Rights*, passing by the *Development of International Law by the International Court*. It also extends to his consultant work, nowhere more strikingly than in the odd pronouncement at the head of his draft to the opening speech of Sir Hartley Shawcross at Nuremberg in 1945: "[T]he mystical sanctity of the sovereign state is arraigned before the law."[7]

I agree with Loeffler that Lauterpacht joined his Zionist nationalism with his legal cosmopolitanism by an argument that aimed to "tame" sovereignty, that looked not just for a world of nations but specifically law-abiding, good, bourgeois nations. This is certainly the ideal world of most international law professionals. It does not emerge from deep jurisprudential theory or a philosophy of history but from engagement in an existing legal practice that is geared toward making it possible for nations to think of themselves as simultaneously independent and joined by the rule of law. This is a political project of "gentle civilizing" that always looks for the reasonable middle way where the opposites are finally united. It is by reference to that project that I see Lauterpacht's continued and often passionate attack on the ethereal abstraction of "sovereignty" as so problematic. It embodies a refusal to engage with one of the constitutive paradoxes of his profession, opening a vulnerable point in his otherwise impressive argumentative arsenal. Without a powerful view of legal sovereignty, it remained ultimately a mystery as to why Israel needed to become an independent state. Such defense would be sorely needed today to finally decide the fate of Palestine.

---

[7] Martti Koskenniemi, The Gentle Civilizer of Nations: The Rise and Fall of International Law 1870–1960 389 (2001).

PART 2

HANS KELSEN

3

Assimilation through Law

Hans Kelsen and the Jewish Experience

Eliav Lieblich

INTRODUCTION

Hans Kelsen's 1969 biography, written by his former assistant Rudolph Aladár Métall, does not begin – as perhaps expected in the genre – by describing Kelsen's immediate family or early childhood. Rather, Métall takes us many centuries back, to an age when Roman Legionaries defended the borders of the empire, between Germany and Luxemburg. For supplies, the Romans relied on Jewish sutlers,[1] who eventually settled in the area. A small village – "Kelsen über Saarburg" – was one of these settlements. In the eighteenth century, when Austrian Jews were given German surnames, many took the names of their places of origin. In this manner, Métall tells us, the surname "Kelsen" came to be.[2] Hans Kelsen, thus, is not a foreigner: he is of firm Habsburgian-German roots. We even have *maps* to prove it – to convince us, Métall provides the exact geographical coordinates of his ancestral village.[3]

Métall's well-meaning intention was to dispel the long-standing attempts by Austrian anti-Semites to "expose" that Kelsen's true name was Kohn (Cohen) – and that therefore, he can never *really* be German (or Austrian).[4] While Métall immediately qualified that in any case this should not be a cause for shame,[5] this peculiar opening encapsulates the tensions of European Jewish identity, underlying and undermining assimilationist attempts, until the catastrophe of the twentieth century brought them to an abrupt end.

---

[1] Historically, sutlers were civilians who sold provisions to military units.
[2] RUDOLPH ALADÁR MÉTALL, HANS KELSEN: LEBEN UND WERK, 1 (1969).
[3] *Id.*
[4] *Id.* On the perplexities of German and Austrian identities, and in particular among educated Jews, *see* STEVEN BELLER, VIENNA AND THE JEWS, 1867–1938: A CULTURAL HISTORY, 144–64 (1989).
[5] MÉTALL, *supra* note 2, at 1.

This chapter discusses Hans Kelsen in light of these ever-present tensions, with particular focus on his position as an international lawyer. Indeed, recent scholarship recognizes the particular importance of questions of identity when discussing international law, precisely because of the latter's ambiguities.[6] To be sure, since the "cause" of international law was consistently driven, in its formative years, by committed individuals,[7] it is of special interest to explore their motivations, as well as the uses and constructions of their identities.

In this context, Kelsen's life trajectory is truly representative of the tragedy of European Jewry in the twentieth century. He was born in 1881 in Prague – then part of the Austro-Hungarian Empire – to assimilated Jewish parents, who moved shortly after his birth to Vienna.[8] The world of his childhood and young adulthood was described by his contemporary Stefan Zweig as "the Golden Age of Security," where everything in the "thousand-year-old Austrian Monarchy seemed based on permanency."[9] However, the age of security did not last long. At the closing of World War I and the collapse of the empire, Kelsen, then a young jurist in the ministry of war, became – by force of circumstance – instrumental in forming the new federal order, and is widely credited for authoring Austria's 1920 democratic constitution.[10] Thereafter, he was simultaneously a prominent academic in the University of Vienna's faculty of law – where he developed his immensely influential brand of positivism known as the "Pure Theory of Law" – and a judge in Austria's constitutional court, which he helped to establish.[11] In 1930, with the beginning of the slide toward Austro-fascism and the dissolution of the court, he left Vienna for the University of Cologne, only to escape Germany by the skin of his teeth in 1933, after Adolf Hitler took power.[12] Continuing his academic work from Geneva's Graduate Institute of International Studies, he also attempted, in 1936 – under impossible circumstances – to teach part-time at the German University of Prague, only to leave in 1938.[13] With the outbreak of

---

[6] See Re'ut Paz, *A Forgotten Kelsenian? The Story of Helen Silving-Ryu (1906 –1993)*, Eur. J. Int'l. L. 25, 1123–46 (2015).

[7] For the definitive work on this, *see* Martti Koskenniemi, The Gentle Civilizer of Nations: The Rise and Fall of International Law 1870–1960 (2001).

[8] Hans Kelsen, Autobiografia, 67 (L.V. Borda, trans., 2008); Métall *supra* note 2 at 1–2.

[9] Stefan Zweig, The World of Yesterday, 1 (A. Bell, trans., 1964).

[10] Monica Garcia-Salmones Rovira, The Project of Positivism in International Law, 166 (2013); Re'ut Paz, A Gateway between a Distant God and a Cruel World: The Contribution of Jewish German-Speaking Scholars to International Law, 178–79 (2012).

[11] Kelsen, *supra* note 8, at 119–49.

[12] *Id.* at 150–53.

[13] *Id.* at 153–68.

World War II, Kelsen resolved to leave Europe, fearing that Switzerland would not remain neutral. He left for the United States in 1940, ultimately settling at UC Berkeley's Department of Political Science in 1945.[14] He died in California in 1973.

Kelsen was perhaps the twentieth century's most influential Continental jurist. Encompassing almost eight decades of prolific work, his writings addressed not only fundamental legal problems, but also issues of psychology, sociology, philosophy, and politics.[15] He engaged in intellectual exchanges with figures such as Sigmund Freud,[16] and his debates with Carl Schmitt are canonical in constitutional theory.[17] Especially challenging for commentators is the fact that Kelsen's thought, while returning to some basic premises, was constantly evolving, even well into his eighties.[18] Unsurprisingly, his works are discussed in vast secondary literature, celebratory as well as critical.[19] It is beyond this chapter to address this vastness. Nonetheless, it is still helpful, before moving on, to recount the basic tenets of his legal thought.

Since Kelsen's jurisprudence envisioned all levels of law as unity – this is his famous concept of *monism* – international law was an integral part of his analysis. In fact, it became increasingly dominant as his career progressed and his life circumstances took him away from Europe. His writings on international law can be roughly divided into four periods. Until the mid-1930s, Kelsen mainly addressed the nature of international law within his

---

[14] *Id.* at 168–73; Paz, *supra* note 10 at 183; David Kennedy, *The International Style in Postwar Law and Policy*, 1 Utah L. Rev., 30–59 (1994).

[15] For chronological bibliographies, *see* Métall, *supra* note 2 at 124–55; for a bibliography of key writings on international law, *see* N. B. Ladavac, Hans Kelsen (1881–1973), *Biographical Note and Bibliography*, 9 Eur. J. Int'l. L., 394–96 (1998).

[16] Hans Kelsen, *The Conception of the State and Social Psychology, with Special Reference to Freud's Group Theory*, 5 Int'l J. Psycho-Analysis 1–38 (1924); Clemens Jabloner, *Kelsen and His Circle: The Viennese Years*, 9 Eur. J. Int'l. L., 368–85, 382–83 (1998).

[17] For an overview in English *see* David Dyzenhaus, "*Now the Machine Runs Itself*": *Carl Schmitt on Hobbes and Kelsen*, 16 Cardozo Law Review, 1–19 (1994).

[18] *See, e.g.*, S. L. Paulson, *Four Phases in Hans Kelsen's Legal Theory? Reflections on a Periodization*, 18 Ox. J. L. Stud., 153–66 (1998).

[19] For a bibliography of main secondary literature in English (as of 1992) *see* Hans Kelsen, Introduction to the Problems of Legal Theory, 145–53 (Bonnie Litschewski-Paulson & Stanley L. Paulson, trans., 1992); perhaps the foremost collection of secondary literature in English is Normativity and Norms: Critical Perspectives on Kelsenian Themes (Stanley L. Paulson & Bonnie Litschewski-Paulson, eds., 2007); for secondary literature on Kelsen's international legal theory (as of 1998) *see* Ladavac, *supra* note 15, at 396–400; for recent analysis *see* Jochen von Bernstorff, The Public International Law Theory of Hans Kelsen: Believing in Universal Law (2010); Garcia-Salmones Rovira, *supra* note 10; see also 9 Eur. J. Int'l. L. (1998).

general jurisprudence. Writing against predecessors such as Georg Jellinek,[20] he chiefly dealt, in this period, with *descriptive* theoretical issues such as the nature of the state, of sovereignty, and of international law qua legal system, including its relation with domestic law.[21] Before and during World War II, until the establishment of the UN, Kelsen was preoccupied with *normative* problems of world organization.[22] His writings from these years analyze the failure of the League of Nations, while suggesting a new world order structured around a compulsory world court.[23] In the decade following the founding of the UN, Kelsen mainly engaged critically with the emerging law of the organization,[24] while completing his comprehensive treatise on international law in 1952.[25] Thereafter, until his death, Kelsen returned to revisit the issues he addressed along the years, challenging some of his early assumptions.[26]

Throughout the years, Kelsen's positivist international legal jurisprudence was elaborated on and disseminated by a close circle of students. Together with Kelsen, the "Vienna School" of international law included namely Métall, Josef Kunz, and to a varying extent, Alfred Verdross.[27] Collectively – and in seeming disconnect from Kelsen's normative projects – they offered a "scientific" description of international law as a distinct object of cognition, as a response to what they saw as political abuse of legal concepts.[28] They followed the logic of the Pure Theory, which famously attempted to describe "law" as an independent concept, disconnected from "foreign

---

[20] Von Bernstorff, *supra* note 19, at 44.

[21] *See, e.g.*, HANS KELSEN, DAS PROBLEM DER SOUVERÄNITÄT UN DIE THEORIE DES VÖLKERRECHTS (1920); KELSEN, INTRODUCTION, *supra* note 19, at 107–25.

[22] On Kelsen's dual descriptive/normative legal project, *see* Von Bernstorff, *supra* note 19, at 2–3.

[23] *See, e.g.*, HANS KELSEN, PEACE THROUGH LAW (1944). This period also saw his treatment of international criminal law. *See* Hans Kelsen, *Collective and Individual Responsibility in International Law with Particular Regard to Punishment of War Criminals*, 31 CAL. L. REV., 530–71 (1943).

[24] Notably, HANS KELSEN, THE LAW OF THE UNITED NATIONS: A CRITICAL ANALYSIS OF ITS FUNDAMENTAL PROBLEMS (1950).

[25] HANS KELSEN, PRINCIPLES OF INTERNATIONAL LAW (1952).

[26] Most notably, the 1960 major revision of the Pure Theory. HANS KELSEN, PURE THEORY OF LAW (M. Knight, trans., 2d ed., 1967).

[27] J. L. Kunz, *The "Vienna School" and International Law*, 11 N. Y. U. L. QUAR. REV., 393–94 (1933–1934); VON BERNSTORFF, *supra* note 19 at 4–5; for short "career sketches" of Kunz and Verdross, *see id.* at 281–86; for others in Kelsen's wider circle, *see* Jabloner, *supra* note 16, at 375–85. Verdross deviated, eventually, from the Pure Theory. Other prominent students of Kelsen deviated more significantly, notably Hersch Lauterpacht and Helen Silving-Ryu, *see, e.g.*, Paz, *supra* note 6.

[28] VON BERNSTORFF, *supra* note 19, at 54–55.

elements" such as ethics, theology, psychology, and biology[29] – and, as such, disconnected both from morality and natural facts.[30] To Kelsen, a legal norm, domestically as internationally, is merely a link between extralegal fact (the *Sein*) and an "imputed" coercive consequence.[31] In fact, the coercion is constitutive of the legal norm itself.[32] In international law, coercion is effected through reprisals and war,[33] which can only be undertaken against an international "delict."[34] Law is distinct from morality, since the "ought" (the *Sollen*) in law refers strictly to the link between fact and prescribed coercive consequence, *not* between fact and moral outcome.[35] In this sense, Kelsen emphatically denied "that it can be the task of legal science to justify anything whatever."[36] Law is also distinct from natural science since it is ruled not by "causality" but by normativity (the imputed coercive consequence), and therefore cannot be analyzed and identified by scientific measures.[37] Thus, according to the Pure Theory, every legal norm derives its validity, domestically and internationally, not from ethical ideals but from a higher norm, the highest of which is a presumed *grundnorm* (basic norm).[38] The basic norm of the international legal system is that *custom* is a law-creating material fact.[39] Given the unity of all systems of law, the primacy of international law must be acknowledged, if this unity is to be workable and coherent.[40] If this view is

[29]   KELSEN, *supra* note 19 at § 1; Stanley L. Paulson, *Introduction, in* KELSEN, *supra* note 19 at xix (1934); Kunz, *supra* note 27, at 377–80.

[30]   Paulson, *supra* note 29, at xxi.

[31]   KELSEN, *supra* note 19, at §§ 15–16, § 31(c).

[32]   KELSEN, *supra* note 25, at 7.

[33]   *Id.* § 49(b).

[34]   To Kelsen, if international law is to have a legal character, force can only be used as sanction, and not at will (*bellum iustum*). *See* HANS KELSEN, LAW AND PEACE IN INTERNATIONAL RELATIONS, 13, 34 (1942); later on, he based his just war theory also on positive law. *See* KELSEN, *supra* note 25, at 33–64; for a discussion of Kelsen's *bellum iustum* theory *see* PAZ, *supra* note 10, at 276–77.

[35]   KELSEN, *supra* note 19, at §§ 15–16.

[36]   *Id.* § 48(f).

[37]   *Id.* § 2, § 8, § 15–16.

[38]   *Id.* §§ 27–29.

[39]   *Id.* § 49(a); for a discussion of why *pacta sunt servanda* itself cannot be the basic norm of international law (as Kelsen initially claimed) *see* Kunz, *supra* note 27, at 403–04. Later on, Kelsen clarified that the international basic norm maintains that "states ought to behave as they have customarily behaved." KELSEN, *supra* note 26, at 418.

[40]   KELSEN, *supra* note 19, at § 49(a), § 50(d-e); Kelsen emphatically leaned toward the supremacy of international law, while half-heartedly acknowledging that the primacy of domestic law was also possible. *See* Kunz, *supra* note 27, at 398–403; the choice between the two approaches was "political," but Kelsen clearly implied his own preferences. KELSEN, *supra* note 26, at 428–47. Compare VON BERNSTORFF, *supra* note 19, at 93–107.

accepted, the international basic norm must also be the ultimate norm of states' legal systems.[41]

Beyond the above, this chapter does not offer a comprehensive outline or critique of Kelsen's general or international jurisprudence, except when needed to exemplify the argument – this has already been done by many others. Rather, and since at issue is *Jewish* international lawyering, it only makes sense to restrict the analysis to a point in time when the Jewish condition in Europe came to a boiling point, and to situate Kelsen within these tensions. Accordingly, this chapter focuses, when discussing Kelsen's writings, mainly on the period around the first edition of Kelsen's *Pure Theory of Law*, published in 1934.[42] This work is significant not only on account of its canonical status as the most concise expression of Kelsen's theory, but also because it was written in the last moments of the long-standing attempts by "educated" Jews to assimilate in their surrounding society. It was literally written on the brink: hope still existed, but catastrophe already loomed large.

Before proceeding, a disclaimer is required. Any discussion of an intellectual endeavor in light of a person's collective background – Jewish or otherwise – can collapse into essentialism, if not worse. There is something potentially degrading in attempting to demonstrate that the work a thinker, who – as we shall see – manifestly did not consider himself a *Jewish* thinker, reflects the work of a "Jewish mind." However, it is completely fair to discuss a thinker in light of the challenges his "collective" faced within a certain society; challenges that might translate to common reactions and trends in thought. Thus, I do not aim to discuss the "Jewishness" of Kelsen, but rather his *experience* as a Jew.

That this experience affected Kelsen cannot be reasonably denied. Indeed, while his academic writings adhered to the rational tradition of separating emotion from reason – after all, he saw the "emotional component" as part of "primitive consciousness"[43] – it must be recalled that some of his seminal works were written just as his world was crumbling around him, sometimes under imminent physical danger. The bridge between Kelsen's detached analytical writing and his personal upheavals can be found in the usually

---

[41]   KELSEN, *supra* note 19, at § 50; KELSEN, *supra* note 25, at 446–47.

[42]   This work was translated only in 1992 as INTRODUCTION THE PROBLEMS OF LEGAL THEORY, to distinguish it from the second version of the Pure Theory of Law. *See* KELSEN, *supra* note 19. Kelsen's 1960 rework of the Pure Theory modified some of his previous arguments, specifically in its emphasis on will and volition. *See* KELSEN, *supra* note 26. *See, e.g.*, Kennedy, *supra* note 14, at 35; Paulson, *Introduction, supra* note 29 at v. However, this is less relevant for our purposes.

[43]   HANS KELSEN, SOCIETY AND NATURE: A SOCIOLOGICAL INQUIRY, 1–23 (1946).

overlooked part of great works, the preface. For instance, in the preface to 1934's *Pure Theory*, written in Geneva after Kelsen escaped Germany, he vehemently defends his theory against critics. This would hardly be unusual, had the tone of the defense not been so *emotional*. Kelsen's tone, in fact, is reminiscent of a cry from a drowning vessel: the Pure Theory is "besieged," a victim of an "all-out battle" waged by a hateful opposition.[44] The critics tear at the Pure Theory from opposing ideological angles, simultaneously condemning it as fascist, communist, or liberal.[45] Kelsen laments the state of the world, in which those who "place intellectual values before power" are few, while hoping that the younger generation, "caught in the raucous hue and cry of our times," will not abandon the belief in "independent legal science." Hope and despair are mixed in Kelsen's closing statement, expressing his "firm conviction that in some distant future, the fruits of such a legal science will not be lost."[46] When considering Kelsen's personal circumstances at the time, the thought that he was writing about his own fate when decrying the treatment of the Pure Theory becomes inescapable. Like the Pure Theory, Kelsen was besieged, embattled, and victimized by intense hate. Like the Pure Theory, Kelsen was subject, as a Jew, to propaganda that Jews were simultaneously behind opposing ideologies.[47]

Bearing this in mind, this chapter discusses Kelsen along three interrelating themes especially relevant to the situation of educated Jews – and perhaps, more so, to Jewish international lawyers – in the first half of the twentieth century. The first part is biographical, situating Kelsen in relation to that era's key dilemma of Jewish politics: the tension between Jewish nationalism and assimilationism. As I show, like many Jews in the Viennese intellectual elite, Kelsen's public stance shunned Jewish collectivism, in favor of a supposedly neutral Austrian identity. "Austrian Kelsen" was challenged, however, by two extremes. Both anti-Semitism, and, from an opposing angle, Zionism, rejected the possibility of assimilation and thus constructed Kelsen as a Jew. "Jewish Kelsen," in turn, was utilized both as a legitimizing and delegitimizing figure by collectivist ideologies.

The second theme focuses on the question of assimilationist politics in Kelsen's jurisprudence. Regardless of the attempts to construct a "Jewish

---

[44] KELSEN, *supra* note 19, at 2.
[45] *Id.* at 3.
[46] *Id.* at 4–5.
[47] *See, e.g.,* JOSEPH W. BENDERSKY, A CONCISE HISTORY OF NAZI GERMANY 21, 37 (3d. ed., 2007); *see generally* Izhak Englard, *Nazi Criticism against the Normativist Theory of Hans Kelsen: Its Intellectual Basis and Post-Modern Tendencies*, 32 ISR. L. REV. 183–249 (1998).

Kelsen," Kelsen was an Austrian patriot with strong cosmopolitan leanings, an assimilated Jew par excellence. However, since his "neutral" positivist juris-prudence, on its face, rejected cosmopolitanism as a *legal* construct, it is impossible to place his thought within the strand of assimilationist jurispru-dence that placed universal rights at the basis of the legal system. Still, I suggest that an assimilationist reading of Kelsen's *Pure Theory* is possible, going beyond the rather obvious observation that the mere attempt to construct "neutral" concepts could in itself be an assimilationist endeavor.[48] A profoundly assimilationist vision is revealed if we "reverse" Kelsen's top-down perception of a universal legal system, in which law pulsates dynami-cally from a universal basic norm to individual transactions, to a bottom-up process in which the individual dissolves into the international community. This process can only be described as *assimilation through law* – a starkly different concept from the attempts of some Jewish internationalists to pursue assimilation through *universal rights*.

The third theme pitches Kelsen's Pure Theory of (international) law, which he describes in a striking oxymoron as "radically anti-ideological," against the notion of "progress" – the latter being a key idea in the thought of assimilated Jewish internationalists. As I argue, the notion of "progress" shines through Kelsen's attempts to shun ideological perceptions of law. In particular, it lies in the core of his view of the proper international order, which informed, in turn, his construction of the nature of international law qua legal system. Nonetheless, the tragic events of his time were reflected in his adoption of a pragmatic version of progressivism in his vision for a world order.

AUSTRIAN KELSEN VERSUS JEWISH KELSEN

A. A *Quintessential Jewish Dilemma*

Like other key European Jewish thinkers of the twentieth century, Kelsen's experiences can be discussed in light of the quintessential dilemma of Jewish politics of the time – between assimilation in surrounding society and asserting Jewish identity – whether by positively embracing "Jewish" traits, or as a form of reactive identity politics.[49] Assimilationist politics of Jewish international-ists, in particular, were bolstered by strong cosmopolitanism, as a vehicle to transcend exclusionary nationalisms.[50] These tensions were burning in the

---

[48] E.g., the idea of the ethnically neutral *"mensch."* BELLER, *supra* note 4, at 236.
[49] *See, e.g.,* HANNAH ARENDT, MEN IN DARK TIMES, 18 (1955).
[50] PAZ, *supra* note 10, at 23–28.

extreme public discourse of turn-of-the-century Vienna: local politics were dominated by anti-Semitic mayor Karl Lueger, just as Theodor Herzl founded the Zionist movement, which advocated a solution to the "Jewish problem" in the form of a Jewish state.[51]

Choosing assimilation could entail denying the relevance of one's Jewish background for all practical purposes, or perhaps, one's Jewishness altogether. It could also imply a division between one's public, assimilated identity, and a private, Jewish identity.[52] In any case, it was effected through attempts to integrate in non-Jewish society,[53] and was characterized by the adoption of key Enlightenment tenets, namely liberalism, progressivism, and the value of education (*bildung*).[54] Assimilation was common among the Jews in Vienna's cultural elite and bourgeoisie, as a perceived entry ticket to Austrian society.[55]

Kelsen was described as an "extremely assimilated" Jew,[56] an admirer of the old Austrian Empire, and in particular the empire's multinational ideals.[57] He was said to have treated his Judaism as an "irrelevancy,"[58] although he did not actively deny his Jewish origins or Jewishness.[59] That *formal* religious identity was not central to Kelsen is clearly evidenced by his double conversion – once to Catholicism (1905) and then to Lutheran Protestantism (1912) – although these were not for reasons of faith.[60] As Steven Beller rightly notes, however, actively considering something – such as Jewishness – as "irrelevant" actually implies that the same thing is undesirable.[61] Since there are no transparent social categories, choosing *not* to stress an aspect of one's identity is an active choice of other identities. And indeed, Kelsen did not perceive his assimilation as neutral. In the preface to 1944's *Peace through Law*, he laments the tragedies

---

[51] BELLER, *supra* note 4, at 74.

[52] *See infra*, note 157.

[53] BELLER, *supra* note 4, at 76.

[54] *Id.* at 76, 122.

[55] *Id.* at 84.

[56] Benjamin Akzin, *Hans Kelsen – In Memoriam*, 8 ISR. L. REV. 325, 326 (1973).

[57] GARCIA-SALMONES ROVIRA, *supra* note 10, at 159–60.

[58] BELLER, *supra* note 4, at 76.

[59] GARCIA-SALMONES ROVIRA, *supra* note 10, at 159.

[60] *Id.*, 158–59; PAZ, *supra* note 10, at 178. Conversion to Protestantism – the religion of German enlightenment – was considered a progressive move. BELLER, *supra* note 4, at 153; PAZ, *supra* note 10 at 232–33. Arendt notes that conversion was common among educated Jews for economic reasons, but that this usually did not make them "cease to be Jews, neither in their own opinion nor in that of their environment." Hannah Arendt, *Privileged Jews*, 8 JEWISH SOCIAL STUDIES, 3–30, 21 (1946). Kelsen continued to harbor some Jewish awareness, conversions notwithstanding.

[61] BELLER, *supra* note 4, at 74–75.

of the time, asking dramatically "have *we* men of a *Christian civilization* really the right to relax morally?"[62] Assimilation here is pursued not only by positively adopting "Christian civilization," but is also augmented by juxtaposing this civilization to other, "primitive peoples."[63]

However, assimilation was pressured from two divergent viewpoints. As is well known, twentieth-century anti-Semitism did not base "Jewishness" on subjective perceptions but on ancestry.[64] Thus, Kelsen, like many others, was regarded as a Jew by society and as we shall see, suffered grave persecution. This persecution encompassed not only Kelsen's person but also his work. In an infamous 1936 conference, organized by Carl Schmitt, Kelsen's jurisprudence was condemned as "Jewish."[65] His Pure Theory was even described in a Nazi encyclopedia as a "typical expression of the corroding Jewish spirit" in its "community destroying" nihilism.[66] On the other hand, some strands of Zionism, either essentially or reactively, held that "Jewishness was a matter of the blood" and thus that assimilation was impossible.[67] Ultimately, both stressed the Jew's eternal foreignness.[68]

B. Constructing "Austrian" Kelsen: The Assimilationist Narrative

These tensions of Jewish identity never played an explicit role in Kelsen's work. Still, they can nevertheless be implied from the manner in which *others* constructed his *personal* identity, adopting either an assimilationist or Jewish-collectivist narrative. These narratives have political significance. On the one hand, treating Kelsen as "Austrian" (or "European") places one in firm opposition to the exclusionary discourse of anti-Semitism, while risking, unintentionally, its denial. On the other, incorporating him into a Jewish collective could be a source of political capital, especially for Zionists:[69] indeed, leading jurists – perhaps even more so, prominent

---

[62] KELSEN, *supra* note 23, at vii (emphasis mine).

[63] *Id.*

[64] *See, e.g.,* BELLER, *supra* note 4, at 190–92.

[65] *See, e.g.,* Detlev F. Vagts, *Carl Schmitt in Context: Reflections on a Symposium,* 23 CARDOZO L. REV. 2157–63, 2158 (2001–2002).

[66] Cited in England, *supra* note 47, at note 1.

[67] *See supra* BELLER, *supra* note 4, at 79, citing T. LESSING, DER JÜDISCHE SELBSTHAAS, 68 ff (1930).

[68] Hannah Arendt, *Antisemitism, in* HANNAH ARENDT, THE JEWISH WRITINGS, 54–55 (Jerome Kohn & Ron H. Feldman, eds., 2007).

[69] *See, e.g.,* ZE'EV ROSENKRANZ, EINSTEIN BEFORE ISRAEL: ZIONIST ICON OR ICONOCLAST, 2–3 (2011).

international lawyers – can serve as agents of legitimacy for political aspirations.[70]

Thus, some "Kelsenists" outright object to discussing Kelsen's work in terms of his Jewish identity. Jabloner, for instance, states bluntly that "there is no sense . . . in seeking to detect 'Jewish' characteristics" in Kelsen's thought, both since this will be "ambivalent" and because many in Kelsen's elite circles were not Jewish.[71] Others, likewise, do not emphasize Kelsen's Jewish background as having a substantial impact on his thought, beyond, of course, the objective fact that it triggered anti-Semitic attacks.[72] As Monica Garcia-Salmones Rovira points out, stressing Kelsen's Viennese cultural, political, and philosophical influences, implies the construction of an "Austrian Kelsen."[73] It is clear that in effect, discussing Kelsen as an "Austrian" figure adopts the assimilationist narrative: at the end of the day, his Jewish identity was secondary, if at all relevant.

This is probably loyal to the way Kelsen would have presented himself, at least publicly. Along several phases of his career, Kelsen was simultaneously persecuted not only for being Jewish, but also for being a liberal Austrian jurist. When narrating each of these junctions, one could stress either one of these causes. Interestingly, when presenting himself to the general public, Kelsen chose to emphasize the latter. Although this type of "denial" was criticized by some Jewish thinkers,[74] it could be understandable, since highlighting one's group-based persecution reiterates the same group identity that speaker wishes to transcend. It might also be perceived as a self-compromising act, where the victim admits her weakness and adopts the discourse of the aggressor.[75]

In accordance with these dynamics, in Kelsen's 1947 autobiography, "Austrian Kelsen" is constantly present, while "Jewish Kelsen" is at most implied. Thus, when describing his childhood and his family background, Kelsen tells us of his Galician father, and of his German-Czech mother. He likewise speaks at length of the German literature that influenced his early years. He does not, however, mention that his parents were Jewish, nor does he

---

[70] If international law has a deep relation to legitimacy, prominent international lawyers, arguably, can serve the same function. *See* THOMAS M. FRANCK, THE POWER OF LEGITIMACY AMONG NATIONS (1990).

[71] Jabloner, *supra* note 16, at 368–85, 374–75.

[72] VON BERNSTORFF, *supra* note 19; Kennedy, *supra* note 14, at 36–37 (constantly referring to Kelsen as "European").

[73] GARCIA-SALMONES ROVIRA, *supra* note 10, at 124–25.

[74] Arendt saw this as an illusion, self-denial, and betrayal. Arendt, *supra* note 68, at 46–59, 99.

[75] *See* Arlene Stein, *"As Far as They Knew I Came from France"*: *Stigma, Passing, and Not Speaking about the Holocaust*, 32 SYMBOLIC INTERACTION, 44–60 (2009).

refer positively or negatively to any Jewish experience in these formative years.[76]

Similarly, when explaining Kelsen's 1930 departure from Vienna, one can choose to stress the relevant political-constitutional circumstances – and thus emphasize Kelsen's identity as an Austrian democrat – or, conversely, to emphasize the anti-Semitic underpinnings of the affair. Again, when describing this episode, Kelsen (and others) chose the former. Under this narrative, Austrian Kelsen's leaving was a result of the "strong reaction" by conservatives to a ruling by the constitutional court, authorizing administrative bodies to dissolve Catholic marriages.[77] During 1929, the increasingly influential proto-fascist Christian-Social Party (CSP) reacted wildly to this decision, including by launching personal attacks against Kelsen.[78] As Kelsen writes, this was part of the CSP's plan to eliminate the court altogether.[79] Once the CSP gained sufficient power, it moved to carry out the plan. In order to secure the Social Democrats' support for the move, the new CSP government offered them the opportunity to nominate two of the fourteen judges of the new, "reorganized" court. One position was offered to Kelsen, who was sympathetic to the Social Democrats. He refused decisively.[80] As Kelsen tells it, "these events" angered him deeply and "discouraged me to continue my work in Austria."[81] Kelsen's emphasis of the constitutional-political circumstances surrounding his departure is telling. It is clear that anti-Semitism played a significant part in the attacks on Kelsen and the court,[82] not least because the CSP was overtly anti-Semitic.[83] Nonetheless, in Kelsen's narrative it is "Austrian," rather than "Jewish" Kelsen, who suffers these attacks.

---

[76] KELSEN, *supra* note 8, at 67–72. Conversely, in Kelsen's 1968 biography, Métall devoted considerable attention to Kelsen's Jewish roots. It could be speculated that by that time Kelsen, almost thirty years in the United States, felt more at ease to talk about these issues, or that it was easier to do so through others.

[77] Jabloner, *supra* note 16, at 375. The issue was the most controversial legal problem of Austria at the time. *See* GARCIA-SALMONES ROVIRA, *supra* note 10, at note 51.

[78] KELSEN, *supra* note 8, at 145–46.

[79] *Id.* at 146.

[80] As Kelsen writes, he was requested to serve as the Social Democrats' "confidant" in the new court. Kelsen resisted for obvious reasons. KELSEN, *supra* note 9, at 148; *see also* GARCIA-SALMONES ROVIRA, *supra* note 10, at 166–67; Jabloner, *supra* note 16, at note 29 (adopting this account).

[81] KELSEN, *supra* note 8, at 150.

[82] VON BERNSTORFF, *supra* note 19 at 278; MÉTALL, *supra* note 2, at 54; Democratic Austria was attacked by Christian Socialists as a "vile concoction of indignation against the eternal order" masterminded by "Jewish Professor Kelsen (Kohn)." *See* JOHANNES FEICHTINGER, WISSENSCHAFT ALS REFLEXIVES PROJEKT: VON BOLZANO ÜBER FREUD ZU KELSEN: ÖSTERREICHISCHE WISSENSCHAFTSGESCHICHTE 1848–1938, 478 (2010).

[83] BELLER, *supra* note 4, at 193–97.

We find similar undertones in two other episodes described by Kelsen – his 1933 escape from Cologne and his 1936–1938 experience in Prague. In 1930, he took up a chair at the University of Cologne. When Hitler ascended to power in 1933, Kelsen was one of the first professors dismissed. He managed to escape Germany only through the police connections of a university employee.[84] Of course, the chief reason for his dismissal was his Jewish background: Kelsen's termination was based on the notorious "Law for the Restoration of the Professional Civil Service" of July 1933,[85] which barred Jews (non-Aryans) from German civil service.[86] However, in his description of these events, Kelsen chose to focus on his position as a "pacifist" and the "author of the democratic constitution of Austria."[87] The word "Jewish," while obviously implied, is not directly mentioned.

In late 1936, while holding a professorship at Geneva, Kelsen undertook a part-time position in the German University of Prague – a courageous decision, considering the growing tensions in Czechoslovakia.[88] Kelsen vividly paints the nightmarish scene of his first lecture. The university building was occupied by members of German nationalist organizations. He was barely able to pass through the hostile crowd, only to learn that the lecture hall itself was also overtaken by Nazi sympathizers. "Upon my entrance to the room," writes Kelsen, "no one rose from the chair." As he attempted to start his lecture, the crowd uniformly chanted "down with the Jews."[89] Kelsen was rushed out of the classroom, while his students were beaten and thrown down the stairs.[90] Ultimately, due to repeated death threats, and in light of the deteriorating political climate in the country, Kelsen left the university in 1938.[91] Although he by no means denied the motivation behind these attacks, the *only* reference made to his Jewishness is extrinsic, when quoting the racist chants he encountered. Austrian Kelsen, thus, is made Jewish only through the words of his persecutors.

C. Constructing "Jewish" Kelsen: The Collectivist Narrative

Throughout the years, some Zionist commentators sought to incorporate Kelsen into their *own* collective narrative, perhaps as a legitimizing figure

---

[84] Kelsen, *supra* note 8, at 152–53.

[85] *Id.* at 152 n. 244.

[86] *See* Jürgen Matthäus and Mark Roseman, Jewish Responses to Persecution: 1933–1938, 439 (vol. 1, 2009).

[87] Kelsen, *supra* note 8, at 153; compare with Métall, *supra* note 2, at 57–63.

[88] Kelsen, *supra* note 8, at 160–61.

[89] *Id.*

[90] *Id.*

[91] *Id.* at 162–66.

for political choices. This incorporation requires two steps: (a) constructing a "Jewish Kelsen," either positively by revealing that Jewishness was an active part of his identity, or negatively by stressing that his assimilation failed; and (b) demonstrating that Kelsen ultimately realized that Zionism was the answer to the "Jewish question."

Positively integrating Kelsen into the Jewish collective can entail uncovering a Jewish essence in his jurisprudence. Thus, Izhak England, a law professor and a retired justice of the Supreme Court of Israel, tells of a 1968 conversation between Kelsen and Avigdor Levontin, one of the founders of Hebrew University's faculty of law.[92] Since Levontin (and England) paraphrased the discussion, we can learn about the motivation to construct "Jewish Kelsen" both from the questions posed to Kelsen, as well as through the interpretation they gave to his answers. The discussion, as reported, reveals a Levontin keen to expose Jewish influences in Kelsen's jurisprudence and a rather reluctant but polite Kelsen. Levontin asked Kelsen whether there was a Jewish-cosmopolitan influence in his universal theory of law. As reported, Kelsen "did not object to the direction of the question," but answered that since Austria was a multinational state, it was the *Austrian* influence that was dominant in the Pure Theory.[93] Thereafter, Levontin asked whether Kelsen's hierarchical perception of law was influenced by Jewish law, which gives primacy to the norms of the Torah. As Levontin reported, "it seemed that Kelsen agreed, this time without noting another dominant influence." The third question was whether Kelsen's legal monism was influenced by Jewish monotheism. Here, too, Levontin "thought that Kelsen agreed with him, once again without citing a more dominant influence."[94] The need to stress that Kelsen "did not object" to a question or refrained from citing other influences is above all revealing of Levontin's (and England's) eagerness to recover Kelsen's Jewish essence.

Other examples of positive incorporation could involve searching for manifestations of Kelsen's Jewishness in his day-to-day life. Benjamin Akzin, another founder of Hebrew University's faculty of law and a staunch Zionist, noted, for instance, that a certain Jewish "kinship-feeling" could be implied, perhaps, in Kelsen's cordial treatment of young Jewish students from Eastern Europe.[95] Nathan Feinberg narrates a conversation with Kelsen – to which we return shortly – in which Kelsen admitted that when meeting people, he was

---

[92] Izhak England, God, State, Nature, Man: Hans Kelsen on Political Theology and Natural Law, 15 at n. 15 (2010) (Hebrew).
[93] For a similar statement by Kelsen, *see* Métall, *supra* note 2, at 42.
[94] England, *supra* note 92.
[95] Benjamin Akzin, *Hans Kelsen – In Memoriam*, 8 Isr. L. Rev. 325-29, 326 (1973); But *see* Izhak England, *Haben Kelsens Reine Rechstlehre, seine Faszination für Religion und sein*

interested, "first and foremost, to know, whether they are Jewish or not."[96] Stressing these anecdotes tells us less about Kelsen and more about how others would like to *perceive* him.

A negative construction of "Jewish Kelsen" can be effected by emphasizing his failed assimilation, which could serve to reinforce the basic Zionist conviction that assimilation was impossible, merely a "prelude to a catastrophe."[97] The point is further solidified when the failure is accompanied by "redemption": when the assimilationist realizes his mistake. This archetypical trajectory of failed assimilation and late realization is as old as Zionism itself. Theodor Herzl's 1894 play, *Das Neue Ghetto*, revolved precisely around the key protagonist's realization that his assimilation has failed,[98] implying that the only way for a Jew to assimilate is through an honorable death.[99]

Akzin painted Kelsen's ideological trajectory exactly in this manner.[100] Akzin, who knew Kelsen personally,[101] noted that Kelsen disconnected himself from the Jewish community in Vienna, but that "unlike many extremely assimilated Jews, Kelsen showed no trace of either an inner or an active antagonism" toward Jewish nationalism.[102] Rather, his attitude was one of "distant intellectual curiosity." From the point of view of Zionism, "[h]e neither helped nor hindered."[103] "Austrian Kelsen" thus viewed the Zionist endeavor as a detached spectator. Only with the rise of Nazism, "Jewish Kelsen" emerges: "His attitude changed," as "he proclaimed himself a Jew, showed much interest in Zionism [and the Jewish State], followed its development and expressed anxiety over its future."[104] According to Akzin, Kelsen even agreed to settle in Jerusalem but this failed to materialize.[105]

Even more explicit in terms of this narrative was Nathan Feinberg, early Israeli international lawyer and first dean of Hebrew University's faculty of law. In his obituary for Kelsen, Feinberg generalized Kelsen's experience as

Religionsverständnis einen jüdischen Hintergrund? in SECULAR RELIGION – REZEPTION UND KRITIK VON HANS KELSENS AUSEINANDERSETZUNG MIT RELIGION UND WISSENSCHAFT 101–11 note 57 (Clemes Jabloner et al., eds., 2013) (German), maintaining that Kelsen's Pure Theory was not influenced by Jewish religious thought.

[96]   Nathan Feinberg, *Hans Kelsen and His Judaism*, 5 MOLAD 638–40, 639 (1973) (Hebrew).
[97]   *See* Arendt, *supra* note 68, at 46–121, 51.
[98]   JACOB GOLOMB, NIETZSCHE AND ZION, 28–29 (2004).
[99]   BELLER, *supra* note 4, at 133.
[100]   Akzin, *supra* note 95.
[101]   Akzin was Kelsen's former student. MÉTALL, *supra* note 2, at 85.
[102]   Akzin, *supra* note 57.
[103]   *Id.*
[104]   *Id.*
[105]   *Id.*

"reflecting the tragedy of the life of a Jew in the diaspora."[106] Feinberg tells us of a pseudo-confessional interaction, in which Kelsen symbolizes an arche-typical assimilated Jew, while Feinberg plays the symbolic role of a "Jew from the Land of Israel."[107] This archetypical Kelsen turned his back on his Jewish identity, only to unexpectedly confess, in a 1932 meeting with Feinberg in The Hague, that "the Land of Israel is my miserable love."[108] In Feinberg's narrative, the discussion was cut short by a French colleague who entered the room.[109] The scene of two Jews discussing their mutual fate, silenced by the sudden presence of a gentile, further adds to the archetypical atmosphere of a secret confession.

In a trip to the beach a day later, Kelsen elaborated further. Attributing special importance to his words, Feinberg wrote them down that evening.[110] According to Feinberg, Kelsen regretted that he "was not active in the Zionist movement." "I *confess*," says Feinberg's Kelsen, "that I have made a grave mistake which becomes increasingly clear ... I believed in the possibility of complete assimilation of the Jews; moreover: I condoned assimilation as the solution to the Jewish question ... *today, I am forced to admit that assimilation is impossible.*"[111] As Feinberg notes, Kelsen exclaimed that "the voice of Jewish blood" was speaking through his voice.[112] Feinberg evidences Kelsen's turn to Zionism by a 1939 letter, in which Kelsen agreed that "despite the current difficulties," the Land of Israel continued to be "the only safe haven for Jews." Feinberg sums up Kelsen's experience in dramatic words, invoking a rhetoric of judgment and atonement: "Kelsen's life-story reveals ... the doubts of a Jew, who recognizes and admits, when the final account is made, the mistake in his long path of life."[113] Assimilation is thus portrayed as a colossal mistake, and the realization of Zionism as its remedy. If Kelsen, the "genius,"[114] realizes this, so should everybody else. Kelsen, as a key international jurist and thinker, thus becomes a legitimizing figure for political choices.

Above all, this reveals the complex position of the cosmopolitan Jewish international lawyer in Zionist discourse: on the one hand, he is derided for his

---

[106]   Feinberg, *supra* note 96, at 638. For another short take on this Feinberg-Kelsen interaction, see PAZ, *supra* note 10, at 183–84.
[107]   Feinberg, *supra* note 96, at 639.
[108]   *Id.*
[109]   *Id.* Indeed, Feinberg describes Kelsen's words as a "personal confession."
[110]   *Id.* The fact that Feinberg found it necessary to write these things down reflects his evidence-gathering state of mind, out to prove Kelsen's *true* stance toward Zionism.
[111]   *Id.*
[112]   *Id.*
[113]   *Id.* at 640.
[114]   *Id.*

assimilationist choices, but on the other, revered for his international status, accumulated *precisely* through the same assimilation.[115] In turn, this tension is relieved through a discourse of redemption: Kelsen is "redeemed" from diasporic assimilationism by his latter-day realizations.

Kelsen's potential as an agent of legitimacy was noticed also by Israeli institutions. In 1950, he was invited to teach at Hebrew University, but this failed to materialize for economic reasons.[116] As England notes, Kelsen was even invited to serve as the dean of Hebrew University's nascent faculty of law.[117] He also granted legal advice to the Israeli UN delegation in its first years.[118] Significantly, in 1953 he was invited to advise the Israeli Ministry of Justice on matters of international law, but refused due to his old age.[119] This invitation, extended through a formal government decision, was initiated by a group of jurists who thought that Kelsen's mere presence in Israel – in any role whatsoever – could "add prestige to the young State."[120] We cannot know whether Kelsen's reply was a diplomatic refusal, or rather, that he would have entertained this option under other circumstances: in fact, Kelsen never visited Israel, although his daughter, Hanna, lived there in the 1940s.[121] What is clear, however, from these offers, is that Kelsen was not known in Jerusalem circles as unsympathetic to the state, and that in any case, his legitimizing potential was widely recognized.

Nonetheless, assuming that Kelsen – a cosmopolitan who was known to be "indifferent to nationality"[122] – was not antagonistic to Jewish nationalism, his exact position on the spectrum of opinions concerning the Palestine question remains debatable.[123] Kelsen's interactions with Feinberg do not reveal much in this context. In Feinberg's 1932 meeting with Kelsen, he stressed the need

---

[115]   See BELLER, *supra* note 5, at 84 (pointing out that assimilation was, de facto, a precondition for Jews' becoming central figures in European culture). This position reflects the duality in Zionist discourse between the rejection of Europe on the one hand, and the aspiration to reconstitute it in the Land of Israel on the other, as classically reflected in Herzl's ALTNEULAND (1902).

[116]   Feinberg, *supra* note 96, at 1940; MÉTALL, *supra* note 2, at 85.

[117]   ENGLARD, *supra* note 92, at 14 at n. 12.

[118]   Feinberg, *supra* note 96, at 639; MÉTALL, *supra* note 2, at 85.

[119]   ENGLARD, *supra* note 92, at 15; MÉTALL, *supra* note 2, at 85.

[120]   Feinberg, *supra* note 96, at 640.

[121]   Anne Feder Lee and Thomas Olechowski, *The Kelsen Genealogy*, www.univie.ac.at/kelsen/family/11511_Rolf_Hanna.html (last visited Oct. 25, 2017).

[122]   GARCIA-SALMONES ROVIRA, *supra* note 10, at 158, citing MÉTALL, *supra* note 2, at 18.

[123]   Indeed, at the time, there were different voices within the Zionist movement regarding the desirable model of government in Palestine. *See, e.g.*, Eliav Lieblich and Yoram Shachar, *Cosmopolitanism at a Crossroads: Hersch Lauterpacht and the Israeli Declaration of Independence*, 84 BRIT. Y.B. INT'L. L., 1–51, 14–15 (2014).

for a "wise and just" policy concerning the Arabs in Palestine.[124] In a letter sent
to Feinberg during the 1948 War, Kelsen wrote that he believed a compromise
between Arabs and Jews was possible, and that "under the circumstances . . . it
would be the best available solution."[125] However, he quickly qualified that as
an "outsider," he could not judge the situation, and in any case, did not
elaborate on the nature of such compromise.[126] Perhaps, some parallels can
be drawn from Kelsen's opinions in comparable circumstances. As is well
known, he strongly identified with the multinational nature of the old Austrian
Empire.[127] During the transition between the empire and the Austrian
Republic, he drafted a report advocating the establishment of a federal state,
recognizing the self-determination of its different nationalities.[128] When
Kelsen met with Czechoslovakian President Benes in 1936, he strongly
urged the establishment of a federal state, to better accommodate the Sudeten-
Germans and the Slovaks.[129] Risking oversimplification, if we apply this logic
to Palestine at the time, it is possible – but of course, not certain – that Kelsen
would prefer, at least as an *ideal* solution, a Jewish–Arab binational model
advocated, for instance, by the 1946 Anglo-American Committee of Inquiry.[130]

Last, it is interesting to highlight one more appearance of "Jewish Kelsen,"
from another angle, also demonstrating the legitimizing potential of the
Jewish international lawyer, but this time for those *opposing* Zionism. In
1950, speaking at the UN General Assembly, the Iraqi ambassador contested
the legality of the UN's famous partition plan for Palestine, by invoking
Kelsen's somewhat ambiguous position on the issue.[131] It is far from
a coincidence that he referred to Kelsen as "a great *Jewish* scholar,"[132] while
denouncing the opposing Israeli position as one that "cannot tolerate truth"
even if it "happens to come from a great scholar who is a Jew."[133] The position

---

[124]   Feinberg, *supra* note 96, at 639.
[125]   *Id.* at 639–40.
[126]   *Id.* at 640. Chiefly, it is unclear whether he argued for a territorial compromise with the Arabs
        or, rather, a substantial compromise on the nature of the future state.
[127]   GARCIA-SALMONES ROVIRA, *supra* note 10, at 159–60.
[128]   *Id.* at 166.
[129]   KELSEN, *supra* note 8, at 166–67; GARCIA-SALMONES ROVIRA, *supra* note 10, at 169.
[130]   Anglo-American Committee of Inquiry, Report to the US Government and His Majesty's
        Government in the UK (1946); as is well known, the UN has rejected this idea in favor of
        a two-state solution in its famous 1947 partition plan. See G.A. Res. 181 (II) (Nov. 29, 1947).
[131]   Generally, Kelsen thought that the General Assembly was authorized to recommend parti-
        tion, but not to establish an international commission to execute it. KELSEN, *supra* note 24 at
        195–96, at n. 7. This is reminiscent of the Israeli position that partition was the substance of the
        plan, while the rest was mere procedure. *See* Lieblich and Shachar, *supra* note 123, at note 65.
[132]   U.N. Doc. A/PV.543 (Nov., 17, 1955), ¶ 15.
[133]   U.N. Doc. A/PV.547 (Nov. 21, 1955), ¶ 56. For the Israeli position see *id.*, ¶¶ 58–59.

of the Jewish international lawyer – then as now – is thus presented as especially credible when speaking *against* her perceived collective, since it would presumably be in her personal interest to do otherwise.[134]

ASSIMILATION THROUGH LAW

A. *The Unavailability of Assimilation through Universal Rights*

Kelsen's above reply to Levontin that the Pure Theory was primarily *Austrian* reflects his own personal identification. Since assimilation was a powerful force in Jewish politics, it is fair to ask whether there are assimilationist traces in Kelsen's jurisprudence. Arguably, a convenient method to promote assimilation is by appealing to higher norms of universal rights, since these transcend the local order and redefine sovereignty. Ideally, such norms challenge and deconstruct the categories within a given society, and allow for new, common identities to emerge. Thus, it is unsurprising that Hersch Lauterpacht – a prominent Jewish international lawyer, a student of Kelsen, and a lifetime stranger himself – advanced an understanding of international law as a system of natural law-based individual rights, in which the sovereign state is only an "administrative convenience" for the fulfillment of such rights.[135]

However, this luxury was unavailable to Kelsen. While Kelsen himself definitely held cosmopolitan views,[136] the Pure Theory, at least on its face, negated any substantive characteristics – including cosmopolitan values such as individual rights – as inherent components of either law or sovereignty (which to Kelsen, are essentially the same). Since the legal nature of a norm is independent of its content, the idea of individual rights preceding and constraining the (domestic or international) legal system must be rejected as "ideology."[137] For this reason, Kelsen admitted that his theory could be objectionable for liberals, who found it "intolerable that the system of the Soviet Union is to be conceived of as a legal system in exactly the same way as

---

[134] Some of the debate concerning the Goldstone Report struck this chord. *See, e.g.,* Alan M. Dershowitz, *UN Probe of Israel Will Only Encourage Hamas War Crimes,* Gatestone Institute (July 24, 2014), www.gatestoneinstitute.org/4512/un-war-crimes-hamas-israel.

[135] *See* Hersch Lauterpacht, International Law and Human Rights, 68 (1950); Koskenniemi, *supra* note 7, at 396; Lieblich and Shachar, *supra* note 123, at 19–20.

[136] In fact, Kelsen claimed that cosmopolitan values are "a higher religion which impresses upon us the supreme duty of preserving the life of man." Kelsen, *supra* note 23, at vii.

[137] Kelsen, *supra* note 19, at §§ 18–19; in the context of "state" rights, *see* Kelsen, *supra* note 25, at 148–57.

is that of Fascist Italy or democratic, capitalistic France."[138] In sum, since the Pure Theory, *on its face*, is non-cosmopolitan, it cannot openly rely on the "nature" of law to reconstruct substantive common identities conducive to assimilation. However, the assimilationist potential of the Pure Theory does not end here.

B. Assimilation and the Antinomy between Individual, Community, State, and World

Much of Kelsen's legal theory attacked various "dualisms" that occur if we assume that above positive law there is an additional, superior legal system based on natural law. These dualisms give rise to tensions across the board of legal theory: between "objective" (positive) law and "subjective" (natural law) rights; between public and private; between law and state; and between sovereignty and the international community. In each of these cases, dualism serves the *ideological* function of either legitimizing or constraining the content of law, thus blurring the meaning of law as a distinct object of cognition.[139] Importantly, by pitting individual rights against the positive legal system, dualism assumes an "antinomy" between the individual and the community.[140] Kelsen's theory, conversely, offers a monist approach to law in which, in essence, these seemingly opposing constructs *assimilate* to form a legal unity.

The ideological role, according to Kelsen, of the dualism between "objective law" and natural law-based "subjective rights"[141] is mainly to entrench the pre-political and superior status of *private property* against state interference.[142] Granted, while rebuking the pre-political status of property is a classic endeavor of the excluded stranger against "sole and despotic dominion,"[143] the same logic must also negate extralegal individual rights as a whole. This fact could justify the critique that Kelsen's theory was not conducive to the promotion of universal human rights in the emerging world order.[144] It must be

---

[138]   KELSEN, *supra* note 19, at 25. Thus, while the Pure Theory presumed to be universalist – by suggesting a jurisprudence equally applicable in all societies – it could not be openly cosmopolitan. *Id.* §§ 25–26. For a discussion of non-cosmopolitan types of "universalisms" see SAMUEL MOYN, THE LAST UTOPIA: HUMAN RIGHTS IN HISTORY, 13–24 (2010).

[139]   KELSEN, *supra* note 19, at § 18, 25(f).

[140]   *Id.* § 25(f).

[141]   *Id.* §§ 18–19.

[142]   *Id.* § 19, 21, 22, 11(c); *see also* MOYN, *supra* note 138, at 35–37.

[143]   WILLIAM BLACKSTONE, COMMENTARIES ON THE LAWS OF ENGLAND (Bk. II, Ch. 1, 1765–9).

[144]   *See also* Kennedy, *supra* note 14, at 45.

remembered, however, that superior "subjective rights" in the form of individual rights were not the only transcendental rights invoked at the time – and by
far not the most "dangerous" ones. Pre-political rights could also be used to
enshrine the inherent dominance of a particular group, such as the German
Volk, over others within a given political system.[145] Deconstructing the latter is
a prerequisite for any society in which minorities can integrate. In a sense, this
form of assimilation is an invitation to engage on (liberal) neutral grounds,
rather than one adopting a romantic perception of the dominant group in
society.[146]

Rejecting the "antinomy between individual and community" is another
crucial aspect of the assimilationist leanings in Kelsen's jurisprudence. It is key
to understand, in this context, Kelsen's counter-intuitive perception of the
"person" within the legal system, at least as late as 1934. To Kelsen, a legal
system is simply a self-contained net of obligations and rights. Within this
system, the "person" is merely an artificial construct assisting the jurist in
describing a "unity of a bundle of legal obligations and legal rights."[147] The
person, thus, is only a "common point of imputation" for normative
regulation.[148] As such, it lacks any essential characteristics. Of course, such
characteristics might exist – Kelsen does not deny, or course, the existence of
human beings beyond the legal system – but these are matters for ethics,
sociology, psychology, or biology.[149] The upshot, as aforementioned, is that
there are no extralegal, natural law "rights" attached to the individual qua
person beyond those positively recognized by the community's legal system.[150]
The interesting aspect, however, is that to Kelsen asserting the significance of
the extralegal "person" within the legal system actually places a bulwark
between individual and community. An objective legal system, conversely,
dissolves the person into a bundle of legal obligations and rights, which can

---

[145]   Nazi thought, for instance, claimed that "German racial inheritance gives them [Germans]
inherent superior rights over other peoples." *See* Memorandum from Douglas Miller, Acting
Commercial Attaché to the Embassy on the "Main Purpose of the Nazis" (Apr. 21, 1934), *in*
PEACE AND WAR: UNITED STATES FOREIGN POLICY, 1931–1941, 211–14 (1943); see also
Marsha L. Rozenblit, *European Jewry: 1800–1933, in* THE CAMBRIDGE GUIDE TO JEWISH
HISTORY, RELIGION, AND CULTURE, 169–208, 194 (Judith R. Baskin & Kenneth Seeskin,
eds., 2010).

[146]   In this Kelsen differed from the likes of Adolf Lasson, whose assimilationist tactics involved
adopting German anti-rationalism. *See* STEPHEN C. NEFF, JUSTICE AMONG NATIONS:
A HISTORY OF INTERNATIONAL LAW, 238 (2014). I wish to thank Eyal Benvenisti for this
point.

[147]   KELSEN, *supra* note 19, at §25.

[148]   *Id.* § 25(a).

[149]   *Id.*

[150]   *Id.* § 25(a), 10.

then only be understood as relational vis-à-vis the relevant legal community, in itself a net of obligations and rights.

It is worthwhile to explore this argument further. According to Kelsen, if the "person" is simply "the personification of a norm complex," the person becomes "part of the system of objective law," comprising "the obligations and rights of all 'persons,' and creating among them an organic, that is, a systemic unity – so that the right of one is always the obligation of another, and right and obligation can never be isolated from each other."[151] If this understanding is accepted, "even the pseudo-antinomy between individual and community dissolves."[152] From a proper legal standpoint, therefore, there is no individual person viewed in isolation from the community: both are just subsets of the legal system.[153] Indeed, the argument that the individual dissolves into the community, even if only in the legal realm, is a blunt, albeit legalistic, argument for assimilation. It is in essence the same "renunciation of characteristics" that Arendt identified in radical assimilationism, which sought to transform the Jew into a neutral, pure entity, devoid of any characteristics.[154] If, as Feinberg tells it, Kelsen has reached the harrowing conclusion that in the real world, assimilation was not possible, perhaps *assimilation through law* was.

When the person dissolves into the community, another result is the negation of the dualism between "public" and "private" law. To Kelsen, this dualism is rooted in the "ideology" that individual autonomy somehow precedes the state. This distinction lacks substance, since actions on both levels are "acts of the state" as a unified legal system: private transactions are merely extensions of the state's coercive power, emanating from the basic norm, but exercised through individuals acting as law-creators.[155] This is clearly a statement about jurisprudence. However, it also brings to mind the classic public/private divide that formed the basis of key strands of *moderate* liberal assimilationism.[156] According to the latter, the proper balance between identity and community was reflected in the maxim "be a man in the streets and a Jew at home" – a straightforward application of the

---

[151] *Id.* § 25(f).
[152] *Id.*
[153] *Id.*
[154] Hannah Arendt, Die Verborgene Tradition: Acht Essays, 67 (1976); cited in Beller, *supra* note 5, at 211. As Beller notes, it was "the logic of the assimilation of the Viennese Jews to become *men without qualities.*" *Id.*
[155] Kelsen, *supra* note 19, at §§ 44–45.
[156] *See* Arendt, *supra* note 68, at 99.

Enlightenment's public/private divide.[157] This famous maxim was also critiqued as introducing a subcategory of dualism: that between "Jew" and "man,"[158] the latter supposedly representing a neutral construct of humanity. Kelsen's vision of the dissolving individual is radically assimilationist as it does not only deny, in practice, the bifurcation of "Jew" and "man," but also the claim that a system of law inherently protects one's ability to abide by the maxim.

But assimilation through monism does not end in the domestic legal community. Kelsen's international legal theory went further. Kelsen famously rejected the dualism between state (qua power) and law, meaning, the perception that the "state" exists independently of its legal system. He viewed the latter as ideological apologetics meant to justify state power through law.[159] State power – like the state itself – is merely an expression of the efficacy of its legal system.[160] The individual, thus, when dissolving into the legal community, unites with sovereignty itself. And here the cards are set for Kelsen's final cosmopolitan-assimilationist move: assimilation into the *world* community.

To Kelsen, the international legal system is merely a net of sub-legal systems, differentiated one from another by their "spheres of validity," determined spatially by the effectiveness of each legal system over a certain territory.[161] The separation of the spheres is regulated by international law, which delegates powers to each state to act within its sphere, and can therefore be understood as superior to state legal systems, uniting them all in a "universal legal community" built around a hierarchical normative structure.[162] By virtue of the unity of all legal systems and of international law, and through their law-making capacity delegated by international law, states can be seen as organs of the international legal community.[163] If viewed as an organ of a superior system, the state is thus freed of the "absolutism of the dogma of sovereignty": it is "relativized" into a "continuous sequence of legal structures, gradually merging into one

---

[157] This famous phrase was penned by Judah Leib Gordon in his 1862 (or 1863) poem "Awake, My People!" For the text of the poem and discussion *see* MICHAEL STANISLAWSKI, FOR WHOM DO I TOIL? JUDAH LEIB GORDON AND THE CRISIS OF RUSSIAN JEWRY, 49–52 (1988). Re'ut Paz, for instance, identifies this type of model in the assimilation of Lauterpacht: "a Jew at home and a cosmopolitan outside." PAZ, *supra* note 10, at 198.

[158] STANISLAWSKI, *supra* note 157, at 51.

[159] KELSEN, *supra* note 19, at § 46, 47, 48(a).

[160] *Id.* § 48(e).

[161] *Id.* § 50(g).

[162] *Id.* § 31(g), § 50(b), § 50(g).

[163] *Id.* § 50(h).

another, [which] leads from the universal legal community ... to the legal communities incorporated into the state."[164] Conversely, the idea of absolute state sovereignty, which justifies dualism and a voluntarist approach to international law, is the opposite of assimilation: because it conditions the legal nature of other legal systems, and of international law, on subjective acts of "recognition," it collapses into "solipsism." The "I," the individual, is comprehended as the center of the world rather than an integral part of it.[165]

Here lies a striking realization: since the antinomy of individual and community is negated – and in turn, the antinomy of community qua state and *international* community is too negated – the logical consequence is that the individual dissolves into the international community. Whether this position is convincing, or consistent with Kelsen's other writings, is well beyond this chapter.[166] Important, for our purposes, is to highlight the extent to which Kelsen's seemingly neutral international legal monism bespeaks the discourse of ultimate assimilation. In Kelsen's world, law is a dynamic, fluctuating phenomenon constantly created, applied, and created again, in waves that emanate from the international basic norm. However, it is possible to describe this process also in "reverse": as a countermovement in which the individual dissolves back into the basic norm. Thus, what Kelsen calls a unity of "hierarchically structured, consecutive strata of law"[167] encompassing national and international law, are essentially a consecutive strata of assimilation, in which the individual is assimilated into the world community – *without* the need to invoke a natural law theory of universal human rights.[168]

However, for this perception to be somehow practicable, we need to say something also about institutions. And this leads us to our third and last theme, that of progressivism.

---

[164] *Id.*
[165] *Id.* § 50(d).
[166] For a relatively recent discussion *see* Alexander Somek, *Kelsen Lives*, 18 Eur. J. Int'l. L. 409–451 (2007); the multitude of writings on monism and dualism are listed in Kelsen, *supra* note 19, at 152–53.
[167] *Id.* § 31(g).
[168] Interestingly, Kelsen tempered the language concerning individual and community in the 1960 version of the Pure Theory, written in the United States, to encompass merely the "abolition of the dualism of right and obligation." Hans Kelsen, Pure Theory of Law, 171–74, 191–92 (2d. ed., 1960). This could reflect his changing thought as well as his changing circumstances as a Jew in America. *See* Hannah Arendt, *The Crisis of Zionism, in* Arendt, The Jewish Writings, 335.

PRAGMATIC PROGRESSIVISM

A. Descriptive Progressivism

A central ideal of the Enlightenment, dominant among the Jewish bourgeoisie of Austria, was the perception of history as a linear process of progress, brought about through science and education.[169] Arguably, the idea of progress was inherent to liberalism itself: as put by Leo Strauss, "liberalism implies a philosophy of history," through which humanity "is essentially changing; that this change constitutes History; and that through History man has developed from most imperfect beginnings into a civilized or humane being."[170] In other words, the basic notion of history in liberal thought is related to an idea of progress.

It is easy to understand why a progressive view of history – perhaps a "naïve faith in the future"[171] – was especially appealing to Jewish assimilationists. To say that the realization of liberal ideas is inevitable was a powerful argument that assimilation *is* indeed possible.[172] Progressivism was especially important in the argumentation of Jewish internationalists, and in particular international lawyers such as Lauterpacht. It allowed them to describe the well-known shortcomings of international law as temporary features of a "primitive" legal system, which will eventually develop into a centralized system capable of enshrining individual rights and world peace.[173]

Progressivism's appearance as objective "science" makes it an especially stealthy form of ideology. Nonetheless, it has been increasingly challenged just as such.[174] One critique challenges its supposed value-neutral basis, in order to expose its ideological core: indeed, progressivism does not only endorse a particular, almost religious view of history,[175] but it must also

---

[169] *Supra* note 10 at 3–6; *see* BELLER, *supra* note 4, at 122–43. For a classic manifestation of the progressive view of history *see* GEORG WILHELM FRIEDRICH HEGEL, THE PHILOSOPHY OF HISTORY (1899).

[170] Leo Strauss, *The Liberalism of Classical Political Theory*, 12 REV. OF METAPHYSICS 390–439, 400 (1959).

[171] BELLER, *supra* note 4, at 141.

[172] *See id.* (noting that the basic assimilationist logic was built on the belief "that one day there would be a common humanity"). Contra the Zionist deterministic view of Jewish/non-Jewish relations. ARENDT, *supra* note 68, at 50–52.

[173] LAUTERPACHT, *supra* note 135 at 103–11; KOSKENNIEMI, *supra* note 7, at 356; PAZ, *supra* note 10, at 23–28, 235, 332; Lieblich and Shachar, *supra* note 123, at 20–21.

[174] One famous critic of progressivism was Nietzsche. *See* FRIEDRICH NIETZSCHE, ON THE GENEALOGY OF MORALS (1887); *see also* P. GOULIMARI, LITERARY CRITICISM AND THEORY: FROM PLATO TO POSTCOLONIALISM, 115–16 (2015).

[175] MOYN, *supra* note 138, at 5–6.

encompass a normative claim about what progress means.[176] Thus, while discussing international law in terms of progress was perfectly compatible with the jurisprudence of the likes of Lauterpacht – which contained a strong ideological, natural law-based component[177] – progressivism, if exposed as ideology, could not be available for Kelsen, precisely because it required a statement about the proper content of the legal system.[178] Ironically, however, while Kelsen's theory sought to reveal the political-ideological content of seemingly "neutral" theories,[179] the ideology of progress, concealed as value neutral, permeates the Pure Theory, *especially* when applied to international law, and specifically in its belief in the value of centralized institutions. The deep intertwining between progressivism and the Jewish experience of the time makes it hardly surprising.

Particularly, progressivism emanates from Kelsen's extensive use of the notion of the "primitive."[180] Since, in the Enlightenment's terms, *primitive* is the opposite of the desired – meaning, the progressive or the civilized[181] – the employment of the term in itself implies an ideological choice. Like other progressivists, thus, Kelsen describes international law as a "primitive legal system" chiefly for its lack of central institutions.[182] Granted, a statement about the primitive does not necessarily connote progressivism. Some of Kelsen's contemporaries saw the primitiveness of international law as an unchangeable, even desired feature.[183] However, this was certainly not Kelsen's view. To him, "primitive" was a chronological point along a general continuum of progress. When describing international law, he constantly uses *temporal*

---

[176]   Indeed, holding a progressive view of history has become looked upon as nonprogressive in itself. *See*, for instance, Robert Howse and Ruti Teitel, *Does Humanity-Law Require (or Imply) A Progressive Theory of History? (and Other Questions for Martti Koskenniemi)*, 27 TEMP. INT'L. & COMP. L. J. 377–97 (2013).

[177]   Lieblich and Shachar, *supra* note 123, at 19.

[178]   KELSEN, *supra* note 19, at §§ 15–16.

[179]   *Id.* at 124. Koskenniemi argues that a key weakness in Kelsen's body of work lies precisely in the separation of law from politics, which undermined Kelsen's ability to justify his own cosmopolitan project. KOSKENNIEMI, *supra* note 7, at 247–49.

[180]   For a comparable argument *see* Kennedy, *supra* note 14, at 47–50, 56–58. Kennedy too identifies a "progress narrative" in Kelsen's use of the primitive. However, he refers mainly to Kelsen's *normative* thought rather than his descriptive writings and does not stress the ideological aspect of progressivism.

[181]   *See, e.g.*, FREDERICK G. WHELAN, ENLIGHTENMENT POLITICAL THOUGHT AND NON-WESTERN SOCIETIES: SULTANS AND SAVAGES, 11 (2009); *cf.* KELSEN, *supra* note 43, at vii.

[182]   KELSEN, *supra* note 19, at § 49(b); *see also* Kunz, *supra* note 27, at 412. The notion of the "primitive" is also found in Kelsen's autobiography: his interest in philosophy has been spurned in reaction to the "primitiveness" of religion. KELSEN, *supra* note 8, at 71.

[183]   For a survey of such thought *see* HERSCH LAUTERPACHT, THE FUNCTION OF LAW IN THE INTERNATIONAL COMMUNITY, 411–13 (1933).

language: it is *"still* marked by wide-ranging decentralization"; there are *"still"* no organs to create and apply legal norms; in sum, it is *"still"* primitive, situated "at the *beginning* of a development that the state legal system has already completed."[184] Even international-legal dualism itself reflects "the standpoint of the primitive man,"[185] in relation to which Kelsen's monism must be progressive and thus desirable.

Kelsen's progressivism, in the Pure Theory, does not only imply the desired development of world institutions, but also an underlying perception of the inherent value of individual rights – which seems to run counter to his assault on "subjective rights" elsewhere. In international law, reprisals are undertaken against the "mass of human beings" comprising the state, and not against a specific liable individual. In its emphasis on "the principles of collective and absolute liability" over *personal* liability and fault, international law is "primitive."[186] If collective responsibility is "primitive," an *individual* approach to liability – basically, the idea of fairness and due process – must be progressive, and thus desired. Kelsen makes this argument indirectly through historical progressivism, by claiming that as international law develops, individual liability *"must"* replace collective liability. Simultaneously, in a seemingly automatic process "the development of central organs for creating and applying legal norms" emerges.[187] The "result" of this process "appears to have as its ultimate goal . . . the development of a world state,"[188] as if this goal exists objectively, as an autonomous progressive will.[189] In order to stay clear of value judgments, Kelsen presents these political developments as an "evolution,"[190] meaning, a scientific chain of progress.

The ideology of *cosmopolitan* progress is also found in Kelsen's monism, which leads, as aforementioned, to the dissolution of sovereignty. While Kelsen does not explicitly judge this process – after all, it is only a "cognitive," not normative unity[191] – it is impossible to understand it as disconnected from his idea of international progress. In this context, the closing paragraphs of 1934's *Pure Theory* are the most telling. In a sharp tonal shift from the otherwise detached style of most of that work, Kelsen closes with an argument about its contribution to the "development of world

---

[184] KELSEN, *supra* note 19, at § 49(b).
[185] *Id.* § 50(c).
[186] *Id.* § 49(b).
[187] *Id.* § 49(c).
[188] *Id.*
[189] As Paz points out, in other earlier works, Kelsen explicitly endorsed the normative desirability of a world state. PAZ, *supra* note 10, at 228–29.
[190] KELSEN, *supra* note 19, at § 50(a); *see also* Kennedy, *supra* note 14, at 57.
[191] KELSEN, *supra* note 19, at § 50(g).

law.”[192] Here, he hails the dissolution of the "dogma of sovereignty" as one of the most "substantial achievements" of the Pure Theory: by exposing sovereignty as an ideological construct, it facilitates the centralization of the international legal system.[193] Of course, this achievement was "not arrived by political design," since this would "besmirch" the Pure Theory with ideology; the Pure Theory simply "facilitates" this process without judging it. Again, the notion of progress shines through: just as "progress" is a collateral consequence of natural science, so is a centralized system of world law a coincidental product of the Pure Theory's "cognitive unity of all law."[194]

B. Normative Progressivism

The encroachment of progressivism into Kelsen's descriptive work is unsurprising, as in his openly normative writings he never presumed to be ideologically neutral. Indeed, what makes Kelsen an especially complex thinker is his own dualism: simultaneously advancing a "radically anti-ideological" conception of law *and* vigorously defending ideological-cosmopolitan agendas.[195] In 1944's *Peace through Law*, thus, he outlined the desired *content* of international law as an instrument of cosmopolitan values. Perhaps predictably, these are the same ones that the Pure Theory collaterally facilitated. Again, these values are phrased in terms of "progress": either as an "essential" social goal,[196] or as a construct juxtaposed, on a linear process of development, against "regress."[197] Linear progress, as a "given tendency," appears also as a powerful historical argument as to why legal centralization is possible and even inevitable.[198]

As noted earlier, progressivism was especially central to the Jewish-assimilationist experience of the time. But equally tangible was the fragility of progress, perhaps to the point of despair. To some, like Viennese writer

---

[192] *Id.* § 50(i).

[193] *Cf.* Garcia-Salmones Rovira, *supra* note 10, at 126 (arguing that the political aspect of Kelsen's international legal theory "is revealed in the way he seeks a method for pursuing the evolution of law").

[194] Koskenniemi criticizes this paragraph as reflecting Kelsen's "covert insincerity." Koskenniemi, *supra* note 7, at 247.

[195] Von Bernstorff explores how these opposing pillars interact, revealing how cosmopolitan ideology repeatedly encroached into Kelsen's doctrinal work. *See* particularly von Bernstorff, *supra* note 19 (Pt. II).

[196] Kelsen, *supra* note 23, at vii ("There is no essential social progress as long as no international organization is established" to prevent wars).

[197] *Id.* at vii (in the context of preventing war, history "shows regress rather than progress.").

[198] *Id.* at 21–22.

Stefan Zweig, the catastrophes of the century exposed that progressivism was nothing but a delusion.[199] To international lawyers, however, abandoning hope for progress would render their project meaningless. As a Jew writing in dark times, Kelsen could not adopt a blind belief in the progress of humanity, but also could not abandon it entirely. His progressivism was an increasingly pragmatic one, heavily dependent upon human political action, and undertaken in the shadow of looming regress.[200] Thus, while 1934's *Pure Theory* attacked the dogma of sovereignty as a barrier to world law, in 1944 Kelsen conceded that "[o]pinions may differ as to the value and justification of nationalism; but one must reckon with this phenomenon" when envisioning the post-war world order.[201] He accordingly rejected utopianism, rebuking "intellectuals" who dreamed of "too much," such as establishing a world state. World peace, to Kelsen, was possible, but only through efforts and compromises leading to "a slow and steady perfection of the international legal order."[202] This required, as a first step, a body capable to make binding legal decisions – a compulsory world court,[203] competent to limit the use of force only as a response for international delicts,[204] and to impose individual criminal responsibility.[205]

It is difficult to overlook that Kelsen's suggestion for a new international order built around a world court is reminiscent of his successful attempt, decades before, to introduce a constitutional court in Austria.[206] Perhaps this was an attempt to reconstruct the age of security of his youth. To Kelsen's visible disappointment, however, this idea was not incorporated in the UN Charter;[207] and although he found physical security in the United States, Kelsen always remained a stranger – an "eternal outsider."[208] American

---

[199] ZWEIG, *supra* note 9, at 3–6; *see* BELLER, *supra* note 4, at 122–43.

[200] KELSEN, *supra* note 23, at viii, ix (urging a pragmatic view toward the international order, warning otherwise "there would be no hope for progress."). On Kelsen as a pragmatist *see* Kennedy, *supra* note 14, at 9–10, 33.

[201] KELSEN, *supra* note 23, at 10–11. Kennedy reads this turn to pragmatism in light of Kelsen's move to the United States. Kennedy, *supra* note 14, at 30–42. Nonetheless, this could also be a response to the catastrophes of World War II. As Kelsen writes: "[T]o secure world peace is our foremost political task, a task much more important than the decision between democracy or autocracy, or capitalism or socialism." KELSEN, *supra* note 23, at viii.

[202] *Id.* at ix.

[203] *Id.* at 13–18. Not only did Kelsen claim that the problem of war was chiefly a problem of unsatisfactory law, it seems that to him the main problem was actually one of legal *theory*.

[204] *Id.* at 66–67.

[205] *Id.* at 110–16.

[206] Kelsen was especially proud of that achievement. GARCIA-SALMONES ROVIRA, *supra* note 10, at 166.

[207] *See* VON BERNSTORFF, *supra* note 19, at 9.

[208] PAZ, *supra* note 10, at 230.

scholars of the emerging policy-oriented approaches to international law were rather impatient with his hyper-logical and theoretical mode of argument.[209]

Nonetheless, while uncertainty of progress is a central Jewish lesson from the twentieth century, the belief that a court could substantially improve the world order reflects the essential optimism that characterized many Jewish international lawyers: even if progress was uncertain, it should still be fought for, since the alternative is catastrophic. It is perhaps this frame of mind that led Kelsen to write, during one of the darkest times in history, that "[t]he idea of law, in spite of everything, still seems to be stronger than any other ideology of power."[210]

CONCLUSION: LAW WITHOUT QUALITIES

Kelsen's *Pure Theory* attempted to present a neutral jurisprudence while vigorously defending law as a distinct object, defined precisely by this neutrality. Interestingly, this is remarkably similar to the Jewish assimilationist experience in the first half of the twentieth century. On the one hand, Jewish assimilationists strived to "purify" themselves from "Jewish" characteristics, thus becoming "men [and women] without qualities."[211] On the other, they remained acutely aware of their distinct status as strangers, even if they could not positively define *what* constitutes this foreignness.

Kelsen's separation between his descriptive and normative writings parallels, in a way, the manner in which the seemingly neutral "Austrian Kelsen" was publicly constructed, while "Jewish Kelsen" was reserved mainly for those who utilized his Jewish identity for political capital. Just as Kelsen's cosmopolitan international-legal project crept into his descriptive writings, his Jewish experience, arguably, also found its way into his theory.

Hopefully, these observations shed another light on the identity and work of one of the most important jurists of the twentieth century. Above everything, however, the tensions discussed in this chapter illuminate that we cannot

---

[209]   *Id.* at 183; Kennedy, *supra* note 14, at 21–22, 35–36. Kelsen's American contemporaries attacked his critical approach toward the UN Charter, in particular his restrictive interpretations, which they saw as disregarding the Charter's spirit. *See* L. B. Sohn, *The Law of the United Nations by Hans Kelsen*, 64 HARV. L. REV. 517–19 (1950–1951) (book review); Oscar Schachter, *The Law of the United Nations by Hans Kelsen*, 60 YALE L. J. 189–93 (1951) (book review); A. H. Feller, *The Law of the United Nations by Hans Kelsen*, 51 COLUMBIA L. R. 537–39, 538 (1951) (book review).

[210]   KELSEN, *supra* note 23, at 21.

[211]   *Supra* note 154.

transcend our own experiences, as many international lawyers – in their desire to dissolve into the "invisible college" of their profession[212] – aspire to do.

ACKNOWLEDGMENTS

I am grateful to Eyal Benvenisti, Ron Harris, Roy Kreitner, Anat Rosenberg, Lena Salaymeh, David Schorr, Yoram Shachar, and Adam Shinar for the helpful comments and discussions.

---

[212] Oscar Schachter, *The Invisible College of International Lawyers*, 72 NORTHWESTERN UNIV. L. REV., 217–26, 218–19 (1978).

4

Philosophy beyond Historicism

Reflections on Hans Kelsen and the Jewish Experience

Leora Batnitzky

I'm grateful to Eliav Lieblich for his nuanced and largely convincing interpretation of the relation between Kelsen's legal theory and his experience as a Jew. I'd like to begin by highlighting Lieblich's own disclaimer:

> There is something potentially degrading in attempting to demonstrate that the work of a thinker, who – as we shall see – manifestly did not consider himself a *Jewish* thinker, reflects the work of a "Jewish mind." However, it is completely fair to discuss a thinker in light of the challenges his "collective" faced within a certain society; challenges that might translate to common reactions and trends in thought. Thus, I do not aim to discuss the "Jewishness" of Kelsen, but rather his *experience* as a Jew.[1]

While Kelsen never denied his Jewish origins, Lieblich provides indisputable evidence that he rejected both anti-Semitic and Zionist attempts to label his thought "Jewish." More importantly, Lieblich moves beyond biography to show that the monism of Kelsen's Pure Theory is an attempt to assimilate the individual into the international community. Lieblich's analysis illuminates a tension, if not a paradox, that is at the heart of Kelsen's legal theory, and his conception of international law especially, which is the undeniable appeal to progress embedded within the purported ideological purity of the Pure Theory of Law.

It is worth noting that this tension in Kelsen's Pure Theory parallels another long-recognized tension in his thought that concerns the status of the basic norm, which remains the fundamental unresolved ambiguity in Kelsen's Pure Theory: What is the basic norm if not a political or moral fact? Kelsen's critique of the tradition of *Staatslehre/Staatswissenschaft*, his sublation of concepts of sovereignty to law, and the Pure Theory's scientific status as well as the normative implications of his theory of international law all rest upon

---

[1] This and other quotations, unless specified, refer to Eliav Lieblich, *Assimilation through Law: Hans Kelsen and the Jewish Experience*, Chapter 3 in this volume.

the successful or unsuccessful elucidation of the basic norm. The question that I'd like to pursue in what follows is: Does the tension that Lieblich elucidates so well with regard to Kelsen's experience as a Jew relate to what arguably remains the fundamental conundrum of the basic norm?

Of course, broadly speaking, these tensions are related since they both reflect what many would argue is Kelsen's inability to move beyond normativity in his Pure Theory or, more generally, the difficulty, if not impossibility, of having a legal theory devoid of ideology or normative commitments. Still, following Lieblich, I'd like to suggest that there is a perhaps illuminating difference between what I will call the paradox of progress and the paradox of normativity in Kelsen's thought. I will suggest that Kelsen's experience as a Jew does indeed resonate with the paradox of progress since, as Lieblich notes, the equation of modernity with progress was not just a preoccupation of many European, and especially German-speaking, Jewish intellectuals, but also reflects modernity and the Jewish question as such.

Yet I also wish to suggest that the question of the relation between Kelsen's thought and Judaism (and not just Kelsen's experience as a Jew) is more complex than Lieblich contends. Here I do not aim to show that Kelsen's thought has a particular Jewish character or that Kelsen is a Jewish thinker. I agree with Lieblich that such claims can be degrading, especially when an author does not characterize his thought or himself as such. It is important to add to this observation that characterizing something as Jewish (whether a person or a system of thought) can also be conceptually problematic because such characterizations often essentialize Judaism and Jewishness. So it is not to the Jewishness of Kelsen's thought that I seek to point but rather to Kelsen's conceptual dependence on one particular interpretation of Judaism: that of Hermann Cohen's. I will suggest that recognizing this dependence allows us to understand better the tension at the heart of Kelsen's basic norm. Just as Lieblich shows that Kelsen's experience as a Jew allows us to appreciate the paradox of progress in his thought, so too does Kelsen's admittedly inadvertent internalization of Cohen's interpretation of Judaism allow us to appreciate better the paradox of normativity, that is, the paradox of the basic norm, in Kelsen's thought.

As Lieblich mentions, Leo Strauss equates modern liberalism with a belief in progress. Strikingly, Strauss offers support for Lieblich's argument that not just liberalism as such but more specifically the modern Jewish experience is linked to a hope for progress. Strauss, of course, was a critic of Kelsen's. But before turning to his specific criticism of Kelsen, we must begin with Strauss's more fundamental criticism of modernity's faith in progress and the manner in which he argues that the modern Jewish experience gives lie to this faith. As

Strauss put it in the 1965 preface to the English translation of *Spinoza's Critique of Religion*: "From every point of view it looks as if the Jewish people were the chosen people, at least in the sense that the Jewish problem is the most manifest symbol of the human problem insofar as it is a social or political problem."[2] The context of this claim is Strauss's criticism of Zionism, which he argues shares the modern belief in progress with modern liberalism. Immediately preceding the above lines, Strauss writes: "Finite, relative problems can be solved; infinite, absolute problems cannot be solved. In other words, human beings will never create a society which is free from contradictions." Lurking behind both Zionism and modern liberalism's belief in progress, Strauss contends, is a belief that with time all human problems can be solved. Kelsen's Pure Theory for Strauss would certainly be representative of this perspective.

Now we can turn to Strauss's more direct criticism of Kelsen, which we find in the opening pages of the introduction to *Natural Right and History*. Strauss criticizes Kelsen in a footnote appended to the following sentence: "What Machiavelli did apparently, our social science would actually do if it did not prefer – only God knows why – generous liberalism to consistency: namely, to give advice with equal competence and alacrity to tyrants as well as to free peoples."[3] As support for this claim, Strauss quotes Kelsen's 1925 *Algemeine Staatslehre*, in which Kelsen dismisses defences of natural law and natural right by maintaining that despotism is a valid legal order.[4] For Strauss, Kelsen's Pure Theory epitomizes the moral crisis of twentieth-century social science. As Kelsen claims, the Pure Theory is ideologically agnostic. If this is the case, Strauss maintains that consistency demands that Kelsen and social scientists more generally have no conceptual right to liberalism of any sort. Here is the paradox of progress to which Lieblich points us. Kelsen, like many twentieth-century social scientists, could not remain pure in his ideological agnosticism. Instead, Kelsen, according to Lieblich, could not but sneak a hope for progress into the Pure Theory.

Whether one ultimately agrees with Strauss's evaluation or not, he helpfully connects the paradox of progress to the modern Jewish experience, and hence Kelsen's experience as a Jew. But Strauss also directs us to another point of contact for thinking about Kelsen's relation to Judaism, and that is to Cohen's philosophy. While remaining an admirer of Cohen, Strauss, in his

---

[2] Leo Strauss, *Preface* to Leo Strauss, Spinoza's Critique of Religion 6 (1965).
[3] Leo Strauss, Natural Right and History 4 (1953).
[4] Strauss expresses confusion about the fact that Kelsen omitted a direct statement to this effect in the 1949 English translation of Hans Kelsen, General Theory of Law and State (1949), even though Kelsen's position did not change on the matter.

introductory essay to the 1971 English translation of Cohen's *Religion of Reason Out of the Sources of Judaism*, links Cohen to what he regards as modernity's deluded optimism about progress: "Cohen seems almost to face the possibility actualized not long after his death by national socialism. But his 'optimism' was too strong."[5] And it is Kelsen's relation to Cohen that allows us to consider not just his experience as a Jew but his relation to one particular modern interpretation of Judaism.

To appreciate the potential connection between Kelsen's Pure Theory and Cohen's philosophical account of Judaism we must first recall Kelsen's account of sovereignty. Sovereignty presents an especially acute challenge for Kelsen's Pure Theory. Any notion of a supreme power or political authority would seem to imply that law is and must be authorized from outside the legal system, whether or not this authorization comes in the form of a god, a person, or a state. If we begin from the perspectives of theological or political sovereignty, law is not an autonomous system. Kelsen's solution to this problem is straightforward, if not uncontroversial: he denies any distinction between state and law.[6] If the state is nothing but law, then the legal order provides the holistic organizing framework required by the Pure Theory of Law. By making sovereignty internal to law, Kelsen shifts the burden away from the Pure Theory's need to account for the sovereignty of independent states and replaces it with the Pure Theory's need to account for a unified theory of law. If we accept Kelsen's equation between state and law, and if then sovereignty becomes an issue internal to law, Kelsen's Pure Theory must account for the ways in which seemingly different legal systems of different sovereign states are in fact unified by the Pure Theory of Law.[7] As Kelsen argues in his 1920 *Das Problem der Souveränität und die Theorie des Völkerrechts*, the rejection of the "dogma of state sovereignty" is a precondition for the comprehension of the state as part of an international legal order.[8] "The basic norm" is the answer to the question of how law gains its validity, once any idea of sovereignty as authorizing law from the outside is rejected.[9] Every law, or norm, is, according to Kelsen, predicated upon

---

[5] Leo Strauss, *Introduction* to Hermann Cohen, Religion of Reason out of the Sources of Judaism xxxvi (Simon Kaplan, trans., 1972).

[6] Hans Kelsen, *The Pure Theory of Law and Analytical Jurisprudence*, 55 Harv. L. Rev. 44 (1941).

[7] Hans Kelsen, Das Problem der Souveränität und die Theorie des Völkerrechts (1920; 2d. ed., 1928).

[8] *See* Graham Hughes's helpful analysis on this point in *Validity and the Basic Norm*, 59 Cal. L. Rev. 695–714, especially 708–13 (1971).

[9] Hans Kelsen, Pure Theory of Law 212 (M. Knight, trans., 1967).

another law or norm. The basic norm is the necessarily presupposed norm that the law must be obeyed.

All of this said, it is far clearer what the basic norm is *not* than what it is. The basic norm is not an actual law. It is also not the fact of law's creation, the effectiveness of law's institutional structure, the sovereign, or the ultimate aim of law. For Kelsen, each of these types of conditions or explanations for law would, by definition, betray law's autonomy. Kelsen claims that the basic norm is best understood as a transcendental-logical condition for law, and it is here that we can begin to appreciate his relation to Cohen's philosophical account of Judaism. As Kelsen explains,

> What is essential is that the theory of the basic norm arises completely from the Method of Hypothesis developed by Cohen ... What is the presupposition underlying the very possibility of interpreting material facts that are qualified as legal acts, that is, those acts by means of which norms are issued or applied? This is the question posed in the truest spirit of transcendental logic.[10]

The key phrase in Kelsen's comments on Cohen is "interpreting material facts." The distinctive marker of Cohen's particular brand of neo-Kantianism is to begin with scientific facts and to reason from there. Once we begin, as Kelsen, following Cohen, does, with the fact of law, the question to be answered is not about the validity of law from outside the law but rather about the validity of the law from its own point of view.

But this still does not tell us why the basic norm cannot be a fact. According to Geert Edel, the key to understanding Kelsen's use of Cohen's method is the recognition that the Pure Theory does not make metaphysical claims:

> [T]he basic norm ... is not a foundation (Grundlage) given in and of itself in nature or by God, but the laying of a foundation (Grundlegung), that is, a Hypothesis. Not, however, an empirical hypothesis, which could be verified or falsified through experience, for norms do not describe what is, and thus they cannot be true or false; rather, they prescribe behavior (what ought to be), and thus they are either valid or invalid. The basic norm is, in a Platonic and Cohenian sense, Hypothesis through and through."[11]

Yet despite what he learns from Cohen's method, Kelsen also claims to break with Cohen. In Kelsen's words: "What actually distinguishes the Pure

---

[10]   Hans Kelsen, *The Pure Theory of Law, "Labandism" and Neo-Kantianism A Letter to Renato Treves, in* NORMATIVITY AND NORMS: CRITICAL PERSPECTIVES ON KELSENIAN THEMES 174 (Stanley L. Paulson & Bonnie Litschewski Paulson, eds., 1988).

[11]   Geert Edel, *The Hypothesis of the Basic Norm: Hans Kelsen and Hermann Cohen, in* NORMATIVITY AND NORMS: CRITICAL PERSPECTIVES ON KELSENIAN THEMES, 217 (1999).

Theory of Law from the Cohenian legal philosophy is that Cohen, in this field, was not in a position to overcome the natural law theory . . . "[12] Drawing on the form of Cohen's neo-Kantianism – its method of hypothesis – while rejecting its content (its implicit and explicit moral commitments), the Pure Theory is content to rest with pure formal categories.

What does any of this have to do with Judaism? To begin to answer this question, it is necessary to recognize that Kelsen's split between Cohen's method and the content of his philosophy is problematic for two reasons. First, it is difficult, if not impossible, to divorce Cohen's method of hypothesis from his philosophy of law, which is the pinnacle of his distinctive brand of neo-Kantianism. Second, despite Kelsen's claim to the contrary, Cohen explicitly rejects natural law theory.[13] In fact, by virtue of his very method of hypothesis Cohen's philosophy of law must, by definition, oppose natural law theory. Note that both of these objections to Kelsen's use of Cohen from the perspective of Cohen's thought do not concern morality or ethics per se. Kelsen is certainly correct to note the centrality of ethics to Cohen's philosophy. Yet the ethical import of Cohen's thought is not antecedent to but rather the consequence of Cohen's method. In other words, understood on his own terms, Cohen argues that ethics follows from logic. And Cohen's logic has both theological implications and theological premises.

To appreciate the theological dimensions of Cohen's thought it is necessary to step back and consider his overall project. To state the obvious, Kelsen's concern is with law, and not science, morality, art, or religion. Cohen, in contrast, developed an entire system of philosophy that meant to account for all of these subjects. In the context of Kelsen's focus on law, we have seen that the basic norm is Hypothesis for Kelsen because it is the concept or foundation generated by thought that makes the Pure Theory possible. In the context of Cohen's concern with knowledge and truth as such, the idea of God is Hypothesis for Cohen because, he argues, God is the concept or foundation generated by thought that makes truth and knowledge possible. We might say that for Cohen, the idea of God is the laying of foundation for the laying of foundation. What does this mean?

In his *Ethik des reinen Willen*, the text that Kelsen cites, Cohen clarifies the distinction between science and ethics: whereas the former concerns what is (what Cohen calls the logic of identity), the latter concerns what ought to be

---

[12]   Kelsen, *supra* note 10, at 173.
[13]   For a comprehensive account of Cohen's rejection of natural law *see* Steven Schwarzschild, *Do Noachites Believe in Revelation?, in* THE PURSUIT OF THE IDEAL: JEWISH WRITINGS OF STEVEN SCHWARZSCHILD, 29–60 (Menachem Kellner, ed., 1990).

(what Cohen calls the logic of the ideal). Cohen then tries to account for how it is possible that we can reason about the relation between the real and the ideal (the relation between science and ethics). The idea of God is Cohen's answer to this question. The idea of God, Cohen maintains, bridges without unifying science and morality: "God guarantees complete harmony between being and what ought to be, but it and can be so for reason, only as idea . . . "[14] In an important sense, the idea of God is nothing other than the bridging without uniting of the empirical and the ideal. It is for this reason that Cohen defines God as truth: "*[T]he concept of God becomes the concept of Truth.*"[15] Truth for Cohen is the binding (though not the unification) of the real and the ideal. Note that the idea of God has ethical implications, upon which Cohen elaborates, but the idea of God as such does not have ethical content. Instead, the idea of God for Cohen is a concept generated by thought that makes truth possible. At the same time, the idea of God for Cohen is not a metaphysical construct but rather a product of thought. To paraphrase Edel, the idea of God, like the basic norm, is "not a foundation (Grundlage) given in and of itself in nature or by God, but the laying of a foundation (Grundlegung), that is, a Hypothesis."

Kelsen's Pure Theory of Law is predicated on binding, without unifying, the real and the ideal. Cohen maintains that "the natural will is not the pure will. The natural human being is not the pure human being. The empirical I is not the pure I." And Kelsen contends that the fact of law is not the pure law. To put the matter perhaps too sharply, what Kelsen doesn't want to admit, from the perspective of Cohen's philosophy, is that the idea of God makes the distinction and relation between the empirical and the pure possible in the first place. From the point of view of Cohen's philosophy, the very fact that Kelsen can ask and answer this question presupposes the idea of God.

Throughout his system, Cohen elaborates at length on the centrality of the idea of God for logic, ethics, aesthetics, and (as one would suspect) religion. Just as his understanding of Plato is crucial to his particular brand of neo-Kantianism, so too is Cohen's understanding of the medieval Jewish philosopher Moses Maimonides central to his arguments about God and religion within his system. Cohen credits Maimonides with "detach[ing] the concept of God from the concept of life"[16] and therefore with recognizing that God must be understood only as an idea. In making this claim, Cohen translates Maimonides' doctrine of negative attributes into his neo-Kantian system.

---

[14] HERMANN COHEN, ETHIK DES REINEN WILLENS 466 (2d. rev. ed., 1907; repr. 1981).
[15] *Id.* at 441 (emphasis his).
[16] *Id.* at 453.

While Cohen has much to say about the relationship between God's attributes and human virtue, his discussion of God's attributes in light of the idea of God's creation of the world is directly relevant for our discussion of Cohen and Kelsen. From a biblical point of view, God's sovereignty manifests itself in God's creation of the world. While the topic of God's creation of the world is a central, if not the central, issue discussed in Maimonides' *Guide of the Perplexed*, Maimonides does not explicitly link creation to God's attributes. Cohen, however, argues: "Creation is God's primary attribute . . . If the unique God were not creator, being and becoming would be the same; nature itself would be God. This, however, would mean: God is not. For nature is the becoming that needs being as its foundation."[17]

That Cohen draws on Maimonides' notion of creation allows us to appreciate two important points regarding Cohen's project and its conceptual relation to Kelsen's Pure Theory. First, in making creation an attribute of God, Cohen takes pains to emphasize, in keeping with his neo-Kantianism, that God's creation of the world is not a metaphysical but rather an epistemological issue. While Cohen's contention that Maimonides does not understand God or creation in metaphysical terms is questionable as a reading of Maimonides, we see that Cohen's claims about God and creation are nonetheless in keeping with Edel's description of the basic norm as not "existent and hidden somewhere in nature" and as not "fallen from the heavens in some mysterious way." Second, Cohen's approach to God's sovereignty and its relation to creation is formally parallel to Kelsen's approach to political sovereignty and its relation to the basic norm. Cohen recognizes that God's sovereignty over his creation is an essential component of the idea of God. But just as Kelsen's solution to the problem of sovereignty for legal theory entails making sovereignty internal to law, so too does Cohen's solution to the question of God's sovereignty for his neo-Kantian philosophy – which by definition rejects metaphysics – entail making God's sovereignty over creation internal to the idea of God.

In pointing out the parallels between Cohen's idea of God and Kelsen's basic norm, I do not aim to discredit Kelsen's use of Cohen, nor do I seek to defend, on philosophical or other grounds, Cohen's idea of God. Rather, the parallels between Cohen's idea of God and Kelsen's basic norm tell us something important about the basic norm, on the one hand, and about the perhaps surprising affinity between Kelsen's Pure Theory and Cohen's philosophical account of Judaism, on the other. With regard to the former, the affinity between Cohen's idea of God and Kelsen's basic norm underscores yet

[17]   Strauss, *supra* note 5, at 67.

again the inherent difficulty in Kelsen's conception of the basic norm: What can it be, if not a statement of value (moral or theological) or a statement of fact? Cohen's idea of God, as the hypothesis that makes thinking about the real and the idea possible, raises this question about the basic norm anew.

The parallels between Kelsen's Pure Theory and Cohen's philosophical account of Judaism allow us to return to Lieblich's disclaimer that it is potentially degrading to think about Kelsen as a Jewish thinker because Kelsen did not think of himself as such. But as I suggested above, the reason that labeling someone a Jewish thinker can be problematic is not only because such a label might conflict with a thinker's self-understanding. Such labels can also be conceptually problematic because they can essentialize Judaism and Jewishness. To recognize that Kelsen's basic norm may be dependent upon Cohen's particular philosophical interpretation of Judaism is merely but importantly to suggest that ideas, however pure we would like to make them, are always shaped by their historical contexts. So too, "Judaism" and "Jewishness" are historical constructs.[18] Just as "it is completely fair to discuss a thinker in light of the challenges his 'collective' faced within a certain society; challenges that might translate to common reactions and trends in thought," so too it is completely fair to discuss a thinker in light of the ideas that may have influenced him, inadvertently or not. In the case of Kelsen this is especially relevant, not because he was a Jew but rather because the notion that historical context (whether by way of the challenges faced by his collective or the context of his ideas) tells us something *conceptually relevant* about the Pure Theory challenges the *purity* of the Pure Theory (or any theory). Strikingly, for all their differences, Kelsen shares with Cohen and Strauss the quest to move philosophy beyond historicism of any kind. Kelsen's enduring legacy rests up whether or not his legal theory can in the end succeed in doing so. And again, we return to the conundrum of the basic norm, which, I have argued, Cohen's philosophical account of Judaism, can help us think about further.

---

[18]   On this topic, *see* Gershom Scholem, *Judaism*, *in* CONTEMPORARY JEWISH RELIGIOUS THOUGHT: ORIGINAL ESSAYS ON CRITICAL CONCEPTS, MOVEMENTS, AND BELIEFS, 505–08 (Arthur Cohen & Paul Mendes-Flohr, eds., 1987).

PART 3

LOUIS HENKIN

5

Louis Henkin, Human Rights, and American Jewish Constitutional Patriotism

Samuel Moyn

Louis Henkin (1917–2010) is remembered as the leading American legal advocate of human rights, and a prime or even the premier contributor to the international movement in their name. "There is no person on the planet," observed his follower Harold Koh, dean of Yale Law School and later State Department legal adviser, late in Henkin's life, "who has not found shelter or affirmation in his ideas."[1]

Henkin was also a Jew, and this mattered dearly to him. It is not unthinkable that in considering human rights law one might flirt with whether its norms or practices are a case of "Judaism terminable and interminable," as Henkin's colleague in Jewish history at Columbia University Yosef Yerushalmi famously described psychoanalysis, whatever the modern and secular trappings of both. Henkin himself, however, vigorously denied that the substance of Judaism helps account for what he liked to call the "ideology" of human rights. It seems hard to quarrel with him on this point. The very insistence of his dissociation of Judaism, indeed religion in general, from human rights is itself noteworthy. Yet the role that, if not Judaism, then Jews have played, individually or collectively, in the elaboration of international human rights is clearly a different matter.[2]

The historical relationship between the politics of the Jewish people and the formulation and advocacy of international human rights in the twentieth century is not only impossible to dismiss, but Henkin himself emphasized

---

[1] William Grimes, *Louis Henkin, Leader in Field of Human Rights Law, Dies at 92*, N.Y. TIMES, Oct. 16, 2010 or Emma Brown, *Louis Henkin, Pioneer of Human Rights Law and Columbia Professor, Dies at 92*, WASHINGTON POST, Oct. 21, 2010. Harold Hongju Koh, *The Future of Lou Henkin's Human Rights Movement*, 38 COLUMBIA HUMAN RIGHTS L. REV. 489 (2007).

[2] YOSEF HAYIM YERUSHALMI, FREUD'S MOSES: JUDAISM TERMINABLE AND INTERMINABLE (1992).

it – and illustrated it even more revealingly. In what follows I will revisit it, arguing that Henkin's case suggests the relationship was not long-term and enduring, but temporary and terminable, as was already becoming clear at the moment Henkin made himself the leading human rights lawyer of his time and place.

The year 1948 saw the promulgation of the Universal Declaration of Human Rights. It also saw the birth of the State of Israel. Yet to the extent there was ever overlap of the roads that led Jews in small or great numbers to those twinned events, they have since diverged profoundly: the belief that the creation of international human rights and the overall political interests of the Jewish people are compatible, whatever their earlier, partial, and intermittent contiguity, has largely evaporated. If modern Jewish politics contributed to international human rights, their relationship now looks contingent and highly short-lived. Henkin's case throws special light on it precisely because he threw himself into the cause of human rights when the relationship was about to fray.

That cause emerged for a few Jews – chiefly Europeans – before Zionism took hold, surging in the age of interwar experiments with internationalism. During and after World War II, a few more were attracted to it. Though the founding of Israel has never been uncontroversial, the country was not regularly indicted on human rights grounds in international fora until after 1967, and since then Israel has made itself more an adversary than an ally of the international human rights project, leaving most Jews loyally defensive about its record or even hostile to human rights as a mask for antisemitism, notably at their proprietary UN forum. As for those Jews who support human rights or even devote their lives to its promotion, their Zionism, except for a small subculture in Israel itself, is rare – to the extent they have much of any specifically Jewish politics at all. What coexisted, however uneasily, as potentially overlapping ideals now typically results in a forced choice. Paradoxically, Henkin's own promotion of international human rights began just as they finally became famous in the 1970s – and just when many Jews concluded they might need to turn on the principles because of the opprobrium for Israel that might follow.

To understand Henkin's trajectory through the era, as this parting of the ways loomed, there is no better choice than to provide a super-commentary on his own neglected essay on "Judaism and Human Rights" (1976).[3] I will follow Henkin's essay, in particular, by providing "three short papers" in one – on how Jewish religious thought contained few sources for human rights norms and law, on how it was rather modern Jewish politics that allowed for the

---

[3] Louis Henkin, *Judaism and Human Rights*, 4 JUDAISM 435–46 (1976).

project instead, and finally, on how Jews in turn contributed to the project's progress and breakthrough after World War II and especially as Henkin himself joined in – not coincidentally in the same era when he first considered the relation of Jews and human rights himself. Yet Henkin worried that it was already plain that "there is also, perhaps, a fourth paper needed," and decades on it is clear that he was right: since the 1970s the sad and, so far, permanent story of divergence between Jewish politics and human rights has only accelerated, after a brief period of harmony between them in which Henkin became their American standard-bearer. It was perhaps, I conclude, because he was so fervently American a Jew that he could do so, at this moment of impending crisis and divergence.

A JEWISH LIFE – AND WHY HUMAN RIGHTS ARE NOT JEWISH

Henkin was born in November 1917 in the small town of Smaljany, Belarus, during the complex period between the Soviet seizure of power in Petrograd a few weeks before his birth and the Treaty of Brest-Litovsk a few months after it. Henkin lived his first years in chaotic circumstances as the war ended, a short-lived Belarusian People's Republic was declared, the new Soviet Union conquered it, and (after a war with Poland) formalized international recognition of its annexation of eastern Belarus in the Treaty of Riga (1921).

For a long time he bore the name Eliezer, in remembrance of his grandfather, *rosh yeshiva* in Klimavichy, also in eastern Belarus. Henkin's father, Yosef Eliyahu Henkin, had been born there, trained in Slutsk, in central Belarus, at what had quickly become a renowned satellite of Lithuanian orthodoxy.[4] Living in Smaljany in the late 1910s and early 1920s, Henkin's father was the local rabbi; but after his wife, Eliezer's mother Rivka, died of dysentery, he remarried and migrated to America sometime between 1922 and 1923, where he led a synagogue and assumed the leadership of a recently founded Jewish philanthropic organization, Ezras Torah. Well known as an erudite and pious man, honored as a premier interpreter of Jewish law, and originator of a widely used liturgical calendar, Henkin's father made his home on the Lower East Side of Manhattan and sent his son to a local Orthodox school.

The younger Henkin remained observant to the end of his life, as a member of the Ramath Orah congregation near his Morningside Heights home, partly

---

[4]   All biographical information is from the chapter on Yosef Henkin's life by his grandson (and Louis Henkin's nephew): YEHUDA HERZL HENKIN, EQUALITY LOST: ESSAYS IN TORAH COMMENTARY, HALACHA, AND JEWISH THOUGHT (1999); *see also* the entry on s.v. Henkin, Joseph Elijah in ENCYCLOPEDIA JUDAICA (1971–72).

out of deep loyalty to his remote father, with whom he nevertheless had a powerful connection. That Henkin could become known essentially as a secular professor, after attending Yeshiva College on its new Washington Heights campus, was due – according to legend – to a chance application to Harvard Law School, from which he graduated in 1940. After a clerkship with Judge Learned Hand and army service during World War II, Henkin set off on a stellar legal career that included a Supreme Court clerkship with Justice Felix Frankfurter and service in the U.S. State Department before he entered the legal academy, first at the University of Pennsylvania in 1956 and then at Columbia starting in 1962. In his letter to Frankfurter recommending his clerk go on to the Supreme Court, Hand reported that, on his information, Henkin grew up "extremely poor," for "his father has devoted himself exclusively to the study of the Scriptures." One of Henkin's many points of distinction was that he was born – and, though living a radically different life than his father, always remained – much closer to the worlds of Jewish observance than many other of the Jews who became international lawyers in the twentieth century, and who contributed to the contemporary success of international human rights politics.[5]

Yet in 1976, in one of the few times the compartmentalization of his identities as Jew and international lawyer was bracketed, Henkin staunchly denied the relevance of Judaism to human rights – and presumably his own professional association with them. Neither the notions of a moral or legal right in general nor one against society's otherwise stronger claims in particular, Henkin acknowledged, "is discernible in the Bible or even in Rabbinic Judaism." Like the systems of belief and practice of many traditional societies, Judaism, he added, "knows not rights but duties, and at bottom all duties are to God. (If every duty has a correlative right, the right must be said to be in God!)"[6] This was, of course, not to say that the content of religious morality

---

[5]   Letter from Learned Hand to Felix Frankfurter (Mar. 18, 1941) (Learned Hand Papers, Harvard Law School Library, Box 73, Folder 5). According to his son, novelist Joshua Henkin, Louis Henkin "had hardly any Orthodox Jewish friends, hardly any observant Jewish friends at all, and I suspect many of the people whom he spent time with didn't know or were only dimly aware of the fact that he was observant." He attributes Henkin's highly privatized observance and compartmentalized Judaism to his otherwise secular life-style and less observant wife Alice. Joshua Henkin, *Sleeping on Felix Frankfurter's Couch*, My Jewish Learning, June 22, 2012, www.myjewishlearning.com/members-of-the-scribe/sleep ing-on-felix-frankfurters-couch/.

[6]   Henkin, *supra* note 3, at 436. Henkin wrote this paper as a delegate to a Vatican City meeting in 1975 on Jewish–Christian relations; *see* Joseph H. Lookstein, *The Vatican and the Jews 1975*, 15 Tradition 24 (1975). The paper was later republished with some differences *in* International Catholic–Jewish Liaison Committee, Fifteen Years of

could never align with some of the value commitments of what became the human rights canon, from the very belief in a distinction of right from wrong to a passion for justice, and from the prohibition of murder in the Ten Commandments to the imperative of charitable redistribution in the face of indigence and suffering. If one stressed these parallels – Henkin acknowledged in what reads like a classic exercise in religious apologetics – one could say human rights are "deeply rooted, or have strong parallels" in the Jewish religion. But ultimately Henkin was honest: whatever the concordances, they obtained in vastly different frameworks, since Henkin defined human rights not vaguely in terms of long-term values but specifically in terms of the modern commitment to give individuals recourse against government or society for violation of their moral or even more narrowly legal entitlements. For that very reason, "any attempt to correlate precisely contemporary concepts with ancient ones risks serious anachronism and other distortion."[7]

Even as he found the value congruence he could in a brief array of biblical and Talmudic examples, Henkin was thus far more skeptical than many a recent apologetic argument in the age of human rights about Judaism's role in bringing it about. And it was not just that Henkin denied that Judaism lacked any notion of natural rights, as distinct from the ethic of duties that divine law imposes on the Jewish people. More radically, Henkin cited the Talmudic story of the Oven of Akhnai (which famously assigns interpretation of divine law to humans alone) to prove the proposition that Jews never affirmed a rationalistic conception of law of any sort. Even in the absence of God's presence, law's authority depended on its linear connection back to his long-ago revelation, not its conformity to rationally available moral principles like those in Christian natural law traditions, let alone like those that modern human rights provide. These must have come from somewhere else.[8]

CATHOLIC–JEWISH DIALOGUE 1970–1985 (1988). As he remarked in somewhat lukewarm terms in a 1995 interview, "I have been interested in my Jewish roots. I identify [with] and am interested in the Jewish tradition and its scholarship and I play with that occasionally." ANTONIO CASSESE, FIVE MASTERS OF INTERNATIONAL LAW: CONVERSATIONS WITH R.-J. DUPUY, E. JIMÉNEZ DE ARÉCHAGA, R. JENNINGS, L. HENKIN, AND O. SCHACHTER 224 (2011).

[7] Henkin, *supra* note 3, at 436–38.
[8] *Id.* at 437; compare the general accounts, which along the way protest Henkin's denial of credit to Judaism for the concept of rights, in both Richard A. Freund, *Universal Human Rights in Biblical and Classical Judaism?*, 12 SHOFAR, Winter 1994, 50–66 and LENN GOODMAN, JUDAISM, HUMAN RIGHTS, AND HUMAN VALUES, esp. 49 and 165–66, note 1 (1998); on natural law and for more recent claims about Judaism and human rights, *see* David Novak's many contributions, which correctly make more room for rationalism within Jewish history than Henkin did but are otherwise on shaky ground. For a sample, David Novak, *The Judaic*

If his rare piece of writing for a Jewish audience strategically countenanced partial continuity between religion and human rights, the emphasis was opposite in Henkin's professional writings for an academic readership. In *The Age of Rights* (1990), Henkin took special care to discuss religion as "an alternative ideology" to human rights, indeed one far less amenable to compromise with the principles than twentieth-century secular faiths like development and even socialism allowed. Not Judaism but Protestantism (and then inadvertently) was the main source of the notion that citizens have entitlements against government. After the slow revolution in political understandings that followed – which went far beyond the more basic idea that morality implies limits to the state – religious ideology could no longer claim to be total in a post-Christian world that had given birth to secular human rights. Religion would have to reinvent itself to survive, accepting that traditional adherence would not interfere with the individual protection human rights would provide. "Religion will continue to reject human rights as a total ideology," Henkin concluded.

> It sees that human rights – cold rights – do not provide warmth, belonging, fitting, significance, do not exclude the need for love, friendship, family, charity, sympathy, devotion, sanctity, or for expiation, atonement, forgiveness. But if human rights may not be sufficient, they are at least necessary. If they do not bring kindness to the familiar, they bring – as religions have often failed to do – respect for the stranger.

The conclusion was even stronger when not speaking for publication: "Human rights are not a Judeo-Christian idea." It seemed clear to Henkin that, in spite of biblical concern for the stranger, Judaism nor any other religion had ever provided law to respect her rights.[9]

TOWARD HUMAN RIGHTS

None of these views were (or are) unusual. But they did mean that if Jews were to be credited for human rights, it would not be on grounds of their faith. In contrast, the political experience of Jews made them natural partisans of

---

Foundations of Rights, 47-63, in CHRISTIANITY AND HUMAN RIGHTS (John Witte, Jr. & Frank Alexander, eds., 2011).

9   LOUIS HENKIN, THE AGE OF RIGHTS 186 (1990). This passage was repeated when Henkin returned to his theory of religion as "an alternative ideology" to human rights in *Religion and Human Rights*, 2 J. OF RELIGIOUS ETHICS 229 (Fall 1998). Louis Henkin, *Human Rights and the Judeo-Christian Tradition*, WOODROW WILSON CENTER, June 23, 1988, at 5 (Louis Henkin Papers, Columbia University, Rare Books and Manuscripts Library, Box 17, Folder 14).

originally Protestant and soon secular human rights. To the extent Jews had been well treated over the millennia, whether in Christian or Muslim lands, it had been as a matter of "grace," Henkin wrote. Finally fortunate in their allies, and with a new Enlightenment recognition – Henkin cited Edmund Burke – that the friendless must make "humanity" their friend, it is no wonder that Jews embraced the new human rights that provided them moral entitlement and legal protection where they were emancipated.

Of course, initially, the Jews embraced rights as a matter of their national emancipations. But, Henkin observed, it was not too long after their initial rights-based emancipation in France in 1791 that Jews were "moved . . . to seek external protection against violations by various governments," attempting the pioneering transfer of rights from entitlements vindicated by citizens against their own states to ones Jews and other interested parties could help less fortunate Jews vindicate from the outside and in the name of humanity. What is now called "Jewish internationalism" was born. The rights of Jews, Henkin noted, were discussed directly or indirectly at many of the diplomatic conferences of the century that stretched from the Congress of Vienna after Napoleon's fall to the Versailles Conference after World War I, and great powers undertook bilateral intercessions on behalf of Jews, after the Damascus Affair made the possibility obvious. "The primitive international human rights movement of the 19th Century, much of it in behalf of Jews, proved fertile seed for an international law of human rights," Henkin explained, "undermining the notion that the way sovereign states treat their own inhabitants, even their own citizens, is not the proper business of anyone else."[10]

Still, Henkin papered over the uneasy coexistence from the beginning of what became the major divergence in Jewish politics in the long run. On the one hand, Jews could seek to install human rights above the nations so that international law would protect individuals from states that failed to do so. Most notably, "Jews were prominently both proponents and beneficiaries" of seeking "minority rights, internationally protected," especially after World War I allowed the League of Nations to experiment with a supranational protection regime for the new Eastern European states where most Jews lived. It was then after the Holocaust provided "the principal impetus to the drive to make international human rights law a reality" that anything truly transformative occurred, in what Henkin called "an act of moral reparations." At the same time, however, Jews sought national self-determination for themselves, and indeed "contributed to the triumph" of that principle, after some

---

[10] Henkin, *supra* note 3, at 440–42. Burke: "The Jews have no . . . power and no . . . friend to depend on. Humanity then must become their protector and ally."

Jews earnestly committed to it in 1917 achieved international support for
a Jewish homeland. As the history of the 1940s illustrated, the international
space could provide a platform on which Jews could seek protection from
other states, and one from which they could gain their own state.[11]

Yet even as he worked for the U.S. government as an internationally minded
lawyer, it is not really plausible to argue that for much of his academic career
Henkin was an advocate of human rights directly or even as a topic within
international law congenitally or consistently. Nor, for that matter, is there any
evidence of strong Zionist commitments.[12] If the 1940s were the breakthrough
moment for the Jewish people's twinned strategies of protection – achieving
a supranational project and a national home – Henkin devoted himself to
other things. He recalled that law school made him interested in domestic
politics, and that his experiences in World War II led him to turn to international affairs, and the extension for New Deal politics at the global level that
the United Nations might allow. As a foreign affairs officer in what became the
Bureau of the United Nations at the U.S. State Department, Henkin participated in the negotiation of the refugee convention, and some of his early
academic work "implicitly" might bear on the constitutional acceptability of
the international protection of human rights in treaties.[13] But there is too
much evidence on the other side of the ledger. As he established himself as

---

[11] *Id.* at 442. Henkin provides much less detail on these matters than Nathan Feinberg, *The
International Protection of Human Rights and the Jewish Question (A Historical Survey)*, 3 ISR.
L. REV. 487 (1968), and a whole new historiography led by Abigail Green, Carole Fink, and
others has since filled in the picture, though it is only now reaching the twentieth century. For
more information, *see* Samuel Moyn, *René Cassin, Jewish Internationalism, and Human
Rights, in* THINKING JEWISH MODERNITY: THINKERS, ARTISTS, LEADERS, AND THE
WORLD THEY MADE 278 (Jacques Picard et al., eds., 2016).

[12] In the remainder of this essay I am reprising, augmenting, and correcting my coverage of
Henkin's career *in* SAMUEL MOYN, THE LAST UTOPIA, chap. 5 (2010), published shortly
before Henkin's death. Besides taking on board new evidence and more recent literature, I have
rearranged and supplemented my arguments, but not seriously altered them, other than fixing
my mistaken denial to Louis Sohn of teaching human rights law very early in an American
university (about which I am very sorry).

[13] CASSESE, *supra* note 6, at 189. On Henkin and the refugee convention, *see* LINDA K. KERBER,
LOUIS HENKIN AND THE SHAPING OF THE UN CONVENTION ON REFUGEES AND THE
STATELESS (forthcoming); Louis Henkin, *The Treaty Makers and the Law Makers: The Niagara
Reservation*, 56 COLUM. L. REV. 1151 (1956); and esp. Louis Henkin, *The Treaty Makers and the
Law Makers: The Law of the Land and Foreign Relations*, 107 U. PENN. L. REV. 903, esp. 922–23
(1959). Lori Damrosch makes the claim about the "implicit" bearing of his early work on his later
work: Lori Fisler Damrosch, *Louis Henkin, 1917–2010*, 105 AM. J. INT'L . L. 295, note 48 (2011). *See*
earlier Catherine Powell, *Louis Henkin and Human Rights: A New Deal at Home and Abroad, in*
BRINGING HUMAN RIGHTS HOME: A HISTORY OF HUMAN RIGHTS IN THE UNITED
STATES (Cynthia Soohoo et al., eds., vol. 1, 2008).

a constitutional lawyer and an expert on the foreign relations law of the United States, Henkin gave precious little sign for decades of the emphasis he would suddenly give to international human rights. He was especially distinctive in this regard compared to the now-forgotten Jewish internationalists whose commitment to human rights from the 1940s on is much more demonstrable.

Continuing his admired older colleague Philip Jessup's cautious internationalism through the 1950s and 1960s, Henkin instead pursued a two-track academic agenda of investigating the conditions under which the world might avoid nuclear disaster through arms agreements and the constraints American constitutional law might place on incorporation of international legal norms of any kind. It was for understandable reasons that his scholarship did not revolve around human rights, reflecting the priorities of international law at the time. He did not cover the field in his teaching. His estimation of the United Nations in general (he did not even mention its human rights program in particular) was lukewarm. And if his early scholarship on the treaty power under the U.S. Constitution arguably did have implications for how to make an international human rights regime compatible with or even available within American constitutional law, he did not really draw them. When it came to constitutional law, for example his critique of the opinion in *Shelley v. Kraemer* (1948), the U.S. Supreme Court's famous prohibition of racially restrictive covenants under the Fourteenth Amendment, Henkin did not fault the justices for failing to take advantage of the possibility mooted at the time that the human rights provisions of the UN Charter might have relevance to the case. Serving on an American Bar Association committee on international law in the mid-1960s, Henkin clarified that the impending United Nations human rights covenants would not be unconstitutional for the country to ratify, even as he made sure "not to imply, at all, a view that it is desirable for the United States to adhere to human rights conventions."[14]

---

[14] *See* Louis Henkin, Arms Control and Inspection in American Law (pref. by Philip Jessup, 1958) and *Toward a "Rule of Law" Community, in* The Promise of World Tensions (Harlan Cleveland, ed., 1961). For an argument against utopian hopes in the United Nations, *see* Louis Henkin, *The United Nations and Its Supporters: A Self-Examination*, 78 Pol. Sci. Q. 504 (1963). On Jessup's influence, *see* Cassese, *supra* note 6, at 188–89, 197–98. Louis Henkin, *Shelley v. Kraemer: Notes for a Revised Opinion*, 110 U. Penn. L. Rev. 473 (1962). On invocation of the UN Charter in the run-up to the case, *see* Mark Bradley, *The Ambiguities of Sovereignty: The United States and the Global Human Rights Cases of the 1940s and 1950s, in* The State of Sovereignty: Territories, Laws, Populations (Douglas Howland & Luise White, eds., 2009). Louis Henkin, *Comments on the Report of the Subcommittee on the Human Rights Conventions*, memo to ABA International Law Committee (March or April 1964) (AJC Archives, FAD-IO, Series 1, Box 2, Folder 2). Thanks to James Loeffler for these last documents.

Henkin's first actual publication on the topic of human rights, which appeared only in 1965 (thus, when he was nearing fifty years old), conceded that there was little reason to treat what had once been announced so hopefully two decades earlier as more than moral norms to protect through the indirect strategy of securing peace and offsetting inequality. "Few appear prepared to build a kingdom of rights built with beams taken from their own eye," he acknowledged – and he was not one of them. "The principal hope for human rights," he insisted, "lies in continuing international peace, in reduced international tensions, in internal stability, in developing political institutions, and in rising standards of living. For the most part, human rights can only be promoted indirectly." In other words, the achievement of human rights could not be taken as a legal end in itself; for the community of international lawyers it was best to stick to its continuing mission of establishing a secure world and promoting well-being. Not surprisingly, then, in the first version of Henkin's classic work on observance of international law, *How Nations Behave* (1968), attention to human rights as a subset of the norms most of which – as he famously argued in the book – most nations follow most of the time was nil. (Only the second edition of the book in 1979 added a chapter on international human rights.) None of this is surprising; it was even to draw a sensible verdict in the depths of the Cold War struggle.[15]

As the rest of this volume shows, both in the 1940s and in the deep freeze when Henkin pursued other things, there were a few individuals and institutions attempting to extend the minor legacy for the international protection of human rights that prior Jewish politics had left. As Henkin recalled in 1976, "after the Second World War, Jews – many of them consciously, even explicitly, motivated by emotional Jewish values – were also prominent in the movement" (Henkin mentioned René Cassin, Hersch Lauterpacht, and Egon Schwelb along with "Rudolf" Lemkin, and various institutions). Yet Henkin's career itself is good evidence that they had not been terribly influential, precisely because he would later throw himself into the cause nearly *ex nihilo*. At best, obstacles in the way of hypothetical American participation in a supranational human rights regime due to misinterpretation of constitutional law could be cleared in hopes of some later and better day, as Henkin attempted to do in his other early article on the subject. At this point human rights law remained a boutique and unpromising topic, even for Henkin, and

---

[15]   Louis Henkin, *The United Nations and Human Rights*, 19 INTERNATIONAL ORGANIZATION 504 (1965); Louis Henkin, *International Law and the Behavior of Nations*, 114 RECUEIL DES COURS DE L'ACADÉMIE DE DROIT INTERNATIONAL DE LA HAYE 167 (1965); LOUIS HENKIN, HOW NATIONS BEHAVE: LAW AND FOREIGN POLICY (1968, 1979).

given how little it figured in his career, it is hardly as if he was simply biding his time.[16]

HENKIN AND THE JEWISH CONTRIBUTION TO INTERNATIONAL HUMAN RIGHTS LAW

It would be hard to overstate Henkin's eventual centrality as "grandfather" of human rights in American international law, idol for younger generations, and model of a career in the field. But then it is not beside the point for the whole field that Henkin's initial impulse to engage with human rights came in part through his connection with the world of American Jewish advocacy, not as an organic consequence of his previous scholarly profile. And once it is put in that context, Henkin's enthusiasm as an international lawyer looks late rather than early. More interestingly, the question becomes how it could take root when it germinated. After all, a Jewish internationalism revolving around human rights would soon collapse.

The American Jewish Committee (AJC) had made human rights lobbying at the United Nations one facet of its international political agenda as far back as the 1940s. Tasked by the AJC to evaluate likely political trends in the 1970s by Lower East Side childhood friend Sidney Liskofsky, who directed international affairs for the organization, Henkin signed on – for the first time anywhere in print to my knowledge – to the organization's long-affirmed position that "Jewish rights are human rights." But if so, he immediately insisted, then international law in the new environment after decolonization was unlikely to make the equation work. At an AJC-sponsored 1963 conference, Henkin had been invited to play the realist, rather than the idealist, casting cold water on any optimism that the human rights covenants that were supposed to follow the Universal Declaration were likely to improve enforcement of human rights standards (or were even feasible). As he had argued before, the only hope for the values embodied in human rights remained indirection: arms control in bilateral relations, and keeping a watchful eye on UN theatricality. But in the decade after 1968, things changed rapidly, in a series of nonlinear steps.[17]

---

[16] Henkin, *supra* note 3, at 443; *The Constitution, Treaties, and International Human Rights*, 116 U. PENN. L. REV. 1012 (1968); *see also "International Concern" and the Treaty Power of the United States*, 63 AM. J. INT'L. L. 272 (1969).

[17] Henkin's relationship with Liskofsky is probably the critical one. On Liskofsky's retirement in 1992, Henkin wrote him wondering how there could be a human rights movement without him, given his presence "at the creation, and before, in the days of Eleanor Roosevelt and René

In his earliest serious engagement with the topic of human rights, Henkin shared the general Western skepticism of what human rights had come to mean at the high tide of anti-colonialist sentiment. His arguments were not at all unusual when he registered the common complaint, in his first essay on the topic of 1965, that human rights had now been made unusable, whatever their potential original promise. "[T]he struggle to end colonialism," he wrote,

> swallowed up the original purpose of co-operation for promotion of human rights ... Anti-colonialism ... colored the human rights covenants[:] Self-determination was added to the roster of human rights as an additional weapon against colonialism though there was no suggestion that this was a right of the individual.

He had not addressed the topic before, except in an atmosphere of Cold War skepticism, and now decolonization had made things worse.[18]

In his AJC work on "the world of the 1970s," and no doubt in reference to the recriminations of the recent Tehran anniversary conference of the Universal Declaration in 1968 where anti-colonialism (and criticism of the then-new Israeli occupation) ruled, Henkin understandably advised caution: he remarked on behalf of his committee that the United Nations had proved a highly unreliable forum for rights claims, "although Arabs succeeded in airing their charges that Israel had violated human rights in the occupied territories." Though human rights were gaining in moral authority, if not real legality, they were now indeed proving to be a double-edged sword for Jews. It seemed bitterly ironic but now absolutely necessary that international Jewry, having "been in the forefront of organized efforts to improve international recognition, promotion, and protection of human rights" must now show "signs of discouragement and doubt about their effort," especially given abuse of Israel in the international forum.[19]

Cassin. You were at Montreal, at Uppsala, at Strasbourg, and at a host of other places that were milestones in the slow but irreversible march of the Human Rights Movement." (These events are covered in what follows.) (Henkin Papers, Box 3, Folder 42.) The full 1963 remarks are in the AJC Archives, FAD-IO, Unnumbered Box, and summarized in the discussion after John Humphrey, *Human Rights*, ANN. REV. UNITED NATIONS AFFAIRS 122–24 (1962–1963). Compared to his long-standing involvement with the AJC, Henkin had only minor and unofficial dealings with the more Zionist American Jewish Congress (Henkin Papers, Box 3, Folder 36).

[18] Henkin, *supra* note 15, at 513; *cf.* Henkin, *supra* note 15, at 216.

[19] [Louis Henkin,] *The World of the 1970s: A Jewish Perspective* (Task Force Report, AJC, 1972), 32, 34, 36 and WORLD POLITICS AND THE JEWISH CONDITION (Louis Henkin, ed., 1972). (Henkin wrote the long introduction and short epilogue drawing conclusions for the American Jewish community, while Liskofsky wrote a dedicated chapter on international human rights.)

In spite of this worry, around the same time Henkin took the lead in setting up the American sister to the International Institute for Human Rights in Strasbourg that Cassin had founded with his 1968 Nobel peace prize monies. Like Cassin's outfit, this institute saw its primary mission as educational, at the university level, and its initial activities included sponsorship of the first-ever compilation of a human rights casebook. Henkin taught his and Columbia Law School's first course on international human rights in 1971–72 (both Schwelb and Louis Sohn had taught small courses on the topic at Harvard and Yale Law Schools in the prior decade, with Sohn publishing his pioneering casebook in 1973, together with Thomas Buergenthal, his student). Late the same year, Henkin testified at Minnesota Rep. Donald Fraser's pioneering congressional hearings on American foreign policy and human rights. There, Henkin ruefully reported no real consensus around even what human rights meant, given the developments since the immediate post-war moment when "the U.N. was much smaller and dominated by Western states and Western ideas." Now, except for more general agreement on egalitarianism, the rise of the third world, along with the continuing influence of communism, meant conflict over the very definition of the idea for international purposes. The only imaginable remedy for the "sense of crisis about international protection of human rights" was UN reform. Given that the rise of grassroots NGOs (which Henkin rarely mentioned) and even Fraser's own hearings mattered because they portended bypassing the United Nations as the exclusive forum for the human rights idea, it is a revealing affirmation.[20]

For even at this late date, the die was not yet cast. Participating in a 1974 McGill University colloquium on Judaism and human rights, Henkin – in showing how genuinely radical a conversion in expectations about the

---

[20] Henkin attended a May 1969 meeting at the New York law firm Coudert Bros. with Cassin present to plan the institute, which Henkin announced a year later (Louis Sohn Papers, Harvard Law School, Box 19–9); Louis Henkin, *The United States Institute of Human Rights*, 64 Am. J. Int'l. L. 924 (1970). On behalf of the Institute, Henkin chaired a session on teaching human rights at the American Society of International Law meetings in spring 1971. See *The Teaching of International Human Rights*, 65 Am. J. Int'l. L. 240 (1971). He also attended the Strasbourg institute's summer session in 1972 (Sohn papers, Box 109–12). The casebook is Louis Sohn and Thomas Buergenthal, International Protection of Human Rights (1973). But by 1976, Henkin suggested that the U.S. institute project had reached its limits, writing to Sohn that he was "not happy at our small activity, but I see no prospect for major change and no one around prepared to do more." Letter from Louis Henkin to Louis Sohn (June 3, 1976) (Sohn papers, Box 127–8). (It subsequently closed.) For the Fraser testimony, *see* U.S. House of Representatives, International Protection of Human Rights: The Work of International Organizations and the Role of U.S. Foreign Policy 355, 357 (1974).

viability of human rights there was in the few years of the mid-1970s –
continued to suggest that the main story of human rights protection was
idealistic disappointment, and Henkin explicitly warned that idealists would
only repeat their past mistakes by pining for radical transformation in the
fortunes of their cause. The unavoidable conclusion is that even by that
moment in the mid-1970s, with the percolation of dissidence skyrocketing
and other forces gathering, no tipping point for the championship of human
rights had occurred, for Henkin at least. This was not a personal failing unless
he is forced to play the role of prophet: his inability to imagine an impending
novelty is simply testimony to how unpredictable it really was. Indeed, he was
completely self-aware of his own belatedness, telling Antonio Cassese in a 1995
interview that he "became active" in human rights "about 15 years ago" – even
less time than was actually the case.[21]

Henkin's belatedness, indeed, primarily matters because it reminds us how
late the rest of the world was to human rights, in spite of its pioneers, including
its Jewish ones. For recalling that a few Jews played an indispensable role in
the development of international human rights before also requires that the
phenomenon is not exaggerated. The contributions of Jews like Cassin and
Lauterpacht to the origins of human rights in the 1940s need to be both
understood and kept in their proper place in any story of the origins of the
global and European human rights project, whose progress depended on
a huge range of factors, more important constituencies, and many later con-
tingencies. That Schwelb, that fascinating figure, heroically shepherded
human rights through difficult early decades at the United Nations and
retained optimism in their ultimate success is ultimately a tiny piece of the
overall picture of their post-war vicissitudes. Correspondingly, the marginal
relevance of international human rights to Jewish history and even Jewish
internationalism in the period – for all the interest in it that this volume
exemplifies – is hard to doubt. No one has made the case that many (let
alone most) Jews heard about, let alone committed to, the idea of human
rights in the 1940s, either as a separable body of abstract norms from the
liberalism, socialism, or communism they endorsed in their old nations or
new one, or as the specific project consecrated in the UN program. In
comparison, all of them knew, and nearly all enthusiastically celebrated, the
birth of the State of Israel, and read the affirmation in its Declaration of

---

[21] The draft papers of the McGill Conference are located (among other places) in the Moses
Moskowitz Papers, Columbia University, Rare Books and Manuscripts Library; a version of
Henkin's contribution appears as Louis Henkin, *The United States and the Crisis in Human
Rights*, 14 Va. J. Int'l. L. 653 (1973–74). Cassese, *supra* note 6, at 194.

Independence of "the natural right of the Jewish people to be masters of their own fate, like all other nations, in their own sovereign state."[22] Even within the ambit of Jewish organizations like the AJC that concerned themselves after World War II with international human rights politics in any forum, it was a peripheral topic rather than a major concern, with the possible exception of the era of the campaign to redeem Soviet Jewry; and what is most interesting in retrospect is that those organizations soon deprioritized human rights rapidly as the latter became cudgels to attack the Israeli occupation (or Israel itself), especially after 1967.[23]

It is extremely interesting, nonetheless, that in a passing window of opportunity it was Henkin's association with Jewish internationalism that helped light his own fuse. Perhaps his career would have taken the direction it did anyway – but it seems unlikely, or that Jewish internationalism helped him steal a march on most other liberal internationalists, and become one of their legal icons in, through, and after the human rights revolution. Given Henkin's origins, perhaps the Jewish background of many Soviet dissidents played a role in what Henkin thought human rights could achieve, or the distinct but related reinvention of the cause of Soviet Jewry in human rights terms. Henkin attended the pivotal Uppsala conference in summer 1972 that retrieved "the right to leave and to return" from the Universal Declaration so as to mobilize it on behalf of persecuted Soviet Jewry. It left no discernible impact on his writing, but the larger course of the 1970s and the unexpected explosion in human rights history at the time caused Henkin's optimism and scholarly commitment to the field alike to soar off the charts, to the point of permanently redefining his career and his memory. This redefinition is not anticipated in anything Henkin wrote, even as his publications of the immediate moment register its transformative power. The rise of transnational human rights activism and a huge boost to the prestige of the norms saved them from their perceived anti-colonialist capture. For the lawyer that he was, it clearly also mattered that the international human rights covenants surprisingly came into force in 1976, thanks in no small part to unexpected ratifications from communist nations and postcolonial states. And U.S. President Jimmy Carter's election in 1977, with his storied human rights rhetoric, had

---

[22] Cited in Samuel Moyn, *The Universal Declaration of Human Rights of 1948*, 40 CRITICAL INQUIRY 378 (2014), where the whole problem of popular and Jewish reception of human rights in the 1940s is discussed.

[23] On Cassin, *see* Samuel Moyn, *René Cassin, in* RENÉ CASSIN AND HUMAN RIGHTS: FROM THE GREAT WAR TO THE UNIVERSAL DECLARATION (J. M. Winter and Antoine Prost, eds., 2013), esp. chap. 11, and Chapter 9 in this volume, by Moria Paz; on Schwelb, *see* Moyn, *supra* note 12, at 199 and Chapter 7 in this volume, by Mira Siegelberg.

a galvanizing effect on an American liberal like Henkin. From that exciting time, Henkin threw himself completely into the cause, without ever explicitly reflecting on the conditions that had made his drastic self-reinvention possible.[24]

In 1977, Henkin began a series of colloquia at Columbia University and the next year founded the first American university human rights center. (Around the same time, Henkin's wife Alice joined the Aspen Institute and began a series of influential human rights conferences.) Henkin introduced human rights into a popular international law textbook over which he assumed supervision as well as into the storied restatement of U.S. foreign affairs law for which he served as reporter in these years. In 1978, Henkin published *The Rights of Man Today*, and began writing the series of essays that would eventually appear as his classic work, *The Age of Rights*. In apparent recognition of the previously unanticipated power of forces outside the United Nations – notably nongovernmental organizations – to define and advance human rights, Henkin joined the board of the Lawyers Committee for Human Rights in 1978 and played a guiding role in its early years.[25]

Conveniently for gauging why he threw himself into these activities, when Henkin came to the prospects for international human rights in *The Rights of*

---

[24] At Uppsala, Henkin did not present a paper but he did serve on the drafting committee that generated the meeting's declaration. THE RIGHT TO LEAVE AND TO RETURN: PAPERS AND RECOMMENDATIONS OF THE INTERNATIONAL COLLOQUIUM HELD IN UPPSALA, SWEDEN, 19–20 JUNE 1972, 565, 568 (Karel Vasak & Sidney Liskofsky, eds., 1976); *cf.* Cassese's participant memories in Cassese, *supra* note 6, at 187, reporting that Henkin saved the endeavor from crisis after the Palestinian representative Musa Mussawi withdrew, on the grounds that exit rights for Soviet Jews could not be championed if return rights for Palestinians were ignored. Henkin also traveled to Moscow and Leningrad in the late 1970s. For my larger case about the transformative period of the mid-1970s, *see* Moyn, *supra* note 12, at chap. 4 as well as THE BREAKTHROUGH: HUMAN RIGHTS IN THE 1970S (Jan Eckel & Samuel Moyn, eds., 2013).

[25] This NGO is now known as Human Rights First. Louis Henkin, *The Internationalization of Human Rights*, 6 PROC. GENERAL EDUCATION SEMINAR 1 (1977) and other information on the Center *in* Henkin Papers, Box 3; HUMAN DIGNITY: THE INTERNATIONALIZATION OF HUMAN RIGHTS (Alice H. Henkin, ed., 1978). For the casebook evolution, *cf.* WOLFGANG FRIEDMANN ET AL., CASES AND MATERIALS ON INTERNATIONAL LAW (1969), with almost nothing on human rights, with LOUIS HENKIN ET AL., INTERNATIONAL LAW: CASES AND MATERIALS chap. 12 (1980), which, interestingly, does mention [807] the 1940s attempt to make the UN Charter justiciable in U.S. courts. (Henkin also led a long-standing casebook project for human rights specifically that first appeared in 1999.) Nicholas A. Lawn, "Orthodoxy of the Most Scrupulous Type"?: A Brief History of the Restatement (Third) of the Foreign Relations Law of the United States (2014) (LL.M. thesis, Columbia Law School). *See also* Henkin's response to the Helsinki process, Louis Henkin, *Human Rights and "Domestic Jurisdiction,"* *in* HUMAN RIGHTS, INTERNATIONAL LAW, AND THE HELSINKI ACCORDS (Thomas Buergenthal, ed., 1977).

Man Today, he reprised (often verbatim) but also updated the lecture he had originally given in 1974 at the McGill conference on Judaism and human rights that had once sounded the theme of "disappointed expectations." There was no agreement concerning the value of the rights, there was resistance to bothering states that violated them, states shied away from committing to hard-won new instruments (to say nothing of complying with them), and to the extent human rights were made an issue it was normally in "politicized" form. Yet as he noted at a meeting of the American Society of International Law in the banner year of 1977, the concept of human rights was transformed from a "long-hair, do good, fringe operation" into "daily news." In 1978, Henkin could therefore add a new section to his prior melancholy reflections. Quite suddenly, "the mood of disappointment and resignation that had hung over the international human rights movement lifted in the 1970s, and gave way to renewed determination and commitment." Like so many others who came to human rights through Jewish internationalism, Henkin found much to cele-brate in the surprising breakthrough period for human rights, in which their promise was, if not redeemed, then at least renewed. But for Henkin, it was only shortly before that breakthrough – and in part thanks to Jewish internationalism – that he signed on to a cause newly worth massive investment.[26]

A ZIONIST – AND AMERICAN JEW

Even then, if Jewish internationalism had belatedly led Henkin to human rights, there was always the threat of "reviving fears" that they would have to be qualified in view of crosscutting loyalties. In his 1976 essay, Henkin wrote,

> Jewish ideas outside the framework of traditional religion . . . are in tune with human rights. The State of Israel . . . has effective national laws comparable to those in the most enlightened constitutions. (Exceptions, in the treatment of Arab populations, are seen as temporary and required by national security in war imposed on the state.)

And yet Jews loyal to Israel were not wrong to judge that "Jews have seen international law and institutions designed for the protection of human rights diverted, if not perfected to political ends hostile to Jewish interests." It was not that "Israel can do, and has done, no wrong" but that she "was unfairly singled

---

[26] Henkin, *The United States, supra* note 21 at 654–63; *Human Rights: A New Policy by a New Administration*, 71 PROC. AM. SOC. INT'L. L. 68 (1977); LOUIS HENKIN, THE RIGHTS OF MAN TODAY 113 (1979).

out" and her faults "wildly exaggerated," to the point that "it is no longer possible to identify valid charges against Israel in the mass of false accusations and distortions."[27]

So whatever the new grounds for optimism about human rights were to which Jewish internationalism had led Henkin through the 1970s, they were shadowed by older and impending causes of depression. The short-term presence of Jewish causes like that of some dissidents and then refuseniks, which gave Jewish internationalism a second life and made it a grassroots cause, also concealed the coming mood that would make international norms seem too threatening to be dependable, let alone exhilarating. The question was whether the passing of the conditions that allowed the retrieval of human rights for their international purposes from the fora where they were directed against Israel might make Henkin revert to his old avoidance or even skepticism of the topic. Antisemitism was escalating after its brief post-war moratorium, and governments did not seem set to "depoliticize" human rights so as to "restore" them to "noble purposes." If the 1970s were the decade of human rights, they were also, Henkin recorded, the time of diverse episodes of Jew hatred, a disturbing alliance of Arabs and Soviets in anti-Zionist agitation, and the General Assembly recognition of the terroristic Palestine Liberation Organization – all before it branded Zionism racism. "The faith of Jews in international protection through universal action focused at the United Nations has faltered," Henkin wrote.[28]

In a 1979 article that Henkin contributed to the belated publication of a selection of the McGill conference papers under the editorship of his Columbia philosophy colleague David Sidorsky, Henkin kept hope alive. Continuing his ties with the AJC projects that had originally drawn him into human rights discussions, Henkin argued that abdication was not the answer: "The answer to politicization in international forums is to fight it," Henkin argued, "not to abandon those who do and to leave the field to the enemies of human rights." The Diaspora – which depended on international protection of human rights, should their host nations shift – was permanent not transitory, and "surely, protection for the Jews outside Israel should not be sacrificed from some misguided notion that international human rights must be scrapped lest they be used against the State of Israel." Anyway, Jewish interest in human rights had never been purely strategic, and hardly lasted only so long as Jewish interests were at stake: "Jews will

---

[27]   Henkin, *supra* note, 3 at 439, 445.
[28]   *Id.* at 445–46.

remain dedicated to human rights in principle and program; they cannot do otherwise."[29]

Henkin certainly could not do otherwise after Jewish internationalism helped lead him to the cause, even as Jewish internationalism proved fickler than he did, losing its ideological and practical association with human rights. For it is equally obvious that few followed Henkin precisely, as many more saw a choice open up for them between the defense of the State of Israel and the defense of international human rights. It would also seem to follow that Henkin became the famed human rights lawyer he did on Jewish grounds almost at the last possible moment it was likely for him to do so. And if he could muster the strong commitment to the human rights to which Jewish internationalism had helped lead him, I believe, it must have been because Henkin's true devotion and long-husbanded Jewish identity was much more that of a proud American nationalist, and because he had long since opted to be an American liberal nationalist with fewer complications in his own relationship to internationalism – though not none.

This devotion ran very deep and its most revealing expression is to be found in a wartime letter Henkin wrote to his brother and sister-in-law from Italy, concerning the future of Palestine and whether, as they had apparently suggested, moving there to agitate for the Zionist dream was incumbent upon them. "I don't know whether I'd be willing to exchange on a permanent basis my American roots for those in a Zionist Palestine," Henkin explained.

> For all my Jewishness and tradition, my education and heritage is largely American. You see what I mean? [E]ven my universalism or humanism, as I like to think, it is largely American. I'm not talking now flags and 4th of July but I think you see what I mean. It was its books and mores that molded me and a firm, fervent belief in the principles of a country which *to me* negate any chauvinistic devotion to country – even this country itself.

Elsewhere in the same long letter, he worried that Zionism might even distract American Jews from improving their own experiment:

> I never got the impression that the "average Zionist" was any more liberal than the "average American." I should think they would be, as all minority groups living in glass houses should be. But, for example, I've seen lots of Jim Crow sentiment among Jews . . . I don't mean that you can't be a liberal if you

---

[29] Louis Henkin, *Human Rights: Reappraisal and Readjustment, in* Essays on Human Rights: Contemporary Issues and Jewish Perspectives 86–87 (David Sidorsky, ed., 1979).

also have self-interest in the cause. But the *only* liberal causes I've ever seen
most of the Zionist leaders associated with were the self-interested ones.

He concluded, "I do confess that the Palestine which would perpetuate the
tradition and the culture, the history, the poetry, and the pathos of our past
thousand years, that would be very dear to me. I don't see it yet in modern
Zionism." Instead, it was aspirational beyond the horizon – a commitment to
"an unborn nation." But, he observed "I've always been, and still suffer from it,
devoted to the mere present, to living human beings and those about to be.
I hold no brief for nations and races and their continued existence as such."
America was a nonnational – as he hoped it would someday be a nonracial –
nation. To be sure, after 1948, Henkin routinely cited the dictum of his father,
no Zionist before, to the effect that once it had come to exist, the Jewish state
surely had to be defended and protected. But it was a subsidiary commitment.
In contrast, though his vocation for international human rights came late,
Henkin's American liberalism came early and endured powerfully.[30]

As William Forbath has recently written, "Interpreting and expounding the
U.S. Constitution is a Jewish calling." If Henkin answered to this calling, as
the bulk of his career before he became a human rights scholar indicates, he
also came late enough in an already long tradition of American Jewish legal
liberals to give him a new task. The tradition had formed long before for
American Jewish lawyers whose most meaningful and sometimes sole enactment of Jewish identity was the defense of constitutional liberalism (e.g., in
the irreligious Frankfurter, over whose funeral no rabbi officiated but at
which Henkin did say kaddish). As Henkin remarked in the 1995 interview,
"I am pleased to be identified as a liberal." In and after the 1970s, the
novel challenge was to internationalize the American Jewish dream through
human rights – and to ask America not to contradict its purposes in its habitual
phobia of the international law defending those rights. Henkin's service as
a "G.I. Jew" and his extraordinary success in his adoptive country understandably stoked an ardor for its political traditions; as Jews like him had

---

[30] This handwritten letter, dated May 23, must be from 1944. It is in the possession of the family
      and I am grateful to Alice Henkin for permission to cite it here. A couple of years earlier in
      correspondence with Hand, addressing what might happen to the Nazi order in the distant
      future if the Allies failed, Henkin wrote, "I find no solace in the hope for humanity 500 years
      from now. The human race means rather little, it seems to me, except as it applies to humans
      living now, and suffering and hoping and looking for the light . . . ." Letter from Louis Henkin
      to Learned Hand (Oct. 9, 1942) (Hand Papers, Box 73, Folder 5). Further impressions of
      Henkin's life in the American South and then in Italy, France, and Germany during World
      War II are available in other letters he wrote Hand, preserved in Learned Hand Papers, some
      partly published *in* REASON AND IMAGINATION: THE SELECTED CORRESPONDENCE OF
      LEARNED HAND (Constance Jordan, ed., 2013).

believed for decades, it was its liberal constitutional principles, however honored in the breach, that made it great. Only now, after the Vietnam War, liberalism committed many to international human rights too, suddenly understood as principles – as Carter claimed in his farewell address as Henkin's activism entered high speed – that made America possible in the first place.[31]

Henkin's Americanization of the concept of human rights was plain in the historical narrative he told in *The Rights of Man Today* and ever after. It was mainly here that Henkin diverged from Lauterpacht's 1950 study of human rights, on which his work otherwise leaned heavily. Thomas Paine, presumably for his credentials in setting off the American experiment, loomed especially large in Henkin's understanding of the origins and meaning of human rights. One obvious explanation for Henkin's warmly patriotic universalism is that it was a strategic move. America's commitment to the idea of international human rights since 1945 had been wayward at best, particularly from the perspective of formal treaties like the human rights covenants. The United States – unlike communist and Third World nations, Henkin acknowledged – had ratified none so far. In 1977, in a letter to the *New York Times*, Henkin insisted that the International Covenant on Civil and Political Rights was not simply "an amazing tribute to Western values" but, even more specifically, to congenitally American assumptions. "It has made our ideology the international norm," he wrote.[32] It therefore made perfect sense to join.

But together with strategy, there was heartfelt belief. As *The Rights of Man Today* makes abundantly clear, Henkin felt a genuine investment in the superiority of the American political and social model as synonymous with a commitment to human rights. The United States, Henkin argued, pioneered commitment to the values to which even its opponents were now forced to pay lip service. Henkin, in other words, fits naturally into the general story of

---

[31] WILLIAM FORBATH, JEWS, LAW AND IDENTITY POLITICS IN THE PROGRESSIVE ERA (Mar. 31, 2014) (unpublished manuscript); *Johnson Attends Private Funeral Service; Kaddish Said*, JEWISH TELEGRAPHIC AGENCY, Feb. 25, 1965; NOAH FELDMAN, SCORPIONS: THE BATTLES AND TRIUMPHS OF FDR'S GREAT SUPREME COURT JUSTICES 420 (2010); CASSESE, *supra* note 6, at 194; James Earl Carter, Farewell Address (Jan. 14, 1981). For reasons stated, the standard literature on liberalism and American Jews provides the best framework for understanding Henkin and Jewish participation in much other American human rights advocacy. The progressive and legally oriented liberalism of Henkin's sort, of course, was and remains a large niche option in the overall ecology of American Jewish politics. On the progressive part of the niche on the American scene, *see* STUART SVONKIN, JEWS AGAINST PREJUDICE: AMERICAN JEWS AND THE FIGHT FOR CIVIL LIBERTIES (1997); on the legal part, *see* JEROLD S. AUERBACH, RABBIS AND LAWYERS: FROM TORAH TO THE CONSTITUTION (1978).

[32] *The Case for U.S. Ratification*, N.Y. TIMES, Apr. 1, 1977.

American liberalism of the era, which proceeded into an age of "reclaiming American virtue" in a moment of ideological recovery in the 1970s after a disastrous earlier form of Cold War globalism. As far as I have been able to discover, Henkin did not seriously comment on the Vietnam War, either outraged by America's war in the first place or even, like his colleague Telford Taylor, moved to intervene by its crimes of war after the My Lai revelations. While others did intervene, for no other American international lawyer were human rights relevant to the debate either. In the decisive period a few years later, unlike Carter, Henkin did not reflect on what American liberalism had to recover from, nor did he present human rights as an American ideology that had ever been interrupted, let alone betrayed. Paine "proclaimed the rights of man in national society [but] would have welcomed international human rights," Henkin wrote in 1978, and the legal challenge was to interpret and expound the U.S. Constitution so as to make the American polity that Paine had made possible two centuries before part of an international rights regime.[33]

With his priorities there, Henkin thus skirted the emerging difficulty of reconciling Zionism with international human rights, especially after 1967, in order to take on the still major but undoubtedly more manageable challenge of updating American liberal nationalism instead. Of course, this meant that Henkin had to oppose the more autarkic form of American nationalism and suspicion of international commitments: trying to exorcise what Henkin famously called the "ghost" of Ohio Senator John Bricker, the Cold War opponent of binding America to international treaty. Henkin had called for an America integrated in global law in his scholarship even before human rights emerged as a plausible imperative within it, but now the agenda had new content and new force. Once again, a comparison of the early and late 1970s in Henkin's appraisal of this scene shows barometric change, as the human rights revolution provided more cause for optimism than before.[34]

---

[33] Barbara J. Keys, Reclaiming American Virtue: The Human Rights Revolution of the 1970s (2014); Henkin, *supra* note 26, at 137. On U.S. international lawyers during the Vietnam era, *see* Samuel Moyn, *From Antiwar Politics to Antitorture Politics*, in Law and War (Austin Sarat et al., eds., 2014); *see also* Henkin's correspondence with Lloyd Weinreb, Nov. 28 and Dec. 1, 1967, the former demurring to the latter's invitation to sign a Vietnam protest statement (Henkin Papers, Box 3, Folder 59).

[34] Louis Henkin, *U.S. Ratification of Human Rights Conventions: The Ghost of Senator Bricker*, 89 Am. J. Int'l. L. 341 (1995). So far as I can tell Henkin avoided the topic of Israel in print in later life, but he was anxious after 1967 about its occupation, and (to take one example) noted in a 1988 speech that "[t]he derogation from rights in the occupied territories is – it is to be hoped – a temporary diversion to be justified, if at all, as 'strictly required by the exigencies of

Through the 1960s, Henkin recorded, the constitutional liberals who had agitated for America to commit to international human rights simply did not exist. "The domestic civil rights movement and our foreign policy on human rights have remained discrete and unrelated," Henkin correctly remarked in 1974. "Even the victims of human rights violations in this country have not seriously sought international protection, nor urged U.S. participation in international programs out of sympathy with victims elsewhere." As a matter of fact, to the extent those victims elsewhere blamed not their own regimes alone but American Cold War policy, they almost never did so in terms of "human rights violations," let alone see America's participation in the international regime as the remedy. The argument in the United States had thus long been between two parties who found American participation redundant of its already strong commitment to constitutional rights, with one side arguing that it was worth doing anyway because (in Henkin's words), "U.S. adherence would entail no change in U.S. law, institutions, or practices, … [but would help] to encourage others and to give us the right to intervene in support of human rights in countries where such intervention is needed." Still, as late as 1974, the argument was not winning, "radical transformations in U.S. attitudes [were] not in sight," and it was not foreseeable that the United States would ever supplement its constitutional rights with adherence to "human" ones.

Four years later, however, the intervening human rights revolution had created new openings in Henkin's outlook to advance America's agenda as well as to hone its practices in view of global norms – even when it came to long-neglected economic and social rights. It was to probing and exploiting these openings to which much of the rest of Henkin's labors (not to mention those of his students and followers) were to be dedicated. If he did not sour thereafter on international human rights like so many other Jews between then and now, it was because his American commitments were stronger than his Zionism was and because it was more promising, though never uncomplicated, to regard the age of rights as a chance to update his American liberalism rather than guard it from threats.[35]

---

the situation in a public emergency,'" – i.e., as a derogation from human rights treaty, and not merely under the international law of occupation. Henkin, *supra* note 9, at 4.

[35] *Cf.* Henkin, *supra* note 21, at 663 and 666, to HENKIN, *supra* note 26, at 121–22, 126–32. His later work on the topic includes Louis Henkin, *Constitutional Rights and Human Rights*, 13 HARV. C. R.-CIV. LIBERTIES L. REV. 593 (1978).

CONCLUSION

For Henkin, then, America perfectly suited his compartmentalized identity in which observant Judaism remained a private affair and constitutional liberalism a public faith. "It has been suggested that for generations of Jews the Constitution has been a substitute for the Bible," Henkin mused on the bicentennial of America's "holy writ." There were massive "conceptual differences between the regime of divine commands and that of constitutional rights," but America's true genius is that both systems could coexist: "Some will ask: which system is 'better,' that of the Torah or American constitutionalism? In the United States many Jews seem to opt for both." American liberalism for Jews allowed dual rival commitments because its solution was one faith and scripture in public and another in private.[36]

Henkin innovated a new version of the long-standing romance of this American liberalism for Jews, which also committed him to a surprising extent to the characteristic exceptionalist nationalism of American politics. Belief in improvement within the framework of the law unified his career and life, with American constitutional liberalism providing its signature. As a recent branch of that longer road, Henkin blazed a now-popular trail into interest in international human rights law. In July 1993, then-Supreme Court nominee Ruth Bader Ginsburg wrote Henkin to ask what she should say in her confirmation hearings about international human rights, if given the chance. Henkin provided this suggested text:

> Our Constitution, especially our Bill of Rights, is our national pride, and justly so. It is also our hallmark and lesson to the world. The world continues to watch and learn from us. But we must also pay decent respect to the opinions of mankind, and be prepared to learn from others. In particular, I am pleased to note that we seem to be rejoining the International Human Rights Movement which we helped launch.[37]

The trail Henkin blazed is still mostly pursued by American scholars trained as constitutional lawyers who begin with U.S. foreign affairs law as their prime interest, not international law directly, and hope to redeem the nation in the name of what they regard as its founding principles in the face of a confusing right wing that stands for impregnable sovereignty, go-it-alone unilateralism,

---

[36] Louis Henkin, *The Constitution and Other Holy Writ: Human Rights and Divine Commands*, Jewish Q. Rev. (Supplement: "The Judeo-Christian Tradition and the U.S. Constitution) 60, 65–66 (1989).

[37] Letter from Ruth Bader Ginsburg to Louis Henkin (July 1993) and letter from Louis Henkin to Ruth Bader Ginsburg (July 1993) (Henkin Papers, Box 3, Folder 67).

and disdain for international law and institutions. In its general and legal version, this new liberal internationalism is a species of a broader American exceptionalism that made human rights an American theme in politics and law after the Vietnam crisis.[38]

If Jewish politics helped Henkin to discover human rights in the first place, it was his American ideology that provided him an alternative to a stauncher nationalism – whether American or Jewish – that has tended to treat human rights as dubious constraints in an age of counterterrorism and occupation. Whether it was the best or sole such alternative, only history will judge. But for Henkin, it meant that when it came to the possible tension between allegiance to a particular state and promotion of international human rights, he was lucky never to have to choose.

ACKNOWLEDGMENTS

I am especially grateful to Alice, David, and Joshua Henkin for their assistance with this paper, as well as James Loeffler, Nathan Kurz, Gerald Neuman, Moria Paz, Mira Siegelberg, and Michael Stanislawski for comments or discussion.

---

[38] On the parochialism of American approaches to international law across the political spectrum, *see* Samuel Moyn, *The International Law That Is America: Reflections on the last Chapter of Martti Koskenniemi's* The Gentle Civilizer of Nations, 27 TEMP. INT'L. & COMP. L. J. 399–415 (Fall 2013) and ANTHEA ROBERTS, IS INTERNATIONAL LAW INTERNATIONAL? (2017).

6

Constitutionalism, Human Rights, and the Genealogy of Jewish American Liberalism

William E. Forbath

Samuel Moyn has written a brilliantly detailed yet wide-ranging essay about Louis Henkin's "drastic self-reinvention"[1] as "the leading American legal advocate of human rights." What light, asks Moyn, does Henkin's Jewishness shed on his emergence as "the premier [American] contributor" to the international human rights movement? What did Judaism or Jewishness have to do with it? And what does that, in turn, tell us about the shape and arc of American Jewish politics and identities and their relationship to human rights advocacy in the twentieth century?

Moyn's essay has three main threads. First is Henkin's late-blooming career as the United States's pre-eminent, "iconic" human rights lawyer.[2] Henkin was fifty before he wrote anything on the subject of human rights; and well over fifty before his sudden conversion to the view that fostering international human rights law was a promising avenue for human betterment, and international human rights advocacy an exhilarating, high-powered calling. The conversion happened in the mid- to late 1970s, and this makes Henkin's career a study in the Moyn thesis about the sudden, unpredictable, contingent, and conjunctural take-off of the human rights enterprise in just those years.[3] Henkin is the Moyn thesis as biography. Both before and after his conversion, Henkin tossed off many lines that confirm various aspects of the Moyn thesis.

The essay's second thread concerns whether Judaism should be understood as a seedbed of human rights and a source of Jews' long involvement with

---

[1] This and other quotes, unless specified, refer to Samuel Moyn, *Louis Henkin, Human Rights, and American Jewish Constitutional Patriotism*, Chapter 5 in this volume.
[2] Samuel Moyn, The Last Utopia 193 (2010).
[3] *Id.* at 203–06.

international human rights advocacy. Here, again, Moyn finds much in Henkin to confirm his own powerful take on human rights history. Like Moyn, Henkin firmly rejected the idea that religion is where to look for the origins of human rights, and Judaism, least of all. Religions, generally, and Judaism, in particular, sound in the key of duties, not rights, wrote Henkin. Religions have not been inclined to set up individual rights over against society, government, or God. Henkin was an observant Jew, more steeped in Judaism, by far, than most other Jewish human rights advocates or scholars of his generation. Having set out to explore the commerce between the two, Henkin concluded – and Moyn seems to agree – that Judaism "lacked any notion of natural rights, as distinct from the ethic of duties that divine law imposes on the Jewish people." "More radically," Moyn notes, Henkin denied that Jews ever "affirmed a rationalistic conception of law of any sort," unlike the "rationally available moral principles" found "in Christian natural law traditions, let alone like those that modern human rights provide."[4] Judaism, Henkin emphasized, offers moral and human values of "a very high order," but "not protection for the stranger." Despite Judaism's injunctions to be kind and charitable to the stranger, it offers the stranger nothing like *rights*. For rights, the stranger must look elsewhere. To which Moyn responds, "Amen." But then, insofar as Jews have had a long, intimate involvement with the pursuit of international human rights, why is that so? The answer, both agree, is in virtue of what Moyn calls "the politics of the Jewish people." Jews must care about human rights, not because Judaism enjoins them to; it doesn't. Rather, they must do so because of their historical experience as a vulnerable "minority," because, quite simply, as Henkin wrote his brother and sister-in-law in a terrifically revealing 1944 letter Moyn uncovered, and to which we will return: like other "minority groups," Jews live in "glass houses."

Not the religious tenets, then, but "the political experience of Jews made them natural partisans" of human rights; and it was "no wonder" that in states where Enlightenment brought Jewish emancipation, "Jews embraced the new human rights," and no wonder that soon after, "[w]hat is now called 'Jewish internationalism' was born."[5] From the mid-nineteenth century onward, prominent Jews, residing chiefly in Western Europe and the United States, undertook international advocacy and private diplomacy on behalf of

---

[4]   In his recent CHRISTIAN HUMAN RIGHTS (2015), Moyn complicates his own views about the influence of Protestant theology on human rights – not as centuries-old seedbed, however, but rather as recent ideological shaper of contemporary human rights discourse.

[5]   *Id.* at 121.

oppressed fellow Jews, dwelling in states and imperial regimes that continued to deny Jews the rights that emancipation secured or, at least, promised. These private diplomats proved pioneers of the "primitive international human rights movement of the 19th century," in Henkin's words. This movement's work, in turn, "much of it in behalf of Jews, proved fertile seed for an international law of human rights," Henkin explained, "undermining the notion that the way sovereign states treat their own inhabitants, even their own citizens, is not the proper business of anyone else."

If you find it hard to make out whose potboiler history of Jewish human rights advocacy we are tracing here – Henkin's or Moyn's? – that is because Moyn's essay weaves them together so tightly, they become one. One, that is, until we arrive at precisely this point, where Moyn pauses to underscore a particular feature of that history in relation to which he means to situate Henkin, making Henkin no longer merely a fellow student but an historical subject in his own right. Moyn draws our attention to the dual politics or "twinned strategies" that Jews pursued in the "international space." Jews strove for supranational protection of Jewish rights, seeking "to install human rights above the nations so that international law would protect individuals ... from states that failed to do so ... At the same time, however, Jews sought national self-determination for themselves, and indeed [quoting Henkin] 'contributed to the triumph' of that principle, after ... 1917." These twin goals, Moyn notes, had an "uneasy co-existence" from the start – an uneasiness that "Henkin papered over." And no wonder, for on Moyn's account, the central "puzzle" of Henkin's own history lies in the seemingly blithe way he managed to become "the famed [international] human rights lawyer he did *on Jewish grounds*"[6] at the very moment, in the mid-1970s, when "Jewish internationalism" and its dual politics fell apart.

Whatever uneasiness attended the enterprise, Jewish advocates "in the international space" were relatively comfortable championing both their "twin goals" for many decades, roughly from the 1910s through the mid-1970s. They promoted the international human rights project ("minority rights, internationally protected"), on the one hand, and the Jewish homeland project (the principle or "national right" of self-determination), on the other. Only "after the Six Days War," in the 1970s, did Jews, who were active, like Henkin, in international affairs, see "a choice open up ... between the defense of the State of Israel or the defense of international human rights." The mid-

---

[6] Emphasis added.

1970s may have been the take-off moment, when international human rights became a serious, mainstream enterprise in international affairs, but it was also the moment when the paired goals or "twinned strategies" of Jewish internationalism unraveled.

From this perspective, Henkin's pre-eminent role, commencing in the mid-1970s, in making international human rights a central focus of international legal practice and scholarship, and his newfound, tireless enthusiasm for international human rights as worthy, fruitful legal material, emerge as the puzzle that Moyn's essay sets up and aims to solve. For, as Moyn observes, Henkin's passionate embrace of human rights advocacy arrived just at the moment when escalating attacks on Israel at the United Nations, Soviet-Arab diplomatic assaults, the legitimization of the Palestine Liberation Organization, and the branding of Zionism as racism all led to a profound crisis in the Jewish political world. How was it, Moyn asks, that Henkin could find the energy and conviction to throw himself into the international human rights project and become its most prominent and inspiring legal academic spokesman, at just the moment when international human rights norms had begun to "seem too threatening to be dependable, let alone exhilarating" from the perspective of Jewish internationalism?

How did Henkin emerge and flourish as an icon of international human rights law, while remaining an observant Jew, a Zionist, and a leader in the American Jewish Committee (AJC) – even as Jewish politics and the AJC swung away from the international human rights community? How is it that "Henkin became the famed human rights lawyer he did *on Jewish grounds*" in this dispiriting conjuncture? Just what Moyn means here by "Jewish grounds" is ambiguous. We will return to it, as we will return to the complicated and changing relationship between the AJC and Zionism.

But that is Moyn's question, and the third strand of the essay provides his answer. This seems to me to be the heart of the essay. Shrewd and compelling, it is this strand I intend to develop and, perhaps, deepen, with some brief forays and reflections backward and forward in the history of Jewish American liberalism.

Henkin's devotion to human rights was grounded in his Jewishness, but, argues Moyn, it was a "fervently American" Jewishness. More pointedly, and paradoxically, Henkin's was a "long-husbanded Jewish identity" whose chief expression was not any form of Jewish nationalism nor any other explicitly Jewish values or commitments, but instead "the defense of constitutional liberalism": a Jewish identity, in other words, which was "much more that of a proud American nationalist," an "American liberal nationalist" for whom America's "liberal constitutional principles, however honored in the breach" were what "made it great."

Indeed, much of Henkin's scholarship, from the mid-1970s onward, consisted of a stream of learned but accessible lectures, essays, and books about the affinities and continuities (real and imagined) between American constitutionalism and international human rights. Thus, Henkin would argue, international human rights were American rights writ globally – improved, enlarged, and brought up to date. Americans should get over those strains in our political culture that have viewed international law as foreign matter, and have shunned the notion of binding the United States to charters like the International Covenant on Civil and Political Rights, which the United States would not ratify until 1992.

Strikingly, as both Henkin and Moyn underscore, while the 1960s were a golden age of constitutional liberalism, it was only in the 1970s that it occurred to "constitutional liberals" to press "America to commit to international human rights." And in journalism as well as scholarly works like *The Rights of Man Today* (1978), Henkin did his part, proclaiming that the International Covenant "has made our ideology the international norm"; its forefather was none other than Thomas Paine, who "would have welcomed international human rights."

There is a tender spot here, however. Just what is Jewish about this? Taking Henkin's "heartfelt" efforts to Americanize international human rights and to "interpret and expound the U.S. Constitution so as to make the American polity . . . part of an international rights regime" for all they are worth, how exactly do these efforts express or flow from a *Jewish* American identity?

Steeped in American constitutional law and history, an accomplished constitutional scholar with a long involvement in international law and an intimate familiarity with that particular precinct of domestic law where foreign affairs intersect with constitutional doctrine around matters like the treaty power, Henkin was professionally well equipped for his "drastic self-reinvention" as an international human rights maven. But why should we see Henkin's well-timed investment in the human rights enterprise as an expression of his Jewishness? Why not see it simply as a case of a Jewish liberal who, acknowledging the real perils of international human rights continuing to be wielded as a "cudgel" against Israel, chose to put his liberal commitments ahead of his Jewish ones? That is, after all, how Henkin saw it.

Henkin insisted that Judaism played no part in forging his felt commitment or professional calling to human rights. Indeed, Moyn shows us that Henkin was at pains to insist, privately as well as publicly, that neither his Judaism nor even his Jewishness had much to do with his liberal universalist feelings and ideals – which returns us to the fascinating wartime letter Moyn uncovered from Henkin, then a young G.I. in Italy, writing to his brother and sister-in-law about whether they, or he, ought to replant themselves "in a Zionist Palestine." For his part, Henkin thinks not; he is unwilling to "exchange ... my American roots" for new ones there: "For all my Jewishness and tradition, my education and heritage is largely American ... Even my universalism or humanism, as I like to think, it is largely American." America, he goes on, "molded me" and instilled "a firm, fervent belief in the principles of a country which to me negate any chauvinistic devotion to country – even this country itself." Given this, Henkin was leery about buying into a "modern Zionism," which, should it succeed, might or might not prove any better than the mine run of "self-interested" or "chauvinistic" nationalist projects: "I hold no brief for nations and races and their continued existence as such." Even when he does point to a Jewish affinity for human rights, Henkin ascribes it only to the generic experience of minority group experience, not even the distinctive pathways of Jewish history. Jews, in other words, ought to be devoted to the rights of outcasts, just as "all minority groups ... should," as a simple matter of enlightened self-interest.

Even there, however, Henkin finds his fellow Jews falling short, regarding the pre-eminent minority rights struggle at home – the battle to topple Jim Crow – which had already engaged Henkin's moral imagination: "I never got the impression that the 'average Zionist' was any more liberal than the 'average American' ... I've seen lots of Jim Crow sentiment among Jews ... [T]he *only* liberal causes I've ever seen most of the Zionist leaders associated with were the self-interested ones."

This was a remarkably cynical and inaccurate assessment of American Zionist leadership. (The most prominent figures at the helm of American Zionism, like Stephen Wise, Felix Frankfurter, and Joachim Prinz, were deeply involved in myriad "liberal causes." However, it is vivid testimony to Henkin's feelings about the sources of his own civil rights liberalism, and to his dim view of Jewish nationalism.

But if Henkin was persuaded that the wellspring of his civil rights liberalism was his American "heritage" and not his "Jewishness," Moyn thinks otherwise. And I agree. What Henkin thought of as his Americanness is, in fact, more deeply, historically understood as a Jewish identity, a distinctly *Jewish* way of being American. Moyn's proof text, the letter from Italy, helps situate the young Henkin in a "long tradition of American Jewish legal liberals whose most meaningful and sometimes sole enactment of Jewish identity was the defense of constitutional liberalism."

This seems exactly right, as far as it goes. It does not explain, however, quite what it means to claim that "defending constitutional liberalism" should be understood as a person's enactment of Jewish identity. What is a priori Jewish about this pattern of behavior and thought? Here, we do well to reach back into the "long tradition of American Jewish legal liberals" to which Moyn alludes, and that I have been studying.[7] I want to suggest that Jewish constitutional and international lawyers in the nineteenth and early twentieth centuries produced[8] and passed along some of the basic categories of thought and structures of feeling that Henkin would inhabit and take for granted, and that enabled and constrained him to experience and interpret his Jewishness and Americanness as he did. I'll go further, and briefly sketch how the first couple generations of these Jewish lawyer-leaders invented, fought over, and hammered out some of the basic terms of Jewish belonging and apartness in twentieth-century America, not only for themselves but for "Jewish liberals," generally.[9]

We need to remember that until the late eighteenth and early nineteenth centuries, it was not possible to speak of Judaism as a "private affair" or a "private faith," as Moyn and Henkin do, nor to draw the distinction they draw between "Jewish politics" and Judaism, the religion. For most of its history, Judaism was *not* a "religion" in this (liberal, Protestant) sense at all.

---

[7] Moyn is gracious in quoting a work-in-progress of mine that examines this tradition, and I draw on it here. *See* William Forbath, *Jews, Law and Identity Politics in the Progressive Era* (www .utexas.edu/law/faculty/wforbath/papers/forbath_jews_law_and_identity_politics.pdf). *See also* William Forbath, The Jewish Constitutional Moment, Princeton University, Public Seminar, Program in Law & Public Affairs, Princeton, N.J. (April 1, 2019) (law.utexas .edu/faculty/william-e-forbath/activityfile/3161).

[8] Or, in some instances, translated into an authoritative and vital American idiom.

[9] *See* Forbath, *Jews, Law and Identity Politics, supra* note 7. Jerold Auerbach first explored this terrain in a brilliant and quirky book: RABBIS AND LAWYERS: THE JOURNEY FROM TORAH TO CONSTITUTION (1990). Auerbach, however, is not concerned with the actual work of Jewish attorneys or the forms and structures of legal and constitutional thought. But Auerbach first lit on the centrality of law and lawyers to creating Jewish American identities. His account has much to say about religious and historical authenticity and about traditional forms of Jewish law and life against which the embrace (and, I'll suggest, sacralization) of secular law and lawyer leadership is judged hollow. Examining, without lament, a Jewishness shaped by the ruptures and changes of modernity, Americanization, and reform, I remain deeply in Auerbach's debt.

It was public, not private; compulsory, not voluntary; and a system of laws, practices, and government, not chiefly a matter of belief or faith. What was more: Judaism named a people and a nation, a "race" no less than a - "religion."[10] All these ways in which Jewishness confounded the category of "religion" would remain salient and vexing, even as Judaism was reinvented for a liberal modernity.

That reinvention assumed a particular form in the work of the generations of Jewish lawyers, most of them from German Jewish Reform religious backgrounds, who sought to complete the arduous work of making American Jewishness into a "religion" and a "private affair." From its beginnings, Reform Judaism was, in important part, a constitutional project: a dream of legal and civic equality and equal rights for a subordinate and outcast group. These lawyers sought to realize this dream precisely by embracing the American Constitution as a new sacred text and enacting its interpretation and exposition as a new, sacred calling. Radical and conservative, some speaking for the old Reform Jewish elite and others for the new Jewish immigrant masses, these late nineteenth- and early twentieth-century Jewish lawyers were not simply courtroom advocates but what I have called lawyer-leaders: key founders and representatives of the first national Jewish organizations, who served not only as advocates but as wordsmiths and public intellectuals, powerbrokers and strategists, as well as authority figures and ethnocultural heroes in a time and place when other authority figures and other markers of difference and authenticity had faded.

Two generations of such Reform Jewish lawyer-leaders-*cum*-authority figures had fashioned and passed along this Jewish liberal identity, and this intensely felt investment in liberal constitutionalism and civil rights liberalism, before Henkin inherited it and gave it his own twist.

The liberal offer of individual emancipation in exchange for collective self-effacement yielded mixed, ambiguous results in Europe before World War I. The United States, by contrast, seemed the utopian dream of an enlightened liberal state brought down to earth; here, there were no Jews statutes, and legal and civic equality were facts on the ground. The Civil War instigated the creation of a modern nation-state and an intensified nationalism centered on the reconstructed Constitution, inscribed with equal rights for all persons born or naturalized in the United States. This Constitution, as the leaders of the victorious Union expounded it, promised formal legal equality to all and condemned what was called "class legislation," including

---

[10]   *See* LEORA BATNITZKY HOW JUDAISM BECAME A RELIGION (2011).

laws that classified and burdened individuals on the basis of race, color, nationality, or creed. Brimming with new national guarantees of equality of opportunity and freedom of contract, trade, and conscience, it seemed to embody the Reform Jewish outlook and the Reform elite's social aspirations. If Reform Judaism had been fashioned to outfit Jews for equal citizenship in an enlightened liberal state, this was the liberal constitution it was looking for!

Over the next few decades, Reconstruction Era constitutionalism flowed swiftly into American Jewish public discourse and self-understandings. It also shaped the identities and worldviews of the first generation of Jewish lawyers to emerge at the forefront of the American legal profession. Men like Louis Marshall and Max Kohler attended and excelled at elite law schools in the late nineteenth century, imbibed classical liberal legal and constitutional learning, and emerged as leading constitutional lawyers in the coming decades.[11] Founders of the AJC and pioneers of "Jewish internationalism" in the United States, these men were also the first generation of American Jewish lawyers working at the intersection of constitutional and international law. As they engaged with the issues of the day – immigration; labor strife; racial subjugation; the plight of oppressed minorities at home, at the nation's gates, and abroad, they made defending the rights of the stranger into a Jewish calling that, several decades and two generations later, Henkin would take up.

Let us focus on just one of Henkin's forebears here – Kohler. Unlike Marshall, Kohler is a largely forgotten figure, but a revealing one for our purposes. Marshall is better remembered because he led the AJC for its first two decades, and was also among the country's premier constitutional lawyers, appearing chiefly for business corporations but also for racial minorities, on behalf of the newly founded National Association for the Advancement of Colored People (NAACP), always wielding the language of classical liberalism. Kohler was Marshall's diligent younger colleague, close friend, and fellow founder of the AJC. Unlike Marshall, he worked almost full-time on immigration and what we would call civil rights. From the 1890s through the 1920s, Kohler advocated tirelessly against the Chinese

---

[11]   So too Louis Brandeis, to whom we'll return. Brandeis mastered classical liberal legal and constitutional discourse as a star student at Harvard, and used it brilliantly as a young attorney. *See, e.g.,* Samuel D. Warren and Louis D. Brandeis, *Right to Privacy,* 4 HARV. L. REV. 193, 220 (1890-1891). By the time he enters our story, however, he will have become one of classic legal liberalism's most prominent and biting critics, and will fashion his rival account of the terms of Jewish belonging and apartness out of different constitutional and international legal materials. But that lay decades in the future, during the 1910s and World War I. *See infra* 22–24.

Exclusion Act and other race-based immigration measures, and against Jim Crow. Kohler and Marshall thus were the first of what would become an enduring twentieth-century Jewish American folk hero, the Jewish civil rights lawyer.

What prompted this momentous bit of self-invention? The standard account runs along the same instrumental lines that Henkin and Moyn suggest. "[A]ll minority groups," said Henkin, really ought to be fighting Jim Crow and championing the Constitution's neglected guarantees against discriminatory laws. For "highly assimilated" Reform Jews like Kohler and Marshall, so David Levering Lewis's classic version of this instrumental thesis goes, fighting Jim Crow laws was a "displaced" way to address the threat that Jews too might be legally cast as racial others in the nativist climate of the day. If it seemed reckless even to raise the prospect of anti-Jewish laws in the United States, they could use Jim Crow statutes as a kind of "stalking horse"; if the latter were unconstitutional, then "a fortiori" so would be laws discriminating against Jews.[12]

There is much to this. But there is a deeper story of how and why interpreting and making claims on the U.S. Constitution on behalf of racial others became a Jewish calling. First of all, this instrumental account overlooks a critical fact. Most of the racial outcasts that Kohler and Marshall first defended were not, in fact, blacks; they were Jews being turned away at Ellis Island[13] – not proxy racial others, but Jewish ones. Well before he began to train his fire on Jim Crow, Kohler was litigating and advocating in the press and public hearings on behalf of Jewish immigrants, claiming that they were being subject to "race discrimination" by the Immigration Bureau and nativist lawmakers and pundits.

This revision reminds us that it was the mass immigration of "poor Russian Jews" from the peripheries of Europe and the tsars' empire that brought urgency and depth to Reform Jewry's embrace of the U.S. Constitution as a source of Jewish American identity. But this revision only begins to unfold the deep and thorny problem for which rights lawyering was a solution. How could a well-heeled, proudly assimilated Reform Jew affirm and act upon –

[12]   David Levering Lewis, *Parallels and Divergences: Assimilationist Strategies of Afro-American and Jewish Elites from 1910 to the Early 1930s*, 3 J. AM. HISTORY, 543 (1984).

[13]   "With their vast numbers, their thicker, 'foreign' kind of Jewishness, and all the ancient hatreds clinging to them as Russia's most despised ethno-racial and religious outcasts, the newcomers crowded in New York's Lower East Side and other new 'Jewish ghettoes' became the paradigmatic 'unassimilable' new immigrants in the eyes of growing numbers of native-born Americans during this era of mass immigration from the peripheries of Europe. Leading voices in Congress and in popular and high culture questioned Jews' 'racial fitness' for American citizenship." Forbath, Jews, *Law and Identity Politics, supra* note 7, at 5.

rather than shamefully shun – his fellowship with the despised racial
others, the allegedly "unassimilable," "poor Russian Jews" at the nation's
gates? And how do so without fatally wounding his own claim that his
Jewishness is no ethno-racial marker at all, but simply his religious
"faith," as a full-fledged American? How could he make something
meaningful of his Jewishness, felt and understood as ineradicable membership in a *people apart*, while carrying on the project of assimilation
and unassailable belonging in America?

Kohler's father outlined the beginnings of an answer. Kaufmann Kohler was
late nineteenth-century America's pre-eminent Reform rabbi. He hammered
out American Reform Judaism's first programmatic theological statement, the
canonical Pittsburgh Platform of Reform Judaism of 1885.[14] Anxious in context
but confident in tone, the heart of Kohler's Pittsburgh Platform was the
proclamation that, "We Jews consider ourselves no longer a nation, but
a religious community, and therefore expect neither a return to Palestine …
nor the restoration of any of the laws concerning the Jewish state."[15] Jewish law
only binds us in its moral precepts. Henceforth, Kohler and his fellow Reform
rabbis and lay lawyer-leaders would repeatedly say, "Our Zion is America." As
another 1880s Reform convention put it in a letter to U.S. President Grover
Cleveland, the "pillars" of Jews' belonging to America were "equal rights" and
"assimilation." Indeed, more than one enthusiastic Reform rabbi sermonized:
"[O]ur Torah is the Constitution."[16] These blunt, cartoonish formulas indicate
that Henkin was not wrong when he wrote in 1983, "It has been suggested that for
generations of Jews the Constitution has been a substitute for the Bible." I am
suggesting that for this generation of Reform Jews, as mass immigration began to
stir up Jew hatred in their new Zion, it seemed time to seal the Enlightenment
bargain unequivocally. Henkin may have believed "America's true genius" was
"that both systems" – Torah and American constitutionalism – could coexist. One
could "opt for both," as Henkin put it, and never have to choose. But these Jews
felt they *did* have to choose. Or, perhaps: they both felt they *had* to, and also *chose*
to choose. Most had arrived in the middle decades of the nineteenth century
already estranged from the universe of Jewish laws and traditions that observant
Jews, then and now, deem central and binding; in their baggage was a Judaism
already being recast as a modern, liberal Protestant-style "religion." It was a good
time to proclaim fealty to the U.S. Constitution in no uncertain terms.

---

[14]   Michael Berenbaum, *Pittsburgh Platform*, *in* 16 Encyclopaedia Judaica 190 (Michael
        Berenbaum & Fred Skolnik, eds., 2d ed., 2007).
[15]   *Id.*
[16]   Quotes in Forbath, *Jews, Law and Identity Politics*, *supra* note 7, at 11.

If the "new immigration" spurred Reform Jews to declare that the U.S. Constitution was their new Torah, it also called forth a vast, decades-long campaign of social, political, and legal action. It seemed only a matter of time before the nation's gates would clang shut. The campaign to keep them open thrust Kohler along with Marshall into central roles defining and defending Jews' contested status and identity, on the American scene as well as at the gates. It lent their classical liberal outlook a militant aspect when it came to keeping the law free of racial classifications and assailing those in place, not only regarding Jews but all racialized outcasts. Immigration law and its administration were where Jews' treasured legal invisibility was most threatened in this era, and Kohler responded vigorously to every threat. Enlisted by Lower East Side editors and attorneys, Kohler led successful legal challenges to new regulations in the hearing rooms at Ellis Island, and brought habeas suits in federal district court challenging them.[17] For the next two decades, Kohler and Marshall orchestrated a many-sided campaign of quiet diplomacy and loud protests, sophisticated lawyering, and intense lobbying to halt the "race prejudice," "deportations," and "administrative lawlessness."[18] At the same time, Kohler became the Reform Jewish elite's leading authority on international law and made his own the intersection of international and U.S. constitutional law that Henkin would occupy at Kohler's alma mater, Columbia Law School, half a century later. With Marshall and others, he led a startlingly successful campaign to prod Congress and the White House to terminate the nation's trade treaty with Russia in protest against the empire's official antisemitism.[19]

For his part, on the bimah at Temple Emmanuel, New York's great Reform Jewish cathedral on Fifth Avenue, while Max was still in law school, Rabbi Kohler gave a sermon on "The Wandering Jew"[20] that seemed to predict and prefigure his son's calling – and also answer a question that the rabbi's own 1885 Platform of Reform Judaism had left hanging. Reform Jews were no longer a nation or people with a separate national destiny involving a return

---

[17]   See Forbath, *Jews, Law and Identity Politics, supra* note 7, at 55.

[18]   *Id.*

[19]   See Max Kohler, *The Abrogation of the Treaty of 1832 between the United States and Russia and the International Protection of Religious Minorities, and Louis Marshall, Russia and the American Passport*, in GOD IN FREEDOM: STUDIES IN THE RELATIONS BETWEEN CHURCH AND STATE, 705 (Luigi Luzzatti, ed., 1930).

[20]   *See* Rabbi Kaufman Kohler, The Wandering Jew, Address before Temple Beth-El (April 1, 1888) (American Jewish Historical Society, Box 1, Folder 4).

to Zion, and no longer bound by Jewish law, hewing only to Judaism's universal precepts. "Why then," asked the rabbi, would not Reform Jews "throw down" the "ragged mantle" of the eternal "wandering Jew" and "melt" and be "absorbed" into the larger gentile community? Why not convert? Why not intermarry? Why remain a people stubbornly apart? His answer was the "arduous" and "priestly" work of justice seeking, which Jews had to do "for all humanity."[21] This, according to Rabbi Kohler, was the "mission mapped out by our great seers of yore" – "the godly men ... who consecrated their lives to the practice of the law."[22] Only then, could the "priest-people" fulfill their destiny – scattered amongst the nations in order to "bring the Law forth from Zion," not the old rabbinic law, but the law of the U.S. Constitution: "human rights" and "freedom."[23]

The "practice of law" was an oddly modern way to describe the work of premodern rabbis in rabbinic courts. But this was a distinctly modern, secular, and American reinterpretation of Jews' "mission." Reform Judaism was built around a new conception of Jews' role in history: keeping Judaism's rigorous monotheism and "universal ethics" alive among the nations of the world. But in the hands of Kaufmann Kohler, this idea subtly changed register, into a more secular language of justice seeking – from a calling to keep alive the religious sources of modern liberal ideals to a calling to pursue those ideals themselves. In this, one can sense a double movement: a secularization of religious commitments and a sacralization of a secular calling, a modernist mingling of religious and secular modes of thought and feeling, which Max Kohler was set to enact. Here was a basis for renewing Jewish particularity – resisting "absorption" into the dominant community, and affirming one's identity as, or identification with, the outsider group, one's solidarity with the despised others, outcasts, and downtrodden – but doing so as a member of a respected bourgeois profession and in terms of enlightened, universal values enshrined in the U.S. Constitution.

We can speculate: without this identification with and seeing oneself in racial outsiders, without taking on arduous law work on their behalf, what exactly did one's belonging to a people apart amount to for an earnest young law student praying in English in an elegant Fifth Avenue cathedral? Like his father's modernized "Godly men of yore," Kohler

---

[21] *Id.*
[22] *Id.*
[23] *Id.*

could "consecrate" his life "to the practice of the law" to bring "human rights and freedom" forth from Zion. Representing racial outsiders before the nation's courts, he and other high-powered Jewish lawyers showed that Jews belonged in the temple of America's civic religion. Linking American Jewishness to defending the rights of racial others, they made expounding the Constitution's *universal* promises a way of affirming Jewish American *particularity*: as a justice-seeking people apart. Civil rights lawyering would prove a long-lived way for American Jews – and not only patrician Reform Jewish liberals, but new immigrant Russian and East European Jewish leftists too – to rise in the social order, becoming insiders, while remaining in some morally and imaginatively significant ways outsiders, publicly enacting one's solidarity with the out-cast and the fallen, the stranger.

The greatest challenge to this civic religion, or even political theology, was the rise of the Zionist movement, which made its own claims on Jewish loyalties and offered its own prescriptions for Jewish responses to antisemit-ism. For this reason, among others, the new immigrants on the Lower East Side did not make it easy for the uptown, patrician Reform Jews to represent them and advocate on their behalf – or preside over their Americanization. The newcomers had their own ideas about what it meant to be both American and Jewish. And by the early 1900s, they had their own lawyer-leaders and their own organizations; indeed, they had built an impressive landscape of organizations – not only the Yiddish press; but hundreds of *landsmanschaftn* and scores of great socialist unions. Also afoot were some tiny new Zionist and Jewish nationalist outfits.

These tiny outfits were a big thorn in the AJC's side. Everything that Rabbi Kohler and the AJC insisted Jews were not, these Jewish nationalists insisted Jews were: a distinct nation, a "race," and a people with its own public political creed and claims to a homeland and statehood in Palestine. They had a constitutional vision and vocabulary of their own that polyglot émigré Jewish lawyers and revolutionaries brought back and forth across the Atlantic from legal and constitutional battles abroad. They demanded indivi-dual civil rights and liberties, about which the Lower East Side nationalists and the uptown establishment liberals were on the same page, but they also demanded group rights and "national rights" of communal autonomy and national self-determination – in Palestine, of course, but also in the Diaspora, in Russia, and even in the United States.[24]

---

[24] *See generally* Forbath, *Jews, Law and Identity Politics, supra* note 7.

So, the nationalists assailed what they saw as the Reform Jewish elite's cowardly assimilationism and called instead for race pride and "national self-assertion"; it was high time to create a robust and democratic Jewish public sphere and Jewish politics. Thus, they called for a Jewish Congress, a kind of Jewish para-state: "a representative and sovereign body of American Jewry," with links to similar bodies abroad.[25]

You can imagine, on the Upper West Side, Max Kohler, Louis Marshall, and other Reform Jewish leaders were thoroughly alarmed. Of course, it was essential to respond to the massacres in Russia and the deportations on Ellis Island. But the reckless crowd of radicals on the Lower East Side could not be allowed to speak for American Jewry. This is what brought about the creation of the AJC in 1906. The AJC swiftly became the premier organizational vehicle of the Reform Jewish elite, their rights advocacy, and their Jewish internationalism. And it remained so in the 1960s and '70s, when the AJC proved the site where, Moyn has told us, Henkin found his calling as an international human rights lawyer, reinventing himself at the last possible moment he could have done so "on Jewish grounds" – the last Jewish internationalist, as it were, in the line that began with Kohler.

Moyn, you will recall, describes Jewish internationalism's relationship to the Zionist project of Jewish "national self-determination" and nation- and state-building as one of "uneasy co-existence" until the 1960s and early '70s. That is not how it seemed to the AJC's founders and leading practitioners of Jewish internationalism in the 1900s. Both Zionism and diasporic national-ism were anti-American as far as Kohler, Marshall, and other AJC founders were concerned. Wrote Marshall to a friend and fellow founder, national organization was "in the air" and "we should take the initiative . . . to avoid mischief."[26] And the friend concurred: "Shall we wait until the Russians push us aside and speak for all American Jewry, or shall we lead the move-ment and give it a sane and conservative tone?"[27] At an emergency gathering of Upper West Side and Lower East Side notables, Marshall declared that any national organization must be "some kind of religious body"; it can't smack of Jewish "nationality" or "race." Those ideas were "inconsistent with

[25] *Id.* at 7.
[26] Letter from Louis Marshall to Dr. Cyrus Adler (Dec. 30, 1905) *in* LOUIS MARSHALL: CHAMPION OF LIBERTY. SELECTED PAPERS AND ADDRESSES 20 (Charles Reznikoff, ed., vol. 1, 1957).
[27] Letter from Cyrus Adler to Louis Marshall *in* CYRUS ADLER, SELECTED LETTERS: 1883–1919, 127 (1983).

the American conception of government" and threatened to give rise to "a Jewish question" here in America.[28]

Marshall read out language that soon would find its way into the new organization's charter: the AJC would set its face against "infringement of the civil and religious rights of Jews" and vowed to "alleviate the consequences of persecution."[29] And the AJC, under his leadership and with Kohler's constitutional and international lawyering, positioned itself as the ideal outfit to litigate, lobby, and engage in "quiet diplomacy," speaking behind the scenes in the corridors of power for American Jews and their oppressed "co-religionists" abroad.

The conflict between the AJC and the Jewish Congress movement did not end. Nor did the AJC's anti-Zionism and anti-nationalism soften much for several more decades. Elsewhere, I reconstruct these early battles and rival ideas about Jewish rights at home and abroad in some detail.[30] Here, I have sketched the beginnings of these largely forgotten battles, and will touch even more lightly on some of the later ones, only to suggest some lines of continuity between Henkin and his liberal Jewish internationalist forebears (and successors) that Moyn leaves unexamined; and to suggest that Henkin's deep misgivings and ambivalence about Zionism had a longer lineage, and a longer future "on Jewish grounds," than Moyn seems to see.

To be sure, one central element of the early AJC's adamant attacks on Zionism was the fear that Zionists' outlook and demands for national self-determination and group rights raised the specter of disloyalty and a Jewish "state within the state," and would stoke the fire of antisemitism in the United States. It was essential for prudential reasons to get right what rights American Jews were championing, for Jews abroad and Jews in the United States; and the AJC would hear of nothing but classical liberal ones. But this founding generation of American Jewish internationalists also had principled misgivings about Zionism very much akin to Henkin's. They were crystal clear about the poisonous, illiberal aspects of ethno-racial nationalism and indeed, all nationalisms – with the notable exception of American civic nationalism, whose blind spots they (like Henkin) overlooked. Like Henkin at his most

---

[28] Protocol of Meetings (Feb. 3–4, 1906) (American Jewish Committee Minutes, vol. 1, American Jewish Committee Archives), quoted *in* MATTHEW SILVER, LOUIS MARSHALL AND THE RISE OF JEWISH ETHNICITY IN AMERICA 118 (2013).

[29] UNION OF AMERICAN HEBREW CONGREGATIONS, THIRTY-FIFTH ANNUAL REPORT OF THE UNION OF AMERICAN HEBREW CONGREGATIONS 6258 (1909).

[30] *See* Forbath, *Jews, Law and Identity Politics* and Forbath, *Jewish Constitutional Moment*, *supra* note 7.

withering (in the 1944 letter Moyn discovered), the AJC founders were deeply skeptical about whether Jewish nationalism, if and when it had a state at its disposal, would prove any different – any less tribal, any more liberal than the European nationalisms from which Jewish nationalism drew so much of its inspiration. They were swift to point out that Palestine was not empty land, and they worried about the rights of Arabs in the Jewish state of Zionist imagination. They would have found little to disagree with in the young Henkin's worries about Jewish "chauvinism"; nor with the older Henkin's conviction that once Israel was a fact on the ground, its beleaguered right to exist had to be fiercely defended.

We should note, though, that Kohler, Marshall, and the early AJC did have one important moment of what, following Moyn, one might call "uneasy co-existence" with the Zionists and their Congress movement. That was during World War I, when wartime massacres of Jews in Russia and Eastern Europe brought a rekindling of the Jewish Congress movement in response to the yearning for mass protest and political action on the Lower East Side and in other new immigrant communities, on behalf of Jewish kin and communities abroad, in the killing fields. This time, the Congress movement with its rival vision of "Jewish rights" did not fade away, but instead proved a match for the AJC.[31]

A central reason for the even match-up at this moment was the fortuity of Justice Louis Brandeis's "conversion" to Zionism and his sudden ascent to leadership of American Zionism, shortly after the war in Europe began. The story of Brandeis's "conversion" to Zionism and his assumption of wartime leadership is a familiar one.[32] But Brandeis swiftly grasped that Palestine was not a cause likely to arouse the majority of ordinary Jews into action; what resonated most about Jewish nationalism – on the Lower East Side, as in Russia itself – was not a homeland or state in Palestine, but the dream of diasporic nationalists: safety and better lives, individually and collectively, via modern communal institutions and a panoply of individual *and group rights* for the oppressed Jewish millions *where they actually were*, in Russia and Eastern Europe themselves.[33] So, Brandeis welded his Zionism to

---

[31]   *See* Forbath, *Jewish Constitutional Moment, supra* note 7. *See also* Jonathan Frankel, *The Jewish Socialists and the American Jewish Congress Movement*, 16 YIVO ANNUAL OF JEWISH SOCIAL SCIENCE 202 (1976); SILVER, *supra* note 28, at 265–89, 294–300.

[32]   *See, e.g.,* MELVIN I. UROFSKY, LOUIS D. BRANDEIS: A LIFE (2009); Allon Gal, *In Search of a New Zion: New Light on Brandeis' Road to Zionism, in* AMERICAN ZIONISM: MISSION AND POLITICS (Jeffrey S. Gurock, ed., 1998); Sarah Schmidt, *The Zionist Conversion of Louis D. Brandeis*, 37 JEWISH SOCIAL STUDIES (Winter 1975), 18.

[33]   *See* Forbath, *Jewish Constitutional Moment, supra* note 7; Frankel, *supra* note 31.

diasporic nationalism, and along with becoming chief of the Zionist federation, Brandeis took over the Congress Movement's helm, as well; and he made his own their outlandish vocabularies and visions of group and national rights.[34]

Brandeis made the movement's foes his own, as well. He had never had any use for New York's Reform Jewish elite and had long been inclined to see the lawyer-leaders of the AJC as just another bunch of plutocrats and parvenus, as well as benevolent despots, who deprived the new immigrant masses of the democratic character-forming opportunity to participate as equals in Jewish politics. So, Brandeis welcomed the battle, and brought to Zionism and the Jewish Congress Movement a great access of money and social and cultural capital, a cadre of talented Progressive lawyers like Felix Frankfurter, and his own towering reputation as the "People's Attorney," first Jewish Justice, and greatest of all Jewish lawyers as Jewish folk heroes.[35]

Zionism, said Kohler, Marshall, and the AJC, was *anti-American.* Zionism, Brandeis serenely declared, made Jews *"better Americans."* Pluralism – understood as the idea that law must embrace the significance of groups as sources of power and identity in social and economic life – was already part of Brandeis's philosophy. Already a pluralist and group rights maven in regard to labor and trade associations, Brandeis took hold of the group rights-laden outlook of the Jewish nationalists and wove it into a new group rights-based account of Jewish belonging and apartness in American life.[36] Incorporating Progressives' insistence on the centrality of groups in American life, this account of "group rights" and "group equality" defended American Jews' and other minorities' "right to be different," to assert multiple public loyalties and to be "hyphenated Americans" – loyal to the United States but also to their own "nation," "race," or "people." So it was that Jewish Progressives around Brandeis invented what soon came to be called cultural pluralism. Zionism, Jewish nationalism, and "hyphenated" immigrant identities, more generally, they declared, were all "True Americanism."[37]

When it came to the nation's Jews and other minority "races and nationalities," equal citizenship in America demanded not only individual but "group

---

[34] Forbath, *Jewish Constitutional Moment, supra* note 7.
[35] *Id.*
[36] *Id.*
[37] Louis D. Brandeis, True Americanism, Oration at Faneuil Hall (July 4, 1914), *in* BRANDEIS ON ZIONISM: A COLLECTION OF ADDRESSES AND STATEMENTS BY LOUIS D. BRANDEIS 3 (Zionist Organization of America, 1942).

equality" and freedom of expression, and association demanded not only individual but "group rights."[38] These were essential to a democratic Constitution, said Brandeis, and essential, as well, for the "American Israel," the "hyphenated" Jewish-American identity he championed. The notion that the official U.S. constitutional order embraced any of these things was the purest legal fiction, but when Brandeis declared it to packed meetings across the country, it became a cultural fact. Thus, Brandeis put the thicker, more public, political, and controversial "hyphenated" conception of American Jewish identity that was afoot on the Lower East Side on the road to respectability.[39]

U.S. President Woodrow Wilson, famously, had no use for "hyphenated" Americanism, but he was devoted to his great friend and counselor, Brandeis. What was more, the American Congress movement under Brandeis's leadership had undeniable support among the new immigrant "masses." The Congress movement's heady mixture of Zionism and diasporic Jewish nationalism, with its vision of group and communal rights for the Jews of Eastern Europe, could no longer be sidelined – not if the AJC wanted their brand of Jewish internationalism and their claims to speak for American Jewry on the international stage to remain credible. And that seemed essential as Marshall, Kohler, and the AJC contemplated their role as interceders at the post-war Paris and Versailles peace conference and treaty making. So, they reluctantly agreed to the notion, backed by Wilson, of an American Jewish delegation to the peace talks that combined the rival forces.[40]

So it was that during World War I and its aftermath, the AJC assented to the Zionist demand for a Jewish homeland. Even then, however, the AJC's representatives clashed with their Zionist counterparts. What Moyn calls their "uneasy co-existence" only went so far; and for reasons both principled and prudential, the AJC drew a line between Palestine as a Jewish refuge and haven and Jewish statehood.[41]

I have spent no time in the archives with the AJC's records after this founding generation. However, I am inclined to think that Kohler's and the first generation's focus on classical liberal rights as a touchstone for international as well as domestic advocacy carried on in the next generation – into an era, when, on Moyn's account, this staunchly individualist idea of human rights found no purchase "[e]ven within the ambit of Jewish organizations like

---

[38]   See Forbath, *Jewish Constitutional Moment, supra* note 7.
[39]   *Id.*
[40]   See SILVER, *supra* note 28, at 338.
[41]   *Id.*

the AJC," where he writes, "it was a peripheral topic rather than a major concern" compared to "the natural right of the Jewish people" to "their own sovereign state," which was warmly championed and celebrated. "No one," he tells us, "has made the case" that leading Jewish internationalist outfits like the AJC "committed to [this] idea of human rights in the 1940s . . . as the specific project consecrated in the UN program."

But that cannot be right. For championing just that classical liberal individualist "idea of human rights in the 1940s" is exactly what James Loeffler has argued the AJC did with great zeal in its strenuous politicking around the creation of the United Nations and the crafting of the Declaration of Human Rights.[42] Confronted by their Zionist rivals' post-war push, the second generation of AJC leadership reckoned that simply being against or, at best, ambivalent about, Jewish statehood was not a recipe for continued prominence in post-war America. The old liberal Jewish internationalist outfit also needed something to be for – and what they settled on, in Loeffler's vivid reconstruction, was rebooting the organization's old liberal Reform Jewish mission by championing in the corridors of American power the idea of putting individual, and not group or national, human rights at the center of the UN program and declaration.[43]

Fast forward, now, to the 1960s, when we arrive at Moyn's "last possible moment" and the terminal undoing of Jewish internationalism's twinned goals and the end of their "uneasy co-existence," in Moyn's telling. Again, I am no expert. But I am less confident than Moyn that Henkin's work for the AJC in this period – exploring the promise and perils of international human rights, and getting his brief but decisive head start toward international human rights stardom – was really at the last possible moment, as far as Jewish internationalism is concerned, at least at the AJC. To my amateur eyes, things look different. The old liberal internationalists at the AJC *still* seem to have been fairly riveted on championing human rights – and what is more, on championing human rights in Israel – well after Moyn tells us that the AJC and its kin "deprioritized human rights rapidly as the latter became cudgels to attack the Israeli occupation (or Israel itself), especially after 1967." In the 1970s, it seems, the AJC was still "Jewish ground" where one might find the twinned projects uneasily

[42] James Loeffler, *"The Conscience of America"*: *Human Rights, Jewish Politics, and American Foreign Policy at the 1945 United Nations San Francisco Conference*, 100 J. Am. History 401 (2013).

[43] *Id.*

carrying on. Frustrated by obstacles to defending Israel and human rights, in the '70s, the AJC made a major investment in funding a human rights organization in Israel, modeled on the American Civil Liberties Union. Dedicated to defending the rights of Israeli Arabs and Jews, the Association for Civil Rights in Israel became Israel's pre-eminent human rights outfit and seems a major thorn in the present government's side and a darling of left liberal Jewish American friends of Israel.[44] Moyn's "last possible moment" may have been a longer time in coming than Moyn thinks.

CONCLUSION

And Louis Henkin, with his stubborn misgivings about and skeptical commitment to the Zionist project, seems to have had much more in common than Moyn allows with both past and future Jewish liberal rights mavens. Where Moyn seems to me exactly right, however, is his suggestion that Henkin, as he ushered international human rights work into the legal-professional limelight, was modeling for late twentieth- and early twenty-first-century Jews what U.S. constitutional civil rights advocacy had been in the early and mid-twentieth century: a calling and cultural space for enacting a distinctly Jewish form of belonging and apartness in the American establishment, a consummate insider, who also stands apart, with the outcast and the stranger – a calling that Rabbi Kohler and his son, Max, invented over a century ago.

Which brings us to a final twist and puzzle in the intergenerational tale of Jewish internationalism, which Moyn's brilliant essay evoked and I have tried to fill in. Following Moyn, I have explored the striking continuities of liberal sensibility – of liberal categories of thought and structures of feeling – about one's Jewishness and one's Americanness, which linked Henkin to forebears like Kohler. But in doing so, like Moyn, I have glossed over a rather striking difference and discontinuity, which bears one more moment's worth of attention.

Reform Judaism may have been, as I have suggested, a seedbed of Jewish American liberalism. However, Henkin – unlike Kohler or Marshall and the other founders of the AJC or most AJC leaders of his own generation – was not a Reform Jew. And neither was Henkin like these other figures in being of German or Central European origins. Henkin was an orthodox and observant Jew, and one of the "poor Russian Jews," to boot – one of the very last arrivals of

---

[44] MICHAEL N. BARNETT, THE STAR AND THE STRIPES: A HISTORY OF THE FOREIGN POLICIES OF AMERICAN JEWS 213 (2016).

the mass immigration from the tsars' empire. Born in Belarus, he emigrated with his family to the Lower East Side – where his father remained a rabbi and Talmudic scholar – in 1923, just a year before the gates clanged shut. A last possible moment, indeed!

So, in terms of the standard uptown/downtown narrative, which this essay has done nothing, so far, to unsettle, one might have expected Henkin to line up on the American Jewish Congress side of the battle lines. One might have expected that Henkin would, at some point, at least, embrace the nationalists' thicker, more public-political and "hyphenated" conception of American Jewish identity – much as Brandeis's lieutenant and Henkin's own mentor, Frankfurter did, in his young radical days. Why, instead, did Henkin always seem to hew to the AJC's classical liberal brand of Jewishness?

No doubt, this is a question that scholars may explore as Henkin's life and career become subjects of more sustained study. But permit me this last speculation. Perhaps it was partly because Henkin remained an orthodox and observant Jew that he always felt so at home on the liberal individualist side of these ongoing clashes over Jewish identity politics. One reason Zionism and Jewish nationalism held such great appeal for the restless offspring of orthodox Russian Jews on the Lower East Side was because it was a way to remain faithful to a thick, deeply felt, and communally involving Jewish identity at the same time as one parted ways with the traditional but confining and unwanted world of Jewish observance. That was part of young Frankfurter's story. But if, instead, one made one's ambitious way into the larger world of American life and law, while remaining tied to orthodox Judaism, then secular Jewish nationalism might exert a far weaker tug; for one already had a deeply felt, communally involving Jewish identity in hand, as one set about forging one's life's work and identity in that larger world.

Finally, we may ask: What was it about Henkin's moment that made it possible for an orthodox Jew to attain such heights in the hitherto non-observant world of prominent Jewish constitutionalists and internationalists? We have seen how Reform Jews like the Kohlers in their day felt both impelled and liberated by the idea of putting aside observance of Jewish law and embracing a new sacred law embodied in the U.S. Constitution. This was part and parcel of the nineteenth-century work of reinventing Judaism in America as a "religion," in the liberal mold. This work done, by Henkin's day, it may have been easier to fit observant Judaism into that mold.

Moyn, in his conclusion, writes: "For Henkin, then, [liberal] America perfectly suited his compartmentalized identity in which observant Judaism remained a private affair and constitutional liberalism a public faith." But I rather think that Henkin could inhabit a "perfectly suited . . . compartmentalized identity" (observant Judaism as "a private affair" and "constitutional liberalism a public faith") partly because these earlier generations led the way in crafting just such liberal structures of thought and feeling, and, unlike Henkin, both chose and felt they had to choose between Jewish and American law. If I am right, then we may have a new angle on how it was that Henkin could bear such a striking resemblance in outlook and sensibility to his first-generation forebears at the AJC, across such gulfs of time and social geography.

PART 4

EGON SCHWELB

7

The *Via Media*

Egon Schwelb's Mid-century Stoic Legalism and the Birth of Human Rights Law

Mira Siegelberg

In Shirley Hazzard's biting episodic novel *People in Glass Houses*, the United Nations is known as the "Organization." Staffers meet each other in the halls of the "Organization" on "Human Dignity Day," and one civil servant quits his post because he can no longer bear the endless pile of acronym-laden documents that accumulate on his desk. Hazzard's mordant depiction of the UN's institutional culture during the height of the Cold War derived from her firsthand experience working at the organization in the 1950s. Of the international civil servants populating the UN, Hazzard wrote,

> The Organization had bred, out of a staff recruited from its hundred member nations, a peculiarly anonymous variety of public official, of recognizable aspect and manner. It is a type to be seen to this very day, anxiously carrying a full briefcase or fumbling for a laissez-passer in airports throughout the world.[1]

In an earlier moment, the Jewish League of Nations official Albert Cohen undermined the veneer of glamour that might be associated with the work of global governance in his sardonic depiction of the League's international civil service. Hazzard's account of the UN particularly captured the mood of the post-war decade when *The Organization Man* – William Whyte's sociological study of the arbitrary rules of corporate conformity – ruled the bestseller lists.[2]

Hazzard gathered the material for her biting essays in the same period that Egon Schwelb (1899–1979), a Czech Jewish émigré jurist, labored at the UN elaborating the architecture of human rights law as the deputy director of the Division of Human Rights from 1947 until 1962. Though little known today, Schwelb belonged, broadly speaking, to the sect of Jewish jurists hailing from

---

[1] SHIRLEY HAZZARD, PEOPLE IN GLASS HOUSES 15 (2004).
[2] ALBERT COHEN, BELLE DE SEIGNEUR (1998); WILLIAM WHYTE, THE ORGANIZATION MAN (1956).

the Russian or Austrian empires working toward the advancement of a cosmopolitan legal order in the period after World War II – a group that included better known international legal scholars such as Louis Henkin, Louis Sohn, and Hersch Lauterpacht.[3] After leaving the UN, Schwelb introduced one of the first courses at an American law school on international human rights in 1963.[4] By the 1970s, Schwelb's peers celebrated him as the elder statesman of human rights and an exemplary international civil servant.[5] In his dedication to Schwelb in the 1971 *Human Rights Journal*, Paul Weis, a Jewish legal scholar who served as the legal advisor to the UN High Commissioner for Refugees, offered this resonant image: The UN Secretariat, he stated, was a "silent service," but "the role which international civil servants can play in international proceedings should not be underestimated. Dr. Schwelb has, in his own discreet way, done a great deal to further the cause in which he believes."[6]

It is valuable, however, to reconstruct the particular contours of Schwelb's life and thought because they illuminate how human rights law emerged in the post-war era from the collapse of an earlier faith among international lawyers in the power of law and legal analysis to shape political reality. Operating within the confines of the UN bureaucracy, Schwelb worked to maintain an optimistic perspective on the progressive developments of human rights law when legal internationalism seemed to be under siege.[7] His arguments about the place of international law and human rights in the post-war world are worth close examination because of the self-conscious way he sought to develop a method for preserving faith in the progressive development of a more humane global system. As we shall see, Schwelb had never sought to

---

[3] On this group as a "humanist conspiracy" working to develop international law's potential, *see* David Kennedy, *Louis B. Sohn: Recollections of a Co-Conspirator*, 48 HARV. INT'L. L. J. 25 (2007).

[4] *See* Zachary Steven Ramirez, International Human Rights Activism in the United States in the Cold War (2013) (unpublished Ph.D. dissertation, University of California–Berkeley).

[5] Frank C. Newman, an Associate Justice of the Supreme Court of California, called him the "loving elder brother of us all" and the "chief mentor of human rights." Frank C. Newman, *Correspondence*, 72 AM. J. INT'L . L. 473 (1979). Louis Henkin, the Columbia law professor, introduced him as "Mr. Human Rights" at a meeting of the American Society of International Law; Louis Henkin, *Meeting Notes*, 65 AM. J. INT'L. L. 242 (1971). The July 1971 edition of the *Human Rights Journal* devoted the full issue to honoring his work and legacy. *See Essays in Honor of Egon Schwelb*, 4 HUM. RTS. J. 2 (1971).

[6] Paul Weis, *Diplomatic Protection of Nationals and International Protection of Human Rights*, 4 HUM. RTS. J. 643 (1971).

[7] Samuel Moyn has argued that the "human rights revolution" of the 1940s was a "death from birth." *See* SAMUEL MOYN, THE LAST UTOPIA: HUMAN RIGHTS IN HISTORY Ch. 2, 5 (2010), *passim*, for the post-war history of international law in the United States.

overcome the jurisdiction of the state, but his vision of human rights law in the post-war decades addressed the widely shared post-war conviction that international legal doctrine could not escape the struggle of politics. On the "realist" side of the spectrum, émigré lawyers and American diplomats such as Hans Morgenthau, John Herz, and George Kennan in this period preached the dangers of relying on international law to govern an anarchic international system. International law, they argued, was only an expression of power politics, and states could not be held to arbitrarily dictated rules. Rival visions of the future of international legal order meanwhile split the members of the idealist camp, including figures such as Lauterpacht and Sohn, who argued that international law remained vital for reconstruction of a more progressive international system even as they lost faith in its prewar promise to protect vulnerable individuals and groups.[8]

Before human rights gained wider popularity and political salience, Schwelb worked from within the UN to develop a flexible doctrine of international law attentive to custom and domestic practice that strove to balance the two pillars of the UN Charter – sovereign equality and respect for human rights. More profoundly, he linked the project of expanding principles of human rights into binding law to the jurist's character and his emotional affect. Schwelb argued that in order to work toward the legalization of human rights principles and avoid the turn toward realism or despair about moral progress, legal scholars would need to control the passions, as though they were latter-day Stoics. In his teaching and writing, Schwelb likewise promoted a philosophy of moderation and gradualism that appeared outmoded by the time mass social activism in the name of human rights took hold in the 1970s.

This essay therefore seeks to situate Schwelb's vision of human rights law in the context of the generational response to two world wars. Anglophone political theory in the period when Schwelb worked to expand the jurisprudence of human rights was dominated by anti-utopian thought and his framing of post-war human rights resonates with trends in Cold War liberalism more broadly.[9] However, though it is crucial to recognize Schwelb's contributions to a particular mid-century debate about the future of international legal order, it is equally important to grasp how Schwelb's intellectual project to rescue the supranational promise of human rights marks the beginning of a style of thought now de rigueur for human rights lawyers. Examining his life

---

[8] MARK LEWIS, THE BIRTH OF THE NEW JUSTICE: THE INTERNATIONALIZATION OF CRIME AND PUNISHMENT, 1919–1950 (2014).

[9] On the mid-century liberal critique of utopia and the separation between concepts of utopia and liberal legality, *see Introduction* to LAW AND THE UTOPIAN IMAGINATION (Austin Sarat, Lawrence Douglas, & Martha Umphrey, eds., 2014).

and intellectual career indicates that human rights law was born out of a spirit of hopeful caution – of a utopia deferred – rather than exuberant idealism. Schwelb's life and thought reveal the origins of human rights law in the anti-utopian mood of the post-war decades and in the broader transformation of legal thought after the Second World War.

Legal cosmopolitans who aspired to establish a supranational legal order in the wake of World War II faced disappointment first in the failures of the Nuremberg trials, and then in the creation of a nonbinding Universal Declaration of Human Rights in 1948. Raphael Lemkin, the Polish Jewish jurist who created the Genocide Convention, left Nuremberg disheartened because the trials failed to identify genocide as a crime outside the context of aggressive war. Lauterpacht, the eminent British émigré international legal scholar, meanwhile responded bitterly to the General Assembly's acceptance of the UDHR in 1948. Rather than a legal convention that would at least formally assign its signers particular obligations, the Universal Declaration represented a statement of principles without legal force.[10] Moreover, the Allied powers committed themselves to the principle of sovereign equality in the Atlantic Charter and in the domestic jurisdiction clause in the UN Charter from 1945. It thus quickly became clear that the UN was not a particularly promising place to envision the legalization and enforcement of human rights or the creation of law beyond the jurisdiction of the state.

It is in light of the pessimistic reactions toward the non-legally binding Universal Declaration that we must comprehend Schwelb's argument during his years as head of the Division of Human Rights that international lawyers focus on developing the proper emotional affect in order to further the cause of human rights. As the assistant director of the Human Rights Division, he cautiously sought to rebuild international law on its post-war foundations. Schwelb did not simply believe in the optimistic faith in social progress that had defined the profession of international law since its formation as a discipline. Instead, he suggested that it was necessary to structure one's attitude and perspective in order to be open to hope for a more progressive future. His insistence that the principles of the Universal Declaration would become legally relevant relied on the idea that patience and intellectual labor would reveal the gradual instantiation of principles into international and domestic law. This approach culminated in the publication of a book-length study, *Human Rights and the International*

---

[10]   Hersch Lauterpacht, International Law and Human Rights (1950).

Community: The Roots and Growth of the Universal Declaration of Human Rights.[11]

Analyzing the emergence of new law required emotional control as much as it demanded analytical skill and technical competence. In essays and speeches from the 1950s and 1960s, Schwelb often quoted the Viennese émigré jurist Josef Kunz, who argued, "in the field of human rights as in other actual problems of international law, it is necessary to avoid the Scylla of a pessimistic cynicism and the Charybdis of mere wishful thinking and superficial optimism."[12] It is striking that Schwelb invoked Kunz's dictum since Kunz's intellectual evolution testifies to the broader transformation of legal internationalism from the interwar to the post-war era.[13] Kunz had never been a "superficial optimist," but in the 1920s he had promoted a legalist solution to the crises of the post-World War I period, crises that included the growing number of stateless people in the Central European successor states. Kunz had written and lectured on the proper legal interpretation of the peace treaties and advocated for the legal inclusion of people excluded from new states after the war and had served as the legal secretary of the Austrian League of Nations Union.[14] By the 1950s, however, Kunz concluded that the diversity of ideologies in the post-war world destroyed the ambition to resolve international crises by reference to a gapless international legal order. Kunz described international order as marked by "the decline of Europe" and the "the deep split between the free and communistic worlds."[15] The expectation that legal scholars deploying juridical techniques could resolve political and social crises had given way to a more critical perspective on the real-world power of legal analysis. Responding to the post-war crisis of internationalist idealism, Schwelb seized on the idea that the elaboration of human rights law depended on the character of the jurist who could, as Kunz suggested, avoid the extremes of excessive optimism or pessimistic doubt.

---

[11] EGON SCHWELB, HUMAN RIGHTS AND THE INTERNATIONAL COMMUNITY: THE ROOTS AND GROWTH OF THE UNIVERSAL DECLARATION OF HUMAN RIGHTS (1964).

[12] Egon Schwelb, *International Conventions on Human Rights*, 19 INT'L & COMP. L. QUAR. 654 (1960); Egon Schwelb, *Teaching the Law Relating to the International Protection of Human Rights: An Experiment*, 17 J. LEG. EDUC. 451 (1964–1965); Egon Schwelb, *The Teaching of the International Aspects of Human Rights*, 65 AM. J. INT'L L. 242 (1971).

[13] MARTTI KOSKENIEMMI, THE GENTLE CIVILIZER OF NATIONS: THE RISE AND FALL OF INTERNATIONAL LAW 1870–1960, 474 (2004).

[14] On Kunz's interwar legal activism and the broader emphasis in interwar international legal thought on international legal personality, *see* Mira Siegelberg, The Question of Questions: The Problem of Statelessness in International History 1921–1961 (2014) (unpublished Ph. D. dissertation, Harvard University).

[15] Josef Kunz, *Pluralism of Legal and Value systems and International Law*, 49 AM. J. INT'L L. 373 (1955); On Kunz and the mid-twentieth century crisis of international law, see Mark Mazower, "An International Civilization? Empire, Internationalism, and the Crisis of the Mid-Twentieth Century," 82 *International Affairs* 3 (2006).

Yet Schwelb's post-war approach to the development of human rights law did not signify an abrupt transition from his interwar and wartime professional commitments. Born in Prague in 1899, he served in the Austrian army during World War I, where he was stationed in Montenegro during the Austrian occupation of the kingdom. After the war, Schwelb studied briefly in Vienna before returning to Prague to complete a law degree. Committed to progressive causes, he worked as a lawyer in the newly formed Czechoslovakian republic, litigating labor disputes and civil liberties cases, and served on the Prague city council. In his private legal practice he represented trade unions, newspapers, and workers' compensation cases, and later refugees fleeing fascism. Before the Jewish refugee crisis of the 1930s, Schwelb's primary academic and professional focus was not international legal scholarship but rather the jurisprudence and implementation of the welfare state. In his early legal writing from the 1920s, Schwelb examined the administrative law of Czechoslovakia, as well as the state's nationality and citizenship laws. Like many liberal lawyers at that time, he worried about the tightening boundaries of citizenship and sought interpretive legal solutions to exclusionary legislation that left many without the protection of the state.[16] He also participated in the construction of the state's social welfare regime as a member of the Prague city council. In the 1930s, he represented refugees from Germany who sought asylum in Czechoslovakia. After the Anschluss in 1938, Schwelb began writing about the legal questions over nationality and citizenship that arose from the treaty between Czechoslovakia and Germany.

International legal argument became more significant in Schwelb's personal and professional life once he was forced to flee Nazi Europe. After facing arrest and imprisonment by the Gestapo in 1939, Schwelb left Prague with his family and lived in refugee-designated quarters in London before finding his professional and political footing. He joined the Czech government in exile in London, serving as a consultant on military law for the Czechoslovakian army and as a member of the Czechoslovakian legal council under the leadership of Eduard Benes.[17] For new states after World War I, international law was as much a means to legitimize political status as a potential restriction of sovereignty. U.S. President Woodrow Wilson had favored Czech independence in part because Benes and Thomas Masaryk had presented a strong case for Czechoslovakia's bona fides as a democratic state on the model of

[16] On Schwelb's writings on nationality and constitutionalism *see* Egon Schwelb, *Staatsbürgerschaft: Verfassungsgesetz mit Erläuterungen*, in PRAGER ARCHIV FÜR GESETZGEBUNG UND RECHTSPRECHUNG (1926); *Die cechoslovakische Staatsbürgerrechtsnovelle vom 1 Juli 1926*, ZEITSCHRIFT FÜR OSTRECHT (1927).
[17] Telephone Interview with Frank Schwelb (Sept. 16, 2009).

Mazzini's cosmopolitan nationalism. The importance of international legal argument was particularly clear after 1938, when Czech nationalist leaders including Benes and Masaryk functioned as a government in exile. As a legal advisor to Benes's government in exile, Schwelb developed legal arguments to justify the continuing existence of the Czechoslovakian state. He reported on the international legal status of the Czech government in exile as well as other jurisdictional issues that emerged from the presence of allied troops in Britain for the 1942 *Czechoslovak Yearbook of International Law*.[18] Like the *Jewish Yearbook of International Law*, which published only one issue in 1948 with contributions from prominent Jewish international legal scholars including Lauterpacht and Kelsen, the *Czech Yearbook of International Law*, with articles written in English, was designed to demonstrate the close relationship between international law and democratic statehood.[19]

The members of Schwelb's expat circle in London had already begun to express their doubts about whether international lawyers would play any role in shaping the post-war world. One of Schwelb's colleagues, Joseph Weyl, wrote in the *Czechoslovak Yearbook*, the same issue for which Schwelb had contributed, that international lawyers would have to adapt if they were to remain a relevant force in international affairs. In the essay, Weyl counseled that if international lawyers accept the importance of social and economic realities, they will "be esteemed by society as sober social technicians of a specific kind" and they will no longer face the common objection that they are "out of touch with reality."[20] We cannot know whether he took this assertion to heart, but it is clear that Schwelb was aware early on of the perceived powerlessness of international lawyers in directing international affairs. Allies of the Benes regime later claimed that the emphasis on legalistic argumentation left an indelible mark on Benes's capacities as an effective political actor. Looking back on Benes's ill-fated reign, Edward Taborsky – a legal scholar who had been part of Benes's government in exile – assessed that Benes had spent too much time in the "League's peculiar atmosphere of wordy legalism in which disagreeable problems were disposed of by polished but ineffective

---

[18] See Egon Schwelb, *Zur Anerkennung der Tschechoslovakischen Regierung in England. Eine staatsrechtliche Studie* (1940); Egon Schwelb, *The Jurisdiction Over the Members of the Allied Forces in Great Britain*, CZECHOSLOVAK Y.B. INT'L. L. 147 (1942); Egon Schwelb, *The Competence of Foreign Governments Institute in Great Britain over Civilian Persons, in Particular the Allied Powers*, CZECHOSLOVAK Y.B. INT'L. L. 198 (1942); Egon Schwelb, *Legislation in Exile: Czechoslovakia*, J. COMP. LEG. & INT'L. L. 120 (1942).

[19] 1 JEWISH Y.B. INT'L. L. 1 (1949).

[20] Joseph Weyl, *Some Suggestions for a Future Covenant*, 1 Czechoslovak Y.B. INT'L. L. 196 (1942).

resolutions."[21] In other words, Benes's political struggles at the end of his career, when the communist party overtook Czechoslovakia, derived in part from his reliance on legal argument.

In addition to working as a legal advisor for the Czechoslovakian government in exile, Schwelb continued to reflect in his writing and speeches on the rise of administrative law and the legal provisions required for welfare distribution, which had been central to his career in Prague after World War I. Schwelb delivered a lecture before the Association of Czechoslovak Lawyers in Great Britain in December 1942 on the subject of the "Rule of Law" and the comparison between legal guarantees in English law compared with Continental and Czechoslovak law. In his lecture, Schwelb paid homage to the British legal scholar A. V. Dicey's treatise on the concept of the rule of law in relation to a discussion about the system of administrative courts for delivering and adjudicating social services in Czechoslovakia. A reviewer at the *Solicitor* noted that the discussion of Czech law was relevant for England since the Beveridge report from 1942 had outlined a comparable system for implementing a welfarist order in the United Kingdom.[22] Schwelb thus entertained the legal and constitutional questions prominent in this period among those trying to reconcile the rule of law with the expansion of the administrative state.

Indeed, prior to joining the international civil service, Schwelb remained a committed citizen of Czechoslovakia. Schwelb only decided not to return to Europe once it became clear that the communists would take over Czechoslovakia. He made plans for his family to remain in the United Kingdom by completing a separate law degree in London and then naturalizing as a British subject. Schwelb already expressed interest in international organizations in a 1944 note on the Diplomatic Privileges act of 1944 and its application to international organizations.[23] He made the transition from legal advisor for a national government to international civil servant when he obtained a position as a legal officer for the UN War Crimes Commission in London from 1945 to 1947.[24] In the course of the Nuremberg trials, the adoption of the concept of "crimes against humanity" captured Schwelb's imagination. It was at this time that he began to present the protection of individuals outside of states as the major site for future hope in a more just

---

[21] Edward Taborsky, *The Triumph and Disaster of Eduard Benes*, 36 FOREIGN AFFAIRS 669 (1958).

[22] *"The Rule of Law" Lecture Summary*, 10 THE SOLICITORS 19 (1943).

[23] Egon Schwelb, *Diplomatic Privileges (Extension) Act 1944*, 1 MOD. L. REV. 8 (1945).

[24] According to his son, Schwelb expected Czechoslovakia to become part of the communist sphere. Schwelb, *supra* note 17.

international order. In the Nuremberg principles, elaborated in August 1945, the Allies defined violence against individuals or minorities on political, racial, or religious grounds as a "crime against humanity" but only in the context of aggressive war. In his landmark essay from 1946 on the concept of "crimes against humanity," Schwelb investigated whether Article 6 of the Charter of the International Military Tribunal from 1945 actually made a "radical inroad" into the "sphere of the domestic jurisdiction of sovereign states."[25] The reason, Schwelb argued, that the "crimes against humanity" clause was so potentially radical was that it held out the promise of instituting external limitations on sovereign power. One objective of Schwelb's piece was to trace the implications of the Nuremberg principles and trials for international law, especially the orthodox view that individuals were not directly connected to international law. Schwelb expressed particular interest in whether the "far reaching and revolutionary nature of the notion of crimes against humanity" was borne out by the proceedings and the results of the trial.[26] The principles adopted at Nuremberg indicated more judicial interference into the area of domestic jurisdiction compared to the period after World War I. He wrote,

> It must be said that the jurisdiction over crimes against humanity of occupation and municipal courts in Germany and elsewhere has little bearing on the great principle which it is the desire of many to see embodied in the law of crimes against humanity, namely, the principle that the protection of a minimum standard of human rights should be guaranteed anywhere, at any time, and against anybody.[27]

Schwelb's essay on the concept of "crimes against humanity" contained the seeds of the theory that would characterize his post-war approach to the development of human rights law. Despite the failure of the trials to encroach fundamentally on sovereign right, Schwelb nevertheless presented the results of Nuremberg as progressive because they provided a pathway toward the development of crimes against humanity beyond its original narrow remit. The statement of the principle itself created an opening for new developments in international law. By contrast, Hans Kelsen, the premier European jurist before World War II, claimed that the judgment at Nuremberg did not constitute a precedent in international law because it only applied pre-existing rules and was not established as a general principle of law "but as

---

[25]   Egon Schwelb, *Crimes Against Humanity*, 23 BRIT. Y.B. INT'L. L. 178 (1946), republished in PERSPECTIVES ON THE NUREMBERG TRIALS, 121 (Guenael Mettraux, ed., 2008).

[26]   *Id.* at 148.

[27]   *Id.* at 166.

a rule applicable only to vanquished states by the victors."[28] Unlike Kelsen, Schwelb assessed the legal significance of the trials in terms of their inchoate legal merits rather than their immediate contemporary force.

Impressed by the detailed reports Schwelb submitted from the War Crimes Commission, John Humphrey, a Canadian international law expert who became the first director of the Human Rights Division of the UN, hired him in 1947 to serve as his second in command.[29] One of Schwelb's first tasks at the UN was to translate the work undertaken in the war crimes trials into the language of human rights. He sought to generalize the concept of crimes against humanity, a wartime charge, to acts committed by governments against their own people in peacetime. The work undertaken by legal scholars to extract and collate the laws emerging from the post-war war crimes trials constituted, Schwelb wrote, "the development of a new science – the science of the law concerning crimes against humanity of which I am one of the charter members."[30] In the service of this project he hired John Fried, an émigré jurist from Vienna and Kelsen's nephew, as a consultant. Schwelb gave Fried strict instructions to produce a study that would be the first to articulate in clear, nontechnical language the status of human rights protection in the trials during and after the war. Schwelb proposed an organizational scheme for the study based on the rights protected or vindicated, rather than according to the trials in particular countries.[31] Looking to build a new legal concept of human rights, he insisted that Fried keep a tight focus on the implications of the trials for the doctrine of human rights and pay less attention to its implications for international law in general.[32]

The project to expand the legal remit of "crimes against humanity" set Schwelb on a collision course with Raphael Lemkin, the inventor of the term "genocide" and the principle author of the Genocide Convention. Schwelb's

[28] Hans Kelsen, *Will the Judgment in the Nurember Trial Constitute a Precedent in International Law? in* PERSPECTIVES ON THE NUREMBERG TRIALS 275 (Guenael Mettraux, ed., 2008).

[29] Some Czech members of the secretariat protested Schwelb's appointment due to his Jewish and social democratic background. Humphrey described it in his memoirs as "one of the first human rights cases within the Secretariat." JOHN HUMPHREY, HUMAN RIGHTS AND THE UNITED NATIONS: A GREAT ADVENTURE 33 (1984).

[30] Letter from Egon Schwelb to George Brand (Jan. 5, 1949), SOA 317/03 (United Nations Office at Geneva).

[31] Letter from Egon Schwelb to John Fried (Nov. 30, 1949), SOA 317/03 (United Nations Office at Geneva).

[32] Schwelb persisted even after the creation of a separate convention banning genocide to try to bring the category under the general rubric of human rights. In an article from 1960, he cited the Genocide Convention as an example of the "humanitarian instruments" produced by the United Nations. *See* Egon Schwelb, *International Conventions on Human Rights*, 19 INT'L & COMP. L. QUAR. 654 (1960).

conflict with Lemkin reveals two distinct conceptions of how to create law binding upon states. In his campaign to pass and ratify the Genocide Convention, Lemkin emphasized the legal power of a ratified treaty that enshrined the value of groups in international life. Before the General Assembly voted on the convention, Schwelb told Lemkin that it would be better to develop the legal concept of crimes against humanity brought against the Nazi war criminals at Nuremberg rather than burden the international community with a redundant instrument. "It will be necessary," he told Lemkin, "to unite the two rivers flowing under two different names, namely 'genocide' and 'crimes against humanity' into one broad and solid bed."[33] The discussions on genocide in the General Assembly, Schwelb told a colleague, "amounted to a retrograde step compared with the law as laid by the Nuremberg Charter."[34] Schwelb considered the Genocide Convention a step backward because it represented a missed opportunity to build on the groundwork established at Nuremberg. For Lemkin, however, the Genocide Convention was vital because it specified crimes not necessarily committed during a war and provided a clear statement of legal sanction.[35]

Schwelb's position at the UN gave him particular insight into the limits of looking to the United Nations for the development of supranational law. As a legal advisor to the Czechoslovakian leadership, Schwelb grasped the political implications of the displacement of minority rights with human rights as the governing principle in the post-war reorganization of Europe. As Mark Mazower has shown, Benes cannily turned to the language of individual human rights in order to facilitate the quiet death of the more legally forceful minority rights protection treaties, which had been a condition of Czech statehood in the period after World War I.[36] Within the Human Rights Commission, Eleanor Roosevelt urged the commission to renounce any power to investigate the thousands of complaints from individuals alleging human rights violations. The accumulation of such petitions led to the creation of a system for filing complaints that John

---

[33] Letter from Egon Schwelb to John Humphrey (June 7, 1947), SOA 17/03 (United Nations Office at Geneva).

[34] Schwelb described his exchange with Lemkin in a letter to George Brand, a member of the UN War Crime Commission. Letter from Egon Schwelb to George Brand (Nov. 18, 1948) SOA 17/03 (United Nations Office at Geneva).

[35] *See* Lewis, *supra* note 8, at 224 (2014); on Lemkin's self-perception as an outsider compared to the professional international bureaucrats *see* Mira Siegelberg, *Unofficial Men, Efficient Civil Servants: Raphael Lemkin in the History of International Law*, 15 J. OF GENOCIDE RES. 297 (2013).

[36] Mark Mazower, *The Strange Triumph of Human Rights, 1933–1950* 47 HIST. J. 379 (2004).

Humphrey called "the most elaborate wastepaper basket ever created."[37] Humphrey himself offered the empty-sounding promise of an International Bill of Human Rights when W. E. B. Du Bois petitioned the Human Rights Commission to take up the struggle for African American civil rights in the United States.[38] Civil rights activists who initially saw the Human Rights Commission as a potential arena to promote their cause quickly realized that the project of legalizing human rights norms could be deployed as a tactic to avoid UN involvement in the struggle for civil rights in the United States.

Schwelb's role at the UN likewise provided a unique perspective on the collapse of interwar plans for the expansion of supranational law. Jurists who had dreamed in the era of the League of Nations about a robust system of law beyond the jurisdiction of the state wrote to Schwelb after 1948 to inquire whether the implementation of such visions was on the horizon. Vespasian Pella, a Romanian jurist who had championed an international criminal court in the interwar period and assisted in the drafting of the Genocide Convention, asked Schwelb in September 1949 whether there were any plans for an international court of human rights, and whether it would treat the question of the stateless.[39] Such a court above the nations could cater to those without their own states and Schwelb knew that such proposals had been quickly snuffed out. The United States turned away from formal treaty obligations after 1953. Allies of the cause like the émigré political scientist Erich Hula meanwhile documented the loss of faith in international treaties as instruments for promoting human rights.[40]

Avoiding the turn to rule-skepticism and realism, or the collapse into despair, thus required the careful pruning of hopeful expectation and careful control over the emotions. In the two decades after the General Assembly adopted the Universal Declaration of Human Rights, Schwelb focused his attention on the gradual interpolation of principles outlined in the UDHR

---

[37] BARBARA KEYS, RECLAIMING AMERICAN VIRTUE: THE HUMAN RIGHTS REVOLUTION OF THE 1970S 28 (2014); CAROL ANDERSON, EYES OFF THE PRIZE: THE UNITED NATIONS AND THE SUPRA AFRICAN AMERICAN STRUGGLE FOR HUMAN RIGHTS 101 (2003).

[38] ANDERSON, *id.*

[39] Letter from Vespasian Pella to Egon Schwelb (Sept. 11, 1949), SOA 317/03 (United Nations Office at Geneva).

[40] Erich Hula, *International Law and the Protection of Human Rights*, 162 *in* LAW AND POLITICS IN THE WORLD COMMUNITY: ESSAYS ON HANS KELSEN'S PURE THEORY AND RELATED PROBLEMS IN INTERNATIONAL LAW (George Lipsky, ed., 1953), cited in Egon Schwelb, *International Conventions on Human Rights*, 9 INT'L & COMP. L. QUAR. 654 (1960).

into domestic law in order to rescue it from the charge of legal irrelevance.[41] Together with Humphrey, Schwelb developed a creative response to the marginalization of the legalization of human rights at the UN. He sought to expand international human rights law by drawing out the rules implicit in international treaties and international practice. Schwelb collected documents from around the world to demonstrate the long-term effects of the declaration. He preached the importance of the afterlife of the UDHR in numerous contexts and exhaustively catalogued any reference to it. Wilfred Jenks, a prominent international legal scholar and a legal advisor at the International Labor Organization, described Schwelb in a letter to Lauterpacht as "the backbone of the human rights work of the U.N." who "has a real grasp of practical possibilities."[42] Maintaining faith in such a project proved difficult. When Humphrey received the proofs of Lauterpacht's article in the *British Yearbook of International Law* on the disappointment of the UDHR from Schwelb, he wrote in his diary, "nothing could be more negative or more unsympathetic to our work. It is destructive criticism of the worst kind, and coming from such an authority, will undoubtedly do us much harm."[43] He remarked in his memoir that Lauterpacht was simply too impatient to anticipate the gradual legalization of the principles of the UDHR. If "sparks of legality were to be kindled in it," Humphrey stated, it would only be through its inclusion in customary law and through the slow evolution of legal consensus.[44] Schwelb tried to acquire Lauterpacht's ex post facto approval by insisting that had Lauterpacht lived, he would have recognized the cascading power of the declaration, and insisted that Lauterpacht had revised his initial negative response to the Universal Declaration before his death in 1960.[45]

Schwelb thus turned toothlessness into a virtue by urging a Penelope-like patience – weaving together declarations, statements, and treaties that together added up to a new image of conventional state practice. He sought to resolve

---

[41] Beth Simmons refers to the UN Human Rights Commission as an early agent of the legalization of the doctrine of international human rights. BETH SIMMONS, MOBILIZING FOR HUMAN RIGHTS: INTERNATIONAL LAW IN DOMESTIC POLITICS 24 (2009).

[42] Letter from Wilfred Jenks to Hersch Lauterpacht (Feb. 16, 1960), Jenks Collection, ILO, Geneva. Thanks to James Loeffler for sharing this source.

[43] John Humphrey, ON THE EDGE OF GREATNESS: THE DIARIES OF JOHN HUMPHREY, FIRST DIRECTOR OF THE UNITED NATIONS DIVISION OF HUMAN RIGHTS 216 (A. J. Hobbins, ed., vol. 3, 1994).

[44] *Id.*

[45] Moyn, *supra* note 7, at 199. There is in fact evidence to support such a claim: according to Jenks, Lauterpacht planned to collaborate with Schwelb on a new edition of *International Law and Human Rights.* Jenks to Lauterpacht, *supra* note 42.

the problem of the proper restraints on state behavior by making the principle actors intrinsically changeable and moldable. At times he moved beyond recording references to the UDHR in order to deliberately advocate for the production of textual connections between the declaration and international treaties.[46] Schwelb argued that the UDHR had succeeded in blurring the line between "binding conventions" and "non-binding pronouncements."[47] The realist international legal scholar Georg Schwarzenberger asserted in no uncertain terms that the search for an international *jus cogens*, fundamental principles of international law, amounted to an international public policy dictated by powerful states. For Schwelb, however, progress occurred gradually behind the scenes, once the difficult labor undertaken by legal experts of discovering underlying consensus could begin.[48]

Indeed, in his behind-the-scenes role at the UN, Schwelb sought to preserve the organization's delicate diplomatic balance, especially as new states joined the General Assembly. During the debates at the UN over the right to self-determination, Schwelb argued against the establishment of a commission to survey the status of the permanent sovereignty of peoples and nations over their natural resources. It would, he stated, "confirm the worst apprehensions of anti-United Nations groups that the United Nations is a kind of supra national arbiter over national sovereignty. It would also tend to complicate relations among the under developed countries and those economically more advanced."[49] Schwelb thus proposed that international human rights are not trumps to transcend domestic institutions; instead they are enriched and transformed through domestic struggles.

A debate between Schwelb and Moses Moskowitz over plans for the international human rights covenants demonstrates Schwelb's commitment to explicating the cascading power of the Universal Declaration to shape domestic law rather than to establish a separate supranational enforcement mechanism. Moskowitz, a Jewish émigré from the Russian Empire who operated under consultant status as a member of a nongovernmental organization at the UN, saw the UN's emphasis on state sovereignty as an essential limitation on the idea of human rights. In 1959, Moskowitz stated, "as it is, the covenants leave the individual at the mercy of the state as ever." They failed to identify

---

[46] Egon Schwelb, Memo (Sept. 22, 1953), SOA/317/1/02 (United Nations Office at Geneva).

[47] HUMAN RIGHTS IN NATIONAL AND INTERNATIONAL LAW 144 (A. H. Robertson, ed., 1968).

[48] Georg Schwarzenberger, *International Jus Cogens?* 43 TEX. L. REV. 455 (1965); Egon Schwelb, *Some Aspects of International Jus Cogens as Formulated by International Law Commission*, 61 AM. J. INT'L . L. 946 (1967).

[49] Egon Schwelb, Memorandum to M. De Seynes Annex (Feb. 24, 1955), SO261/413 (United Nations Office at Geneva).

the "inalienable rights of man as distinguished from the rights of citizens."[50] Moskowitz claimed that only the recognition of the right of individual petition could correct this problem by providing individuals with a supranational legal forum to assert rights against their states, and by providing a forum for individuals who had no state to which they could assert their demands or express their grievances.[51]

In his rejoinder to Moskowitz, Schwelb rejected the supposition that state sovereignty and individual human rights represented either/or propositions. In his review of Moskowitz's *Human Rights and World Order* from 1959, Schwelb argued that Moskowitz's enthusiasm led him to ignore the gradual accumulation of achievements. The assumption that sovereign authority represented the antithesis of human rights reinforced, Schwelb argued, the worn-out doctrine of domestic inviolability. Anyone interested in the international protection of human rights, Schwelb wrote, would support comprehensive, legally binding treaties combined with international supervision. Moskowitz had missed how the UDHR had become incorporated into international conventions and subsequently influenced national constitutions and legislation.[52] Schwelb insisted that one could document the slow diffusion of human rights law into states and then down into the citizenry.

It was as if by continually softening the edges of sovereign authority the problem of those who butted up against its boundaries would diminish over time. In his time at the Human Rights Division, Schwelb served as an informational node for lawyers who wanted to bring human rights developments at the UN into their domestic legal arguments. After he spoke in 1959 at the American Society of International Law on recent developments relating to expatriation and statelessness, American lawyers involved in cases involving the involuntary loss of nationality wrote to Schwelb asking for material prepared by the Human Rights Division on the subject of statelessness. Leonard Boudin, a prominent civil rights attorney, asked Schwelb to send him materials while preparing an article for the *Harvard Law Review* on the

---

[50] Moses Moskowitz, *The Covenants on Human Rights: Basic Issues of Substance*, 53 PROC. AM. SOC. INT'L . L. 230 (1959). On Moskowitz *see* Moyn, *supra* note 7, at 122–26.

[51] *Id.*

[52] Egon Schwelb, Book Review, 57 MICH. L. REV. 791 (1959) (reviewing MOSES MOSKOWITZ, HUMAN RIGHTS AND WORLD ORDER: THE STRUGGLE FOR HUMAN RIGHTS AT THE UNITED NATIONS (1958)). On Louis Sohn and Egon Schwelb as part of the "first generation of academic students of human rights" who hoped to "assimilate the declaration and other pronouncements of international organizations into domestic law or by a kind of judicial osmosis," *see* José A. Cabranes, *Customary International Law: What It Is And What It Is Not*, 143 DUKE J. COMP. & INT'L. L. 22, note 29 (2011–2012).

constitutionality of the involuntary loss of nationality.[53] Schwelb argued, for example, in 1962 that the Convention on Marriage and Human Rights represented a positive achievement because it added to the body of conventional international law in the human rights field that had come into being since 1945. He admitted that the convention had not immediately transformed domestic practice and called attention to Israel's lack of civil marriage as an example of national legislation that did not yet match the promise of the convention. Rather than rejecting the convention as useless, he suggested that it would eventually bear upon domestic law.[54]

The conflict between Schwelb and Moskowitz – seemingly quite scholastic in light of their broader agreement about the importance of human rights – only appears coherent in light of the prewar international legal goal of asserting the fundamental supremacy of international legal order over domestic legal regimes. Moskowitz had studied with the American international lawyer Philip Jessup and shared Jessup's long-term goal to define the state's legal regime as subordinate to international law. The UN Charter's foundation on the principle of sovereignty was bound to seem like a retrograde step because it affirmed the supremacy of state sovereignty. Moskowitz recommended an amendment to the UN Charter that clarified the supremacy of human rights over the principle of sovereignty. Schwelb gently suggested that Moskowitz continued to fight old battles over the boundary between domestic and supranational spheres of authority by railing against the UN's structural commitment to state sovereignty, missing the opportunity to achieve practical progress in other realms. Schwelb insisted, "[S]o delicate a problem as domestic jurisdiction is beyond the realm of practicability." It was all a matter of keeping it in perspective. Appreciating the slow evolution of progress demanded maintaining the proper temperament. Schwelb concluded his review by identifying himself with Marcus Aurelius and the willingness to accept "even slight progress in human affairs." Though the Stoics famously emphasized the brotherhood of humanity and world citizenship, Stoicism seems to have been less significant for Schwelb's rhetorical purposes for its cosmopolitanism than for its emphasis on avoiding emotional extremes.[55]

---

[53] Letter from Leonard Boudin to Egon Schwelb (Apr. 23, 1959), SOA 373/1/04 (United Nations Office at Geneva); Leonard Boudin, *Involuntary Loss of American Nationality*, 72 HARV. L. REV. 1510 (1960); Letter from David Carliner to Egon Schwelb (May 6, 1959) SOA 373/1/04 (United Nations Office at Geneva).

[54] Egon Schwelb, *Marriage and Human Rights*, 12 AM. J. COMP. L. 337 (1963).

[55] Egon Schwelb, *International Conventions on Human Rights*, 9 INT'L & COMP. L. QUAR. 654 (1960). Stoic doctrine also demanded that adherents cultivate the proper affect in order to feel affiliated with everyone; *see* KATJA VOLK, LAW, REASON AND THE COSMIC CITY (2008).

It was not easy to maintain faith in the gradualist promise. Humphrey noted in a diary entry from October 3, 1957, "Schwelb sulks because, according to his lights, the programme [*sic*] has gone to pieces, the output of resolutions and draft conventions having diminished; and he only feels at home with legal problems."[56] Schwelb's vision of the jurist carefully keeping his passions and enthusiasm at bay bore a similarity to the image of the international civil servant cultivated at the UN in this period. Since Weber, sociologists had theorized that bureaucracies demanded the negation of personality in order to function properly. Dag Hammaskjold's address on "the international civil servant in law and in fact" from 1961 discussed how the secretary general could reduce his own level of personal discretion. Self-surveillance was a requirement of the responsible international civil servant.[57] If the United Nations were to become an effective organ for governance, it required emotional restraint and stoic conviction on the part of the civil servants devoted to its success. Schwelb emphasized the need to control the emotions but added the idea that focusing on the technicalities of legal work represented an additional step to maintaining such equanimity.

Schwelb's association with legal scholars at Yale Law School promoting a "legal realist" approach to international law such as Myres McDougal suggests a different interpretation of Schwelb's particular brand of legalism and his devotion to the expansion of human rights law. After leaving the UN, Schwelb spent a number of years teaching at Yale, and thus seems to have been part of McDougal's legal realist orbit.[58] In the 1950s and 1960s, McDougal promoted the idea that international lawyers should serve as peripatetic policy experts, providing legal arguments in the service of higher moral causes. Richard Falk, another member of this school, outlined the new approach to international law that tried to meld international relations and international law. As Martti Koskeniemmi vividly portrayed in *The Gentle Civilizer of Nations*, realism captured American international law and helped authorize the move to deformalized moralism among American international lawyers.

---

56 Humphrey, *supra* note 43, at 245.
57 *See* Guy Fiti Sinclair, *The International Civil Servant in Theory and Practice: Law, Morality, and Expertise*, 26 EUR. J. INT'L. L. 747 (2015).
58 Kunz, *supra* note 15, at 474. Samuel Moyn, *The International Law that is America: Reflections on the Last Chapter of the Gentle Civilizer of Nations*, 29 TEMP. INT'L & COMP. L. J. 399 (2013). *Also see* Richard Falk, *New Approaches to the Study of International Law*, 61 AMER. J. INT'L L. 477 (1967). Jochen von Bernstorff argues that Schwelb was an ally of the New Haven school, though it remains unclear whether he agreed with their approach or just saw it as a way to make "an affirmative reading of political events possible." Jochen von Bernstorff, *The Changing Fortunes of the Universal Declaration of Human Rights: Genesis and Symbolic Dimensions of the Turn to Rights in International Law*, 19 EUR. J. INT'L. L. 903 (2008).

Yet Schwelb's obsessive focus on documentation and the scholastic interpretation of texts does not easily fit a policy-oriented perspective that embraced
the politicization of international law. The concept of what law is, and
especially the conceptual boundaries of international law, transformed in
the mid-twentieth century away from an idealization of an autonomous
legal order (or law that is separate from morality or politics) toward the general
acceptance of the idea that law involves particular judgment and is often
purpose driven.[59] The period after the second world war is when, broadly
speaking, the vision of a more formal international law based on treaties and
state consent begins to change, and to authorize a more eclectic or deformalized approach to law. Though he associated with the more policy-driven
scholars at Yale, Schwelb's approach remained more aligned with the legalist
perspective characteristic of the Central European lawyers who worked with
Schwelb in London during World War II. In an article titled "Czechoslovak
Philosophy of Law," from the Czech *Journal of International Law* from 1942,
Adolf Prochazka examined the role of legal interpretation in the Vienna and
Czech schools of law. Prochazka – the chairman of the legal council of the
Czechoslovak government in exile – argued that a highest norm is required in
order to pull acts, utterances, legislation, court judgments, and administrative
organs into the field of legal vision (what constitutes a "fact"). But these data
points then determine what norms actually are.[60] These facts in turn revealed
conventional or customary norms. Prochazka was an interlocutor in the
interwar period with Kelsen and his theory bore a certain similarity to
Kelsen's idea that all new rules are logically related to old ones. For Kelsen,
even though legal systems evolve over time in a piecemeal fashion, all new
rules are logically related to old ones. A number of commentators have
observed that this theory reflected the jurisdictional and constitutional com-
plexity of the late nineteenth-century Habsburg Empire. The multiplicity of

---

[59]   Duncan Kennedy, *Three Globalizations of Law and Legal Thought: 1850–2000, in* THE NEW
LAW AND ECONOMIC DEVELOPMENTS: A CRITICAL APPRAISAL, 19–73 (David Trubek &
Alvaro Santos, eds., 2006); Jean d'Aspremont, *The Politics of Deformalization in International
Law*, 3 GOETTINGEN J. INT'L. L. 503 (2011); MORTON HORWITZ, THE TRANSFORMATION
OF AMERICAN LAW 1870–1960: THE CRISIS OF LEGAL ORTHODOXY (1992); on the "loss of
law's special status" since the nineteenth century, *see* DAVID KENNEDY, A WORLD OF
STRUGGLE: HOW POWER, LAW, AND EXPERTISE SHAPE GLOBAL POLITICAL ECONOMY
(2016); David Kennedy, *International Law and the Nineteenth Century: History of an Illusion*,
17 QUINNIPIAC L. REV. 99 (1997); ROBERTO UNGER, LAW IN MODERN SOCIETY: TOWARD
A CRITICISM OF SOCIAL THEORY (1976); KOSKENIEMMI, *supra* note 13; ALDO SCHIAVONE,
THE INVENTION OF LAW IN THE WEST (Jeremy Carden & Antony Shugar, trans., 2012);
Moyn, *supra* note 58.

[60]   Adolf Prochazka, *Czechoslovak Philosophy of Law*, 1 CZECHOSLOVAK J. INT'L. L. 89 (1942).

jurisdictions in the empire led to legal conflicts that generated the need for some basic rules that created the foundation for a legal whole to bring each jurisdiction into common regulatory understanding.[61] According to this juristic logic, trained legal specialists can discern and clarify the underlying normative principles shared across the empire.[62] Schwelb's legal approach to the UDHR in turn appears consistent with Prochazka's model since he sought to circumvent widespread "rule-skepticism" by proving the existence of a legal groundwork that would justify overriding domestic sovereignty in the name of a higher norm. According to this view, the UDHR functioned as the highest norm from which to evaluate and identify relevant "facts." Even if the UDHR did not count from a more positivist legal perspective as "law," it provided a legitimate textual basis for evaluating and interpreting an eclectic range of sources and did not depend on the moral sensibility and mission of the individual jurist.

Schwelb's formal approach to the creation of human rights law likewise set him apart from the broader reframing of international law at the UN during the height of decolonization. Postcolonial states likewise turned to a more pragmatic and deformalized conception of international law. As the community of independent states expanded, many argued that the possibility of anything like a common law of mankind was increasingly distant. Legal scholars from the global south pursuing the sovereign recognition of their own states at the United Nations promoted a conception of international law beyond the adaptation and adoption of a Western-imposed normativity. Lawyers, jurists, and civil servants at the UN in this period developed arguments to respond to the charge that international law is irrelevant or utopian, and the accusation that international law is a form of Western hegemony, by promoting more open-ended ways of making the law with the idea that international law could become a commonly shared language that could encompass a kind of agonistic form of global politics. Rather than presenting the development of international law as a source for limiting state power, those who promoted the UN as a site for the expansion and codification of international law began to argue that international law is always a form of political argument.[63]

---

[61] Gerhard Stourzh, *The Multinational Empire Revisited, in* GERHARD STOURZH, FROM VIENNA TO CHICAGO AND BACK: ESSAYS ON INTELLECTUAL HISTORY AND POLITICAL THOUGHT IN EUROPE AND AMERICA 145 (2007); JOHN DEAK, FORGING A MULTINATIONAL STATE: STATE MAKING IN IMPERIAL AUSTRIA FROM THE ENLIGHTENMENT TO THE FIRST WORLD WAR (2015).

[62] SALLY FALK MOORE, LAW AS PROCESS: AN ANTHROPOLOGICAL APPROACH 10–11 (1978).

[63] On decolonization generating an anti-formalistic international law *see* Umut Özsu, *Determining New Selves: Mohammed Bedjaoui on Algeria, Western Sahara, and Post-*

Indeed, critics seemed to be speaking directly to Schwelb when they addressed the hazards of an overly formal approach to international law. In a presentation on the "Implementation of International Instruments of Human Rights" at the American Society of International Law, Stanley Hoffman cautioned lawyers not to fall into the two main pitfalls of the profession: "the gratifying but perfectly vain exercise in moral sermonizing which finds a gloomy delight in exposing the wickedness of states, or the touching obstinacy of Orwell's horse – the horse which in Animal Farm drew from its constant failures the one and only lesson: 'I shall work more.'"[64] Hoffman distinguished between legalistic formalism, which "makes the researcher grateful for every reference to a "universal principle" in laws, codes, and constitutions, and sociological formalism, which "purports to bring about world order by emphasizing not any substantive principle, but mere procedures, patterns, 'interaction.'"[65] Schwelb fit Hoffman's description of the steadfast formalist, committed to the idea that laboring over existing texts would yield favorable results. At the same time, he scoured the texts for evidence of shared norms, which brought him closer to the sociological school and its emphasis on discerning patterns of belief through empirical study. Unlike McDougal, however, his interpretive doctrinal project was wrapped up in the problem of political hope, in the possibility of progress in relation to international order, rather than an apologetics about American power for the sake of a better world. He thus remained a formalist but conceived of what he was doing as disciplinary practice that would ward against dangerous emotional extremes that threatened to destroy the possibility of hopeful expectation altogether.

His commitment to textual interpretation as a safeguard against cynicism is further evident in his arguments for the development of a legal curriculum to teach international human rights in the 1960s. Schwelb was one of the first to introduce a course at an American law school on international human rights and he was part of a group of legal scholars who promoted the inclusion of international human rights in legal education.[66] Teaching his 1963 course at Yale provided the opportunity to spread his particular message about the

---

Classical International Law, in THE BATTLE FOR INTERNATIONAL LAW IN THE DECOLONIZATION ERA (Jochen von Bernstorff & Philipp Dann, eds., 2019).

[64] Stanley Hoffman, *The Implementation of International Instruments of Human Rights*, 53 PROC. AM. SOC. INT'L. L. 244 (1959).

[65] *Id.*

[66] *See* Ramirez, *supra* note 4, at chap. 5. Louis Sohn pointed out that Harvard Law School had offered a seminar on the international protection of human rights since 1962. *See* Louis Sohn, *Teaching the Law Relating to the International Protection of Human Rights: An Addendum*, 18 J. LEG. EDUCATION 221 (1965).

preservation of cautious idealism through obsessive documentation and legal interpretation. By continuing to promote – and to educate a new generation – in his textual method, Schwelb introduced a subversive contrapuntal note into the realist house. In an essay from 1964 on teaching the law relating to the international protection of human rights, Schwelb argued that it was vital to show law students that "the protection of the properties of enterprise of capital exporting countries in the less developed areas of the world is not the only, or main, purpose of public international law."[67] Once again, Schwelb addressed the threat of cynicism and called attention to the accusation that international law only served commercial interests. Later, he claimed that such a course was necessary because it was simply a fact that "conferences and projects, charges and counter-charges in regard to human rights dominate to a large extent the international life of our time." At the same time, those (presumably like himself) who were aware of the difficulties of trying to make international machinery matter "believe that the persistent and tireless efforts" may lead to some success.[68]

Resistant to the politicization of human rights law, and worried about its association with neocolonialism and Western capitalist exploitation, Schwelb developed a view of professional practice that allowed the human rights lawyer to imagine herself standing apart from politics. Schwelb implicitly tried to respond to the charges of apology and utopia, alternately distancing the work of right-minded legal scholars from politics and from the charge of intemperate idealism. At a panel discussion of the American Society in September 1971, the same forum in which the Columbia law professor Louis Henkin introduced Schwelb as "Mr. Human Rights," Schwelb described his course as a contribution to the heroic effort to live the *via media* by quoting Kunz on the difficulty of avoiding pessimism or dangerous optimism. It was the task of institutions of higher learning to collect, clarify, present, and analyze the facts and developments that alone can bring about the avoidance of extreme attitudes. One of his goals in teaching the class was to prove the modest proposition that international law could stand above the protection of global capitalism and thus to nurture idealism as such. By presenting human rights law in this fashion to his students, Schwelb contributed to the ideology that allows human rights lawyers to see their work as removed from the struggle of politics at a moment when law was seen to be politicized in a way it had not been before.

---

[67] Egon Schwelb, *Teaching the Law Relating to the International Protection of Human Rights: An Experiment*, 17 J. LEG. EDUCATION 451 (1965).
[68] Egon Schwelb, *Human Rights and the Teaching of International Law*, 64 AM. J. INT'L . L. 355 (1970).

What was the legacy, then, of Schwelb's self-conscious adoption of the Stoic ethos for the new generation of students trained in human rights law? José Cabranes – a judge on the U.S. Court of Appeals and one of Schwelb's students at Yale – recently called Schwelb's approach "European" because he practiced a rigorous scholastic approach to the analysis of documents. Cabranes describes how Schwelb introduced his students to the unglamorous and tedious task of textual investigation in the service of holding up a mirror to states in order to reveal their underlying convictions and promises. It is worthwhile to cite Cabranes's reflections at length because they testify to the linkage between Schwelb's method and his overarching philosophy of human rights law:

> It was in Dr. Schwelb's seminar that his students were introduced to the intense, scholastic reading of international human rights treaties. We were introduced also to their drafting history (*travaux preparatoires*) and amended drafts, year-by-year, article by article. The course did not encourage celebration of one's politics or sanctimonious comments on world affairs, no political arias, and no *Ode to Joy*. In sum, this was an unusual enterprise for us, an enterprise very much in the European tradition of legal education, and a form of education wholly foreign to the agitated activism that we associate with the human rights movement about to be born.[69]

As Cabranes notes, Schwelb introduced the methods that would allow Cabranes and his generation of legal practitioners to insist that international human rights principles play a role in domestic legal disputes. Schwelb demonstrated the labor required to determine customary international law, the body of law composed of the records indicating state consent to particular rules or norms. The true adherent, Cabranes states, must rely on the "laborious but authoritative compilations of state practice" and resist the temptation to develop creative readings of customary international law. The tedious work of recording and cataloging the practices of individual states not only provides the evidence for what the law is but also, according to Cabranes, represents a disciplinary practice that can ward off the temptation to veer from the path of such careful labor. By framing the professional habitus in this way, Cabranes echoes Schwelb's own arguments that emotional self-control was a precondition for a certain progressive view of international life.

As I have argued, Schwelb directed his attention toward the traumatized cosmopolitan legal imagination of the post-war era. Yet Schwelb helped establish the method that today provides legal internationalists with the

---

[69] Cabranes, *supra* note 52, at 145–46.

conviction that international law informs domestic legal procedures. Cabranes argues, for example, that the kind of labor Schwelb taught in his human rights course provides federal judges today with the confidence to appeal to international law by demonstrating the consensus that develops around particular norms.[70] Such textual alchemy remains distinct, however, from the model of "norm socialization" developed by later theorists of human rights who emphasize the necessity of transnational advocacy networks to diffuse international norms.[71] The content of this cosmopolitan ambition is markedly different from an activism focused on mobilizing a network of international human rights advocates in the name of distant human suffering. It does, however, resemble the chastened version of human rights legalism outlined by Cabranes.[72]

In the context of post-war legal thought, Schwelb's legalist approach to international politics was clearly not entirely unique: he derived the same sense of security from anchoring himself in documents and textual detail as the other members of the "sect" of Jewish émigré legal scholars who did not turn to study power politics and instead tried to discover the flickers of life within the gray literature produced by international organizations. David Kennedy, for instance, recalls that Louis Sohn was also an obsessive collector and reader of UN documents in his search for a new, better, order peeking over the horizon.[73] Schwelb's post-war career is nevertheless striking because he did not simply cling to the conviction that the promulgation of rules could ensure respect for human rights in international and national settings. Instead, he promoted the particular view that the practice of studying and recovering existing material would itself prevent the pessimism that seemed to plague his peers. He advocated the cultivation of an anti-utopian sensibility in the name of rescuing faith in the possibility of future grace. Examined in the broader setting of Cold War thought, Schwelb's vision of human rights law highlights the

---

[70] Cabranes, *supra* note 52, at 149. On Schwelb's role in "incubating a progressive fiction of the unfolding of human rights across the postwar era," *see* Moyn, *supra* note 7, at 260.

[71] *See, e.g.,* THE POWER OF HUMAN RIGHTS: INTERNATIONAL NORMS AND DOMESTIC CHANGE (Thomas Risse, Stephen C. Ropp, & Kathryn Sikkink, eds., 1999).

[72] *Also see* Seyla Benhabib on recent attempts to balance democratic sovereignty and human rights and the compatibility between pluralism and legal cosmopolitanism. Seyla Benhabib, *Claiming Rights Across Borders: International Human Rights and Democratic Sovereignty,* 103 AM. POL. SCI. REV. 691 (2009). On international human rights law as a "pessimistic reformist hope," *see* Samuel Moyn, *Do Human Rights Treaties Make Enough of a Difference? in* CAMBRIDGE COMPANION TO HUMAN RIGHTS LAW 329 (Conor Gearty & Costas Douzinas, eds., 2012).

[73] Kennedy, *supra* note 3, at 25.

importance of reconceiving the intellectual history of "realism" and "idealism" in the post-war era that takes into account a wider spectrum of agents than previously supposed.[74]

---

[74] On the political theology implicit in post-war international relations realism, *see* THE INVENTION OF INTERNATIONAL RELATIONS THEORY: REALISM, THE ROCKEFELLER FOUNDATION, AND THE 1954 CONFERENCE ON THEORY (Nicolas Guilhot, ed., 2011).

8

"Emotional Restraint" as Legalist Internationalism

Egon Schwelb's Liberalism After the Fall

Umut Özsu

Egon Schwelb is an intriguing figure in the history of international law – a key member of a generation of jurists, diplomats, state functionaries, and international civil servants who devoted their lives and careers to the project of securing peace through law. He is also a largely forgotten figure. Aside from sporadic references to his work in the growing literature on the histories of international criminal law and international human rights law, Schwelb enjoys little recognition for the years he committed to the United Nations and the international legal order it signified and spearheaded. Siegelberg's analysis of this Czech Jewish émigré jurist is thus most welcome, providing a nuanced and well-researched study that sheds significant light upon the shift from minority protection to individualistic human rights following World War II.

Siegelberg situates Schwelb's personal and professional trajectories alongside those of a number of other key figures in the post-war transformation of international law. Louis Henkin, John Peters Humphrey, Hersch Lauterpacht, and Louis B. Sohn understandably enjoy pride of place in this regard. Each of these jurists has either already been studied in some detail (the case with Lauterpacht and Humphrey) or is widely regarded as a pioneer of human rights law, destined for the kind of triumphalist hagiography enjoyed by only the most prominent international lawyers (the case with Henkin and Sohn). Schwelb is a glaring exception, here as elsewhere. Few today are aware of his scholarship. Fewer still bother to examine his tireless advocacy at the United Nations or his role in the gradual normalization of human rights in U.S. legal education. This is unfortunate not simply because Schwelb's contribution to the early development of the UN human rights system continues to be neglected – in itself, that is an omission that could be addressed without much difficulty. More fundamentally, it is unfortunate because Schwelb illustrates with especial clarity the transition from Geneva to New York, from the collective to the individual, from the League of Nations's attempt to institutionalize elements of the Concert of Europe's elite managerialism to the United Nations's drive to craft a more "socialized" international order, one in which principles of sovereign equality and nonintervention would be tempered by strong insistence upon economic coordination and individual human rights.

This brief response does not address the details of Schwelb's life and work. These are matters about which Siegelberg has written revealingly, and I have little of substance to add to her insightful discussion. Instead, my response engages with the incisive argument that Siegelberg makes about the role of "emotional restraint" in Schwelb's conception of post-war international law.[1] Notwithstanding Siegelberg's invitation to develop a fractured or splintered account of liberal internationalism, I argue that Schwelb is emblematic of a broader, more systemic shift in the ideological posture of those lawyers who invested themselves in human rights after the second "great war." Ultimately, I suggest that this posture was grounded in and nourished by a class project driven by a fundamentally bourgeois understanding of law's relation to order and justice.

NUANCED LEGALISM AND HUMAN RIGHTS

In a recent article, Duncan Bell argued that attempts to define liberalism – a tradition of social, legal, and political thought that he rightly regards as having "expanded to encompass the vast majority of political positions regarded as legitimate," such that "[m]ost inhabitants of the West are now *conscripts of liberalism*"[2] – tend more often than not to be marked by certain standard shortcomings. When they are not overtly prescriptive, specifying and patrolling the term's denotative parameters with the hope of fixing its content once and for all, they frequently aim for exhaustiveness, mapping the competing ways in which the term has been used in the hopes of generating a complete taxonomy. Yet another set of approaches is driven by the desire to explain the historical and conceptual development of liberalism, whether in predominantly prescriptive or taxonomic terms.[3] In the place of these and related perspectives, Bell suggests that we prioritize the categorization and explicit recognition of certain claims as specifically liberal in character. As he

---

[1]   Unless otherwise specified, all quotations refer to Mira Siegelberg, *The Via Media: Egon Schwelb's Mid-century Stoic Legalism and the Birth of Human Rights Law*, Chapter 7 in this volume.

[2]   Duncan Bell, *What Is Liberalism?*, 42 POL. THEORY 682, 689 (2014) (original emphasis).

[3]   *Id.* at 685.

himself puts it, "the liberal tradition is constituted by *the sum of the arguments that have been classified as liberal, and recognised as such by other self-proclaimed liberals, across time and space.*"[4]

I cannot help but wonder whether a broadly similar approach might not be the most helpful means of assessing Schwelb today. Undertaking a detailed critique of Schwelb's romantic faith in the possibility of building a better world through hard legal work would be as facile as it would be pointless. Schwelb's world is no longer our own. More to the point, the world that Schwelb believed himself to inhabit – one purportedly characterized by the slow, steady, and incremental move from war to peace, conflict to cooperation, independence to interdependence – was never actually the world in which he himself operated. Schwelb was an aspirational idealist – one in a long line of internationalists who have been fixated on one or another mythopoetic vision of juridical cosmopolitanism, in his case one that would be assembled and preserved through assiduous analysis and collection of texts. To debunk such a vision, with its insufficient attention to material conditions and its implicit reliance upon Whiggish progress narratives, would be to accord it a significance and sustainability it simply does not deserve. Far more useful – and far more interesting – is to approach Schwelb's understanding of law from within, excavating its core commitments and underlying assumptions in light of the broader forces and dynamics in response to which they emerged and developed. Ironically, it is also through such an immanent investigation that the political and economic underpinnings of Schwelb's (recognizably liberal) vision of legal life are likely to reveal themselves.

First, it must be emphasized (and I do not think it can be emphasized enough) that Schwelb understood himself to be an international lawyer, and that he was also widely understood as such. This, of course, is to state the obvious. Yet it is precisely this most evident of facts that anchors and integrates Schwelb's otherwise tempestuous and rather eclectic career. Unlike so many of his contemporaries, most famously Hans Morgenthau, Schwelb did not abandon or attenuate his commitment to international law after World War II. In particular, Schwelb resisted the temptation to jettison legal formalities and embrace the task of developing the new, United States-centric, and chiefly functionalist field of "international relations" – a field that grew to no small degree through the efforts of international lawyers, frequently of European extraction, who had turned against their original discipline out of frustration with what they saw as its inability to constrain aggression and coordinate interstate relations. If anything, the cumulative experience of the two "great

---

[4] *Id.* at 689–90 (original emphasis).

wars" seems only to have augmented Schwelb's commitment to law, albeit with certain qualifications. Aside from his early work on Czechoslovakian public law, he wrote prodigiously on a variety of issues, from the use of force to the Partial Test Ban Treaty, from the laws of occupation and diplomatic protection to international criminal law and, of course, international human rights law. Schwelb was a true believer, a lawyer's lawyer who saw his discipline and profession as the key to global peace and prosperity. This, of course, is indicative of a quintessentially liberal predisposition, a penchant for situating rights – and, by extension, rights-based political strategies and movements – at the center of social relations more generally.

Interestingly, though, Schwelb's devotion to international law was also a capacious and socially sensitive one. Trained in Continental legal positivism, Schwelb placed a premium on the traditional legalist insistence on attentive, borderline obsessive analysis of treaties and other instruments, as well as systematic documentation of varying patterns of state practice. He regularly made a point of touting the need for such legalism when teaching human rights and international law, and his writings are testimony to the depth of his faith in law's role in the construction and preservation of a world that is both just and orderly. Yet this legalism was not as pure – or even, for that matter, as strictly "legalistic" – as some may have expected, particularly given Schwelb's close association with Kelsenians like Josef Kunz. Siegelberg argues that Schwelb stressed the need for "stoic conviction," consistently pushing his readers, students, and collaborators to find ways of avoiding "emotional extremes" and maintaining the "proper affect" in order to remain open to a progressive vision of international order.[5] This conviction was central to Schwelb's self-understanding as an international lawyer. To practice moderation, approaching legal practice with an eye to its social and even sentimental power, was not simply to underscore the need for the kind of evenhandedness expected of a civil servant; it was also to reassert law's distance from the extralegal, particularly from political and economic power. Far from standing at a remove from Schwelb's commitment to international law, then, "emotional restraint" went hand in hand with legalist internationalism, grounding its insistence upon texts and state conduct in a personalized, affectively charged model of impartiality and egalitarianism. Schwelb was a formalist, but his formalism was not without its nuances.

This brings us to a second basic aspect of Schwelb's conception of international law and order, namely his defense of human rights. At root, Schwelb

---

[5] As Siegelberg notes, Schwelb anchored his commitment to emotional moderation in Stoicism.

believed that his controlled form of liberal legalism was essential to international law's future. Total war had proven to be just that: total. The brutality and comprehensiveness of the carnage unleashed in 1939 had done much to undermine traditional faith in the tenability of formal distinctions between civilian and combatant, neutrality and belligerence, the domestic and the international. Such distinctions increasingly struck many as little more than technicalities, fundamentally out of step with a world in which legal formalism – and the largely bourgeois and Eurocentric sensibilities that produced and sustained it – had been transformed into a bad joke. Of course, the onset of wave upon wave of legal realism, particularly of the purposive and social-scientifically reinforced variants of Karl Llewellyn, Jerome Frank, and Felix Cohen, had already done much to fuel such skepticism. But whereas legal realism was still a comparatively elite phenomenon, confined for the most part to a select group of U.S. law schools and an equally select cadre of legal practitioners, the war belonged to all, both product and reflection of a generalized system of imperial competition and capitalist exploitation. The League's inability to craft a meaningful response to the Great Depression, coupled with its lack of effectiveness in response to war and intervention in Spain, Abyssinia, Manchuria, and elsewhere, had undermined the international law it championed and represented.

Schwelb's preponderantly formalistic reaction against these suspicions – suspicions about the impartiality of decision-making bodies, the coherence of law's normative architecture, and, above all, the capacity of law to withstand "the social," "the political," and "the economic" – came to the fore most clearly in his unflagging support for human rights. As Siegelberg notes, "[a]voiding the turn to rule-skepticism and realism, or the collapse into despair, ... required the careful pruning of hopeful expectation and careful control over the emotions," and it was just such "careful pruning" that inspired Schwelb's "insistence that the principles of the Universal Declaration would become legally relevant" over the long run, notwithstanding that instrument's abstract and formally nonbinding character. Similarly, when writing of Schwelb's contributions to legal pedagogy, particularly his innovative course on international human rights law at Yale in 1963, Siegelberg suggests that "[o]ne of his goals in teaching the class was to prove the modest proposition that there could be international practice apart from the protection of global capitalism and thus to nurture idealism as such." Serving as a bulwark against flippant deformalization, such idealism would encourage the gradual expansion, consolidation, and institutionalization of international human rights. The human rights project was thus tightly conjoined to the emotionally restrained formalism for which Schwelb agitated so relentlessly. And what, Schwelb must have wondered, could be any more logical than this? Natural and human rights, integral to the liberal tradition, had long been reproached for their vagueness and loose generality. A sufficiently finessed legal formalism seemed like the perfect response, promising a degree of precision and specificity that would otherwise be unavailable.

Of course, none of this was unique to Schwelb, even when refracted through the prism of the flexible and broad-minded formalism for which he hoped to win converts. International law has always been nourished by liberal legal and political thought, and the insistence upon human rights, particularly of the "civic-political" variety, was a standard feature of post-war liberalism. Besides, Schwelb was hardly the only international lawyer with extensive interwar experience to place human rights at the center of his work after 1945. Consider once more the figures who find their way into Siegelberg's narrative: Henkin, Humphrey, Lauterpacht, Sohn. Three of the four subscribed to the Jewish faith and hailed from the borderlands of Galicia and present-day Belarus; all four identified with the interests of upwardly mobile bourgeoisies and eventually made significant investments in the claim that international human rights constituted a viable counterweight to (though not necessarily a strict antagonist of) state sovereignty.[6] And one could, of course, offer any number of other examples. Consider, as a somewhat heterodox case, Nicolas Politis, another oft-forgotten Continental jurist and servant of the League project. A leading scholar and diplomat, comfortable spilling ink in defense of legal solidarism and Greek foreign policy alike, Politis was among the most active and influential in an ambitious generation of interwar legal idealists, shuttling between Athens, Geneva, and The Hague for years. Rather than casting this idealism into the dustbin of history, or letting it go by the wayside during the 1930s, Politis cultivated his "social" variant of liberal legalism – gleaned largely from the legal thought of the French Third Republic – until his death in 1942, including in his posthumously published *La morale internationale*.[7] In some respects, his public profile tracks that of Schwelb even more closely than the other figures (and this despite the fact that Politis didn't live long enough to insert himself directly into the post-war reconstruction of international law). Tellingly, the ethno-religious differences

---

[6] For a narrative account of this common origin and shared investment in international human rights law, *see* PHILIPPE SANDS, EAST WEST STREET: ON THE ORIGINS OF "GENOCIDE" AND "CRIMES AGAINST HUMANITY" (2016).

[7] NICOLAS POLITIS, LA MORALE INTERNATIONALE (1944).

between Schwelb and a figure like Politis pale in comparison to their common class affiliation: in sharing Schwelb's polite activism, Politis (like Henkin, Humphrey, Lauterpacht, and Sohn) also shared his membership in a transnational network of well-heeled and predominantly social democratic lawyers and legally trained activists with close ties to political elites in the states from which they hailed or in which they ultimately settled. It is this class affiliation – typically elided, frequently misunderstood – that lies at the root of the kind of cosmopolitan humanism that Schwelb championed and that so many others, including Politis, similarly espoused.

A POLITICAL ECONOMY OF "PROPER AFFECT"

Samuel Moyn may very well be justified in situating the operational "breakthrough" of human rights in the 1970s. But as he too has admitted, much of the ideological terrain for the programmatic shift to this "last utopia" was prepared during the tumultuous years that followed World War II – and this in spite of the centrality of state sovereignty, not to mention the enormous resonance of political and economic self-determination, in a world marked by rapid decolonization and growing Cold War rivalry.[8] Schwelb's humanism is significant here, shedding light on the "cautious idealism," the "traumatized cosmopolitan legal imagination of the postwar era," that would eventually make it possible for human rights rhetoric to be absorbed, mobilized, and weaponized by both state authorities and nongovernmental organizations. To be sure, such humanism manifested itself in a variety of forms after 1945, some of which were not as obviously humanist as others. For instance, as Mark Mazower has shown, Raphael Lemkin's drive to secure legal recognition for the concept of genocide ran counter to Joseph Schechtman's suggestion that recourse be had to mass population transfer as a means of forging politically stable and economically viable states.[9] Nevertheless, the basic tenets and assumptions of the post-war human rights project are intelligible only against the background of the rarified and multilingual diplo-legal world of the United Nations. It is only within a world of this sort that the slow workings of international human rights law can be viewed as the linchpin of human progress.

---

[8] *See generally* SAMUEL MOYN, THE LAST UTOPIA: HUMAN RIGHTS IN HISTORY (2010).
[9] *See* MARK MAZOWER, NO ENCHANTED PALACE: THE END OF EMPIRE AND THE IDEOLOGICAL ORIGINS OF THE UNITED NATIONS ch. 3 (2009).

This point holds the key to Schwelb and his generation. Ultimately, if Schwelb's devotion to "emotional restraint" truly "reveals the origins of a style of thought now *de rigueur* for human rights lawyers," this is so mainly with respect to his belief that patient, meticulous, and often unabashedly pedantic work would ultimately reduce the messiness of international politics to the nominal order of international law – a belief that is exceedingly difficult to entertain by anyone who is not immersed in (and also benefiting from) a coordinated and largely self-reproducing network of elite lawyers and bureaucrats. Like so many of his contemporaries, Schwelb was not only a "person with a project,"[10] but a member of a transnational class of legal actors with a vested interest in a particular brand of cosmopolitan justice, with the always nebulous idea of *jus cogens* perched at the top, the concept of permanent sovereignty over natural resources relegated to the margins, and proposals for the global redistribution of wealth and power (like the New International Economic Order) dismissed as unrealistic and potentially dangerous. Siegelberg's splendid chapter provides us with much to ponder. Perhaps what is now needed, though, is a *political economy* of the kind of "proper affect" that she associates with the progressive vision of international order behind which Schwelb and others threw their weight after 1945. Among other things, such an account would help to explain why the kind of bourgeois internationalism to which Schwelb dedicated his life has failed as spectacularly as it so clearly has to yield the more stable, egalitarian, and democratic world that it promised us. Nuanced though it was, Schwelb's was a thoroughly bourgeois international law – an international law in which the formalistic prioritization of the individual rights-bearer (and, by extension, the state as a rights-bearer) went hand in hand with economic inequality and ever-growing environmental degradation. Its failure is the failure of post-war human rights.

---

[10]   The expression belongs to David Kennedy. *See, e.g.,* David Kennedy, *Tom Franck and the Manhattan School*, 35 N.Y.U. J. INT'L L. AND POL. 397 (2003); David Kennedy, *The Last Treatise: Project and Person (Reflections on Martti Koskenniemi's* From Apology to Utopia), 7 GERMAN L. J. 982 (2006); DAVID KENNEDY, A WORLD OF STRUGGLE: HOW POWER, LAW, AND EXPERTISE SHAPE GLOBAL POLITICAL ECONOMY (2016).

PART 5

RENÉ CASSIN

9

A Most Inglorious Right

René Cassin, Freedom of Movement, Jews, and Palestinians

Moria Paz

INTRODUCTION

This chapter is concerned with a particular type of myopia in human rights law – namely, a myopia about the role that mobility plays in the lives of refugees. Rights that regulate mobility offer protections that are incomplete. And those incomplete protections are also incongruous: the interests protected under the law often do not correspond to the motivations of the refugees who seek to avail themselves of the law.

Curiously, this myopia has a history. It can be traced directly back to the French Jewish jurist René Cassin, the "Father of the Declaration of Human Rights."[1] In the genealogy of human rights, the 1968 Noble Peace Prize laureate plays an important role; he was one of the drafters of both the Universal Declaration of Human Rights ("UDHR") and the European Convention of Human Rights ("ECHR").[2] In addition, Cassin also contributed to the creation of the United Nations Educational, Scientific and Cultural Organization ("UNESCO"), was a member (1959–65) and president (1965–68) of the European Court of Human Rights ("ECtHR"), and the Vice Chairman and Chairman of the Commission on Human Rights of the United Nations.

---

[1] Sam Grant, *Remembering René Cassin, Father of the Universal Declaration of Human Rights*, available at: https://rightsinfo.org/remembering-rene-cassin-father-universal-declaration-human-rights/.

[2] Note, however, that Cassin's importance in the drafting efforts of the UDHR is contested. For a view of Cassin as the father of the Universal Declaration of Human Rights ("UDHR"), *see, e.g.*, MARC AGI, RENÉ CASSIN: FANTASSIN DES DROITS DE L'HOMME (1979). For a minimal view of Cassin's role, see SAMUEL MOYN, THE LAST UTOPIA: HUMAN RIGHTS IN HISTORY (2010). Jay Winter possibly summarizes it best: "It would be wrong ... to say that ... [Cassin] was the author of the document. He created one of its personae, that which arose from the French republican tradition." *See* JAY WINTER, DREAMS OF PEACE AND FREEDOM. UTOPIAN MOMENTS IN THE TWENTIETH CENTURY 119 (2006).

Here, I recount two separate stories. The first offers a functional interpretation of the right to freedom of movement. I selected this right because it is the human right that most explicitly involves cross-border mobility.[3] And, moreover, it was also the right that for Cassin – as he wrote in a 1973 editorial in the *New York Times* – was the "indestructible core of all human rights."[4] I discuss two shortcomings of this right: one having to do with the limitation of the return right of nonnationals and one having to do with the unavailability of an entry right for refugees.

My second story draws on René Cassin and the evolution of his thinking regarding human rights and the regulation of cross-border mobility. In particular, I focus on the way he applied the right to mobility to Jewish and Palestinian refugees after 1948. It is this case involving the two main post-WWII refugee populations, I maintain, that foreshadows the present myopia regarding the role that mobility plays in the lives of refugees and also makes concrete the point at which it is exposed. And so, rereading Cassin's Jewish legal biography today forces us to recognize how susceptible to historical contingency legal thought truly is, and how yesterday's legal myopia drives today's ethical dilemmas.

THE FREEDOM OF MOVEMENT RIGHT V

Let us turn to the first story. The right to freedom of movement involves two functions: exit and entry. For this right to have practical meaning, both functions must be protected. In other words, to cross a border, an individual must be able to leave a state and settle in another.

Under human rights law, the exit function is always in effect. It is universal and unlimited; anyone can leave any country. This is confirmed by both the UDHR[5] and the ICCPR.[6]

---

[3] The other two human rights that assume mobility are the right to seek asylum and the right to nationality.

[4] *See* René Cassin, *For a Right to Leave and a Right to Return*, N.Y. TIMES, March 23, 1973. Indeed, Cassin co-organized an international colloquium that produced the first "expression of expert opinion" on the status of this right. THE RIGHT TO LEAVE AND TO RETURN: PAPERS AND RECOMMENDATIONS OF THE INTERNATIONAL COLLOQUIUM HELD IN UPPSALA, SWEDEN, 19–20 JUNE 1972 (Karel Vasak & Sidney Liskofsky, eds., 1976).

[5] Art 13(2) UN General Assembly, *Universal Declaration of Human Rights*, 10 December 1948, 217 A (III), available at: www.refworld.org/docid/3ae6b3712c.html. ("Everyone has the right to leave any country, including his own.")

[6] Art. 12(2) UN High Commissioner for Refugees (UNHCR), *ICCPR International Covenant on Civil And Political Rights: Quick Reference Guide – Statelessness and Human Rights Treaties*, October 2016, available at: www.refworld.org/docid/58c25e3a4.html. ("Everyone shall be free to leave any country, including his own.")

As for the entry function, it is limited to three main situations.[7]

(i) **Entry under the right of return.** Human rights law provides any individual with a right of return, or entry, to "his own country."[8] The United Nations Human Rights Committee ("UNHRC") defines the scope of "own country" as protecting nationals in a *formal* sense, i.e., citizens. This relationship between an individual and her country does not depend on physical-territorial presence; formal nationals bear the right of return even if they were never present in the state prior to the return.[9] Protection here is robust, regulating *both* aspects of return: the actual entry (a mobility right), as well as the person's status after entry (a continuity right).

The UNHRC also extends protection to nationals in an informal sense, i.e., individuals who are not nationals but "who, because of . . . [their] special ties to or claims in relation to a given country, cannot be considered to be a mere alien."[10] In contrast to nationals, however, protection in this case is a function of an ongoing personal-territorial continuity in the country. The determination of this continuity invites, the UNHRC explains, consideration of such matters as "long standing residence, close personal and family ties and intentions to remain, as well as to the absence of such ties elsewhere."[11] Now protection is thin and attends only to the right permitting an informal national to remain or not to be expelled (a continuity right). This protection is the opposite of mobility, leaving the exit and entry functions irrelevant for the operation of the right. So while formal nationals bear a return right (a mobility right), informal nationals bear what I call the right of a domicile – the right to remain in the place where they live.

---

[7] There may be a fourth variation: a right for entry under family unification. I do not include this variation in my discussion because under human rights law this entry is mainly limited to family members of migrants lawfully present, while under humanitarian law it is only aspirational in nature.

[8] UDHR, *supra* note 5, at art. 13(2); ICCPR, *supra* note 6, at art. 12(4); 1965 International Convention on the Elimination of All Forms of Racial Discrimination, art. 5(d)(ii), 660 U.N. T.S. 195 (1969).

[9] Hurst Hannum, the Right to Leave and the Right to Return in International Law and Practice 56 (1987).

[10] Para 20 UN Human Rights Committee (HRC), *CCPR General Comment No. 27: Article 12 (Freedom of Movement)*, 2 November 1999, CCPR/C/21/Rev.1/Add.9, available at: www.refworld.org/docid/45139c394.html.

[11] UN Human Rights Committee, *James Warsame v. Canada*, Communication No. 1959/2010, UN Doc. CCPR/C/102/D/1959/2010 para. 8.4 (2011); UN Human Rights Committee, *Nystrom v. Australia*, Communication No. 1557/2007, UN Doc. CCPR/C/102/D/1557/2007 7.5 (2011). But *see* the strong joint dissent of Gerald L. Neuman and Yuji Iwasawa's in *Nystrom, Dissent*, at 3.1–3.3.

This type of entry is narrowly constrained. The return function is limited only to formal nationals, and the domicile right is constrained by location: because of the requirement of physical continuity on the land, an informal national can only bring a claim from within the state to remain in the state.

(ii) **Entry under refugee status.** Some instruments guarantee vulnerable individuals a right of entry into host states as refugees.[12] However, the vast majority of international treaties – including, most importantly, the Refugee Convention and the Convention Against Torture – only create a right for a refugee to remain in the host state ("non-refoulement"). But they do not include a right to enter the state in order to seek asylum in the first place.

As a result, the opportunity to enter as a refugee is constrained territorially: an individual can only be considered for entry *after* she has established a territorial presence, either inside the state, or under the effective control of the state or its agents, even if beyond national borders.[13] At the same time, this form of entry is also imprecise: the legal meaning of territorial presence changes over time.[14]

(iii) **Entry under a deliberate decision of the host country.** Public inter-national law permits the state to offer entry to selected individuals and/ or subgroups that the state wishes to take in.[15] Much like entry under the right of return, this entry imposes a duty only on a *particular* state. But, unlike the right of return, entry here depends on that state's

---

[12] E.g., UDHR, *supra* note 5, at art. 14.; G.A. Res. 217 (III); Regional Refugee Instruments & Related, *Convention on Asylum*, 20 February 1928, available at: www.refworld.org/docid/3a e6b37923.html.

[13] See, e.g., Art. 33(1) UN General Assembly, Convention Relating to the Status of Refugees, 28 July 1951, United Nations, Treaty Series, vol. 189, p. 137, available at: www.refworld.org/docid/ 3be01b964.html [accessed 15 April 2019]; Art. 3 UN General Assembly, Convention Against Torture and Other Cruel, Inhuman or Degrading Treatment or Punishment, 10 December 1984, United Nations, Treaty Series, vol. 1465, p. 85, available at: www.refworld.org/docid/3a e6b3a94.html [accessed 15 April 2019]. Regional bodies, moreover, stretched entry to also include prohibition for collective expulsion of asylum seekers on the high seas. *See, e.g.,* the European Court of Human Rights in *Hirsi Jamaa and Others v. Italy*, Application no. 27765/ 09, Council of Europe: European Court of Human Rights, at 84, 23 February 2012, available at: www.refworld.org/cases,ECHR,4f4507942.html.

[14] For the expansion in their meaning in only the past ten years, *see* Moria Paz, *Between the Kingdom and the Desert Sun: Human Rights, Immigration, and Border Walls*, 34 BERK. J. INT'L L. 1 (2016).

[15] *Advisory Opinion No. 4, Nationality Decrees Issued in Tunis and Morocco*, 4, Permanent Court of International Justice, at 36, February 1923, available at: www.refworld.org/cases,PCIJ,44e5c9fc4 .html; *Nottebohm Case (Liechtenstein v. Guatemala); Second Phase*, International Court of Justice (ICJ), 6 April 1955, available at: www.refworld.org/cases,ICJ,3ae6b7248.html.

consent. This state-based definition of nationality is supported by human rights law,[16] and is considered valid so long as it is not challenged by another state.[17] This type of entry, once again, is restricted; it is circumscribed by the will of the state. An individual has no ability to enter without the state's consent.

The result is that while a right of return obliges states not to expel nationals, either formal or informal, it does not require them to allow the reentry of informal nationals if they were not originally expelled. This offers meaningful protection for refugees who are formal nationals and who ask to return to their "own country," regardless of the reasons why they are not there. It also covers first-generation informal nationals who were expelled from the state after they had established their physical continuity.

But second-generation refugees who seek to return to their "own country," from which their parents were expelled, but of which they are not formal nationals, find themselves without protection. Human rights law guarantees them what I call a domicile right, a right to remain where they are, but makes this right a function of territorial presence. Without the ability to show physical continuity, they are unable to return to the place of original dispossession.

At the same time, this return right can amount to a death sentence for other refugees who do not seek to remain (a continuity right), but rather to flee their "own country" (a mobility right). The right to free mobility mandates that states permit them to exit, but it does not require states to allow them to enter, unless they are nationals.

For some, the universal right to exit, by itself, is indeed meaningful. If they could leave, they could live. By leaving, they would have the possibility, at the very least, to file an entry claim somewhere, and perhaps some state would let them in. But a large percentage of refugees who exercise their freedom of movement right find themselves in limbo. Human rights law guarantees them universal exit, but

---

[16] *See, e.g.*, UN Human Rights Committee (HRC), *CCPR General Comment No. 15: The Position of Aliens Under the Covenant*, 11 April 1986, available at: www.refworld.org/docid/45 139acfc.html.

[17] *Nationality Decrees in Tunisia and Morocco, supra* note 15; *Nottebohm, supra* note 15, paras 20–12. Population exchange may be a second possible form of a non-obligatory entry under a deliberate decision of a host state. A state may undertake population exchange in order to offer entry to a particular subsection of the population, whose ethnicity and/or religion aligns with that of the state.

without a state that consents to take them in, they are on a journey that ends nowhere.

This configuration of the right to mobility operates within an international legal system that places the state as the center of corrective legal processes. Victims of human rights abuses bear private rights as individuals with respect to a state. States, in turn, owe protection to individuals *within* their territory after they have established territorial presence in the state.[18] Under certain circumstances, they may also accrue extraterritorial responsibilities; states could also owe duties toward individuals that come under their effective control.[19]

This framework eschews mobility as a formative part of the regime. It leaves without protection those second-generation refugees who are not formal nationals of the state of expulsion as well as those refugees who have fled their state and are unable to reach a host state or its agents. They are permanently stuck in transitional locations such as refugee camps or territorial borderlands.

THE RIGHT OF DOMICILE

Did the architects of this system realize what they were building? If not, why? A look at the work of Cassin provides answers. Thus, we arrive at our second narrative. In 1930, René Cassin conceived of human rights in terms of a universal system that incorporates cross-border spatial movement as a corrective mechanism: individuals and/or groups could remedy their situation by leaving a bad or an incompetent state and entering another state. In that newly adopted host state, their status was regulated under what Cassin called the *"right of a domicile."* This right drew on a domicile – or the establishment of cultural, social, economic roots in a host state – as a possible replacement for citizenship.

In thinking about the notion of domicile, Cassin began with a problem. The legal system constructs the "relations of the state with its subjects and with other states, on the sole basis of … sovereignty and of nationality."[20] But sovereignty is "limited,"[21] and so a legal system that confers on sovereignty "a monopoly of competence" is "too exclusive, simplistic and weak to satisfy the

---

[18]   Hirsi Jamaa, *supra* note 13, para. 71.
[19]   *Id.* at 74.
[20]   René Cassin, *La nouvelle conception du domicile dans le règlement des conflits de lois*, 34 RECUEIL DES COURS À L'ACADEMIE DE DROIT INTERNATIONAL À LA HAYE 768 (1930–IV).
[21]   Cassin repeats this idea often. *See, e.g., Id.* at 767 and 769.

complex needs of international life."[22] Nationality, in turn, is also insufficient; it is "not a primary or a unique bond among the members of a nation: there are other more elementary ones ... the district, the region, the province, and so on."[23] This leaves individuals "masked by the state,"[24] or, in other words, "subservient to an abstraction," that of the nation-state, which in turn is "a veritable idol to powers without check other than the illusory 'self-limitation.'"[25] The result is "the denial of human right."[26]

To make the individual a legal person cognizable under the law, Cassin articulated a novel international right: *the right of domicile*. This right would govern the status and capacities of a resident alien by reference to the state of his domicile rather than the state of his nationality.[27] Cassin wrote:

> Precisely because the right of a domicile rests on universal and permanent fact, the concreteness of a place where one lives, a place where families reside, it has been taken into consideration everywhere to determine the point of juridical attachment of persons and to order more or less completely the status of the individual.[28]

Over time, Cassin added, nationality – a "political"[29] tie between a citizen and her state – would "exhaust its beneficial effects."[30] It was "destined to be weakened to the benefit of the law of domicile."[31]

The League of Nations and its efforts at collective security and disarmament played a key role in this inevitable transition from the principle of nationality to the right of domicile. During Cassin's tenure at the League, he served on the Disarmament Conference and for close to a decade worked toward "the immediate reinforcement of collective security." This, Cassin insisted, was "the only way forward" in order to "avoid a return to absolute sovereignty."[32]

In articulating the right, Cassin expressed two *separate* ideas of what domicile means, each of which corresponds to a different positive good. He remained oblivious as to the difference between these two goods. Cassin's

---

[22]   *Id.* at 771.
[23]   *Id.* at 740.
[24]   *Id.* at 769.
[25]   *Id.* at 768.
[26]   *Id.*
[27]   *Id.* at 655, 760.
[28]   *Id.* at 740.
[29]   *Id.* at 678.
[30]   *Id.* at 801. For Cassin, the principle of nationalities played an important role during the cycle of national emancipations but over time it became "degenerated." (*Id.* at 768.)
[31]   *Id.* at 767.
[32]   Georges Scelle and René Cassin, Mémoire sur l'opinion française et le problème de la sécurité collective, in LA SÉCURITÉ COLLECTIVE, April 1935, 73.

first meaning aligned domicile with its dictionary definition as a permanent dwelling place and treated an individual as a right-bearer in the place where he continuously lives. The right of domicile, Cassin explained, meant that where the individual was located, as a matter of "fact"[33] – i.e., where he had established his "place of dwelling, the center of interests"[34] – would take precedence over his formal nationality in the regulation of international legal status. States, he wrote, are prohibited from "widely ... expel(ing) foreigners who are already established on national grounds."[35] Under this interpretation, a person obtains the legal status of "domicile" where he already is.

Here, Cassin's right to a domicile resembles the thin protection of the informal national under the right of return: it attaches protection to physical existence on a particular land and is about *continuity*, or the right not to move, not mobility. The exit and entry functions are irrelevant for the exercise of the right.

The second meaning that Cassin gave to domicile, however, is the opposite of its conventional definition. This version of domicile regulated an individual's entry into a new host state and his personal status after entering. An individual, Cassin wrote, would have the right to "create ... a new domicile without changing nationality, whether ... [his] expatriation has been made with or without an intention of returning."[36] In the new place of domicile, moreover, he would enjoy "all or part of the private rights normally reserved for nationals."[37] This more robust right tracks the protection of formal nationals under the right of return: it supports cross-border mobility instead of continuity. Here, a person bears a right to create a new domicile by moving, and the exit and entry functions are directly relevant to the operation of protection.

For Cassin, the exit function was universal – a tenet later incorporated by the human right for the freedom of movement. Cassin envisioned multiple forms of protected exit: individuals and collectivities would be free to cross a border when they sought to "group themselves together, across frontiers, in order to realize religious, moral, economic, etc. ends ... "[38] (exit by preference); World War I veterans would be free to cross borders, even into countries that had been on the opposite side of the war, to obtain better welfare and

---

[33] Cassin, *supra* note 20, at 664.
[34] *Id.* at 685.
[35] *Id.*
[36] *Id.* at 682.
[37] *Id.* at 685.
[38] *Id.* at 768.

care[39] (exit as redistribution); and vulnerable minorities and refugees would be permitted to cross borders to protect themselves from nationalist movements and other political upheavals. Here, Cassin specifically referred to the plight of the "Armenian refugees and the Russian émigrés" whose personal status was thrown into doubt by war and revolution[40] (exit as protection).

The entry function in Cassin's second meaning of a domicile, however, diverged from that incorporated by human rights law. Instead of entry limited by nationality, he advocated for universal protection. But in construing such a broad entry, Cassin confused different degrees of protection. Sometimes, he argued that the entry right was constrained by the extent to which a foreigner established roots in the territory. A foreigner has domicile, Cassin explained, when he does not enter briefly as a "visitor,"[41] but rather "enters and sojourns in the territory of the state," and therein he "fixes" himself "in a durable manner,"[42] including, for example, establishing "familiar patrimonial, social relations."[43] Under this view, the right of a domicile protects only those foreigners who enter the state and establish therein long-term affiliations. This rule regulates both entry and personal status and makes *"rootedness"* in the land a replacement for formal citizenship under the law.

At other times, however, Cassin's approach to entry was absolute. "The acting principle," he declared, is that "the choice of domicile is free."[44] Mobility was to be based on the individual, and it permitted him to choose his geographical location according to his needs and preferences: "An isolated individual and even a family have the freedom to . . . go and settle in a country where the customs would be better for them."[45] Under this view, there is something like a universal right to mobility (anyone has a right to enter any country and establish residence there).

This second articulation of the right of domicile is bounded up with a utopian vision of a borderless world. At the moment, Cassin explained "states consider themselves virtual masters of permitting or banning entry and

[39] Jay Winter and Antoine Prost, René Cassin and Human Rights: From the Great War to the Universal Declaration 3–80 (2013). For more on Cassin's work on behalf of veterans, see Antoine Prost, *René Cassin and the Victory of French Citizen-Soldiers, in* The Great War and Veterans' Internationalism 19–32 (Julia Eichenberg & John Paul Newman, eds., 2011), and Bruno Cabranes, The Great War and the Origins of Humanitarism 1918–1924, 18–76, esp. 52–53 and 74 (2014).
[40] Cassin, *supra* note 20, at 749.
[41] *Id.*
[42] *Id.*
[43] *Id.* at 691.
[44] *Id* at 672.
[45] *Id.* at 739.

residence for foreigners on their territory."[46] They prohibit entry by placing "restrictions on the access of immigrants."[47] But the application of the right of domicile "constitutes ... the best way of avoiding ... [the] draconian processes ... [of] frontier closings or other artificial obstacles to immigration, harmful for all countries."[48]

And so, while Cassin's first articulation of a right of a domicile was about continuity, his second definition correlated to an international order that incorporates (to different degrees) *exit*, or voluntary spatial movement, as an ordinary mechanism of protection. Individuals and groups who were dissatisfied with the quality or benefits of their state of nationality could exit, withdraw from any relationship with their state, and migrate to a different state where they could better defend their welfare or improve their position.[49]

The internal coherence of Cassin's 1930 articulation of human rights was conditional on loosening the power of nationalism, including state control over membership and borders, and on a limitless capacity for states to absorb new entrants. Cassin took both these structural requirements for granted: nationalism was "destined to be weakened," he wrote. States would, he assumed, be able to absorb "approximately a million and a half Armenian refugees and Russian émigrés."[50] Cassin was oblivious to the question of numbers and never referred to mass migration and/or small receiving states. In less than a decade, however, he would drop his law of domicile in the face of the realities of nationalism and scarce resources. Cassin no longer mentioned his right to domicile as a possible substitute for citizenship. Perhaps the war taught him that a borderless utopia is, literally, "nowhere."

THE SECOND WAR WORLD: A BREAK

Then came the winter of despair. In 1933, Hitler rose to power. After 1936 and the Germans' occupation of the Rhineland, Cassin wrote, "the floodgates are open" and "the tide of violence and ... war raises more and more powerfully."[51]

---

[46] *Id.* at 673.

[47] *Id.*

[48] *Id.* at 747.

[49] For more on exit, *see* Charles Tiebout, *A Pure Theory of Local Expenditures*, 64 J. POL. ECON. 416 (1956) and ALBERT O. HIRSCHMAN, EXIT, VOICE, AND LOYALTY (1970).

[50] Cassin, *supra* note 20, at 748.

[51] René Cassin, *Salutaires avertissements*, CAHIERS DE L'UNION FÉDÉRALE, Dec. 10, 1938, cited *in* WINTER AND PROST, *supra* note 39, at 97.

Nationalism was not "weakening," but getting ever stronger. And it was the worst type of nationalism at that: nationalism guided by "the German romanticism of the eighteenth century," reflecting "irrational and mystical aspirations" about languages rather than "the rationalization of Immanuel Kant, the humanism of Goethe, [or] the generous liberalism of Schiller."[52] Similarly, the "old dogma" of sovereignty did not "disappear." Instead it grew more monstrous. Cassin now spoke of the "Leviathan state,"[53] of which Hitler's totalitarianism offered merely the "most developed, but not only, representative"[54] case. This state, Cassin reflected, pursues "an ideology of violence and terrorist methods applied on a huge scale."[55] It was a state that stood "against man and the human community."[56]

The rise of the Leviathan state brought about a profound rupture in Cassin's thinking. "Thus," he declared, "[I] arrived at a dramatic turning point."[57] After fourteen years of serving as a delegate to the League of Nations, and spending a month every summer in Geneva,[58] Cassin gave up on the League and discarded the policy of collective security and disarmament that he had developed for over a decade. In 1934, he argued that the League had become "a great machine without a motor,"[59] and in 1938 he said it had received its "coup de grace."[60] After the surrender at Munich, Cassin never returned to Geneva.

"[It] is time to decide," Cassin announced two years later, between either an earth "shared between a few Leviathan-states ... each living respectively in political and economic autarchy" and keeping its "dominant race" under "iron discipline" and its "subservient races" under "the inhuman treatments already inflicted by the Germans unto the Jews, the Czech, and the Polish," or

---

[52] René Cassin, *L'État Léviathan contre l'homme et la communauté humaine*, Nouveaux Cahiers, April 1940, rpt. *in* René Cassin, La pensée et l'action 63–79 (1972). Cassin used the term in reference to Thomas Hobbes, Leviathan (1651).

[53] *Id.*

[54] *Id.* at 63.

[55] *Id.*

[56] *Id.*

[57] Cassin, *supra* note 51, at 98. For a discussion of the rupture in Cassin's thinking in this time frame, *see* Winter and Prost, *supra* note 39, at 84–94; Prost, *supra* note 39, at 29–31 ("1935 marked a significant change in Cassin's attitude").

[58] Ethan Katz, Crémieux's Children: Joseph Reinach, Léon Blum, and René Cassin as Jews of French Empire (unpublished manuscript; copy on file with author).

[59] René Cassin, *L'effondrement d'une politique*, Cahiers de l'UF, Oct. 1938, cited *in* Winter and Prost, *supra* note 39, at 93.

[60] René Cassin, *Dure alerte, terrible leçon*, Notre France, Oct. 1938, 4, cited *in id.* at 93.

war, until "France and England will manage to win in the name of the oppressed nations for which they entered into this war."[61]

After France lost, Cassin was among the first who joined Charles de Gaulle and the "Free France" movement in London. From London, he played a critical role in De Gaulle's resistance government until the end of the war.[62]

From that point on, Cassin ceased to allude to the right of domicile. With it, he abandoned his vision of an international order with the right to exit as a fundamental element. But, as he had in 1930, Cassin continued to call for the accession of the individual to "the rank of subject of international law."[63] Making the individual a legal person would now take a different route, however. Protection would derive from processes *within* the state, and no longer from a right to cross-border spatial mobility.

By 1940, Cassin had placed the sovereign state, which he had referred to in 1930 as an "old dogma," at the center of the legal system: "any program for the international implementation of human rights must, at the present state of the law of nations, be in a form acceptable to states."[64] Indeed, he wrote, the "new international order" was to be "based on the principle of national sovereignty."[65] And the principle of nationality that in the 1930s Cassin had thought would soon have "exhausted its beneficial effects" and would "disappear," now became a condition for bearing rights. Cassin declared that "everyone has the right to be integrated into a determined state" and no one can "be deprived of nationality without being accorded another one."[66]

Starting from the nation-state, Cassin's goal was the "curtailment of the absolute sovereignty of states."[67] Human rights law, he explained, constrains the jurisdiction of the state.[68] But he did not go as far as the universal application of human rights obligations. Cassin drew instead on the concept of territory to limit the jurisdiction and responsibility of states. States, he explained, must only "insure respect for fundamental rights and liberties in

---

[61] Cassin, *supra* note 52, at 69.

[62] For discussion of Cassin's role in Free France, *see* Agi, *supra* note 2.

[63] René Cassin, *The Charter of Human Rights Nobel Lecture* (Dec. 11, 1968), www.nobelprize.org/nobel_prizes/peace/laureates/1968/cassin-lecture.html.

[64] René Cassin, *From the Ten Commandments to the Rights of Man*, http://renecassin.over-blog.com/article-from-the-ten-commandments-to-the-rights-of-man-72080499.html ("the pre-eminent form of social organization").

[65] Cassin, *supra* note 52, at 70.

[66] Cassin's draft *Declaration on the Rights of Man and Citizen* from February 1943, cited *in* Marco Duranti, *The Holocaust, The Legacy of 1789 and the Birth of International Human Rights Law, Revisiting the Foundation Myth*, 14 J. OF GENOCIDE RES. 169 (2012).

[67] Cassin, *supra* note 52, at 71.

[68] Cassin, *supra* note 63 ("jurisdiction of the states ... will no longer be exclusive").

the territories under [their] jurisdiction."[69] They ought to "set up, within the sphere of their jurisdiction, systems of appeal to judicial administrative bodies, in order to prevent and, if necessary correct or suppress such violations of human rights as may have been committed within their territory."[70] Under Cassin's 1930 enunciation of human rights, when he held to a utopian vision of a world without states, borders were "draconian." By 1948, however, after Cassin no longer imagined that states were going to disappear, borders became essential: they capped states' duties to engage in humanitarian intervention wherever rights were violated around the world.

This strategy conflates protection with territorial presence and corresponds to an international legal system that locates the state as the site of correction and forgoes geographical mobility as a formative part of the regime. Individuals and groups who are dissatisfied with the quality or benefits of their state of nationality can repair the state from *within* the state. They can do so through state-centered strategies, turning to political mobilization or to human rights, with international enforcement bodies supervising the effective execution of these rights within the state.

Here is a structural tension, however. Cassin's expression in 1948 of human rights was universal and unqualified; the law, he said, guarantees "fundamental liberties" and "rights" that are "common to all human beings, without possible discrimination."[71] But he also focused on national sovereignty. Cassin worked *through* the state to provide protection. Recall a state must only "insure respect for rights in the territories under [their] jurisdiction." But in a world of nation-states and sovereign control over borders, where protection is equated with the state structure, human rights are not universal. Children of refugees who were expelled from their place of ongoing domicile and refugees who have fled their state but have not yet reached another state (or come under its effective control) bear an exit right. Alas this right is nonoperational: no state owes them an entry duty.[72]

In 1948, Cassin was acutely aware of this lacuna. He warned that "it is impossible to recognize a right . . . if no one was bound to respect it."[73] Cassin

---

[69] Cassin, *supra* note 63.
[70] Cited *in* WINTER AND PROST, *supra* note 39, at 249.
[71] Cassin, *supra* note 63.
[72] Famously on this, *see* HANNAH ARENDT, THE ORIGINS OF TOTALITARIANISM (1951). For a different perspective, *see* Louis Henkin, *Introduction, in* LOUIS HENKIN, THE INTERNATIONAL BILL OF RIGHTS 18 (1981) (any state that is party to the ICCPR has legal standing to bring a claim against any other state for violations of core rights such as the right not to be tortured regardless of whether or not it has other connections to the case).
[73] Second Session's Working Group Discussion, *Drafting of the UDHR* (1948), cited *in* JOHANNES MORSINK, THE UNIVERSAL DECLARATION OF HUMAN RIGHTS: ORIGINS, DRAFTING, AND INTENT 77 (2000).

accepted this tension, but only as a pragmatic first step, or, in his words, a "way to move ahead."[74] "[G]radually," he insisted, "member states ... [would bring] their legislation into conformity with the principles formulated in it."[75] States, in other words, would in time supplement the negative exit with a positive duty.

FROM INTERNATIONAL VETERAN TO JEWISHNESS

Cassin's transition between the two systems of human rights is reflected in the move he made from thinking about WWI veterans to Jews. Cassin was a veteran and had been seriously wounded during the Great War. After the war, he became concerned with the rights and welfare of veterans. For Cassin, veterans were owed "rights not charity."[76] But the states that had sent soldiers to the "butchery"[77] of 1914–18, he explained, could not be trusted to vindicate those rights upon the veterans' return. Instead, their recovery was a duty shared by all states. Cassin translated this into a doctrine that permitted veterans to cross borders, even into countries that had been on an opposing side in the war, in search of better health care and welfare.[78] This system incorporated spatial exit as a corrective measure.

Into the late 1930s, however, Cassin, secular and atheist ("not committed to holding [Jewish] rituals"),[79] had turned his attention to the plight of Jews. But, as he explained later, he always qualified this allegiance:

> [M]y loyalty to Judaism is quite specific, for I do not attend synagogue frequently. Only since the persecution of 1933 have I stood in solidarity among the persecuted. But if one day they became the persecutors, I will no longer be with them.[80]

---

[74] E/CN.4/147, *Exposé de M. René Cassin*, cited *in* WINTER AND PROST, *supra* note 39, at 249.

[75] *Id.*

[76] Cassin, *supra* note 63 ("I was not able to accept the idea that national solidarity with those victims should limit itself to a kind of charitable aims. This is why I soon joined those who fought ... for the recognition of the right to compensation for personal damages incurred in the service of national community").

[77] CABRANES, *supra* note 39, at 74.

[78] WINTER AND PROST, *supra* note 39, at 3. For more on Cassin's work on behalf of veterans, *see* Prost, *supra* note 39, at 19 *and* CABRANES, *id.* at 18–76, esp. 52–53 and 74.

[79] René Cassin, *BBC Radio Address by Rene Cassin to the "Israelites of France,"* BBC (April 1941), *in* JEWISH RESPONSES TO PERSECUTION: 1941–1942, 24 (Jürgen Matthäus, ed., 2013).

[80] Letter from René Cassin to Sam Lévy, directeur des Cahiers Sfaradis, in Neuilly (April 12, 1948) (Alliance Israélite Universelle, AM Présidence 001e), cited *in* Jay Winter, *René Cassin between humanitarian rights and human rights* 4 (2012) (unpublished manuscript; on file with author).

With the shift of his focus to the Jews, Cassin began to imagine protections coming from within the state and supervised by international enforcement bodies. He attributed this change in his thinking to the influence of the Bernheim Petition. Franz Bernheim, a German Jewish citizen in Upper Silesia, had been discharged in 1933 from his employment following the introduction of the Nazi anti-Jewish laws.[81] He invoked the protection of the League to argue that his discharge was in breach of the Minorities Treaties.[82] In contrast to the case of WWI veterans, responsibility was particularized; one state, Germany, was accountable for Bernheim's situation. Bernheim's harm awakened Cassin to the need, as he wrote, for rights supporting "external interference [in the state's] policies towards its nationals."[83]

Around the same time, Cassin set out to harmonize the status of the Jews with the emerging statist definition of human rights. Interestingly, Cassin did so by drawing on the institutional framework of a cross-border anti-Zionist Jewish network that stood outside these very same definitions.

In 1943, while still in London, Charles de Gaulle appointed Cassin as the President of the *Alliance Israélite Universelle*.[84] The Alliance was a transnational Jewish network founded in 1860 in Paris. It was born out of a particular need: "... all other important faiths," its manifesto explains, "are represented in the world by nations – embodied, that is to say, in governments that have a special interest and an official duty to represent and speak for them. Ours alone is without this important advantage ... "[85] To fill this vacuum, the Alliance set up a "political force preoccupied with Jewish interests."[86]

---

[81] René Cassin, *La Declaration universelle et la mise en oeuvre des droits de l'homme*, 239 ACADEMIE DE DROIT INTERNATIONAL DE LA HAYE: RECUEIL DES COURS 324 (1952), cited *in* Greg Burges, *The Human Rights Dilemma in Anti-Nazi Protest: The Bernheim Petition, Minorities, Protection, and the 1933 Session of the League of Nations*, CERC Working Papers Series No. 2/2002, www.academia.edu/20240407/The_Human_Rights_Dile mma_in_Anti-Nazi_Protest_The_Bernheim_Petition_Minorities_Protection_and_th e_1933_Sessions_of_the_League_of_Nations.

[82] In particular, the minorities protection provisions of Part III of the *German-Polish Convention*.

[83] Burges, *supra* note 81 (Cassin noted the simultaneity of Franz Bernheim's petition and Joseph Goebbels's entry into the Assembly Hall, signaling "his sovereign country could not support any external interference in its policies towards its nationals").

[84] This was unusual. It was the prerogative of the Central Committee of the Alliance, not the French president, to appoint a president. For more, see WINTER AND PROST, *supra* note 39, at 310.

[85] "Manifeste de juillet 1860."

[86] *Alliance Israélite Universelle* 19 (1858): 692–99; AIU 19 (1858): 624–45; AIU 18 (1857): 200–202, cited *in* MICHAEL GRAETZ, THE JEWS IN THE NINETIETH CENTURY FRANCE – FROM THE FRENCH REVOLUTION TO THE ALLIANCE ISRAÉLITE UNIVERSELLE 277 (1996) (quoting the founders).

This Jewish "political force" completely rejected the idea of a Jewish state. "A work like that of the Alliance cannot and should not be shut in the borders of one country," explained one of the prominent personalities who presided over the creation of the Alliance and the elaboration of its ideological platform.[87] Instead of a nation-state, the Alliance organized world Jewry into a *network* that cut across territorial boundaries. "[A] link," declared its manifesto, must be "created, a solidarity established, from country to country, embracing in its network all that is Jewish."[88] Their network, again from the manifesto, corresponded to "neither a state, nor a society, nor a determinate territory."[89]

Conflict between the Alliance, a transnational Jewish "political force," and Zionism, the Jewish nationalist-territorial movement, was inevitable. While the Zionists were committed to establishing a Jewish national home in Palestine, for the Alliance, in the words of its president in 1919, it was "unconscionable to expel the Palestinians from the land where they have lived for centuries to house Jews flocked from all parts of the world."[90]

By the time of Cassin's presidency, the Alliance had performed the "official duty" of representing and speaking for world Jews for almost a century.[91] As president, Cassin continued on this path; he was, in his words, a "Jewish statesman."[92]

In 1947, Cassin sent a memorandum to the United Nations's Secretary-General, "Memorandum of the Alliance on the Palestinian Problem,"[93] in which he outlined the Alliance's strategy for fitting world Jews into the new international legal system that guarantees individuals rights primarily as citizens of their respective states.

---

[87] GEORGES J. WEILL, ÉMANCIPATION ET PROGRES: L'ALLIANCE ISRAÉLITE UNIVERSELLE ET LES DROITS DE L'HOMME 64 (2000) (quoting Narcisse Leven).

[88] Manifeste de juillet 1860.

[89] *Id.*

[90] Sylvain Lévi, Presentation before the Supreme Allied Council on the question of Palestine, Process-Verbal of 46th Session, Paris (Feb. 27, 1919), *in* THE LETTERS AND PAPERS OF CHAIM WEIZMANN, SERIES B – PAPERS, VOL. 1, AUGUST 1898–JULY 1931 228 (Barnet Litvinoff, ed., 1983).

[91] On the representation capacities of the Alliance on the international stage, *see* Moria Paz, *A Non-Territorial Ethnic-Religious Network and the Making of Human Rights Law: The Alliance Israélite Universelle.* 4 INTERDISCIPLINARY J. HUMAN R. L. 1 (2010) and MORIA PAZ, NETWORK OR STATE? INTERNATIONAL LAW AND THE HISTORY OF JEWISH SELF-DETERMINATION (forthcoming).

[92] WINTER AND PROST, *supra* note 39, at 318–19.

[93] René Cassin, "Mémorandum sur le problème Palestinien," June 9, 1947, AM Présidence 030a, AIU Archives. My sincere thanks to Nathan Kurz for providing this document.

In general, Jews were to be integrated in their respective nation-states. To facilitate this integration, the Alliance would "defend the Jews wherever they suffer because of their being Jews," and would "obtain for them full rights of citizenship in the countries in which they live."[94] This was an extension of the Alliance's tradition; for the "last 85 years," the memorandum read, the Alliance's work was "aimed at Jewish emancipation" and the network has "always tried to obtain to Jews ... the rights and duties of a citizen."[95]

As for "the general majority of the 'Remnant of Israel' who still live in Central and Eastern Europe" – those who have "escaped the slaughter" and "live in the Displaced Persons camps"[96] – integration was neither practical nor rational. Instead, Cassin wrote to the Secretary-General, they were "to build a new life in Palestine" where they should gain "the status of independence."[97] To support them, the Alliance demanded of the U.N. "the provision of facilities for Jewish immigration and colonialization in Palestine."[98]

In embracing the establishment of a Jewish national home in Palestine, Cassin was the first president who broke away from the Alliance's long tradition of anti-Zionism. But his adoption of the Zionist answer to the plight of Jewish refugees was a matter of expediency rather than an ideological commitment. It was an ad hoc solution to a particularly horrifying reality. After the Holocaust, the memorandum read, the creation of a national home "is a right humanity cannot refuse them."[99] *Moreover*, it was only a second-best remedy; the Alliance, Cassin insisted, "will continue this struggle [to secure Jewish citizenship in their existing states of residence] wherever it believes it possible to achieve its aims."[100] Indeed, around the same time, Cassin vowed that the Alliance was "committed to the complete incorporation of Jews in the countries where they live (A Statement of the Alliance's principles, 1944)."[101]

In the 1940s, René Cassin crafted a universal system of rights at the same time that he presided over a "political force" that was concerned with the protection of one particular people ("I am a Jewish statesman") and, moreover, was a devoted Republican patriot who took the French political order as superior to all other systems (what Cassin called the "brilliance of

---

[94]   *Id.*

[95]   *Id.*

[96]   *Id.*

[97]   *Id.*

[98]   *Id.*

[99]   *Id.*

[100]   *Id.*

[101]   René Cassin, "Une declaration de l'Alliance Israelite Universelle," Nov. 11, 1944, AM Presidence 001b, AIU Archives, cited *in* WINTER AND PROST, *supra* note 39, at 322–23.

France")[102]. Cassin was able to reconcile the universal with the particular because he saw them as a single unified whole.

For Cassin, after the Holocaust, Jews represented a test case for all victims. "Never," he wrote, "will Jews in particular obtain real equality until the totality of human rights are respected for everyone."[103] Solving the problem of the Jews, therefore, was a symbolic victory of human rights for all victims. At the same time, the French Republic stood for the universality of the law. "If in all my life I have fought for the existence and brilliance of France," Cassin explained, "it has been for the France of human rights and not for an ordinary nation."[104]

Cassin's equation of Jewish interests, human rights, and French ideals was viable only insofar as it did not erase the interests of any other people. In particular, Cassin saw no conflict between the needs of Jews and those of the indigenous Arab population in Palestine. Jewish "work and ... creative spirit," he argued in the memorandum, can only benefit Arab Palestinians, and "the democratic spirit of the Near East can only but prosper through the influence of Jewish accomplishments in Palestine." Indeed, should strife emerge, it would only be due to "outside influence" that may raise "difficulties between the various elements of the population."[105] And, even in that extreme case, Cassin was optimistic. The Alliance ran a massive network of schools across the Muslim world that educated students, both Jewish and non-Jewish.[106] It had gained a "long experience in relations between Jews and [Muslims]." This extensive knowledge, Cassin concluded, "encourages the hope that equitable solution of the whole problem can be achieved."

In fact, the Alliance under Cassin did everything it could to harmonize the status of *both* Jews and Arab Palestinians with the emerging state-based definition of human rights. "If," Cassin wrote to the U.N. Secretary-General, "a general solution for the entire country appears impossible, the Alliance would be willing to accept any other proposal which would permit large scale immigration and colonialization and the free development of the Jewish National Home in Palestine."[107]

---

[102]   Cassin's 1974 testament cited *in* WINTER AND PROST, *supra* note 39, at 301.
[103]   René Cassin, *Discours de Jérusalem, in* CASSIN, LA PENSÉE ET L'ACTION *supra* note 52, at 159, 161.
[104]   *Id.* at 302.
[105]   *Id.*
[106]   On the Alliance school system, *see* PAZ, NETWORK OR STATE, *supra* note 91.
[107]   *Id.*

While in 1930 Cassin had argued that nationalism was "destined to be weakened," in 1947 he still believed that it was possible to legally and politically differentiate two separate peoples within the same single territorial home, Palestine. It was only much later, after Cassin realized that a conflict between Jews and Arabs was inevitable, that he would choose a side.

CASSIN, THE FREEDOM OF MOVEMENT RIGHT AND JEWISH AND PALESTINIAN REFUGEES

Over time, René Cassin's pragmatic capitulation to the political realities of the world became the status quo. In 1948, he adopted the UDHR as a practical first step to move forward with the law. He was, however, aware that to vindicate mobility in a meaningful way requires providing for the entry function: "it is impossible to recognize a right . . . if no one was bound to respect it." Still, by 1972 he had already accepted human rights as "a whole in time and in space."[108]

Similarly, in 1947 Cassin considered Zionism merely an expedient solution for those who had "escaped the slaughter" of the Holocaust. Yet by the 1973 war, when Israel had already been occupying East Jerusalem, the West Bank, and the Gaza Strip for six years, Cassin described his and the Alliance's relationship with the Israeli nation as one of "complete admiration."[109] This admiration was a far cry from Cassin's earlier temporizing: "[I]f one day they became the persecutors, I will no longer be with them."

In taking both human rights and Zionism, the best we can do in 1948, as the best we do by the 1970s, Cassin neglected to see how in the case of refugees they reinforced each other: under the freedom of movement right, the protection of Jewish refugees, but not that of Palestinians who were expelled from Israel by Israel, was grounded in the moment of legal sovereignty and the specific way in which the British Mandate over Palestine dissolved.

In 1972, Cassin co-organized in Sweden an international colloquium on "The Right to Leave and to Return."[110] For him, this right to movement was foundational, indeed the "indestructible core of all human rights."[111] He later reflected on the colloquium for the *New York Times*, in a piece he titled: "For a Right to Leave and a Right to Return." In that piece, Cassin discussed the

---

[108] Cassin, *supra* note 4.
[109] Letter from René Cassin to Katzir, Oct. 29, 1973 (AIU, AM, Présidence 015a). *See also* letter from Cassin to Asher Ben Natan, Oct. 10, 1973, cited *in* WINTER, *supra* note 80.
[110] On the Colloquium, *see* THE RIGHT TO LEAVE AND TO RETURN, *supra* note 4.
[111] Cassin, *supra* note 4.

operation of the right in relation to Jewish refugees, especially those seeking to flee the USSR, and Palestinian refugees.

For Soviet Jews – and other Russians – Cassin wrote, the right to freedom of movement carried "particular meaning":[112] it guaranteed them the right to leave any state, both in situations where they faced a danger to their life and security,[113] and also when they did not confront the risk of physical persecution, but were faced with the lesser threat of losing their separate culture.[114]

But Cassin was wrong to assign the mobility of Soviet Jews to the freedom of movement right. A majority of Soviet Jews sought to exit their state of nationality permanently, because conditions there were intolerable, and to enter into another state with which they had no prior relationship. They, therefore, needed an exit right and an entry right as a duty imposed on *all* states. A minority of Soviet Jews, in turn, wanted to exit their state of nationality permanently and enter into the State of Israel, with which they shared common cultural roots. This group needed an exit right, as a universal duty and entry duty imposed only on Israel. Both of these groups' claims were associated with mobility, and they required the exit and entry functions.

Yet Cassin focused only on the exit function. Emigration, he said, is within the framework "of the protection of human rights."[115] Where would these Jewish refugees go? Cassin was able to ignore the contingency of the exit function under human rights law because in this particular case the State of Israel had already solved the entry problem for world Jewry. In 1950, Israel passed the Law of Return securing the right of "[e]very Jew . . . to come to the State of Israel as an immigrant,"[116] and, in 1952, it passed the Law of Nationality, making "[e]very immigrant in the sense of the Law of Return of

---

[112] *Id.* (Cassin's NYT Opinion).

[113] For example, from the summer of 1954 onward Cassin, together with other Jewish international organizations, mobilized the right to leave for Moroccan Jews who became subject because they were Jews. For discussion, *see* NATHAN KURZ, "A SPHERE ABOVE THE NATIONS?": THE RISE AND FALL OF INTERNATIONAL JEWISH HUMAN RIGHTS POLITICS, 1945–1975 (2015) (Unpublished Ph.D. Dissertation, Yale University), at 200–73.

[114] Louis E. Pettiti, *The Right to Leave and Return in the USSR, in* THE RIGHT TO LEAVE AND TO RETURN *supra* note 4, at 182 ("Opposition to mass emigration of a cultural group is perhaps understandable as a way of avoiding the loss of the group's social and cultural contribution. But it should be counter-balanced by maintaining and encouraging the cultural development of the group. This is not the case with the Jewish minority in the USSR, which has constantly been deprived of publications in its own language, of synagogues, of schools and so on.").

[115] AD-HOC COMMITTEE ON MOROCCAN AFFAIRS, "PROCÈS-VERBAL DE LA SÉANCE DU COMITÉ," SEPT. 10, 1954, AM PROCÈS-VERBAUX, BOÎTE 17, AIU ARCHIVES. CITED IN KURZ, *supra* note 115, at 241.

[116] The Law of Return, 5710–1950, July 5, 1950, Art. 1, www.refworld.org/docid/3ae6b4ea1b.html (Isr.).

1950 . . . an Israeli citizen."[117] In these twin laws, Israel exercised its discretion as a state to secure Jews a landing place. This permitted Soviet Jews a robust entry right, including – like the human rights for the right of return of nationals – both a return (entry) function and a domicile function (regulating personal status post-entry). But, as opposed to the right to return, Israel drew on common ethnic and cultural attachments, not nationality, as a proxy for "own country." This echoes Cassin's second definition of the right of a domicile, which took cultural roots as a replacement for citizenship.

Cassin, therefore, missed that Soviet Jews were, in fact, atypically situated: they had a pre-exiting landing place. Ultimately, the entry of Russian Jews was the result of Israeli law. They, therefore, enjoyed the right of mobility by virtue of legal claims of a nonuniversal nature. Moreover, those who did not really desire to go to Israel had to transform their actual motivation to exit the USSR into a legally cognizable collective cultural-political attachment with Israel. And so, what Cassin called a universal right, is, practically speaking, particular: the right is only functional for these refugees who, like Soviet Jews, have a place to go, as a result of national domestic law.

At the same time, for Palestinian refugees, Cassin wrote in his *New York Times* opinion piece, the freedom of movement right did not guarantee a right of return to Israel. Their predicament presented an "important problem."[118] But this problem was a non-event from a human rights perspective. It called for a political answer, or, in Cassin's terminology, "a humane solution."[119]

In asserting that human rights law denies Palestinians a right of return, Cassin relied on the argument of Paul Weis, a leading refugee scholar. Of the two functions that make up the right to free mobility, Weis focused only on that of entry; Palestinian refugees did not raise an exit problem. He proceeded in two steps.

First, Weis differentiated between waves of refugees: what he named the "old" refugees, the result of the exodus during the war of 1948,[120] and the "new" refugees, the result "of the occupation of certain areas by Israel"[121] in 1967. He explained that neither wave was made up of individuals who had ever been nationals of the State of Israel. The old refugees were divided between

[117] Nationality Law, 5712–1952, July 14, 1953, Art. 2, www.refworld.org/docid/3ae6b4ec20.html (Isr.).
[118] *Cassin, supra* note 4.
[119] *Id.*
[120] Paul Weis, *The Problem of the Arab Refugees from Palestine, in* THE RIGHT TO LEAVE AND TO RETURN, *supra* note 4, at 134.
[121] *Id.* at 315.

nationals of Jordan and those who had lived under the former Mandate of Palestine and then under military administration (first Egyptian and then Israeli).[122] The new refugees were nationals of Jordan.[123]

Second, Weis offered a detailed examination of the legislative history of both the UDHR and the ICCPR to ascertain what the drafters had in mind in upholding the right of an individual to return to "his own country":

> [T]he legislative history shows that the words "his own country" refer to the state of which the person is a national. They may also include the state whose nationality the person possessed and of which he has been arbitrarily deprived.[124]

Weis concluded that since neither the old nor the new refugees were ever nationals of the State of Israel, and as the right of return requires nationality, "the problem of the return of the Palestine refugees [is not related to] the right of return."[125] Palestinian refugees presented, Weis ended, a "most grave humanitarian problem."[126] But this problem required a political, not a legal, remedy.

The unarticulated concept implied in the arguments of both Weis and Cassin is that of "political continuity." Palestinian refugees did not have a right of return to the State of Israel – and Israel lacked a corresponding duty to let them in – because there was no political continuity between the entity the Palestinians fled and the entity to which they now sought to return.

Although Weis and Cassin failed to articulate the criterion of political continuity, they did not invent it to benefit Jews. Rather, they were operating within the fundamental distinction in international law between state continuity and state succession.[127]

Broadly speaking, if the State of Israel was a successor to the British Mandate in Palestine, then the acquisition of Israeli independence would

---

[122]   *Id.* ("As to the "old" refugees, they found themselves in Jordan, the Gaza strip, Lebanon, and Syria. In 1950 the Eastern part of Palestine was made part of the Kingdom of Jordan. The inhabitants and residents of the Eastern part, including the refugees, became nationals of Jordan. 1) As to the Gaza strip, formerly part of Palestine, it was under Egyptian military administration and is at present under Israeli military administration.")

[123]   *Id.* ("As to the "new" refugees, they have mainly fled from Cisjordan to Transjordan, i.e. a movement within the state of their nationality.")

[124]   *Id.* at 318.

[125]   *Id.*

[126]   *Id.*

[127]   JAMES CRAWFORD, THE CREATION OF STATES IN INTERNATIONAL LAW 667 (2d. ed., 2006). (International law "embodies a fundamental distinction between state continuity and state succession ... The law of state succession is predicted on this distinction.")

only mean a change in sovereignty and would have left unaffected the original legal personality. Israel would be considered the same entity as the mandate, and the inhabitants of the territory under the mandate would have become ipso facto nationals of Israel.[128]

But, if the State of Israel was not a successor to Palestine, then at the moment of independence it would have become an entirely new legal personality. In this view, Israeli independence would have been a "break in the chain of legal continuity."[129] As such, Israel would have started its life with a "clean slate," free of the sum of its predecessor's rights and liabilities,[130] and Palestinians would not automatically have become Israeli nationals.[131]

At the time Cassin and Weis were writing, there was a widespread consensus, shared by all sides to the conflict,[132] that there was no political continuity between Israel and the mandate. Israel argued that continuity was broken because the Partition Plan had never been implemented[133] and the British Parliament unilaterally terminated the mandate before Israel declared its independence.[134] Until as late as 1967, Palestinians, in turn, demanded a return to the entity that existed prior to Israel, also implying that Israel was entirely different from the previous Palestinian entity.[135] This consensus, moreover, was confirmed by the language of the UN Resolution 194(III),

[128] For a discussion on the effect of succession on nationality, *see* DANIEL PATRICK O'CONNELL, STATE SUCCESSION IN MUNICIPAL LAW AND INTERNATIONAL LAW 499–506 (1967).

[129] Arnold McNair, *Aspects of State Sovereignty*, 26 BRIT. Y.B. INT'L. L. 6, 8 (1949).

[130] This is a broad picture. In reality, new states rarely discredited all the duties and rights that were incumbent on the previous sovereign, just as much as it is rare that the new state does not alter some of the legal positions of the previous sovereigns. *See* Matthew C. R. Craven, *The Problem of State Succession and the Identity of States under International Law*, 142 EUR. J. INT'L. L. 148–49 (1998).

[131] A former Palestinian citizen could only return to Israel as an immigrant subject to Israeli immigration laws.

[132] This consensus is significant for in thinking about continuity "the view of the state or states concerned ... will be highly influential." CRAWFORD, *supra* note 129, at 671.

[133] G.A. Res. 181 (II), 2 U.N. GAOR, Resolution 131, 132, U.N. Doc. A/519 (1947) (a plan of Partition with Economic Union for the future Government of Palestine).

[134] Palestine Act, 1948. For the position of Israel, *see, e.g.*, Ambassador Shabtai Rosenne, *The Effect of Change of Sovereignty Upon Municipal Law*, 27 BRIT. Y.B. INT'L. L. 267, 272 (1950); NATHAN FEINBERG, PALESTINE UNDER THE MANDATE AND THE STATE OF ISRAEL: PROBLEMS IN INTERNATIONAL LAW (1963).

[135] HOWARD ADELMAN AND ELAZAR BARKAN, NO RETURN, NO REFUGEES 204 (2011). *See also* Howard Adelman, *Palestinians and the Right of Return*, *in* PLURALITY AND CITIZENSHIP IN ISRAEL: MOVING BEYOND THE JEWISH/PALESTINIAN CIVIL DIVIDE 42–43 (Dan Avnon & Yotam Benziman, eds., 2010).

1948, which construes return as a recommendation, not a right, conditional on permission.[136]

Today, this consensus is questioned.[137] What is clear, however, is that the law of state succession is "largely confused,"[138] to the extent that it can be successfully used to serve conflicting positions.[139] This leaves the argument supporting the absence of political continuity between Israel and Palestine at least as doctrinally plausible as its opposite.

For Cassin, the right of return depended on the political continuity of a state, and in the case of the State of Israel, this continuity did not exist. This historical anomaly left Palestinian refugees deprived of an obligatory right of entry into one's "own country" under the universal human right of return.

Alas, in analyzing the suffering of Palestinian refugees as a question involving the freedom of movement right, Cassin was, again, wrong. He misidentified the nature of the claim. Palestinian refugees did not raise an exit issue, nor did they focus on a general right of entry. Their claim was about continuity, not mobility. They asked to return, or to enter, permanently, into Israel, the place where they had long-standing roots and from which they were expelled by Israel. Unlike Jewish refugees, then, who primarily needed a "right to enter" as a duty imposed on *all* states, Palestinian refugees required entry as a duty imposed only on a *single* state, Israel – the state responsible for their dispossession. Consequently, holding Israel particularly liable for their return did not have to do with the freedom of movement right (otherwise, under the "right to entry," their plight could have been laid at the door of every single country in the world that refused to let them in en masse). Instead, it was a violation of their right to a domicile in Cassin's first meaning of domicile: a right to remain, or not to be expelled.

Cassin misread the nature of the Palestinians' legal harm because he underestimated the difference between entry to one's *"own country"* (state of

---

[136] G.A. Res. 194 Section 11, Dec. 11, 1948, GAOR, 3rd Session part I, 1948, Resolutions, 21–24 http://unispal.un.org/UNISPAL.NSF/o/C758572B78D1CD0085256BCF0077E51A. On the restrictive meaning of the resolution, *see*, *e.g.*, Ruth Lapidoth, *The Right of Return in International Law, with Special Reference to the Palestinian Refugees*, 16 ISRAEL YEARBOOK ON HUMAN RIGHTS 103 (1986); Yaffa Zilbershats, *International Law and the Palestinians' Right of Return to the State of Israel*, *in* ISRAEL AND THE PALESTINIAN REFUGEES 194 (Eyal Benvenisti, Chaim Gans, & Sari Hanafi, eds., 2007).

[137] For a good summary, *see* Kathleen Lawand, *The Right to Return of Palestinians in International Law*, 8 INT'L J. REFUGEE L. 532, 551 (1996).

[138] Craven, *supra* note 132, at 143; O'Connell, *supra* note 130, at 179.

[139] MARTTI KOSKENNIEMI, FROM APOLOGY TO UTOPIA: THE STRUCTURE OF INTERNATIONAL LEGAL ARGUMENT 582–3 (1989) (the "law of state succession . . . produces a fully contextualized normativity").

nationality or citizenship) and entry to one's *"place of domicile"* (a place of long-standing roots) in the context of decolonization. He drew on nationality as a proxy for return and made return a function of formal political ties with a state. But a person who was expelled at the end of the colonial order could not go back to her "own country." That political entity was the colonized rule that was now dissolved. She could only return to the new legal sovereign that emerged out of the colonial order. In other words, in cases involving the return of refugees and decolonization the relevant proxy for return is domicile; return as a function of existing roots in a *place*, rather than formal political ties in a *state*. By insisting on return to one's "own country" as the legal framework, Cassin abandoned Palestinian refugees in an impossible situation. Israel expelled and dispossessed them. But it does not have a duty to permit their entry, or return, to the very place from which it barred them.

Today, moreover, after the UNHRC has expanded the definition of one's "own country" to include also informal definitions, first-generation Palestinian refugees would have likely qualified for return under the freedom of movement right. But their children would not: protection derives from ongoing continuity in the land and they are two, three, or even four generations away from "domicile," in the usual sense (or Cassin's first meaning), in Palestine. And, at the same time, this same threshold might *also* give second-generation Jewish settlers strong claims to the occupied territories; they were born and continue to reside there.

Perhaps Dr. Musa Mazzawi – the only expert invited to Cassin's Colloquium on the Right to Leave and to Return who opposed the denial of the right of return for Palestinian refugees – summarized it best. In contrast to Cassin's conclusion that the Palestinian plight is only a "humanitarian problem," Mazzawi insisted that their "problem" is, in fact, "a legal problem."[140] But the relevant harm was one of continuity, not mobility, making freedom of movement the wrong right to apply. In terminology almost perfectly mirroring Cassin's 1930's articulation of the right to domicile, he insisted:

> A person's "country" is that to which he is connected by a reasonable combination of such relevant criteria as race, religion, language, ancestry, birth and prolonged domicile. Governments come and "go," and their political fluctuations and vagaries should not affect the fundamental rights of human beings, such as the right to return to one's own country and to have a homeland ... A person's relationship to his country should not be at the mercy of politicians.[141]

[140] Dr. Musa Mazzawi, *Comment on The Middle East, in* THE RIGHT TO LEAVE AND TO RETURN, *supra* note 4, at 343–44.
[141] *Id.*

René Cassin applied the freedom of movement right to Jewish and Palestinian refugees. But he evinced a myopia regarding the role that mobility plays in Palestinian refugees' lives. Their claim was associated with continuity (to remain), not mobility (to withdraw), and had nothing to do with exit/entry rights. By applying the freedom of movement right, Cassin misconstrued their harm. The appropriate right in the case of first-generation Palestinian refugees was the right to domicile in Cassin's more familiar meaning, the right to stay put ("right to domicile"). And, in the case of second-generation Palestinian refugees, the correct right was Cassin's less familiar articulation – the right to take the establishment of cultural roots in a host state as a possible replacement for citizenship ("the right to establish a domicile by moving").

The claim of Jewish refugees, in contrast, was to withdraw territorially, to escape, and it required both the entry and exit functions. Here, freedom of movement was the correct right. Alas, Cassin was wrong about the breadth of its protection. He missed the fact that Soviet Jews were atypically situated because their mobility was meaningful without symmetry between the exit and entry functions of the right.

Cassin embraced the human rights definition of mobility because the Holocaust taught him that open borders were not a plausible reality. But, at least in 1948, when the issue of Jewish refugees was most pressing, he was sensitive to the practical limitations of the right, understanding that it is "impossible to recognize a right if no one was bound to respect it." By 1972, however, he had accepted the right to freedom of movement as the "indestructible core of all human rights," and no longer seemed to concern himself with the shortcoming of the right to mobility. It is difficult to know what Cassin was thinking. But after world Jews already had an entry place, Cassin no longer appeared to care about how this right actually operates on the ground. He seemed indifferent that his core right was, in fact, incomplete. And this incomplete right leaves second-generation refugees born to noncitizens and refugees who lack an entry right under national prescription stranded between states. Without a state to take them in, they have rights but no protection.

ACKNOWLEDGMENTS

I am thankful for Nathaniel Berman for his careful engagement with this text. The argument benefitted tremendously from his comments. I am also thankful to Gabriella Blum, Barbara Fried, Tom Ginsburg, Mark Kelman, Amalia Kessler, Martti Koskenniemi, Peter Kozodoy, Nathaniel Kurz, David Luban, James Loeffler, Itamar Mann, Samuel Moyn, and Robin West for their generous comments on earlier drafts. This paper could not have been written without the help of the Stanford Law Library. In particular, I thank Sonia Moss, Rich Porter, and Sergio Stone for invaluable assistance. Finally, I am deeply grateful for Nadia Asancheyev and Laura Donohue and the Centre on National Security and the Law at the Georgetown University Law Center, which was my home for the past three years.

10

There's No Place Like Home

Domicile, René Cassin, and the Aporias of Modern International Law

Nathaniel Berman

Refugees: quintessential subjects of international law or its eternal pariahs? Does their legal treatment vindicate internationalism's humanism or prove its contamination by power? In periods when a large portion of humanity becomes transfigured into refugees, as in the aftermath of the two world wars, as well as during our post-Cold War agonies, these questions become more than academic curiosities. They become matters of life and death for millions.

The collapse of empires and the birth of new states: foundational moments of international legal order or episodes of its deepest crises, as its pillars disappear into quicksand? Do such periods provide opportunities for reconstructing global society or show the futility of such projects? Again, it has been in the three global post-war periods that such questions have taken on their vital, and lethal, urgency.

It is at the intersection of these two fundamental conundra that Moria Paz's essay is situated. The conditions they evoke overlap to a great extent, for political chaos tends to cause massive refugee flows. But if the dissolution and reconstitution of states engender what Paz calls the problem of "mobility," they also engender the problem she calls "continuity," the legal status of people who remain in territories where changes in sovereignty destabilize citizenship.

The issues of "continuity" and "mobility," however different, are both symptoms of the dissociation of human beings from states. This dissociation makes possible, indeed demands, reflection on the very nature of international law. In what follows, I situate Paz's essay in a more general theoretical and historical framework, while reexamining certain aspects of the career of René Cassin (1887–1976), particularly as it relates to the "law of domicile." I offer a different interpretation of Cassin than Paz, though ultimately converge with some of her general conclusions.

International law, like all law, is a complex force field of heterogeneous rights, doctrines, and institutions, crackling with latent tension among them. At least since World War I, that force field has included, with varying emphases depending on the decade: the rights of states to sovereignty, the rights of groups to self-determination and minority rights, the rights of individuals to human rights, the authority of international institutions, and so on. As is true of all legal fields, it is real human beings who stand at the point at which the vectors of these conflicting forces converge, with unpredictable and divergent consequences for their lives and deaths.

Nowhere is this more true than in relation to refugees and those threatened with statelessness, whether the latter have fled or have remained in destabilized territories. The appearance of either as a massive phenomenon strikes at the ability of states to serve as international law's pillars. The assumption that individuals are always subject to the legitimate jurisdiction of some sovereign is shared by two conceptions that are otherwise diametrically opposed: the notion that international law should take no notice of individuals' rights as such due to the sacrosanct veil of territorial sovereignty (an extreme form of nineteenth century positivism) *and* the notion that international law's central duty is the protection of individuals' rights by restricting the actions of states (the post-World War II human rights vision). Massive phenomena of mobility and/or loss of citizenship, by undermining this shared assumption, throw both of these conceptions into question.

When the international order is destabilized by *both* massive refugee flows *and* a substantial redrawing of borders, as in the three global post-war periods, conditions are ripe for an explosion of the latent conflict among heterogeneous legal principles. They also provide fertile ground for contestation among legal visionaries advancing novel ways of organizing the divergent principles. Taking as their point of departure the displacement of the centrality of states, such visions often have both urgent and utopian dimensions.

Freed of the practical and imaginative constraints posed by stable sovereign power, creative legal minds propose visions foregrounding other values, such as the self-determination of peoples or the human dignity of individuals. Such visions often flounder when state power dynamics re-emerge. Utopian vision is then confronted by apologetics for state sovereignty (Martti Koskeniemmi), "normativity" by "relevance" (Richard Falk), principle by power. The death of the political possibilities afforded by post-war instability often also spells the retreat of legal imagination.

Paz's essay suggests that we examine these dialectics through the career of Cassin, an exceptionally emblematic twentieth-century figure. Like so many of his era, Cassin's early adult life had been decisively marked by the traumatic rupture of service in World War I. After being gravely wounded, he returned home to become one of the founders of a left-of-center veterans' organization with strong pacifist leanings (L'Union Fédérale).[1] Paz invites us to begin observing Cassin when he is delivering his 1930 lectures to the Hague Academy of International Law: "The New Conception of Domicile in the Resolution of Conflicts of Law."[2] At the time of these lectures, Cassin was already in his forties and the holder of a chair at the University of Paris, a status befitting one invited to speak before the venerable academy.

Cassin situated his lectures against the backdrop of the "great upheaval provoked by the war," which "imposed on all the task of methodical reconstruction."[3] In terms similar to those of other innovative jurists of this era, Cassin declared that state sovereignty must be dramatically attenuated, for it had become a "veritable idol," "strongly contributed to exalting imperialist policies," "led to the War," and "covered the Earth with material and moral ruin."[4] Moreover, like a number of his contemporaries, Cassin coupled this war-guilt indictment of statism with a strong valorization of the new "legal organization of the shared life of Nations" epitomized in the League of Nations – a "great institution" established on the "ruins left by the Great War."[5] This shift "upward" of ultimate legal authority from discredited states to the League made it possible to give individuals a place in the international order based on their actual lives, rather than on artificial legal doctrines, a "downward" shift from states to individuals:

> If the state has rights vis-à-vis the international community, ... it also has obligations of which the positive character is being increasingly affirmed ... state sovereignty also has its limits on the side of the individual. In domestic public law, these are outlined by Declarations of Rights, specified by law.[6]

It is within this "transitional period in which we are living,"[7] that Cassin situated his theorization and advocacy of the "return of the law of domicile." To be sure, in "positive international law, the individual is still masked by the state,"[8] and "the time is perhaps far-off when the principles of [a 'Declaration

---

[1] "Hommage à René Cassin," L'UNION FÉDÉRALE, http://union-federale.com/presentation/hommage-a-rene-cassin/.
[2] René Cassin, *La nouvelle conception du domicile dans le règlement des conflits de lois*, 34 RECUEIL DES COURS À L'ACADEMIE DE DROIT INTERNATIONAL À LA HAYE 768 (1930-IV).
[3] *Id.* at 659.
[4] *Id.* at 768.
[5] *Id.* at 801.
[6] *Id.* at 769.
[7] *Id.* at 767.
[8] *Id.* at 769.

of the International Rights of Man'] will enter into positive international law."
Nonetheless, an "appreciable progress" might be accomplished if the "law of
domicile" assumed a more important role in private international law.[9]
According to Cassin,

> Domicile is the place where a man has established his domestic household
> and concentrated the ensemble of his interests ... It ... responds to an
> elemental need, that of marking legally the link which attaches the individual
> to a point of the surface of the earth, a link where he is presumed to be
> present, even if he absents himself temporarily. The existence of this legal
> headquarters [*siège légal*] of a person constitutes a universal and permanent
> phenomenon of legal life.[10]

In jurisdictions where the "law of domicile" prevails, a whole host of private
law issues are determined for noncitizen domiciliaries by that jurisdiction's
rules: rules affecting real property, contracts, families, civil status, judicial
jurisdiction, and so on. Cassin's emphasis on the links between individuality,
universality, and the union between real life and legal life in his advocacy of
the "law of domicile" marks his discourse as quintessentially of its period.

Before exploring further Cassin's understanding of the "law of domicile,"
I note that his lectures stand out from other contemporaneous re-imaginings of
the international order precisely because they focus on private, rather than
public, international law. Cassin shared with many of his contemporaries the
general structure of the double shift away from sovereignty – "up" to the
international plane, "down" to the infra-state level (which, for Cassin, was
the individual, though for some of his contemporaries, it consisted of non-state
groups like "peoples" or "minorities"). Cassin's distinctiveness consists in
showing the relationship of *private* law to the broader political-historical
trends to which others had pointed in relation to public law.

The rival principles to the "law of domicile" were the "law of nationality"
(that of the state of the individual's formal citizenship) and the "law of
territory" (that of the place where the individual resides, without regard to
the center of his domestic and economic life). While both of these rival
principles were state-centric, it is the "law of nationality" whose importance
increased in the nineteenth century with that of the ethno-national state.
Cassin attributed this growing importance to events such as the growth of
nationalism in the wake of the French Revolution and theories of the state
such as that of Pasquale Stanislao Mancini (1817–88). Mancini advocated both

---

[9] *Id.* at 770.
[10] *Id.* at 664.

the public international law "principle of nationalities," the forerunner of the twentieth century's "self-determination of peoples," and the private law rule of the "law of nationality."[11]

Cassin pointed to two opposite post-World War I trends, which together implicate the two phenomena with which I started this essay – refugees and the statelessness threatening those remaining in territory whose sovereigns were displaced. On the one hand, states that emerged from the ruins of the Hapsburg, Ottoman, Romanov, and Hohenzollern empires, and formed to realize the aspirations of ethno-nationalist movements, emphasized the "law of nationality."[12] On the other hand, states that had received many refugees, immigrants, and foreign workers in the wake of the war grappled with the need "to take account of a large influx of a foreign population settled permanently on their soil."[13] Such states, and Cassin clearly had France in mind, increasingly favored the "law of domicile." Thus, no less than the changes in public international law, the "return of the law of domicile" and its continuing rivalry with the "law of nationality" touch upon the "essential problems" of the new international order.[14]

For Cassin, the "law of domicile" had two advantages, for states and for individuals. On the one hand, it ensured legal uniformity in states with large populations of residents holding foreign citizenship. On the other hand, unlike the "law of territory," it accorded the real lives of individuals a decisive role in determining which law would apply to them. It was thereby "best adapted to the needs both of the person and the social group where she lives."[15] Cassin declared that the "choice of domicile is free," by which he meant the following:

> Every foreigner who has been *permitted to enter* and to dwell in the territory of any state can establish his principal place of establishment and acquire his domicile therein, entailing all the normal prerogatives that flow from it.[16]

As this passage indicates, the 1930 Cassin did not propose a legal right to move across state borders, either to exit or to enter. The "law of domicile" concerned the rules applicable to immigrants *in the place where they lived* and to individuals who had not moved but whose citizenship had been destabilized. While Cassin's tone was clearly unfavorable toward excessive use of

[11] *Id.* at 712–15.
[12] *Id.* at 732.
[13] *Id.*
[14] *Id.* at 767.
[15] *Id.* at 740.
[16] *Id.* at 672 (emphasis added).

sovereign power to banish noncitizens, he nowhere broached the notion of a *right* to cross borders. On the contrary, the application of the "law of domicile" to foreign residents was a way to deprive states of the incentive to expel foreigners out of fear of a large population on their soil not subject to their laws.[17] But he nowhere questioned states' legal right to undertake such expulsions.

One of Cassin's justifications for the "law of domicile" concerned his stance toward ethno-nationalism, which I discuss later in relationship to Zionism. Nationalist theorists defended the "law of nationality" on the grounds that state law and ethnic cultural norms are closely related or identical. Cassin denied this claim, citing the new nation-states of central Europe, whose large ethnic minorities were guaranteed equal protection of the laws by international treaties.[18] More generally, Cassin declared that people who move to foreign countries "'quickly take on the customs [*moeurs*] of the country in which they have established their habitual residence.'"[19] The "foreigner settled in a country in a stable manner intends to live like the natives, to submit himself to the same civil laws … even concerning the organization of his family."[20] Such statements express a strong antipathy to ethno-nationalism.

Finally, I note that Cassin did not envision a complete abolition of the "law of nationality," at least not in the short term, but only a greater emphasis on the "law of domicile." A variety of cultural, political, and religious factors entered into this view. In his words,

> The inequality of the development of the peoples of the Earth and the differences in civilization still justify … a personal law based on race or nationality for Europeans domiciled in a milieu governed by Koranic or Soviet law concerning the organization of the family. Moreover, are there not, among the civil legislation of nations of Christian civilization, all members of the League of Nations, … a profound division on the subject of … divorce … ?[21]

In particular, and depressingly, Cassin asserted that the "law of domicile" was not applicable in conflicts of laws in the colonial context, conflicts due to the fact that different laws apply to Europeans and "natives": "[E]vidently, it is according to race and customs that such conflicts must be decided."[22]

---

[17] *Id.* at 747.
[18] *Id.* at 742.
[19] *Id.* at 740. Cassin does not give the source of this quoted adage.
[20] *Id.* at 741.
[21] *Id.* at 764.
[22] *Id.* at 693.

This preservation of the "law of nationality" alongside the "law of domicile" corresponded, at the public law level, to the maintenance of state sovereignty alongside heightened international authority and a heightened role for the individual. Cassin acknowledged, as I noted above, that a state had "rights," as well as "obligations," in relation to the international community – "notably," the right to "maintain its existence."[23] To this structural preservation of sovereignty within the international order, Cassin also added a historical dialectic: when the national state and its private law correlate, the "law of nationality," first appeared, they had an emancipatory function, which then became transformed into its opposite when it became absolutized. The "law of nationality" had sought, "in the name of human dignity," to loosen the automatic application of the "law of territory." Yet, it "degenerated after having served as an instrument of emancipation and, in the end, subjugated individuals to an abstraction [*i.e.*, the state]."[24]

Cassin's 1930 lectures show him to be an exemplar of the progressive, though by no means radical, European legal thought of his time. He celebrated the new authority of international law, welcomed auguries of a greater internationalization of individual rights, and preserved a continuing, though more limited, role for states. He also exemplified a progressive French republicanism, emphasizing those aspects often highlighted by assimilated French Jews: hostility to ethnic determinism and veneration for the rule of law whose protection is guaranteed to all, whatever their ethnicity. And, finally, he also exemplified a key deformation, at least from our perspective, of this vision: the taken-for-granted legitimacy of some form of colonialism, with its dual legal systems based on "race and customs."

If we fast-forward through Cassin's career, from the forty-three-year-old Parisian professor lecturing at the Hague to the eighty-one-year-old international icon delivering his 1968 Nobel Peace Prize Lecture in Oslo, we might tell a linear narrative. Cassin's Nobel lecture was a paradigmatic statement of the modern conception of human rights. Interpreted in light of his 1930 lectures, it may be read as an explication of themes Cassin had pursued for decades. The impending "veritable juridical revolution" heralded by the adoption of the "Charter of Human Rights" (the two human rights covenants and the Universal Declaration) had been made possible by a new *après-guerre*, "the confusion, not to say anarchy, from which the nations of the world have just emerged." This "Charter" resolved the "fundamental question," that of "whether the various sovereign states have retained or lost their traditionally

[23] *Id.* at 769.
[24] *Id.* at 768.

exclusive sphere of authority" over "those under their jurisdiction." If the "jurisdiction of the states will always be a fundamental principle," it will, however, "no longer be exclusive." Indeed, in some instances, "as in the case of a complaint ... presented before certain international agencies," it will be possible to transfer that jurisdiction to "the whole of juridically organized mankind." This "revolution" signified: "first, the permanent accession of every human being to the rank of member of human society ... the rank of subject of international law; second, it will mean that the states consent to exercise their sovereignty under the authority of international law."[25]

Many of Cassin's interwar themes were reprised in this 1968 passage: legal transformation in an *après-guerre*; the restriction of state sovereignty, while not abolishing it altogether; the valorization of the international community, particularly as embodied in adjudicatory institutions; and the aspiration to accord individuals a firm international legal status. This latter aspiration, which seemed utopian to Cassin in 1930, now seemed within reach. In 1968, this goal was still in the future, for no state had yet ratified the covenants. But the 1968 Cassin optimistically anticipated the reconfiguration of the international order that he prophesied in the earlier *après-guerre*.

This continuity can be seen even through the differences. In 1930, Cassin was lecturing about private law; in 1968, about public law. In 1930, he was advocating the "law of domicile," which is, after all, the law of a sovereign state; in 1968, he was advocating internationally codified human rights. Most significantly, while the 1930 Cassin limited the equality principle underlying the "law of domicile" by an acceptance of colonialism, the 1968 Cassin embraced the right of self-determination codified in the human rights covenants – a right he described as "the political emancipation of territorial entities," a "logical outcome of the victorious libertarian principles fostered in the course of the Second World War."[26] This last point should not be taken for granted, for most French international lawyers had long contended (at least before 1962) that liberation from the Nazi yoke did not entail self-determination for territories under French colonial rule – for some, indeed, it was quite the contrary.

Like Paz, though on somewhat different grounds, I would be wary of this linear narrative. The rise of fascism and Nazism caused a shift in Cassin's political alliances in the late 1930s. He clashed with some of his erstwhile comrades in the veterans' movements who persisted in their pacifism despite

---

[25] René Cassin, *Nobel Lecture* (1968), www.nobelprize.org/nobel_prizes/peace/laureates/1968/cassin-lecture.html.

[26] *Id.*

impending catastrophe. Rupture became unavoidable, especially in the wake of the 1938 Munich Accords. In Cassin's telling, some declared that "we no longer recognize our peaceful Cassin." Most wounding of all for the advocate of foregrounding human life over legal formalism, they claimed: "Obsessed, for several years now, with the observance of international agreements," as French delegate to the League of Nations, "the jurist has, within him, supplanted the realist, the ardent adversary of war." They accused him of fetishizing the League as he had accused others of fetishizing the state: "Is [his move away from pacifism] due to the disappointment about . . . his League of Nations?" And, finally, a racist edge: "Have the anti-Semitic persecutions of Germany and Italy altered his faculty of reasoning . . . ?"[27] In response, Cassin narrated his tireless efforts to fight for peace in the League and elsewhere. But he also recited the various depredations of Italy, Germany, and Japan that mandated firm, even forceful opposition, maintaining that he had stayed true to his principles.

In April, 1940, shortly before the fall of France, Cassin returned to the dialectical transmogrification of the national state. In an essay significantly entitled, "The Leviathan State against Man and the Human Community," Cassin wrote:

> The conception of the national state has undergone a deformation. . . . Initially, . . . it was based on the sovereignty of the people, that is, an idea of emancipation in relation to all internal and external oppression. Its bond is the will of all citizens to act together, whatever the differences of temperaments, race, language, religion, etc. But as fate would have it, the German Romanticism of the 18th century oriented the national idea toward mystical, irrational aspirations, based on community of language or race . . .[28]

Cassin listed a variety of proposed remedies – among them a "universal declaration of the rights of the human person." But, he declared, while all these suggestions had merit, none "would be efficacious unless they all converge toward the same goal, the return to moderation and the down-grading of the absolute sovereignty of states."[29]

I now turn to Cassin's relationship, much discussed by Paz, to the Palestinian "right to return," taking his 1930 valorization of the "law of domicile" as my guiding thread. This analysis must be prefaced by a short note about his relationship to Zionism, whose vicissitudes have been outlined

---

[27] *Avertissements Salutaires*, Oct. 1938, reprinted *in* René Cassin, La Pensée et L'Action (F. Lalou, ed., 1972).

[28] *L'Etat-Léviathan*, Apr. 1940, *in* La Pensée et L'Action, 63, 66–67.

[29] *Id.* at 71.

by Paz. Prior to World War II, Cassin, a French Jew imbued with assimilationist ideals, had little contact with Zionism, except for a brief 1930 visit to
Palestine. Cassin took no part in organized Jewish life, let alone its nationalism. His concern with Jewish issues was provoked by the Nazi persecutions, which he protested in universalist terms. His participation in
organized Jewish life only began, fittingly enough for this true French
republican, with his appointment by Charles de Gaulle, in London, to
the presidency of the Alliance Israélite Universelle (AIU), a Franco-Jewish
network devoted to the transnational condition of Jews, particularly in
North Africa and the Middle East.[30] The AIU had always been hostile
toward Zionism and was imbued with the spirit of a taken-for-granted
identification of French patriotism; the equality ideals of the French
Revolution; concern for downtrodden Jews; and a certain complicity with
French imperialism. That the AIU's main activity consisted in the establishment of French-language schools for Jews in places ranging from Morocco
to Turkey encapsulated this identification. Although Cassin took no part in
AIU activities before the war, its ideals were congenial to his sensibility:
hostility to ethno-nationalism; loyalty to French republicanism and complicity with its imperialism; and devotion to the status of individuals *in their
domicile*. Zionism had no place in such a configuration.

It took the plight of the Jews in the wake of the war to move Cassin, and thus
the AIU, to support the establishment of a Jewish state. Cassin's 1947 memorandum to the United Nations on behalf of the AIU was the moment of
transition, as Paz shows. It reaffirmed that the principal aim of the AIU was
to obtain for Jews "full rights of citizenship in the countries where they live" –
i.e., in their domicile, the principle dear to the 1930 Cassin. But it went on to
foreground the impossible position of Jewish survivors of the war, located in
displaced persons camps – human beings dissociated from any existing state.
As an internationalist, Cassin concluded that this dissociation called for an
international trusteeship for Palestine, replacing the British Mandate and
focusing on the facilitation of Jewish immigration. Cassin appeared to have
held out hope for a resolution of the conflict between Jews and Muslims in
Palestine, but, at the same time, supported (a bit ambiguously) the notion that
the "Jewish community in Palestine ... deserves" the "status of
independence."[31]

---

[30] *See generally* MORIA PAZ, NETWORK OR STATE? INTERNATIONAL LAW AND THE HISTORY
OF JEWISH SELF-DETERMINATION (forthcoming).

[31] *Alliance Submits a Memorandum to U.N. Palestine Committee*, 12 ALLIANCE REV. (July,
1947).

Although support for a Jewish state marked a departure for Cassin, and certainly for the AIU, it was perhaps not as great a rupture as it may seem. Cassin's 1930 vision preserved a role for state sovereignty, even as it advocated its attenuation. Indeed, as I have noted, modern international law has always been a field of tension among heterogeneous principles, and thus any particular arrangement of those principles is always contingent. The national state, according to Cassin, had begun its career as an emancipatory political form. It could, perhaps, have continued to play that role had it not been deformed by "mystical, irrational aspirations." Yet, Cassin always envisioned a continuing role for the state, once downgraded from its absolute status.

A Jewish state, midwifed by the international community in the emergency situation after the war, might meet Cassin's criteria on certain conditions. In particular, Cassin's portrayal of two forms of the national state, liberal-emancipatory and communitarian-oppressive, could serve to distinguish between two forms of Zionism, liberal-democratic *versus* national-chauvinist. Of course, as I have argued elsewhere, such distinctions between "good nationalism" and "bad nationalism" are precarious, often incoherent, and subject to a variety of forms of historical, theoretical, and normative critiques.[32] But something like that distinction underlay Cassin's 1930 portrayal of the vicissitudes of the national state and probably continued to subtend his post-1947 stance toward Zionism and the State of Israel.

I now turn directly to the right of movement across borders, particularly as it relates to Palestinians. Oceans of legal ink have been spilled debating the Palestinian right to return, whether to the territory within Israel's 1949 borders or the territories occupied in 1967. I am not going to intervene directly in that general debate here, but will limit myself to the implications of Cassin's evolving framework for this issue.

While Cassin's 1930 lectures were not concerned with a legal right to cross-border movement, a form of this right was incorporated in Article 13(2) of the 1948 Universal Declaration of Human Rights, co-authored by Cassin: "Everyone has the right to leave any country, including his own, and to return to his country." In the 1966 International Covenant on Civil and Political Rights, Article 12(4), this phrase reappears, in slightly more equivocal form: "No one shall be arbitrarily deprived of the right to enter his own country."

As it relates to Palestinians, the issue is the definition of the phrase, "his country." Is the phrase the equivalent of the formal-legal "state of which he is a national," or does its informal, non-legalistic form mandate a more "real-life"

---

[32] *See, e.g.,* Nathaniel Berman, *Nationalism "Good" and "Bad": Vicissitudes of an Obsession,* 90 PROC. AM. SOC. INT'L. L. 214 (1996).

analysis? To put it in "Cassinian" terms: Should the 1930 Cassin's humanistic "domicile," advanced as a substitute for citizenship as the point of connection between law and a person's existential location, be used to interpret the phrase "his country," giving noncitizen domiciliaries a right to return? Recall that the 1930 Cassin declared that domicile links "the individual to a point of the surface of the earth ... even if he absents himself temporarily." Palestinians who fled their homes, for whatever reason, during the 1948 and 1967 wars would incontestably meet Cassin's criteria for domicile.

Does the logic of Cassin's work justify the leap between the private rights entailed by domicile and the public law rights of cross-border movement? Recall that the 1930 Cassin saw the "return to the law of domicile" as marking an "appreciable progress" toward according the individual a firm international legal status, even if a "declaration of the international rights of man" was still a utopian hope. The 1930 Cassin thus made it quite clear that the "law of domicile" was only a first step, realizable under then-current conditions, toward an eventual internationalization of the "rights of man."[33] It would, therefore, be well within the spirit of Cassin's career, as it moved from the 1930 lectures to the Universal Declaration to the Nobel lecture, to transmute the private "law of domicile" to a public law right of a noncitizen domiciliary to return to "his country."

To be sure, ICCPR Article 12(4) does not make this right absolute, but only provides a safeguard against "arbitrary" deprivation. Israel might argue that the refusal to allow the Palestinians to return after the 1948 (or 1967) war was not "arbitrary," but based on security exigencies. From a legal perspective, how-ever, individual rights cannot generally be "non-arbitrarily" deprived collec-tively, but only on the basis of individualized due process.

The link between "domicile" and the "right to return" might even plausibly be read into the "Uppsala Declaration," adopted by a 1972 conference of international lawyers, organized in part by Cassin. Article 12 states that "re-entry of long-term residents who are not nationals, including stateless persons, may be refused only in the most exceptional circumstances." Again, a normal legal interpretation would view "exceptional circumstances" as only determin-able on a case-by-case basis.

However, as Paz recounts, the Uppsala Conference heard an analysis by Paul Weis, a refugee law expert, arguing categorically that the right to return

---

[33] I note that this reading, which has the interwar Cassin dedicated to the internationalization of human rights, departs from that of Samuel Moyn, *René Cassin (1887–1976): Human Rights and Jewish Internationalism*, in MAKERS OF JEWISH MODERNITY: THINKERS, ARTISTS, LEADERS, AND THE WORLD THEY MADE 278 (Jacques Picard, Jacques Revel, Michael P. Steinberg, & Idith Zertal, eds., 2016).

was limited to citizens, specifically excluding Palestinians returning to what became Israel.[34] From the available records, it seems that the only dissenter from this view was Musa Mazzawi, a Palestinian-British scholar, whose views bear partial affinity with the Cassinian spirit outlined above. Mazzawi contended that a "person's 'country' is that to which he is connected by a reasonable combination of such relevant criteria as race, religion, language, ancestry, birth and prolonged domicile."[35] Of course, this statement goes far beyond the link of domicile to include biological and cultural factors disfavored by the 1930 Cassin. Presumably, in the Palestinian context, domicile alone was insufficient in 1972, since it would not cover the *descendants* of the 1948 refugees.[36]

Cassin does not seem to have publicly pronounced on this exchange. Some, including Paz, infer that he stood with Weis from his later statement that the "problem of Arab refugees" needs a "humane solution," making no reference to any legal rights.[37] Such an inference, though rather speculative, is plausible, and troubling.

This plausibility could be interpreted in two ways. If we indulge in speculative psychologizing, we could see it as the collapse of the ideals of a man near the end of his life, shaken by a series of traumatic ruptures that serially destabilized his worldview: World War I, fascism, the Holocaust, and, finally, the post-1967 demise of the Franco-Israeli alliance at the hands of Cassin's old comrade, de Gaulle. This series of shocks may have brought the eighty-five-year-old Cassin to fall back onto "raison d'état," however at odds with the spirit of his entire life's work.

From a broader perspective, the possibility that even a Cassin might abstain from one further reconfiguration of the international legal order can be seen as inscribed in the heterogeneous fabric of that order itself. State sovereignty, the rights of groups and individuals, the authority of international institutions, the uncertain status of those unmoored from sovereign jurisdiction – so much is possible, so much may be dared, but no particular move is compelled.

---

[34] Paul Weis, *The Middle East, in* THE RIGHT TO LEAVE AND TO RETURN, 275, 315–19 (Karl Vasak & Sidney Liskofsky, eds., 1976).

[35] Musa Mazzawi, *Comment on the Middle East, in* THE RIGHT TO LEAVE AND TO RETURN, *Id.* at 343.

[36] I would interpret the 1999 commentary of the U.N. Human Rights Committee on ICCPR Article 12(4) in very similar terms. Noting that the provision "does not distinguish between nationals and aliens," the committee declared that the phrase "his own country" is "not limited to nationality in a formal sense," but rather, includes "an individual who, because of his or her special ties to or claims in relation to a given country, cannot be considered to be a mere alien." General Comment No. 27, CCPR/C/21/Rev.1/Add.9, para. 19 (Nov. 2, 1999).

[37] René Cassin, *For a Right to Leave and a Right to Return,* N.Y. TIMES, Mar. 23, 1973.

And so I conclude with the observation I made at the outset: in the face of the twin phenomena of massive refugee flows and the displacement of sovereign stability, international law is tested. Will it vindicate its highest aspirations or prove its complicity with power? The heterogeneity of legal principles makes both possible; the choice is always in the hands of those who situate themselves in the "transitional moment," at the intersection of law and life, of home and the open road.

PART 6

SHABTAI ROSENNE

11

Shabtai Rosenne

The Transformation of Sefton Rowson

Rotem Giladi

PROLOGUE: A CLASH OF ALLEGIANCE

On Saturday June 29, 1946, the British mandatory government of Palestine placed Jewish towns and villages under curfew, conducting an extensive search for arms and documents. More than 2,700 people were arrested during Operation Agatha – Black Sabbath, in *Yishuv*[1] parlance. Among them were members of the Jewish Agency Executive, including the director of its Political Department, Moshe Sharett (Shertok), Israel's future first foreign minister.[2] His Majesty's government's promise of November 2, 1917 to "view with favour the establishment in Palestine of a National Home for the Jewish people" had, evidently, gone sour.

Back in London, the allegiances of a former Royal Air Force flight lieutenant, now employed by the Jewish Agency's Political Department at 77 Russell Square, were clashing. He developed "anti-British" sentiments;[3] memories of Black Sabbath and the attendant disillusionment would resurface, more than four decades later, in an interview for the UN oral history project.[4] He was born, in London, on November 24th, three weeks after the Balfour Declaration. His son tells how, the year after Black Sabbath, using forged travel orders and leaving behind a wife and two young children, he traveled to Palestine illegally.[5] In the last days of 1947 he arrived in Palestine, keeping his

---

[1] Pre-independence Jewish community in British Mandatory Palestine.
[2] David Ben-Gurion, the future prime minister of Israel, was in Europe.
[3] Interview with Janet Davis, in the United Kingdom (Oct. 25, 2014); I am grateful to Mrs. Davis for her cooperation and her son, Mr. Adam Davis, for conducting the interview on my behalf.
[4] The Labor party "reneged on its own ... electoral campaign [promises and] ... its traditional position": Interview by UN with Shabtai Rosenne, UN Oral History Project, ST/DPI/Oral History (02)/R673, 6 (June 12, 1990).
[5] Interview with Daniel Rosenne, in Jerusalem (July 22, 2014), discussed *infra*.

employ with the Jewish Agency's Political Department. He soon changed his name. Thus ended one chapter in the life of Sefton Wilfred David Rowson. Another, as a "student of international law" – had begun.[6]

THE TWO ENGAGEMENTS OF SEFTON ROWSON

Shabtai Rosenne passed away in 2010. The obituaries, in Hebrew and English, were many. There was also a eulogy, followed by a minute's silence, by the president of the International Court of Justice (ICJ) while the Court was in session.[7] These celebrate the known accomplishments of a renowned international jurist. Rosenne's engagement with international law requires no demonstration.

Rosenne's engagement with Jewish affairs, however, remains entirely unknown, as are early chapters of his life and career. How these two engagements related to one another is, necessarily, entirely unexplored. His career choices present an overlap evident in his service as the first legal adviser of the Ministry of Foreign Affairs (MFA) of the Jewish state (1948–67).[8] This career path, then, appears to attest to a perfect synthesis of his two engagements. In this essay, rather than reproduce or supplement records of achievement and accolade, I argue that appearances are misleading. Rosenne's two engagements – international law and Jewish affairs – undoubtedly coexisted; this was, however, no peaceful cohabitation. Synthesis came late, and was the product of a personal, and ideological, transformation; it came, moreover, with a cost. By and by, I hope to shed some light on less familiar sides of Rosenne's early life and work; here, I acknowledge my indebtedness to Daniel and Jonathan Rosenne for their readiness to share their father's papers, life, and person.[9]

---

[6] Which he entered for "function" in the Peace Palace Library visitor registration card in 1992: Ingrid Kost, *Shabtai Rosenne, London 1917–Jerusalem 2010*, PEACE PALACE LIBRARY, Oct. 8, 2010, www.peacepalacelibrary.nl/2010/10/shabtai-rosenne-london-1917-jerusalem-2010/.

[7] Territorial and Maritime Dispute (Nicaragua v. Colombia), Verbatim Record, President Hisashi Owada (Oct. 11, 2010), www.icj-cij.org/files/case-related/124/124-20101011-ORA-01-00-BI.pdf; Malcolm N. Shaw, *Obituary*, http://legal.un.org/avl/pdf/ls/Rosenne_obituary.pdf; Stephan M. Schwebel, *In Memoriam: Shabtai Rosenne (1917–2010)*, 105 AM. J. INT'L. L. 91 (2011).

[8] Yoram Shachar, *Jefferson Goes East: The American Origins of the Israeli Declaration of Independence*, 10 THEOR. INQUIRIES L. 589, 593 (2009).

[9] All papers cited as Rosenne Papers (RP), kindly supplied by Daniel Rosenne, on file with author.

AN EARLY INTERNATIONAL LAW ENGAGEMENT

Consider, first, Rosenne's early engagement with international law. What must have been his first *legal* works, in the *Law Times* of London in 1940, appears to have been "Prize Law and Aircraft" and "Some Legal Aspects of the Asama Maru Incident,"[10] a naval incident involving *HMS Liverpool* and a Japanese ocean liner. More on naval warfare followed: an early 1945 survey on "British Prize Law 1939–1944" appeared in the *Law Quarterly Review*. In twenty-two pages, S. W. D. Rowson canvased "Enactments," "Reprisals," "Contraband," "Judicial Decisions," and "Procedure." "[N]o other country can boast," the introduction averred, "a clear and comprehensive body of Prize Law" such "as England to-day" could.[11] This survey continued, two years later, in a piece covering British prize practice 1944–46.[12] In between, he published in 1946 three shorter pieces: a "Note on Scottish Prize Law," again in the *Law Quarterly Review*, "Modern Blockade: Some Legal Aspects," and "Italian Prize Law during the Second World War," both in the *British Yearbook of International Law*.[13] Naval warfare occupied him still in 1947, with another long *British Yearbook* essay on "Prize Law during the Second World War."[14]

All these directly concerned the war. None, however, touched on Jewish matters, directly or indirectly. Nor did, for that matter, his 1941 "Domicile of Political Refugees," in the *Law Times*, or a single-page 1944 "Note on the Punishment of War Criminals."[15] The former discussed English law: "an examination of the possibility, according to the principles of English law, of their acquiring a domicile of choice in this or any other country."[16] Jewish refugees were not alluded to in any way. The latter was not concerned with putative post-war trials: it merely reported a 1944 amendment of the *British Manual of Military Law* in respect of "superior orders." If Rowson had a Jewish interest, it seems to have played no role in his early international law leanings. Methods of naval warfare were, simply, not quite a Jewish concern.

---

[10]   LAW TIMES, Apr. 23, 1940; LAW TIMES, June 22, 1940.
[11]   S.W.D. Rowson, *British Prize Law 1939–1945*, 61 LAW QUAR. REV. 59 (1945).
[12]   S.W.D. Rowson, *British Prize Law 1944–1946*, 63 LAW QUAR. REV. 337 (1947).
[13]   S.W.D. Rowson, *Note on Scottish Prize Law*, 62 LAW QUAR. REV. 132 (1946); *Modern Blockade: Some Legal Aspects*, 23 BRIT. Y.B. INT'L. L. 346 (1946); *Italian Prize Law during the Second World War*, 23 BRIT. Y.B. INT'L. L. 282 (1946).
[14]   S.W.D. Rowson, *Prize Law during the Second World War*, 24 BRIT. Y.B. INT'L. L., 160 (1947).
[15]   S.W.D. Rowson, *Domicile of Political Refugees*, LAW TIMES, July 19 and 26, 1941; S.W. D. Rowson, *Note on the Punishment of War Criminals*, 60 LAW QUAR. REV. 225 (1944).
[16]   Rowson, *supra* note 15.

Why study law? And why, specifically, international law? Rosenne left us no answer to these questions; it may be that his headmaster suggested "he might do well in international law."[17] The evidence suggests that what drove his early legal career was *not* Jewish concerns. Compared to the nature of engagement with international law by Jewish practitioners in those Holocaust years, his early writings display, if not detachment from Jewish interest, at least an intention to exclude it from his professional engagement. The Robinson brothers, Nehemiah and Jacob, Raphael Lemkin, Nathan Feinberg (future mentors, collaborators, colleagues, and, at times, rivals), and many others had their attention focused on refugees and genocide, human rights and war crimes, reparation claims and the future of minority protection, world organization, and post-war order – and the place any post-war settlement would hold for the Jewish people.[18] Rowson's international law engagement seems markedly different, more universally British than particularly Jewish.

Only in 1947, Rowson's *legal* writings started edging closer toward Jewish interests. That year appeared a *Modern Law Review* piece titled "Some Private International Law Problems arising Out of European Racial Legislation, 1933–1945."[19] The piece discussed discriminatory legislation against Jews; its function, however, was the assessment of such "foreign law" from an English legal perspective. A similar short note in the 1948 issue of the *Jewish Yearbook of International Law* dealt with "The Abolition of Nazi and Fascist Anti-Jewish Legislation by British Military Administrations of the Second World War." It asked "whether The Hague Convention permits an occupying Power to repeal anti-Jewish legislation in occupied territory."[20] The perspective remained as much British as it was Jewish, more general than particular. Rowson's answer, incidentally, was that it would be "morally and psychologically inconceivable" for the Allies not to somehow affect "repeal of anti-Semitic legislation as a matter of high priority" once in occupation of enemy territory. Still, in law,

---

[17] His sister recalls overhearing this, but was "quite sure Sefton could have worked it out for himself": *supra* note 3; Rosenne's daughter-in-law recalls a similar account: Interview with Zippi Rosenne (Apr. 2015).

[18] Even Hersch Lauterpacht's *International Law and Human Rights* (1950), bereft of any Jewish reference, unmistakably echoed Jewish concerns: Elihu Lauterpacht, The Life of Hersch Lauterpacht (2010); Martti Koskenniemi, The Gentle Civilizer of Nations: The Rise and Fall of International Law 1870–1960 (2002).

[19] S.W.D. Rowson, *Some Private International Law Problems arising Out of European Racial Legislation, 1933–1945*, 10 Mod. L. Rev. 345 (1947).

[20] S. W. D. Rowson, *The Abolition of Nazi and Fascist Anti-Jewish Legislation by British Military Administrations of the Second World War*, 1 Jewish Y.B. Int'l. L. 261 (1948).

[t]here is no doubt that The Hague Convention gives an occupying Power the right to repeal local anti-Jewish laws if their continued enforcement would be detrimental to its own military interests. If not, such a far-reaching step could only be taken on the assumption, which is questionable, that anti-Jewish legislation is contrary to international law in general. However that may be, it seems that from the point of view of the Convention an occupying Power does nothing wrong if it merely refuses to enforce discriminatory legislation to which it objects.[21]

This would be the last piece authored by "S.W.D. Rowson LL.B. (London)." What international law essays followed were written after he immigrated to Palestine – in fact, after Israel's establishment in May 1948. Now, penned by "Rosenne," his writings would reflect – for some time, still indirectly – the preoccupations of the legal adviser to the new state's MFA: a 1949 *British Yearbook* piece addressed "Recognition of States by the United Nations";[22] Israel was admitted to the organization in May that year. 1950 saw, again in the *British Yearbook*, "The Effect of Change of Sovereignty upon Municipal Law";[23] and, again on state succession, "Israël et les traités internationaux de la Palestine."[24] There were, in addition, two short Hebrew essays: "International Law and the Domestic Law of Israel" appeared in the Israeli Bar Association professional journal;[25] a lecture reprint on "Law and Justice in International Relations" was part of a government publication.[26] The 1951 "Israel's Armistice Agreements with the Arab States: A Juridical Interpretation" emerged from his involvement in the negotiations.[27] Even in later years, the place of Israeli affairs in his vast international law production would remain modest.

If the preceding paragraphs give the impression that Rowson's early Jewish awareness was lacking, or that he could be described as a "crypto-Jew" (as Jacob Robinson would describe Joseph Kunz to Rosenne in

---

21 *Id.* at 262.
22 Shabtai Rosenne, *Recognition of States by the United Nations*, 26 BRIT. Y.B. INT'L. L. 437 (1949).
23 Shabtai Rosenne, *The Effect of Change of Sovereignty upon Municipal Law*, 27 BRIT. Y.B. INT'L. L. 267 (1950).
24 Shabtai Rosenne, *Israël et les traités internationaux de la Palestine*, 77 JOURNAL DU DROIT INTERNATIONAL (CLUNET) 1140 (1950).
25 Shabtai Rosenne, *International Law and the Domestic Law of Israel*, 7 HA-PRAKLIT 258 (1950).
26 Shabtai Rosenne, *Law and Justice in International Relations*, THE WORK OF GOVERNMENT MINISTRIES, 17–20 (1950) (Hebrew), RP.
27 Blumstein's Bookstores, Tel Aviv, 1951.

1950),[28] that impression is utterly wrong. He may have, for all we know, elected to play down his identity in professional life emulating, perhaps, the example of Hersch Lauterpacht whom he came to consider his mentor.[29] Yet the evident transformation – from Rowson's *legal* disinterest in Jewish questions to Rosenne's position as legal representative, on the world scene, of the Jewish state – demands tracing and reflection. These require an introduction to the Rowsons – formerly Rosenbaums – and to Sefton's early life.

MEET THE ROWSONS

Harry Rowson (1876–1951), Sefton's father, grew up in an Orthodox Manchester family. His own father fled Czarist Russia to evade conscription, making a living as a workshop laborer.[30] The family was poor; Harry's general education, nonetheless, was supplemented with private Jewish schooling. By his own recollection, he was always "top of my class."[31] His first hero was a local cricketer, one Joe Showman; here was one signpost of Anglicization. His parents, he would recall, "Always ... urged us to be good citizens, and never to do anything which could hurt the race to which we belonged."[32] Harry's coming of age speech promised to repay them "by becoming a worthy citizen of this country and a good Jew."[33]

One of six siblings, he left school at thirteen to help "towards the upkeep of the home,"[34] starting as an errand boy for the Cheetham Rubber Company. Later he became a chess editor for the *Saturday Review* and took a keen interest in a debating club. This led, in turn, to political interest and reading.[35] In the 1906 elections, he volunteered as a canvasser[36] for the Liberal Party candidate for North-West Manchester district, one Winston Churchill. Later in life, comparing chess with politics, he wrote: "Words are nothing and force has become the only deciding factor in International

---

[28]   Letter from Jacob Robinson to Shabtai Rosenne (May 31, 1950), FM-1816/1 ISA.

[29]   *Acceptance Speech by Professor Shabtai Rosenne*, 51 NETH. Y.B. INT'L. L. 475 (2004).

[30]   HARRY ROWSON, 'IDEALS' OF WARDOUR STREET, 1, 5 (unpublished autobiography, n.d., *circa* 1950) RP.

[31]   *Id.* at 4.

[32]   *Id.* at 174.

[33]   *Id.* at 14.

[34]   *Id.*

[35]   *Id.* at 17.

[36]   At the behest of Nathan Laski, father of Harold and Neville: *Id.*, 20.

Politics."[37] Sefton's own interest in politics, and his realism, may well have been home-grown.

So was hard work. In 1906 Harry left for New York. Kindness to a stranger took him to the celluloid trade, selling scrap to patent leather manufacturers.[38] This led to selling blank film to "moving pictures manufacturers";[39] one of the Lumière brothers convinced Harry of "the future of films."[40] He founded the Ideal Film Renting Company: scrap reels bought in the United States as blanks turned out to be rentable to independent cinemas in the United Kingdom. Film distribution expanded to advertisement. The firm expanded and branched out: Rowson became a name in the silent movie industry on both sides of the Atlantic. A 1915 encounter with Red Cross nurses took Ideal into the production business, starting with *Florence Nightingale* (1915). Now a family business, Ideal was part of the silent film industry boom during WWI, while Harry was doing war work for the ministry of information.[41]

By the time the armistice was declared, his idea of making a movie about Lloyd George – "I had been a follower of his all my life" – came to fruition. *The Man Who Saved the Empire: The Life Story of David Lloyd George* met, however, war xenophobia and partisanship. *John Bull* magazine pronounced the "Rosenbaums" German, and, as such, unfit to produce so British a film. Ideal's slander suit was countered with contempt proceedings. "Great pressures" were put on the Rowsons "to prevent this, at any cost, from becoming a Jewish question."[42] Ideal won the legal battle; it lost, however, the campaign. Lloyd George became dissuaded. The government suppressed the film, reimbursing Ideal's production costs.[43] In 1920, the Hudson Bay Company took over Ideal, retaining Harry and his brother as minority directors for some time.

Harry married late. Vera Miriam Davis, whose mother owned several movie theaters in London,[44] was nearly eighteen years his junior. Sefton was born in late 1917, followed by Leonard George, then Janet. A well-to-do "bourgeois" family in North London, the Rowsons supported the Liberal Party, but otherwise seemed unengaged in politics, British or Jewish. Loyal British,

---

[37]   *Id.* at 18.
[38]   *Id.* at 23.
[39]   *Id.* at 24.
[40]   *Id.* at 25.
[41]   *Id.* at 130.
[42]   *Id.* at 141.
[43]   Long considered lost, a complete negative was found in 1994 in an attic. Restored, it was first screened in 1996: *Id.*, 140; DAVID LLOYD GEORGE: THE MOVIE MYSTERY (David Berry & Simon Horrocks, eds., 1998).
[44]   *Jewish Woman Furthers Big British Film Combine*, JTA, Apr. 6, 1927.

consciously Jewish ("observant ... not ... religious")[45] and not quite Zionist perhaps best describes their worldview.[46] They were, however, certainly involved: Vera was active in the Jewish Girls Guides' Association (serving as chairman for two years),[47] catered for HaBonim camps,[48] and, since childhood, was in the Mermaid Swimming Club.[49] Service was another Rowson value.

Of Sefton's early years little is known. Only some of his studiousness or knack for languages showed early: "[Y]our boy," Reverend Loveday, headmaster of the Cranleigh School (later Bishop of Dorchester) in Surrey reported to Vera Rowson, "did one very good paper in Greek, one very fair and one tolerable paper in Latin, and we were favourably impressed by his French." Loveday, however, deemed "his work ... not sufficiently distinguished" to merit "a major scholarship": "his Mathematics were extremely poor, and English undistinguished though not without promise."[50] Attending Cranleigh from 1931 to 1935, Sefton became a house prefect and a lance corporal in the OTC, playing clarinet in the band. He did well enough to obtain a university scholarship.[51]

He read law at the University of London, Kings College, "taking among other subjects the Law of Palestine and private international law,"[52] and earned a bachelor of laws degree on July 27, 1938. A year later, he passed the Law Society's final exam to become a solicitor.[53] He started postgraduate studies, reading "property, private international law, and public international

---

[45] Davis, *supra* note 3. Apart from the Sabbath and the high holidays, the family also celebrated Christmas and, typically, employed a non-Jewish nanny: Shabtai Rosenne Interview by Gabriela Spector-Mersel, School of Social Work, Sapir Academic College, April 2010; I am grateful to Dr. Spector-Mersel for the permission to use this source from her research on "Identity and Experience of Older Men from Israeli 1948's Generation Cared by Foreign Live-in Caregivers"; Anon., ZIONIST Rev., Feb. 15, 1946 ("Although he comes from an assimilated family, he is passionately interested in Jewish life.").

[46] Harry did discuss boxing with Israel Zangwill in the buildup to the Dempsey-Carpentier 1920 New Jersey Heavyweight World Championship fight. Rowson, *supra* note 31, at 185. In 1905, Zangwill broke away from the Zionist movement to advocate Territorialism, the establishment of Jewish homeland in any territory found available.

[47] *Jews in the Forces*, JEWISH CHRONICLE, Apr. 19, 1941; Davis, *supra* note 3.

[48] Founded in 1929 as a non-Zionist Jewish youth movement, later becoming Zionist.

[49] *Jews in the Forces, supra* note 48.

[50] Letter from Rev. Loveday to V. Rowson (July 6, 1931) (RP).

[51] *School Scholarship announcement* [n.d., unknown newspaper], RP; author's correspondence with Martin Williamson, Cranleigh School Archivist, 2015.

[52] Letter from Rowson to L. Bakstansky, Zionist Federation of Great Britain and Ireland (Jan. 12 1945), F13/2/2103, Central Zionist Archive.

[53] *Id.*

law."[54] He could not complete his LLM but was later admitted to a PhD program. His thesis was to discuss prize law.[55]

THE ROWSONS AT WAR

The war – "the most influential event of my life"[56] – scattered, then shattered, the Rowsons. Vera, Sefton's mother, joined the Women's Auxiliary Air Force as early as February 1939. Janet, who was attending "a young ladies' school" in Switzerland at war's outbreak, was called home. She followed her mother in March 1940, "as soon as she was old enough," to serve as a WAAF radar operator. Leonard George joined the Royal Army Service Corps in October 1939, and "was among those who escaped at Dunkirk." "Invalidated out of the army" after the evacuation, he died in 1950. The London bombings damaged the Rowson house.[57] Sefton, who was working as a solicitor, joined the RAF Volunteer Reserve in the summer of 1940; his newlywed wife Esther "was also engaged" in war work.[58] Harry, Sefton's father, now in his sixties, did not enlist. In December 1942, Section Officer Vera Rowson died of "incurable disease."[59] Janet would recall: "The family disintegrated in the outbreak of war ... there was no family at home."[60] Rosenne recalled: "The family altogether dispersed"; it was "the end of the family."[61] The Rowson home was no more.

After some time in Scotland, Sefton was posted in Sierra Leone. Of this time, all that is left are a few Freetown photos in uniform and a letter titled "Yom Kippur on the Equator": "Sargent L. Solomon, serving in West Africa," told how "a young airman, named Sefton Rowson, from Hendon ... thought it would be a good idea to try & have" High Holidays services for Jewish servicemen – and of his success despite "many difficulties."[62] This was no single incident: Rowson took to rectifying

---

54   *Id.*
55   *Id.* A subsequent 220-page draft was titled "The Development of Prize Law during the Second World War, 1939–1948," Tel Aviv, 1949, RP.
56   Spector-Mersel, *supra* note 46.
57   *Id.*
58   *Jews in the Forces, supra* note 48; Sefton married Esther Schultz, whom he met at *HaBonim,* on Nov. 17, 1940.
59   *Proud Record of the Rowsons,* EVENING STANDARD [n.d.]; *[Deaths] On Active Service,* JEWISH CHRONICLE, Dec. 11, 1942, at 3, 9.
60   Davis, *supra* note 3.
61   Spector-Mersel, *supra* note 46. He first lived with his future in-laws.
62   "Yom Kippur from Hell," [m.s.], RP; 2(7) THE TORCH, November-December 1941; *From Iceland to Abyssinia, Jewish Soldiers Hold Their Own Services,* JEWISH CHRONICLE, Dec. 26, 1941.

"the wholesale ignorance concerning the Jews" among his "non-Jewish comrades" and satisfying their "anxiety to learn."[63]

After a spell back in England, Sefton was transferred to Egypt. Reportedly, he was tasked with providing RAF servicemen stationed all along the Suez Canal with legal advice on their civil affairs.[64] There was opportunity, to be proven useful later, to acquire intimate knowledge of the local geography[65] and take Arabic classes at the Cairo University.[66] Geography also made it possible to visit Palestine: in 1944, Rowson sent his firstborn son a photo of himself from "Jerusalem, the Holy City." To the readers of the *Zionist Review*, he later sent more elaborate impressions. "What Is It Like in Eretz Israel," by "Shabtai Rowson, who just returned from Palestine," exposed his dilemmas – but also foretold a turning point.[67]

JEWISH ENGAGEMENT – AND ZIONISM

International law, clearly, was not Sefton's only preoccupation. Of the Rowson children, Sefton had the greatest "leaning towards Judaism." He had "developed his religious interest quite early, several years before the war" and "was remarkably more observant than the rest of the family," taking his father away from the family high holidays shul to an orthodox synagogue. The Rowsons were "not particularly Zionist";[68] Sefton, however, became discontent with moderate assimilation. Jewish identity mattered; *how*, precisely, was a question that preoccupied him for nearly two decades.

His search must have started at school in the early 1930s. Cranleigh expected its students to adhere to the Church of England worship and "made no special allowances for services ... for other religions." If Rowson protested, the only remaining telltale was the index card entry inscribed by Headmaster Loveday: Sefton, he wrote, was a "very conscientious Jew ... I rather liked him but he was tiresomely controversial."[69]

---

[63] Shabtai Rowson, *Some Impressions of Service Life*, ZIONIST REV., July 9, 1943.
[64] Daniel Rosenne Interview, July 22, 2014; Spector-Mersel, *supra* note 46.
[65] UN Interview, 74 ("I knew quite a bit about the Suez Canal ... So did Eban ... I'm not sure that we didn't know it better than some of the Egyptians ... "; discussing his first UNSC appearance during the Suez crisis).
[66] Alan Stephens Interview, Apr. 6, 2015.
[67] Shabtai Rowson, *What Is It Like in Eretz Israel*, ZIONIST REV., Mar. 1, 1946.
[68] Davis, *supra* note 3.
[69] Williamson correspondence, *supra* note 52.

By his own testimony, Sefton became Zionist at the age of sixteen, in 1933.[70] How precisely is unclear: his sister, chuckling, says he "probably went looking for it."[71] What is clear, however, is the extent of his Zionist engagement. In 1936, after graduation, Sefton joined the editorial board of the *Young Zionist*, of the Federation of Zionist Youth (FZY); in 1937 he became its editor, a role he held until 1939. He chaired the FZY Hebrew Department, was an FZY honorary secretary, and served as secretary of the Hebrew Youth League.[72] As a student, he volunteered at the London offices of the Jewish Agency for Palestine. He regularly contributed to London Jewish and Zionist press – writing essays, commenting on new books, surveying Jewish politics and culture and, quite often, courting controversy.[73] Defending Zionism against its diverse detractors, Jews and Gentiles, was one common thread.[74]

Jewish nationalism, however, presented its own dilemmas and demanded choices. His Zionism was itself a journey. The early Zionism of "Shabtai Rowson" – this is how he often appeared in this sphere – was broad, inclusive, "all-embracing":[75] it could, at first, contain his dual identity and reconcile his allegiances. He took to Zionism studiously: in a 1943 speech, he confided to his Hendon audience that during the past decade, he had "made quite a deep study of its theories and philosophies."[76] This produced numerous publications in various Jewish and Zionist journals. Their gist, early on, was that one could be both British[77] and Zionist. Subscribing to Zionism, in other words, could

---

70 [Shabtai Rowson,] *Youth and Reconstruction: Speech delivered at Hendon Young Zionist Society* (Oct. 18, 1943), 2, RP; in 1935, he took to learning Hebrew: Yaacov Morris, *Britons in Israel: Shabtai Rosenne*, JEWISH VANGUARD, Sept., 11, 1953.

71 Davis, *supra* note 3.

72 *Jews in the Forces*, *supra* note 48. For Jewish and Zionist activities, see JEWISH CHRONICLE, June 3, 1938; Nov. 4, 1938; Nov. 11, 1938; Dec. 16, 1938; June 9, 1939.

73 Shabtai Rowson, *The Jews of Soviet Russia: Some Facts and Figures*, THE NEW JUDÆA 120–121 (1942); Shabtai Rowson, *The Jewish Revolution 1789–1896*, THE NEW JUDÆA 153–154 (1943). For controversy, *see* S.W. Rowson, *My Patience Is Exhausted*, JEWISH CHRONICLE, Jan. 19, 1945.

74 Shabtai Rowson, *The Only Way*, letter to the JEWISH CHRONICLE, Jan. 7, 1944, where he protested the "defamatory" treatment of Zionism in Joseph Stalin's *Marxism and the National and Colonial Question*; or his lambasting the American Jewish Committee: Shabtai Rowson, *Isolationist Move*, ZIONIST REV., Dec. 5, 1943.

75 Shabtai Rowson, *Zionism in the Period of Herzl* (Speaker's Notes No. 5, Zionist Federation of Great Britain & Ireland, London, 1944), at 4.

76 Rowson, *supra* note 71, at 2. *See, e.g.*, Shabtai Rowson, *An Early Zionist Document*, [m.s.], Aug. 8, 1943, RP.

77 Specifically British: Note Rowson's account of Herzl's attitude to Great Britain–and of Lloyd George. Rowson, *supra* note 75, at 8.

easily coexist with life in the Diaspora.[78] Jewish nationalism, while oriented at Palestine, could equally be directed at fostering national consciousness and developing a national life at home.

Britain's mandatory entanglement in Palestine and its impact on British Jewish politics, in which Rowson became embroiled while posted in England in the later years of the war, started undermining his faith. The Anglo-Jewish Association resolved to submit a separate Palestine memorandum, decried as anti-Zionist, first to the British government, then to the Anglo-American Committee of Inquiry. He loudly opposed this, resigned from the AJA council in protest, and campaigned to discredit the association.[79] As his allegiances became more conflicted, he turned to the works of Simon Dubnow in search of a national role and justification for the Diaspora. And yet, as the fate of the Diaspora in Europe under Nazi rule was revealed, his own dual allegiance was becoming less and less tenable. He came to disavow, more and more, Dubnow's diasporic Jewish nationalism.

DIASPORA NATIONALISM: APPEAL AND DISENCHANTMENT

Simon Dubnow's (1860–1941)[80] answer to the "Jewish Question," rooted in his historical philosophy, was a response to Herzlian Zionism. Dubnow identified "spiritual-cultural determinants" of Jewish existence as indicia of a model of nationalism more advanced than that associated with its territorial expressions.[81] At the turn of the century,[82] Dubnow proceeded to advocate "Diaspora Nationalism." This model of Jewish nationalism rejected both individual assimilation in local culture or political structures and collective

---

[78]   Rowson, *supra* note 70; Rowson, *Early Document, supra* note 76; Shabtai Rowson, *Book Review: Justice for My People, by Ernst Frankenstein*, YOUNG ZIONIST MAGAZINE, July 1943, [m.s.] RP.

[79]   JEWISH CHRONICLE, Jan. 28, 1944; Dec. 15, 1944; Dec. 22, 1944; Jan. 19, 1945. S.W.D. Rowson, *Memorandum on the Anti-Zionist Stance of the Anglo-Jewish Association*, [n.d.], F13/77, CZA; STEPHAN WENDEHORST, BRITISH JEWRY, ZIONISM, AND THE JEWISH STATE, 1936–1956 (2012).

[80]   SOPHIE DUBNOV-ERLICH, THE LIFE AND WORK OF S. M. DUBNOV: DIASPORA NATIONALISM AND JEWISH HISTORY (1991).

[81]   OSCAR JANOWSKY, THE JEWS AND MINORITY RIGHTS, 1898–1919 58–59 (1933). SIMON DUBNOW, NATIONALISM AND HISTORY: ESSAYS ON OLD AND NEW JUDAISM 80 (Koppel Pinson, ed., 1961). This work began in 1897, the year of the first Zionist Congress, and was largely Dubnow's reaction to Zionism, assimilation, and alternative solutions for the Jewish problem: Koppel Pinson, *Simon Dubnow: Historian and Political Philosopher, id.* at 1–69.

[82]   Marcos Silber, *S. Dubnow, the Idea of Diaspora Nationalism and its Dissemination*, 15 IYUNIM BITKUMAT ISRAEL: STUDIES IN ZIONISM, THE YISHUV AND THE STATE OF ISRAEL 83 (2005) (Hebrew).

return to territorial-political nationalism.[83] Rather, it sought to secure the maintenance of collective Jewish autonomous existence in the Diaspora.[84]

Autonomism, per Dubnow, "recognize[s] Jewry, not only as a nation of the past or of the future, but also as a nation that is, of the present." "Work of the present" – *gegenwartsarbeit* – became Autonomism's writ.[85] This was one source of its appeal: it offered an immediate, if ongoing, political program for Jewish elites and a national solution for the Jewish masses in Central and Eastern Europe – unlike the distant, uncertain utopia of Herzl.[86] In the first decade of the twentieth century, after the failure of political Zionism to obtain "a home for the Jewish people in Palestine secured under public law,"[87] Dubnow's Autonomism had gained enough popularity to be adopted, ideologically or instrumentally, by nearly all Jewish national parties in Eastern Europe.[88] Even the Zionist movement, despite its negation of the Diaspora and emphasis on territorial national revival, was forced to come to terms with Autonomism's call for "national rights" – either as an ideological synthesis[89] or, especially after Herzl's death, as an interim *bildung* instrument.[90]

Programmatically, Autonomism called for "striving for national rights or cultural autonomy in the Diaspora."[91] "[I]n the Diaspora," Dubnow wrote, "we must strive, within the realm of the possible, to demand and to attain national-cultural autonomy for the majority of the nation."[92] This "became the basis for the practical program of Jewish national minority rights in the

---

[83]   Pinson, *supra* note 81, at 40.

[84]   JEWS AND DIASPORA NATIONALISM: WRITINGS ON JEWISH PEOPLEHOOD IN EUROPE AND THE UNITED STATES (Simon Rabinovitch, ed., 2012).

[85]   Hence the competing prescriptions: Zionism was concerned with "work of the future"; Autonomism, with "work of the present" or *Gegenwartsarbeit*. *See* M. Mintz, *Work for the Land of Israel and "Work in the Present": A Concept of Unity, A Reality of Contradiction*, 161-70 in ESSENTIAL PAPERS ON ZIONISM (Jehuda Reinharz & Anita Shapira, eds., 1996).

[86]   *Supra* note 82; James Loeffler, *Between Zionism and Liberalism: Oscar Janowsky and Diaspora Nationalism in America*, 34 AJS REV. 289 (2010).

[87]   This was the "Basle Program" adopted by the 1897 First Zionist Congress.

[88]   Silber, *supra* note 82, at 95–96.

[89]   Dimitry Shumsky, *Zionism in Quotations Marks, or To What Extent Was Dubnow a Non-Zionist*, 77 ZION 369 (2012) (Hebrew); ISRAEL BARTAL, COSSACK AND BEDOUIN: LAND AND PEOPLE IN JEWISH NATIONALISM (2007); and, with regard to Robinson, JAMES LOEFFLER, *"The Famous Trinity of 1917": Zionist Internationalism in Historical Perspective*, 15 SIMON DUBNOW INST. Y.B. 211 (2016).

[90]   GIDEON SHIMONI, THE ZIONIST IDEOLOGY 114–15, 169 (1995); DAVID VITAL, ZIONISM: THE FORMATIVE YEARS 467–75 (1982); MINTZ, *supra* note 86; JONATHAN FRANKEL, PROPHECY AND POLITICS: SOCIALISM, NATIONALISM, AND THE RUSSIAN JEWS 1862–1917 (1981).

[91]   DUBNOW, *supra* note 81, at 186.

[92]   *Id.*

succession states after World War."[93] Dubnow's ideas underscored Jewish minority politics, legal advocacy, and diplomacy. They drove internal as well as international[94] praxis: Autonomism underscored the Jewish involvement in the 1919 Versailles Conference, at which minority protection provisions were imposed on the succession states of the Habsburg and Ottoman empires.[95] With that, Diaspora Nationalism became "guaranteed by common public law."[96] "[N]ational minority rights," Dubnow wrote in 1929, "have been guaranteed by national and international law."[97] His answer to the Jewish Question could be, and indeed was, furnished by international law.

Dubnow's answer to the Jewish Question did not necessarily entail hostility to territorial Jewish nationalism in Palestine (i.e., Zionism); it certainly could be, and sometimes was, so interpreted. At first, he treated Zionism as modern messianism;[98] later he mitigated his critique. Even when sympathetic, he emphasized that Zionism was no solution for the Jewish masses.[99] Yet, at the core, Dubnowism and "political Zionism represented mutually opposing doctrines."[100] Zionism insisted on negating the Diaspora; Dubnow sought to reaffirm it. Zionism emphasized territory; Dubnow largely dismissed it. And both ideas competed for followers, resources, voice – and the sanction

---

[93] Pinson, *supra* note 81, at 49.

[94] Verena Dohrn, *State and Minorities: The First Lithuanian Republic and S.M. Dubnow's Concept of Cultural Autonomy, in* The Vanished World of Lithuanian Jews, 155–73, 157 (A. Nikžentaitis, S. Schreiner, & D. Staliūnas, eds., 2004) (Dubnow "anticipated an international solution of the Jewish minority problem in Eastern Europe").

[95] Dubnow, *supra* note 81, at 371, note 31 (note by Pinson) ("the theories of Dubnow had a great deal to do with shaping the thought of the Jewish leaders" at Versailles); Janowsky, *supra* note 81, at 264; Carole Fink, Defending the Rights of Others: The Great Powers, the Jews, and International Minority Protection, 1878–1938 (2004) 193–235; Mark Levene, War, Jews, and the New Europe: The Diplomacy of Lucien Wolf, 1914–1919 (1992); Mark Levene, *Nationalism and its Alternatives in the International Arena: The Jewish Question at Paris, 1919*, 28 J. Cont. Hist. 511 (1993); "Committee of the Jewish Delegations at the Paris Peace Conference, Memorandum of 10 May 1919," discussed by Stanislaw Sierpowski, *Minorities in the System of the League of Nations, in* Ethnic Groups in International Relations, 13–37 (P. Smith, ed., 1991); Rabinovitch, *supra* note 84, at 156.

[96] Dubnow, *supra* note 81, at 179.

[97] *Id.* note of 1929; "We succeeded," he wrote, "in winning such liberty after World War I, but only in a juridic sense, in the treaties of the League of Nations with the east-European states": Pinson, *supra* note 81, at 69; Dubnow, *supra* note 81, at 357.

[98] *Id.* at 157 ("Political Zionism is merely a renewed form of messianism ... In it the ecstasy bound up in the great idea of rebirth blurs the lines between reality and fantasy").

[99] Pinson, *supra* note 81, at 53–57; Josef Fraenkel, *Simon Dubnow and the History of Political Zionism, in* Simon Dubnow: The Man and His Work 140–61 (Aaron Steinberg, ed., 1963).

[100] Fraenkel, Id., at *supra* note 99, at 141. *Cf.* Shumsky, *supra* note 89.

of "public law." Circumstances forced, for a brief while, a compromise. *Gegenwartsarbeit* in the Diaspora and "work of the future," directed at building a Jewish National Home in Palestine, could cohabit the Zionist agenda, if only for a while.[101]

Rowson, born and raised in liberal Western Europe, had little need for or interest in minority protection.[102] The writs of Autonomism, however, presented a program that could furnish justifications for Zionist life in the Diaspora. By his time, he knew well, Autonomism's program was widely practiced by "Palestine Zionism."[103] He nonetheless took care to note, and advocate, a synthesis. In a piece published in 1944 (but probably written earlier), he observed that by the end of the nineteenth century, "the conflict between" Palestine nationalists and Diaspora nationalists

> was bitter, owing to the prevalent Zionist theory of the "Negation of the Diaspora," i.e., that there is no possibility for Jewish revival in the Diaspora, and its vehement denial by men like Dubnow and Zhitlovsky, etc. But, as we shall see in the course of this note, the gulf between them has so narrowed that since the last war the chief spokesmen of the two movements (though not necessarily the theorists) have been one and the same (Weizmann, Sokolow, Motzkin, Judge Mack, etc.).[104]

Having described the history of the gulf, he prescribed synthesis: "Zionism would only colonize Palestine, and at the same time it would support Jewish nationalism in the Diaspora so long as the first and main aim was not prejudiced."[105]

Earlier, in January 1943, he wrote an eighteen-page synopsis of Dubnow's *Letters on Ancient and Modern Judaism.* He tried to describe "Dubnow's general theory of nationalism ... his theories of the nature and functions of Jewish nationalism, and finally his attitude towards Zionism."[106] His aim was to demonstrate the persisting relevance of Dubnow's theories. Evidently, he planned a book; an incomplete manuscript, or parts thereof, survived. Shorter

---

[101]   Mintz, *supra* note 85.
[102]   Consider Shabtai Rowson, *Were the Minorities Treaties a Failure?*, ZIONIST REV, Oct. 20, 1944, reviewing JACOB ROBINSON, OSCAR KARBACH, MAX M. LASERSON, NEHEMIAH ROBINSON, & MARC VISHNIAK, WERE THE MINORITIES TREATIES A FAILURE? (1943).
[103]   Rowson, *supra* note 75, at 3.
[104]   *Id.*
[105]   *Id.* at 12.
[106]   S.W.D. Rowson, *Simon Dubnow–Letters on Ancient and Modern Judaism, A Synopsis,* 2, RP; Shabtai Rowson, *Jewish Nationalism: Simon Dubnow's Theory,* THE NEW JUDÆA, June–July 1944, 152–54.

pieces remain in manuscript form; others were published in the London-based Zionist literature.

For Rowson, at first, Autonomism was a source of current relevance and inspiration. Late in 1943, he moved that "today Dubnow's theories can offer valuable light in facing the problems of Jewish reconstruction after this war."[107] The Diaspora was still a site of national life; it still could play a part in national revival. An August 1944 short essay on Dubnow's theory professed adherence to Dubnow's "dream of the political renaissance of ten million Jews of the Diaspora!"[108] He remained, however, conflicted; his search for synthesis persisted. In an October 1943 speech, he maintained that "the only secure future for the Jewish people is to be found in a Jewish Palestine, where a Jewish National Home is to be established in accordance with international law."[109] He envisioned a liberal, tolerant, and egalitarian "Jewish community in Palestine" and professed his own "fervent" nationalism while warning, just like Dubnow, against "flag waving jingoism" of "degenerating" nationalism. For him, he argued, nationalism was "primarily a cultural matter."[110] He continued to preach a strong Diaspora for some time.

Yet his emphasis was shifting; soon, he abandoned the search for synthesis. This transformation was fuelled by the realization of the Jewish Diaspora's fate under the Nazis, the clash of his Jewish and British loyalties, and his own radicalization during the AJA affair. He had to reconsider the proposition that Jewish *national* life could take place in the Diaspora. His own disenchantment with Diaspora Nationalism was evident. In what was to become the epilogue of his work on Dubnow (titled "Jewish Nationalism Today") he came to admit that Dubnow's observations on the Jewish condition in Europe and his "diagnosis of the sickness from which the Jewish national idea is suffering were essentially correct."[111] Nonetheless, the "cure he prescribed, namely autonomy in the Diaspora, cannot be said to have met with success ... his own tragic death at the hands of the Nazis is symbolic of the weakness of the Diaspora."[112] "The Diaspora still exists," Rowson acknowledged, "but it is a dying force."[113] It became a liability, and could no longer "be included as

[107]   Shabtai Rowson, *Simon Dubnow's Theory of Nationalism*, London, December 1943, 1, RP.
[108]   Shabtai Rowson, *Dubnow's Theory of Jewish Nationalism: Practical Problems*, THE NEW JUDÆA, August 1944, 172–74 . This was based on earlier manuscripts: Shabtai Rowson, *Simon Dubnow on Jewish Nationalism*, London, December 1943; and *Simon Dubnow's Views on Zionism and His Controversy with Ahad Ha-Am*, London, January 1944, RP.
[109]   Rowson, *supra* note 70, at 2.
[110]   *Id.*
[111]   S. W. D. Rowson, *Epilogue: Jewish Nationalism Today*, London 1944, 95/238, RP.
[112]   *Id.* at 95/238.
[113]   *Id.* at 108/251.

an asset on the national balance sheet." Still, he found it hard to write the Diaspora off entirely. If "the old controversy concerning the possibility of Jewish national survival in the Diaspora is now largely superfluous" – rendering his own book project superfluous – he still searched for some role for the Diaspora to play. His persisting dilemmas and lingering contradictions could no longer be reconciled through reflection:

> The duty of Jewish nationalists is to concentrate all Jewish endeavours on the rebuilding of Eretz Israel, reconstructing as strong a Diaspora as is possible, strong physically, strong economically and strong culturally on the basis of true national Judaism. Only in this way can Jewry be fully integrated in the human family and Jewish life lose its bitter misery.[114]

Rowson's way out of the dilemma was to relegate a reconstructed Diaspora to a subordinate role. It no longer had a value of its own: it became an instrument. The Diaspora would only be "an essential hinterland for the Yishuv," a "reservoir ... [for its] reinforcements."[115] The Diaspora had to be rebuilt, but "Jewish nationalism can only be centred in Palestine and not in the Diaspora." Objective conditions made it impossible to pursue national life in the Diaspora. Accordingly, for Rowson, minority protection was no writ for Jewish *national* life; in fact, it was "capable of prevent[ing] national revival."[116] The minority treaties, he concluded, were a bar to Jewish nationalism: they were a demonstration of the unequal, inferior status of the Jewish nation.[117] In 1945, Rowson presided over a London meeting where Sir Leon Simon pronounced Diaspora Nationalism a "contradiction in terms."[118]

Disenchantment with Diaspora Nationalism carried with it a seed of disillusionment with international law, insofar, at least, as it purported to furnish answers to the Jewish Question. The limits of minority protection, secured by international law, revealed the limits of international law itself. With these conclusions, Rowson was ready to abandon intellectual reflection in favor of action; his negation of the Diaspora would now be expressed through praxis, not scholarship.

---

[114] *Id.* at 108/251.
[115] *Id.* at 99/242. The secondary role of the Diaspora would continue to shape Rosenne's attitude to international law impinging on Jewish affairs in his diplomatic career: Shabtai Rosenne, *Basic Elements of Israel's Foreign Policy*, XVII INDIA QUAR., 328 (1961), and *infra*.
[116] Rowson, *supra* note 111, at 100/243.
[117] *Id.* at 100/243; he also had doubts as to the power of law to improve the position of "European," non-Jewish minorities after the war: *supra* note 102.
[118] *Fallacy of Diaspora Nationalism*, JEWISH CHRONICLE, Mar. 16, 1945.

PRACTICING POST-WAR ZIONISM

"I was demobilized from the Royal Air Force – I remember the date very well – on the first of April 1946. On which date I went into the Political Department of the London office of the Jewish Agency for Palestine."[119] The war "just made him more sure of his Zionism"; disillusionment with the British government's anti-immigration policies in Palestine made him "quite anti-British."[120] "I saw no future in England ... the Empire was gone," he recalled in later years.[121] Rowson no longer had "any violent feeling either way" about "domestic politics."[122] A month earlier, he had published his impressions of "What Is It Like in Eretz Israel?" At that point, he already knew he wanted to "end up at home – at Eretz Israel."[123]

"I visited Palestine on many occasions," he reported, "my stays lasting from a day to over a fortnight." While "life in Eretz Israel should not be compared with life in England," it could be contrasted with European life in the Middle East: "[T]he Europeans in the Middle East have an economy based on the master-race principle: they are the masters and the Arabs are their servants. None of this exists in Palestine." "Our Jews," he reported, "are very hard working"; "[f]ood is good and plentiful, though somewhat expensive"; everywhere there is, however, an "unexpressed 'national purpose.'" He took care to note "some undesirable features of life in Palestine": "[t]here are queues" and "conductors are ill-mannered"; "officials show scant respect for the public, whom they regard as a nuisance." He was "a little disappointed that with all the abundance of wines and liqueurs the *Yishuv* does not yet seem to have developed a habit of delicate wine-bibbing. Despite cheap drink, drunkenness is almost unknown." But society was democratic, and "[a]ll are equal because all are Jews ... The average standard of culture and common decency is high ... Life in Palestine," he concluded, was no "bed of roses," and not "everything which the Yishuv produces [or] every new idea which comes from it is above reproach or criticism." All that, however, mattered little. In the last paragraph, Rowson switched to the first person, plural:

---

[119] *Supra* note 4, at 1.
[120] Davis, *supra* note 3; Shabtai Rowson, *The First Passover of Peace*, ZIONIST REV., Apr. 19, 1946, comparing Bevin to Pharaoh. Elsewhere, he anonymously wrote of "a wicked policy ... universally detested", Anon., *New Delhi-New Jerusalem?*, ZIONIST REV., Aug. 22, 1947, RP; Rosenne, *supra* note 116, at 332.
[121] Spector-Mersel, *supra* note 45.
[122] Letter from Rowson to L. Bakstansky, Zionist Federation of Great Britain and Ireland (Jan. 12, 1945), F13/2/2103, CZA; he did consider applying for Foreign or Colonial Office jobs, but wanted "to devote myself to Jewry."
[123] *Id.*

"Our lives are normal"

We have our own peculiar customs and can observe them without restraint. Not only do we not work on the Sabbath, a prized right of all Jews everywhere, but we also work on Sunday as a normal working day, and the 'Monday morning feeling' makes its appearance with sundown on Saturday night. A Jew cannot know what freedom really is for himself and his people until he has been in Palestine. Our lives are normal. We are not on the defensive. We do not have to think all the time 'What will the Gentiles say?' The children are brought up in natural surroundings, free from artificial inhibitions and prohibitions. This is worth far more than the physical disadvantages, which anyhow are not so many, of living in Eretz Israel.[124]

Asked, many years later, whether the Zionist negation of the Diaspora marked a difference between him and Jewish soldiers of Palestine, his answer was emphatically negative: "We have turned our backs to Europe."[125]

Working for the Jewish Agency, Rowson practiced his revised faith. As a junior, it fell on him to take notes during the 1947 Palestine Conference convened by the British government: "One has to start somewhere."[126] He often spoke before Jewish audiences,[127] drafted questions in Parliament,[128] dealt in legal matters, made connections, and wrote on all matters Jewish. In August 1947, he represented the Jewish Agency in its intervention in the *Exodus 1947 habeas corpus* proceedings in the Court of Appeal.[129] His work, evidently, was appreciated.[130] Much of his early international law scholarship was published during this period; little of it, recall, touched on Jewish affairs. His greatest engagement in this period, however, involved begging all who would listen to be allowed to be transferred to Palestine. He was eager to live what he preached.

An extensive campaign ensued. The surviving correspondence attests to a growing desperation.[131] In January 1947, his effort seemed to bear fruit. The Jewish Agency decided to transfer him to Jerusalem: "I later received ... a cable that Mr. Ben-Gurion would desire me to come as soon as possible."

[124] Rowson, *supra* note 67, at 4.
[125] Spector-Mersel, *supra* note 45.
[126] Rosenne, *supra* note 4, at 7.
[127] In August 1947, for example, Mr. Sefton Rowson of the Political Department of the Jewish Agency gave "a Political Survey" to the Theodor Herzl Society: *AJR Information*, 2 ASSOCIATION OF JEWISH REFUGEES IN GREAT BRITAIN, August 1947, 63.
[128] Spector-Mersel, *supra* note 45.
[129] Morris, *Britons*; *R. v. Secretary of State for Foreign Affairs and Secretary of State for the Colonies, ex parte Greenberg*, 2 ALL E.R. 550 (Aug. 29, 1947).
[130] Letter from Eytan to Rowson (Aug. 8, 1946), S25/1189, CZA.
[131] Letter from Rowson to Shertok (Apr. 25, 1946); Letter from Rowson to Reuven [Zaslani] (Nov. 19, 1946), S25/1189, CZA, and other correspondence in this file.

In March, however, Shertok directed him to "postpone departure until further instructions." He pestered the Jewish Agency Executive in London, and others, to no avail. In early June, he raised "once again ... the question of my transfer to Jerusalem" with Shertok.[132] Some "assurances" came in late July, but it was decided he would stay in London until the end of the year.[133] At last, an early October 1947 cable informed him that "immigration certificates [to] you and family [are] granted."[134] These were permanent – and licit. After disentangling logistical complications, the Rowsons arrived in strife-ridden Palestine, via Geneva, on December 30, 1947.

Did Rowson immigrate to Palestine, alone, illegally, before? This is his son's recollection. He points to an air ministry letter, from October 1947, approving Rowson's application to travel to Palestine.[135] The letter, he reports, was forged; Rosenne ever remained "not proud" of the subterfuge. Rowson's Jewish Agency files do not mention any of this – but, then again, would they? A letter dated January 13, 1947, from the Jewish Agency's London office, only adds to the mystery. It was addressed to Rowson, using the Political Department's post office box in Jerusalem; the author expressed the hope that "you have settled down by now."[136] Whatever the answer to this riddle, the outcome was transition.

TRANSITION IN PALESTINE

"I arrived in Jerusalem in December [1947]" to work in the Jerusalem office of the Jewish Agency, and was "immediately put to work in the newly formed legal section of the Political Department,"[137] predecessor to Israel's MFA. His employment as a lawyer was not, however, a foregone conclusion. Elihu Sasson, director of the Jewish Agency's Arab Department and, clandestinely, an intelligence chief, sought to have Rowson, who spoke Arabic, posted in the department's "research" section, with a view to a career in this field.[138] Rowson was not averse;[139] Dov Joseph, the Jewish Agency's newly appointed legal

---

[132] Letter from Rowson to Shertok (June 6, 1947), S25/1189, CZA.
[133] Letter from Rowson to Sharif (Aug. 1, 1947), S25/1189, CZA.
[134] Letter from Scharf to Rowson (Oct. 3, 1947), S25/1189 CZA.
[135] Letter from Air Ministry, London [signature illegible] to Flight Lt. S.W.D. Rowson LL.B. (Oct. 14, 1947) RP ("With reference to your letter of 10th Oct, 1947, I am directed to convey approval of your application to leave the United Kingdom and proceed to Palestine").
[136] Letter from Michael to Rowson (Jan. 13, 1947), S25/1189, CZA.
[137] Rosenne, *supra* note 4, at 13–14.
[138] Letter from Berman to Scharf (Dec. 19, 1947); Letter from Rowson to Berman (Nov. 24, 1947), S25/1189, CZA.
[139] Letter from Rowson to Sharif (Aug. 1, 1947), S25/1189, CZA.

adviser, insisted however that "he remain in the law."[140] Soon after arrival, he reported to Lauterpacht of "legal work here, mostly in connection with the legal problems which arise from the creation of the Jewish State."[141] He became involved in the work of the legal secretariat of the Preparatory Commission tasked "to prepare for the independence of the Jewish state."[142] This involved work on "transitional documents," in secrecy, including early drafts of Israel's declaration of independence.[143] He rendered day-to-day legal advice, improvised a manual on the laws of war, helped the planning for the establishment of the foreign office, and helped set up its law library. Although cut off, in besieged Jerusalem, from the center of political activity in Tel Aviv, his work must have attracted enough attention: in June 1948, he was "asked by Moshe Sharett" to become the foreign ministry's legal adviser. Having adopted "Rosenne," shortly afterward, his transformation was complete.

TERMS OF ENGAGEMENT

The two engagements of Shabtai Rosenne – Jewish nationalism and international law – ran separate courses; they rarely met. The one did not drive the other; if anything, each existed *despite* the other. In the Jewish sphere, Rowson was suspicious of internationalism: he confessed ambivalence toward it. "Internationalism" was "a red herring to distract the mind from the real issues." Being citizens of the world "must not become an excuse for our failing in our duty to our own kind and kin." Even if internationalism was "the ultimate ideal," for the Jewish people it was a luxury they could not afford: "Those nations which are not yet firmly established" would be mistaken "to think that they can cut out one step in their natural evolution."[144] His involvement in this sphere rarely touched on or, even more rarely, invoked international law. Conversely, the international law sphere had, for Rowson, little place for Jewish questions.

A rare convergence occurred in 1947. The forthcoming Palestine Special Session of the UN General Assembly occasioned a revealing three-page essay, in Hebrew, on "International Law and the Jewish People." This came a few

---

[140] Interview by Elliot Tucker with Esther and Shabtai Rosenne (January 2010).

[141] Letter from Rowson to Lauterpacht (Jan. 28, 1948), S25/1189, CZA.

[142] Rosenne, *supra* note 4, at 18–19; Yehudit Karp, *The Legal Council: The Story of Early Legislation, in* IN MEMORIAM: URI YADIN 209 (Aharon Barak & Tana Spanic, eds., vol. II, Bursi, 1990). He was one of the secretaries to several subcommittees.

[143] Rosenne, *supra* note 4, at 18–19 (which "curiously enough . . . does not have an anti-British passage . . . like the US Declaration"); Shachar, *supra* note 8.

[144] Rowson, *supra* note 70, at 4.

months before Rowson would complete his transformation by immigrating to Palestine; at that time, the tension between his two engagements was, in all probability, at its highest. Introducing international law to laymen, Rowson noted the special meaning assigned to the term "nation": "only legal-formal recognition can elevate a people to a nation possessing rights and obligations based on international law." Thus, "in Palestine, neither the Jews nor the Arabs constitute 'nations' from a legal viewpoint," and the Jews' relations with the Arabs "or even with the English are not regulated by international law." Not possessing a state, the Jewish people did not constitute, legally speaking, a "nation"; and in the absence of "nationhood," the Jewish people could not possess their own state.[145] Subjecthood was a vicious circle.

This was followed by a standard realist critique of international law: it exists, but its validity is only recognized and sustained by political force. In the absence of sanctions, international law is "like a servant, not master" of world politics. "In this state of affairs,"[146] Rowson observed, "the position of the Jewish people is very weak":

> We do not constitute a recognized nation in the legal sense, and thus we have none of the rights that international law bestows on such nations. For this reason we cannot even have the right to insist that our matter be brought before an international court. And even if so brought before it, there would be no guarantee that it would agree to deal with our concerns, being devoid of authority to deal with the demands of an unrecognized nation. Moreover: we don't even have the right to appear on any international stage to defend our demands even at a time of debate on an issue so important and sacred to us as our national existence in *Eretz Israel*. Before the UN Assembly in New York, the representatives of the Jewish people appeared as "beggars" relying on the charity of the righteous nations of the world, seeking their benevolence in order to ensure the existence of our people.[147]

International law was an obstacle to be surmounted. The standard against which Rowson tested it was Zionism: the establishment of a Jewish state in Palestine, which was to furnish the Jewish people with equal legal status. Even the role of international law in achieving Zionism's goal, alluded to specifically (if advertently vaguely) in the Zionist program since 1897 ("secured under public law"),[148] was hardly present in Rowson's writings.[149]

---

[145] Shabtai Rowson, *International Law and the Jewish People*, Tarbut, 4–6 (1947) (Hebrew).
[146] *Id.* at 5.
[147] *Id.* at 6.
[148] *Supra* note 87.
[149] A rare example, *supra* note 109.

Yet from this perspective, international law was more than a mere impediment. It suffered from, and attested to, an "inherent defect" as regards the Jewish people. Unless and until a Jewish state was established, international law entrenched their inferior legal status.[150] Until then, the Jewish people, bereft of legal subjecthood, were condemned to be beggars relying on charity and the benevolence of others. From this perspective – prevalent in Zionist diplomacy in the pre-independent period and thereafter[151] – international law was part of the problem, not its solution. It had no power to transform the legal status of the Jewish people. The following, and final, passage prescribed the only answer to the Jewish predicament – and pronounced on the futility of international law in furnishing it:

> It is a vital necessity for the Jewish people that its international position is made equal to the legal position of all other "recognized" nations. As long as this has not been achieved, all rights that will be granted to Jews and to our people, whether in *Eretz Israel* under a new trusteeship instrument or in the Diaspora under new minority treaties, would be hallow and lack any meaningful value. Under present conditions, the Jews cannot even be assured that they would benefit from the famous "Four Freedoms" or from the "humane rights" that many now talk of. For this reason, in the present state of international law the Jews have no other way of securing their rights and achieving their demands than the establishment of an independent Jewish state whose international status would be equal to that of all other states.[152]

International law, in short, could liberate neither individual Jews nor the Jewish people from the trap of inequality and objecthood: it could not furnish the answer to the Jewish Question. Rowson accordingly viewed international minority protection as a bar to Jewish national development.[153] His critical assessment of Jewish rights under the peace treaties with Germany's European allies led him to conclude that "the treatment of the Jews in the peace conference is the best justification for a Jewish state, demonstrating like no other that on the international sphere, the Jews are subject to the greatest

---

[150] This, recall, was his perspective on minority treaties: *supra* note 117.

[151] MOSHE SHARETT, AT THE THRESHOLD OF STATEHOOD: 1946–1949, 161 (1958) (Hebrew) (rejecting the "status of a minority depending on the charity of others"; a "frozen and shrinking minority ... taking solace in paper guarantees"); *cf.* Rowson, *Epilogue*, 100/243 ("The minorities Treaties of 1919 did give on paper some measure of national rights to national minorities in some multi-national states").

[152] Rowson, *supra* note 145, at 6.

[153] "The lesson of the twentieth century is that treaty and constitutional rights are insufficient so long as the ideal of Jewish emancipation is not firmly implanted in the national tradition": Shabtai Rowson, *The Lessons of History*, ZIONIST REV., Apr. 16 1943, at 9.

inequality before the law."[154] Individual, or "humane rights," as he mentioned in that 1947 piece, would be another false promise. Earlier that year, he was equally skeptical toward proposals for an international convention against antisemitism: "Such legislation, whether municipal or international, could be no more than a semi-efficacious palliative for a disease requiring more radical treatment."[155] Even for that "radical" treatment – a Jewish state in Palestine – international law had little to offer. Reviewing Ernst Frankenstein's 1943 *Justice for My People* – a defense of the Jewish case for Palestine – Rowson criticized the author for the "undue stress placed upon the legal side of the question at the expense of the political."[156] In another review of the same piece he practically distanced himself from the profession: "Whether or not the Arabs have any legal claim to Palestine is a question for international lawyers. But our problems do not arise from that."[157]

EPILOGUE

Rosenne has kept his two engagements apart. Early, this separation of Jewish affairs and international law may have been a simple matter of prudence. Later, with his transformations, it became entrenched in ideological choices. His transformations, often fueled by the losses and consequence of the world war – in London and Palestine, in Dunkirk and in Africa – were many. Disillusionment turned him from a loyal British subject, proudly practicing English law, into a Jewish nationalist who turned his back to the empire he had served. His search for an answer to the Jewish Question brought with it disenchantment with Diaspora Nationalism; this led him to negate the Diaspora by casting his lot with his people in Palestine. There, he had found a new home. His journey brought him, all on his own, to profess what became the foundational ideology of the state he helped found.[158] The Jewish state, the only guarantee of the Jewish people's existence, would take precedence and priority.[159]

[154] Shabtai Rowson, *Jewish Rights under the Peace Treaties*, DAVAR, Feb. 14, 1947 (Hebrew).
[155] S.W.D. Rowson, [Book Review] An International Convention Against Antisemitism by Mark Vishniak, INT'L AFFAIRS, January 1947 [m.s.], RP.
[156] Shabtai Rowson, *A Plea for Justice*, ZIONIST REV., Aug. 20, 1944, at 5.
[157] Shabtai Rowson, Book Review: Justice for My People, by Ernst Frankenstein, YOUNG ZIONIST MAGAZINE, July 1943, at 10 [m.s.], RP.
[158] Spector-Mersel, *supra* note 46.
[159] Rosenne's early MFA career, and the role Zionism played in shaping his approach to international law in the service of the Jewish state, is the subject of my forthcoming book: ROTEM GILADI, JEWS, SOVEREIGNTY, AND INTERNATIONAL LAW: IDEOLOGY, IDENTITY, AND AMBIVALENCE IN EARLY ISRAELI DIPLOMACY (Oxford University Press, forthcoming).

With the founding of the Jewish state, international law could be dealt with on normal terms, unencumbered by false hopes or unwarranted expectations. It no longer marked Jewish inferiority. The Jewish people, having acquired an "international status ... equal to that of all other states,"[160] could now approach international law as equals. This, precisely, is what allowed Rosenne to pursue his international law engagement: with the establishment of the Jewish state, international law was no longer a bar to the practice of Zionism.

Rosenne's skepticism toward international law as a platform of Jewish – as opposed to Zionist or Israeli[161] – interests did not decline after 1948. On the contrary: it could now find expression in the diplomatic practice of an official representative of the Jewish state. And this practice demonstrated Rosenne's ambivalence – often aversion and hostility – toward international law whenever it was conceived to impinge on Jewish interests or on the role of the Jewish state as their representative or guarantor. Rosenne's first ICJ appearance, in the 1951 *Reservations to the Genocide Convention* Advisory Opinion, was not meant to promote this instrument but, rather, second-order Israeli foreign policy interests. He did not think much of the convention: its "practical value," he thought, was "negligible,"[162] and "there was no doubt that the Convention does not safeguard the [Jewish] people against a holocaust."[163] Similarly, between 1951 and 1954 Rosenne stalled Israel's ratification of the 1951 Refugee Convention: it was of "little practical value for us."[164] Quintessentially, as he told Paul Weis, the UNHCR Jewish legal adviser, "We are not very interested in ratifying this Convention as we have no need for it."[165] In both cases, his objection was rooted in ideological considerations.[166] The interests of the Diaspora were not only subordinate to those of the Jewish state; they were also defined by its own foreign policy imperatives.[167]

---

[160]   Rowson, *supra* note 145, at 6.
[161]   In a 1949 MFA consultation, Rosenne insisted: "[W]e are a *Zionist*, not a Jewish, state"; emphasis in the original: Record of Meeting with Minister of Foreign Affairs, May 8, 1949, FM-87/11, ISA, 5.
[162]   Letter from Shabtai Rosenne to Jacob Robinson (Feb. 28, 1951), FM-1832/3, ISA.
[163]   Letter from Shabtai Rosenne to Jacob Robinson (Feb. 15, 1951), FM-1840/2, ISA.
[164]   Letter from Shabtai Rosenne to Leo Cohn (June 25, 1954), FM-1847/2, ISA.
[165]   Letter from Shabtai Rosenne to Ben-Meir (Oct. 27, 1953), FM-1847/2, ISA.
[166]   Rotem Giladi, A *"Historical Commitment"? Identity and Ideology in Israel's Attitude to the Refugee Convention 1951–4*, INT'L. HIST. REV. 745 (2014); Rotem Giladi, *Not Our Salvation: Israel, the Genocide Convention, and the World Court 1951*, 26 DIPLOMACY & STATECRAFT 473 (2015).
[167]   Rosenne, *supra* note 116, at 339–40; GILADI, *supra* note 159.

Synthesis, however, came with a cost. If Israel's establishment freed Rosenne, as its legal representative in the world arena, to deal with international law on its own terms, the terms of the synthesis of his two engagements also produced some short-sightedness toward past Jewish reliance on, and benefit drawn from, international law. This was patent in a Hebrew 1957 piece.[168] "The Influence of Judaism on International Law: A Preliminary Assessment"[169] sought to identify the influence of Jewish thought on the intellectual development of international law.[170] The effort itself was a signifier of Jewish sovereignty: it made a historical-cultural claim, emulating recent claims made by "ancient India, ancient China, and above all Islam" to have made a contribution to the making of international law that, otherwise, was the exclusive product and marker of European civilization. "The Jewish national movement," Rosenne wrote, hardly dealt with this question and had not "participated in that competition";[171] "now, with Israel's independence, it is time to rectify this state of affairs and to try a more profound analysis of the influence of Jewish legal thought."[172]

The survey that followed, faithful to the article's aim and title, demonstrated the benefits of the study of Judaism's contribution to international law. The influence it portrayed was entirely one-sided: it was blind to any benefit that Jews may have drawn from international law. The article noted, instead, the "disappointment in light of the poor achievement."[173] It glossed over, in slightly more than one page, the terms of the Jewish engagement with international law since the nineteenth century.[174] Aware of Zionism's original invocation of international law in the Basle Program, what Rosenne

---

[168] Translated and republished in Shabtai Rosenne, *The Influence of Judaism on the Development of International Law*, 5 NETHERLANDS INT'L. L. REV. 119 (1958); also in SHABTAI ROSENNE, AN INTERNATIONAL LAW MISCELLANY, 509–48 (1993); and in THE INFLUENCE OF RELIGION ON THE DEVELOPMENT OF INTERNATIONAL LAW, 63–94 (M. W. Janis, ed., 1991).

[169] 14 HA-PRAKLIT 3 (1957), drawing on and developing SHABTAI ROSENNE, PUBLIC INTERNATIONAL LAW, WITH A REFERENCE TO THE PRACTICE OF ISRAEL, esp. 71–76, 85 (1956, unpublished m.s.), RP.

[170] ROSENNE, INFLUENCE, *supra* note 168, at 4–5. Stoyanovsky, former editor of the *Jewish Yearbook*, thanked Rosenne for sending him a reprint with "mixed feelings": "the topic attests to an attachment I have not so far, for some reason, ascribed to you": Letter from Stoyanovsky to Rosenne (June 16 1958), RP.

[171] ROSENNE, INFLUENCE, *supra* note 168, at 4.

[172] *Id.* at 5; he proposed to do so by sketching a research agenda combining three "branches of science": public international law, Jewish law, and Jewish history.

[173] *Id.* at 14.

[174] *Id.* at 14–15.

emphasized was the "tendency of philosophers who had influenced the development of the Zionist idea to belittle the value of international law."[175] Familiar with the interest of "a vast number of Jewish scholars" in the mandates system and in minority protection, he took care to note that "only a few of them have had the benefit of a direct, living connection with the Jewish project in Palestine." Even the benefit to be drawn from the study of pre-state Jewish diplomacy was nationalized by Rosenne: what could be gained here was a more perfect understanding of the "international philosophy of the Jewish revival movement."[176] Even after 1948, international law could not be allowed to take credit for answering the Jewish Question. This outlook, it appears, persisted in Rosenne's later years.[177]

Rosenne's transformation and his ability to synthesize or, rather, compartmentalize his two engagements suggest that, alongside the Jewish *engagement*, we must consider sites of Jewish *disengagement* with international law. Renewal of Jewish sovereignty was one such site; there may well have been others. In the aftermath of the Holocaust, the question to ask, perhaps, is not on which terms did Jewish lawyers approach international law but, rather, how could they approach international law at all. Rosenne's answer to this question was confined to the dictates of the Zionist creed. Those not adhering to that creed had to have had other answers, awaiting discovery by future research.

Rosenne's transformation and the terms of his international law engagement underscore the significance of 1948 as a cusp in the interaction between international legal and Jewish history. Exploring this cusp promises important insights: it raises, for one thing, the question of Israel's original international legal outlook – Rosenne, after all, was first among its founders – its

---

[175] *Id.* at 14.

[176] *Id.*

[177] Shabtai Rosenne, *The Protection of Certain Jewish Interests in the Statute of the Permanent Court of International Justice*, 3 ISR. Y.B. HUM. R. 136 (1973), *repr.* in MISCELLANY, 577–620 is no exception: note the multiple reservations and qualifications in the concluding paragraph. In a short 1990 intervention on "The Protection of Minorities and Human Rights," he discussed the League of Nations minorities system without mentioning its Jewish aspect. And he remained critical of that portion of international law: "the generalization or universalization of human rights ... has not had any direct beneficial effect on the various minorities around the world. If anything ... it has brought harm to the general status of minorities ... " Shabtai Rosenne, *The Protection of Minorities and Human Rights*, 20 ISR. Y.B. HUM. R., 359 (1990). Time saw this perspective transmute into UN-skepticism: what started "with an undercurrent of goodwill toward the [UN]," he wrote, became a "story ... of bitterly dashed hopes and expectations"; 1948 UN mediation, *e.g.*, "was to sow the seeds of profound disillusion": Shabtai Rosenne, *Israel and the United Nations-Changed Perspectives, 1945–1976*, AM. JEWISH Y.B. 3 (1978).

transmutations and its place, if any, in Israel's legal diplomacy today. Conversely, if 1948 generated a diversity of Jewish vantage points on international law, then international law, before or after 1948, must itself be considered as a field of political Jewish contestation. [178]

---

[178]   For further elaboration, see GILADI, *supra* note 159.

12

Shabtai Rosenne

A Personal Aspect

Philippe Sands

Shabtai Rosenne was among the early figures who came into my life at the formative period of being a young student of international law, in the early 1980s. I first met him in Cambridge, as he was a friend of one of my teachers, Eli Lauterpacht, whose father Hersch he regularly cited as one of his mentors. Our teachers spoke of him as a scholar of renown, not least for his encyclopedic knowledge of the minutiae of the practice and procedure of the International Court of Justice, and for his role as a legal adviser to the Israeli government. Those were the labels he wore, or at least the ones we allowed ourselves to see. Of Rosenne's past, so elegantly evoked by Rotem Giladi in his fine-tuned and thoughtful portrait-essay, we students knew little. Back in those days we did not seek to better inform ourselves of the personal history now described by Giladi, one that tends not, upon a closer reflection, to follow Giladi's idea that Rosenne's personal and professional engagements somehow moved along distinct lines.

Only later did I come to know more about his roots. Little snippets of information emerged about him, as of other notable seniors in the conservative and carefully structured hierarchy into which I was being drawn, a professional and intellectual space in which the personal tended to be squeezed out. Much of what we heard about Rosenne turned out to be wrong. He was not a solicitor in the city of Leeds, in Yorkshire, and he never was called Sidney Rosenberg. In that pre-internet age – when it took months for a Security Council resolution to snail its way from New York to the Squire Law Library – information about individuals was hard to come by so we swept up what we could find. Giladi has helped inform us as to the facts: The family started as Rosenbaum, then became Rowson and, after the move to Israel, settled on Rosenne. Sefton Wilfrid David, the English Jewish lawyer, became Shabtai, the Israeli legal adviser. A "transformation," as Giladi calls it.

By the time I came to know him the transformation, such as it was, had been completed. I recall a physically imposing figure, a man of a seemingly gentle disposition who would amble amiably among us, sounding gruffer than he was, always happy to engage with younger colleagues. The accent that was not easily placeable, rooted in England but tinted with an Israeli edge. He had a twinkle in his eye, and gave the impression of being at home when in Britain, yet also somehow of another place. For me, the child of an Austrian-French Jewish refugee mother and a father with roots in London's East End, he cut a reassuring figure.

Yet my defining memory of him was formed a few years later, in the spring of 1993, when I happened to be in The Hague during a hearing at the International Court of Justice in the Peace Palace, a case brought by Bosnia and Herzegovina against the Federal Republic of Yugoslavia (FRY), as it was then known, alleging violations of the Convention on the Prevention and Punishment of Genocide.[1]

I arrived on the second day, to observe Rosenne in black robes, a member of the legal team appearing on behalf of the FRY: a Jewish lawyer appearing on behalf of a state defending itself against allegations of involvement in genocidal acts. Nothing wrong with that, I knew, trained as I was at the English bar, where the "cab rank" principle directed its members to act for all and sundry (although the principle does not apply to overseas international practice, I later learned). Curiously, Rosenne was listed not as counsel or advocate, but as one of Yugoslavia's two "Acting Agents" (in a subsequent phase of the case, in August 1993, he was listed as "Counsel and Advocate," and then in the preliminary objection phase, in April 1996, the last time he appeared, as "Counsel," without a speaking role). The agent in a case before the Court is, in effect, the personification of the state, not merely a lawyer appearing on its behalf.

The arguments I heard that day remain in my memory, contributing a permanent impression to my sense of Rosenne, the person and the lawyer. On first reading Giladi's essay I could not recall the exact details, beyond a recollection that in some way Rosenne had introduced a personal note into the proceedings (this is relevant as Giladi draws a distinction in Rosenne's persona, between the personal and the professional, a point to which I will return). I returned to the transcript to jog my memory, and quickly found what

---

[1] This was the second occasion on which Rosenne appeared in proceedings that involved the Genocide Convention, the first having occurred four decades earlier: *see* Rotem Giladi, *Not Our Salvation: Israel, the Genocide Convention, and the World Court 1950–1951*, 26 Diplomacy & Statecraft 473 (2015).

I was looking for. The Court's transcript for that day – April 2nd, 1993 – confirmed that Rosenne had introduced a distinctly personal element into the proceedings, and had done so not once but twice.

Introducing his arguments, Rosenne opened by offering what he referred to as a "personal aspect" to the statement he would deliver on behalf of the FRY. Referring to the application made by Bosnia and Herzegovina by which the proceedings were instituted, he took the Court to a paragraph that referred to the refuge granted to a group of Sephardic Jews who had managed to escape the Inquisition and pogroms in Spain and then, in 1565, formed a community in Sarajevo.[2]

"I myself am descended from one of those Sephardi families," he told the court, "the Fonseca family ... who escaped from Portugal when the Inquisition was extended to that country." Noting the role played by the Ottoman Empire, which held sway over Bosnia and Herzegovina long before 1492 and had long granted refuge to victims of persecution, Rosenne pointed out that the Jewish community of Sarajevo had subsequently "supplied great leaders to Israel today, including two of its Chiefs of Staff."[3]

I found this personal element surprising at the time, and rereading the transcript was surprised once more. Rosenne was signaling to the Court his own sense of identity as a Jew, and one with a historical connection(of sorts) to his client. By referencing that identity and connection he was in effect sending a signal, one that might be seen as eliciting a sympathetic approach from the judges: I know what it means to be oppressed, he seemed to be saying; I know the meaning of genocide; I know what it means to have been weak, and to know now that we are strong; I know what it was to have been stateless, but now we are a state. To do this as counsel or advocate was striking; to do it as an agent, who speaks as the state, not only on behalf of the state, is, to say the least, striking.

Reading the transcript once again, it is easy to see that in full professional flow Rosenne continued to feel a strong "personal aspect," and then a need to share it with the judges, his opponents, and all others present in the Great Hall of Justice that day. In this way, the two engagements of which Giladi writes – the personal and the professional – came together in public expression. In that moment Rosenne melded the being an international lawyer, and the being a Jew.

[2] Verbatim Record (Apr. 2), Application of the Convention on the Prevention and Punishment of the Crime of Genocide (Bosn. & Herz. v. Yugoslavia [Serb. and Montenegro]) 1993 I.C.J. CR 13, at 11.

[3] *Id.*

The few words Rosenne spoke as a "personal aspect" may be sufficient to make the point that I am not immediately persuaded by Giladi's idea that Rosenne's personal and professional engagements moved along distinct rails. Yet there was more to come that day, as the transcript reminded me. Another passage, later in Rosenne's presentation, reinforced the sentiment I describe, this time a reaction to words spoken the previous day by the agent of Bosnia-Herzegovina. Having concluded an aspect of his legal argument, Rosenne interrupted himself to respond to an analogy that had been drawn by Bosnia-Herzegovina, somehow connecting the actions of which the FRY was being accused in these proceedings, and actions of five decades earlier marshaled by the Nazis in the holocaust of European Jews:

> Mr [*sic*] President, while I have the floor I must ask the indulgence of the Court to make one brief personal remark. In his statement yesterday, Ambassador Sacirbey several times referred to the Nazi Holocaust. To any person who has direct knowledge of what the Holocaust was and what it was intended to achieve, such statements are nothing short of blasphemous. Nothing that has occurred since in Europe matches that unspeakable event in European history.[4]

This personal remark – the second – reinforces the first. What is striking, and all the more so in light of Giladi's essay and his account of Rosenne's situation in Britain in the 1940s, is the position in which Rosenne situates himself. Not being a person who had "direct knowledge of what the Holocaust was," he situates himself in a place that allows him to invoke the reactions of others who did have such "direct knowledge," a relocation of the self made possible, one assumes, by the fact that Rosenne is Jewish and has spent much of his life in the service of Israel, the Jewish state (it is difficult to imagine a non-Jew offering a "personal remark" of this kind, particularly one who has no "direct knowledge" of the Holocaust). Irrespective, the point is that the two distinct identities – being an international lawyer, and being a Jew – once again do not operate on parallel tracks. On this occasion they meld into a single course, one in which the agent invokes aspects of his own identity – rather than matters of evidence or law – to underscore the force of a legal argument.[5]

---

[4] *Id.* at 36-37.
[5] In 2014, in proceedings before the same Court, I was involved in a case against Serbia (as the entity that called itself "the FRY" in 1993 was by then known). On this occasion, curiously, it was counsel for Serbia who drew analogies between the actions of the state for which I was acting (Croatia) and those of the Nazis. "[T]here is no doubt about the core of what was decided at Wannsee," Professor William Schabas, counsel for Serbia, told the Court. "Is Brioni any different?" he then asked. The question referred to the minutes of a meeting of the Croatian government held on the island of Brioni. Application of the Convention on the

THE AGES OF ROSENNE

Try as I may, I cannot expunge this personal memory from my reading of Giladi's account of the two "engagements" of Rosenne's early life and work, the engagements of "Jewish nationalism" and "international law" identified as coexisting but running along separate courses that rarely met.[6] Having observed their coming together, in such clear terms, and in a manner that might hardly be considered professionally usual, I will perhaps take a little more persuading that Rosenne's two engagements "existed *despite* the other."[7] Giladi offers a clear thesis, but I wonder if another explanation might also be possible?

I have not engaged in the close reading of the totality of Rosenne's writings across his long and productive life. I always thought of him as being something of a gatherer of materials, an essentially conservative individual who embraced a legal order that placed the artifice of the state at its heart. In this way might one understand his skepticism both of minority rights (which certainly did not offer adequate protections to the Jews or other minority communities in the 1930s) and the later development of individual human rights? In this way, too, one might understand Rosenne's "skepticism toward international law as a platform of Jewish – as opposed to Zionist, or Israeli – interests."[8] Only when Jewish interests are wrapped in the garments of statehood will they be fully protected. The same view is taken today by individuals associated with other communities, including (but not limited to) Kurds, Yazidis, and Palestinians.

What I do now understand better, on the basis of Giladi's helpful and elegant piece, are the three ages of Rosenne. As a speculation, one can see that he began life as a young Englishman who happened to be Jewish, in a country that tended to encourage assimilation and the cloaking of difference as a route to professional progress. (Giladi seems correct in noting that Rosenne may have elected to play down his identity in professional life, emulating his mentor Lauterpacht.)[9]

Prevention and Punishment of the Crime of Genocide (Croatia v. Serb.), 2014 I.C.J. 54 (March 14). Croatia's Agent expressed "deep regret" at the drawing of the analogy (*id.*, Verbatim Record, 15.17 [Mar. 18, 2014, 10 a.m.]), as did I (*id.*, 63.25), but as a matter of fact and evidence, and not invoking any "personal aspect."

[6] Rotem Giladi, *Shabtai Rosenne: The Transformation of Sefton Rosenne*, Chapter 11 in this volume.

[7] *Id.* at 22.

[8] *Id.* at 26. *See* James Loeffler, Chapter 1 in this volume.

[9] For example, in preparing the draft closing speech for UK Attorney General Hartley Shawcross at the Nuremberg trial, Lauterpacht made few references to Jews: *See*

In a second age, at some point in the early 1940s, Rosenne came to learn the details of the horrors that had befallen Jews under the Nazis and their supporters, and confronted a question that many would have asked: Will we be better off – will *I* be better off – as a minority group in a larger state but without the trappings of statehood and all the legal protections that might entail, or as a dominant group in a smaller state with the full "protections" offered by international law? He opted for the latter, a reasonable and rational choice in the circumstances (although one not yet proven to be right or wrong).

Thus, he entered a third age, as legal adviser to the new state, incarnating elements of his own identity and marshaling them into the promotion of his professional engagement. Having made that choice, he took refuge in a classical view of international law, one that integrates the interests of Jewish identity into the interests of the state. And in his view, the interests of the state – and the protection of its sovereignty – were paramount. This too I saw first-hand, toward the end of his career, in a case in which he and I were opposing counsel and where the question arose as to whether a hearing should be held on a preliminary objection raised by Suriname (the state for which Rosenne acted). Invoking two centuries of international arbitration and judicial practice, Rosenne told the tribunal with some force: "I am not aware of a single case in which an international court or tribunal exercising jurisdiction on a compulsory basis has decided on the disposal of preliminary objections to its jurisdiction without a hearing."[10] The case turned out to be the first.

In this way, and in the context of what I observed myself, do I now better understand, and possibly explain, the transformation described by Giladi, "from Rowson's *legal* disinterest in Jewish questions to Rosenne's position as legal representative . . . of the Jewish state."[11] The two engagements apparently existed not despite each other but in connection, perhaps in a sequential and then overlapping sense, the one (representational) because of the other (identification). Two engagements perhaps, but only one, broader course.

Philippe Sands, *Twin Peaks: The Hersch Lauterpacht Draft Nuremberg Speeches*, 1 Camb. J. Int'l. L. 37, 41 (2012).

[10] Proceedings – Day Two, Guyana v. Suriname, U.N. ITLOS, 7th Annex, at 6, U.N. Doc., at 6 (July 8, 2006), https://pcacases.com/web/sendAttach/890.

[11] *Id.*

PART 7

JULIUS STONE

13

Enabling and Constraining

Julius Stone and the Contradictions of the Sociological Path to International Law

Jacqueline Mowbray

Julius Stone was one of the twentieth century's most influential scholars in the field of international law. The Challis Professor of Jurisprudence and International Law at the University of Sydney from 1942 to 1972, Stone also held distinguished positions in the United States, United Kingdom, New Zealand, and Israel. As a public intellectual and adviser to international bodies, Stone was instrumental in shaping international policy, from the creation of Israel to the establishment of a "hotline" linking the White House and Kremlin during the Cold War. Stone's particular contribution to the rapidly changing field of international law, however, was to develop a sociological approach to its study. This approach, which underpinned his meticulous scholarly analysis of the law and drove his insightful and pragmatic contributions in the field of international policy, offered a new way of analyzing international law and understanding how it could be developed so as better to contribute to global justice.

It is generally accepted that Stone's Jewish identity and sympathy for the Jewish cause drew him to the field of international law, through his concern for human rights, justice, and the possibilities for protecting minorities through international legal institutions.[1] In this chapter, I seek to push this argument a little further and suggest that Stone's Jewish identity drove and enabled his development of a sociological approach to international law. In particular, I argue that the three key elements of his sociological approach – the need to analyze law objectively in its social context; the need to adopt an intercultural and inter-systemic approach to the study of international law; and the need to consider law's engagement with broader questions of justice – can be traced to his Jewish consciousness and his experiences as a Jewish man

---

[1] *See, e.g.*, R. Brasch, Australian Jews of Today and the Part They Have Played 223 (1971); Leonie Star, Julius Stone: An Intellectual Life 19 (1992).

in the legal and cultural environment of his time. At the same time, however, I suggest that, in other ways, Stone's Jewish identity limited his development of a complete sociological theory of international law, and also affected the reception of his approach within the international legal community. In other words, I argue that Stone's Jewish consciousness both enabled *and* constrained his development of a sociological approach to international law.

I begin this chapter with an overview of Stone's life and achievements, focusing on his contributions in the field of international law and the influence of his Jewish identity.[2] I then give an overview of his sociological approach to international law, before considering how each of the three key elements of that approach can be attributed to Stone's Jewish consciousness. In the final part of the chapter, I consider the other side of this story and explore how Stone's position as a Jew constrained his development of a coherent sociological theory of international law, and also affected the reception and influence of his work. I conclude that both the contours of Stone's work and the dynamics of its influence and reception were shaped, in profound but sometimes contradictory ways, by Stone's Jewish identity.

BACKGROUND AND ACHIEVEMENTS

Julius Stone was born in 1907 in Leeds, England, to Jewish refugees from Lithuania, who had fled Russian persecution. His early life was "shaped by poverty and family disruption,"[3] but through hard work Stone was able to secure a scholarship to Oxford, where he studied law. Although his time at Oxford was not a happy one, in large part due to antisemitism of various forms,[4] it was there that Stone was first exposed to his two great interests in the field of law: jurisprudence and international law. "Consciousness of Jewish history drew [Stone's] critical mind to the question of how and why laws are made," that is, to jurisprudence.[5] He was also drawn to international law, in part as a result of his position as foreign secretary of the Inter-University Jewish Federation. In this role, Stone wrote his first publication,[6] a pamphlet addressing the issue of numerus clausus provisions, which restricted the entry of Jews

---

[2] For a more detailed overview of Stone's life and achievements, *see* STAR, *supra* note 1.

[3] Adrienne Stone, *Julius Stone: A Reflection, in* JULIUS STONE: A STUDY IN INFLUENCE 13–14 (Helen Irving, Jacqueline Mowbray, & Kevin Walton, eds., 2010).

[4] Star notes, for example, that the "private dining clubs that existed within the college did not admit Jews": STAR, *supra* note 1, at 14.

[5] STAR, *id.*, at 19.

[6] JULES [sic] STONE, THE NUMERUS CLAUSUS IN THE UNIVERSITIES OF EASTERN EUROPE (1927).

to universities in Europe in the 1920s, despite intervention by the League of Nations. This marked the start of Stone's interest in the protection of minorities under international law, an interest that dominated his early academic career.

Upon leaving Oxford, Stone practiced briefly, while completing a BCL from Oxford and LLM from Leeds. He then took up a Rockefeller Fellowship at Harvard, to work on the question of the treatment of minorities under international law. He completed his SJD in 1932, and produced three articles and two books on the question of legal protection of minorities in Eastern Europe. These, together with two articles on evidence, earned Stone a DCL from Oxford in 1936, when he was just twenty-eight, although the degree was rarely awarded to anyone under forty.[7]

Harvard was significant for Stone, as it was there that he first encountered Roscoe Pound, the leading figure in American sociological jurisprudence. Inspired and influenced by Pound, Stone devoted himself to the study of jurisprudence as well as international law, and this is seen by many as the start of his journey toward the development of a sociological theory of international law.

Following the award of his SJD, Stone became an assistant lecturer in jurisprudence at Harvard, where he remained until 1936. However, his efforts to obtain a permanent position at Harvard were frustrated, for reasons which included a degree of antisemitism. As Leonie Star notes, "Stone was overtly Jewish in a way that often made people uncomfortable,"[8] and this affected his efforts to secure an academic appointment, both in the United States and in England.[9] According to former Justice of the High Court of Australia Michael Kirby, Stone's "numerous attempts to secure academic appointments were frustrated, despite his brilliant scholarly achievements on both sides of the Atlantic, by referee reports that cautioned about his Jewish background and attitudes and his Zionist inclinations."[10] In 1939 Stone took up a position as founding dean of the University of Auckland Law School in New Zealand, before being appointed to the Chair of Jurisprudence and International Law at the University of Sydney in 1941. This latter appointment had been strenuously opposed on the basis of more

---

[7]   STAR, *supra* note 1, at 42.
[8]   *Id.* at 40.
[9]   "He was refused post after post, some going to people with academic achievements blatantly inferior to his because of opinions about his personality and because of overt anti-Semitism": Leonie Star, *Julius Stone: Balancing the Story*, 17 ARTS: THE JOURNAL OF THE SYDNEY UNIVERSITY ARTS ASSOCIATION 63, 69 (1995). *See further* STAR, *supra* note 1, at 40–43.
[10] The Hon. Justice Michael Kirby, *HLA Hart, Julius Stone and the Struggle for the Soul of Law*, 27 SYDNEY L. REV. 323, 326 (2005).

or less open antisemitism, of which "there was a strong undercurrent" in Australia at the time.[11]

In spite of the very public controversy surrounding his appointment, Stone remained the Chair of Jurisprudence and International Law for thirty years, during which time he consolidated his reputation as a public intellectual and as an influential scholar in the fields of both international law and jurisprudence. Stone was the author of thirty-four books and more than one hundred shorter works.[12] In the field of international law, he was the first scholar ever to receive two awards from the American Society of International Law: for *Legal Controls of International Conflict*[13] in 1956, and for *Visions of World Order*[14] in 1985. On the basis of his publications, he was elected an associate member of the Institut de Droit International in 1957. In 1962 the American Society of International Law elected him an honorary life member, "an honor given to one person each year among non-American citizens."[15] In 1965 he was the first recipient of the World Law Research Award, made at the World Conference on World Peace Through Rule of Law.

Stone's work on international law focused on big themes of war, peace, and the construction of an international legal order, and adopted his distinctive sociological approach of considering the law in its social context. As a result, Stone's work was characterized by a highly pragmatic outlook on pressing, contemporary problems of international law. Stone's pragmatism and insight (he predicted the scenario of the Cuban Missile crisis six years before it occurred)[16] meant that his work was highly influential in the field of international policy. Perhaps the best-known example of his influence was the

---

[11] STAR, *supra* note 1, at 59. For a detailed description of the controversy and how it played out, *see* STAR, *supra* note 1, at 56–67. For further evidence of the role played by prejudice and antisemitism in the controversy, STAR, Id. at 72.

[12] An almost complete list can be found in the bibliography to LEGAL CHANGE: ESSAYS IN HONOUR OF JULIUS STONE 335 (A. R. Blackshield, ed., 1983). To the list of books should be added: JULIUS STONE AND W.A.N. WELLS, EVIDENCE: ITS HISTORY AND POLICIES – AN ORIGINAL MANUSCRIPT BY JULIUS STONE (W.A.N. Wells, rev., 1991), which was published posthumously. *See also* the list of Stone's major publications in STAR, id., at 280.

[13] JULIUS STONE, LEGAL CONTROLS OF INTERNATIONAL CONFLICT: A TREATISE ON THE DYNAMICS OF DISPUTES AND WAR-LAW (1954).

[14] JULIUS STONE, VISIONS OF WORLD ORDER: BETWEEN STATE POWER AND HUMAN JUSTICE (1984).

[15] STAR, *supra* note 1, at 155.

[16] JULIUS STONE, AGGRESSION AND WORLD ORDER: A CRITIQUE OF UNITED NATIONS THEORIES OF AGGRESSION 99–100 (1958). Stone used this hypothetical scenario in order to explore the possibility of what is now referred to as "anticipatory self-defense." *See further* Edward McWhinney, *Julius Stone and the Sociological Approach to International Law*, 9 UNIV. OF NEW SOUTH WALES L. J. 14, 22 (1986).

implementation of the White House–Kremlin "hotline," a measure Stone first proposed in 1959.[17]

Stone also exercised influence over international law and policy in his role as a public intellectual and as an adviser to international organizations. He frequently made public addresses, both in Australia and overseas. From 1942, he regularly made radio broadcasts with the Australian Broadcasting Corporation (ABC), and in 1960 he delivered the prestigious annual ABC lectures.[18] He represented international organizations, including Amnesty International[19] and the International Commission of Jurists.[20] He also gave advice on questions of international law, particularly those relating to Israel. In 1947, when the question of the creation of a Jewish homeland was being considered, the Jewish Agency in Palestine asked Stone for a legal opinion on the proposals for a Palestine settlement to be considered by the United Nations.[21] Later, in 1979, Stone was asked by Israel's permanent representatives to the United Nations to provide an opinion on the rights of the Palestinian people under international law. His fifty-one-page opinion was presented to the UN Secretary-General, and was considered to have had a substantial effect on the position of the UN Secretariat, and on subsequent actions taken by the Palestine Liberation Organization.[22] Stone is also considered to have played a critical role in the creation of the State of Israel, as a result of the profound influence he exercised over H. V. Evatt, who presided over the General Assembly "at the decisive UN meetings preceding the birth and recognition of Israel."[23]

Overall, the story of Stone is that of an academic who made a remarkable contribution, in both practical and scholarly terms, to the development of international law and policy in his time. It is also the story of a man whose Jewish identity, for better or worse, was always a major aspect of his life. Unlike some other prominent Jews of his time, Stone never sought to keep his identity

---

[17] See STAR, *supra* note 1, at 123. Stone developed this idea further in JULIUS STONE, QUEST FOR SURVIVAL: THE ROLE OF LAW AND FOREIGN POLICY (1961).

[18] JULIUS STONE, LETTERS TO AUSTRALIA: THE RADIO BROADCASTS (1942–72) (Jonathan Stone, Eleanor [Stone] Sebel, & Michael E Stone, eds., vol. II, 2014). *See* Samuel Moyn, James Loeffler, and Joseph Siracusa, *Review, in* H-DIPLO REVIEW FORUM ESSAY 132 (2015), http://tiny.cc/E132.

[19] STAR, *supra* note 1, at 204–06.

[20] *Id.* at 201–03.

[21] As Star notes, "Stone's standing as a spokesperson on Jewish affairs is demonstrated by the fact that the only other international lawyer asked by the Jewish Agency to give an opinion was Sir Hersch Lauterpacht." STAR, *supra* note 1, at 194.

[22] STAR, *id.* at 208–10. Stone ultimately expanded and developed this opinion into his book, JULIUS STONE, ISRAEL AND PALESTINE: ASSAULT ON THE LAW OF NATIONS (1981).

[23] BRASCH, *supra* note 1, at 231. *See further* STAR, *Id.* at 196–98.

to himself: "[His] Jewishness was a central, and never private, aspect of his being."[24] Before considering in detail how this Jewish consciousness played out in the development of Stone's sociological approach to international law, let me first give an overview of that approach.

STONE'S SOCIOLOGICAL APPROACH TO INTERNATIONAL LAW

When Stone studied at Oxford, jurisprudence in England was largely analytical and dominated by legal positivism. Law was viewed as a closed system of rules created by a sovereign body. In contrast, the American sociological school of jurisprudence, which Stone encountered at Harvard, treated law as "a continuing and dynamic process of conflict and competition of the different interests present in society, with specific positive law rules as the end-product of that interaction of social ideas at any particular time."[25] In other words, the focus was on how the law functioned in its social context, and sociological jurisprudence required careful analysis of the law in practice, using empirical, social science methods.[26]

Stone adopted the insights of the American sociological school in his substantial body of work on jurisprudence.[27] Those insights also influenced his approach to international law, from his earliest days at Harvard. His work on minorities, for example, considered not only the relevant legal schemes for minority protection, but also how those schemes functioned in practice.[28] In this respect, Stone was already looking past the narrow legal analysis of those like Hersch Lauterpacht, who sought to characterize international law in positivist terms, as a complete legal order along the lines of municipal law, or a sort of

---

[24] Kirby, *supra* note 9, at 327.

[25] McWhinney, *supra* note 15, at 16–17.

[26] In essence, this approach sought to explore three general issues: the social conditions that lead to the production of law; how law actually functions within society, as an instrument of social control; and how the law *should* operate, that is, how it can be shaped to achieve socially just ends. Sociological jurisprudence thus encouraged experimentalism and pragmatism, with a focus on how law could provide practical solutions to social problems.

[27] *See*, in particular, JULIUS STONE, THE PROVINCE AND FUNCTION OF LAW: LAW AS LOGIC, JUSTICE AND SOCIAL CONTROL (1946), especially the third section entitled "Law and Society"; and JULIUS STONE, SOCIAL DIMENSIONS OF LAW AND JUSTICE (1966).

[28] As one reviewer noted: "One of the chief reasons why Dr. Stone's studies are so excellent is that he has examined the problem on the spot and has therefore been able to give a clear picture of the law in action; he has not confined himself to a study of documents which would merely reveal how the system was intended to work or how it should work." Philip C. Jessup, *Review of Regional Guarantees of Minority Rights by Julius Stone*, 47 HARV. L. REV. 1291, 1292 (1934).

"common law writ large."[29] At the same time, however, Stone did not simply adopt the realist view of those like Hans Morgenthau, who saw international law as pure power politics.[30] Rather, as his sociological approach developed, he came to see international law as "a social fact of cultural life, an objectivization [*sic*] of certain attitudes of certain kinds of groupings of individuals,"[31] such that international law needs to be understood in its social context. This social context includes power politics, but also the "underlying social, economic, psychological, and technological conditions of human life for the time being."[32]

Stone felt that such an approach was essential because "many of our most difficult questions of contemporary international law are not tractable in terms of mere legal technique and ... cry out for further clarification which only a developed sociology can provide."[33] This is, in the first place, because international law as positive law displays "innate shortcomings," characterized by "[g]aps and uncertainties as to content even of everyday norms."[34] This position is complicated by the social and cultural diversity that exists at the international level, as a result of which there is no worldwide consensus on ethical standards, no common cultural or social assumptions underpinning international law. This was particularly the case post-1945, when the creation of the United Nations and decolonization shifted the "Eurocentric" focus of international law toward a new, multicultural world order.[35] As a result, in Stone's view, it was necessary to conduct a careful examination of the diverse "sociological substratum"[36] of international law, in order to understand how international law really operates in practice, and how it can be made more effective as an instrument for preventing conflict and ensuring justice.[37]

---

[29] STAR, *supra* note 1, at 132.

[30] As Richard Falk put it, in relation to Stone's work on use of force, "Julius Stone's special achievement – and it is a notable one – was all along to see through [the] smokescreen of treaties and legal language, and yet not to become a mere advocate of cynical power-wielding." Richard Falk, *On the Recent Further Decline of International Law*, in LEGAL CHANGE: ESSAYS IN HONOUR OF JULIUS STONE, *supra* note 11, at 265.

[31] Julius Stone, *Problems Confronting Sociological Enquiries Concerning International Law*, 89 RECUEIL DES COURS 65, 116 (1956).

[32] *Id.* at 69.

[33] *Id.* at 74.

[34] *Id.* at 69.

[35] *See* Edward McWhinney, *Sociological Jurisprudence and Julius Stone's International Law Thinking*, 10 BULLETIN OF THE AUSTRALIAN SOCIETY OF LEGAL PHILOSOPHY 150, 150–01 (1986).

[36] Stone, *supra* note 30, at 75.

[37] "More broadly formulated, this is the task of defining the conditions under which, and the extent to which international law can conduce to desired results; of ascertaining what we can

Stone applied his sociological perspective to all his work on international law, but the details of his approach are set out most clearly in his 1956 lectures to The Hague Academy, "Problems Confronting Sociological Inquiries Concerning International Law."[38] In these lectures, Stone gave a detailed overview of his proposed approach and methodology, mapping out a program of work for sociological inquiries into international law. Through an analysis of these lectures, together with his broader body of work in international law, it is possible to distill three key features of Stone's sociological approach to international law.

The first, and most obvious, is that a sociological approach requires an examination of the law in its social context. In other words, there is a focus on the *extralegal* factors that shape the law and affect its operation as an instrument of social control. Stone emphasizes the empirical analysis of these factors, which requires, above all, *objectivity*. International lawyers need to position themselves as *outsiders* to the law, in order to observe objectively the relationship between "social facts and legal norms, viewing these latter not as ideal entities of the normative sphere, but as manifestations in the consciousness and emotive life of concrete human beings."[39] Harding has written of Stone's determination "to maintain objectivity, restraint and perspective" and "his refusal to abandon his platform of intellectual detachment."[40] Stone himself, while acknowledging that there "cannot admittedly be absolutely disinterested pursuit of knowledge,"[41] emphasizes the need for lawyers who take a sociological approach to transcend their legal, national, and cultural backgrounds in order to conduct objective analysis, not colored by "the cultural patterns and equipment of the society in which ... [they were] trained."[42]

Secondly, in conducting this sociological analysis, Stone is acutely aware of cultural and social diversity at the international level, as well as the fact that cultures, societies, and legal norms are liable to change over time. As a result, Stone emphasizes the need to conduct *inter-systemic, intercultural analysis*, rather than seeking to construct a unified theory of international law. He acknowledges that "in the instant field at its present phase, the fixing of

---

hope to achieve by international law, and by what speed, and what methods; and of recognizing the limits of effective legal action on particular problems at particular times ...": *Id.* at 119.
[38]   *Id.*
[39]   *Id.* at 67.
[40]   Don Harding, *Reflections on Working with Julius Stone on Sociological Jurisprudence* 10 BULLETIN OF THE AUSTRALIAN SOCIETY OF LEGAL PHILOSOPHY 137, 139 (1986).
[41]   Stone, *supra* note 30, at 159.
[42]   *Id.* at 161. *See generally Id.* at 159–61.

ultimate principles of unity is less important than the recognition of present diversities and incongruities."[43] Stone therefore requires rigorous analysis of different cultures, societies, and legal systems on their own terms, in order to understand the true nature of the international legal order. Such analysis will reveal whether it is indeed possible to speak of one "international community"[44] or whether "there may be separate systems each with common interests, aims, and values among a restricted number of the States and related political entities," that is, the possibility of what Stone terms "partial international legal orders."[45] This intercultural approach also means that Stone consistently adopts a relativist perspective, skeptical of the idea of absolute or universal truths or values, and open to the possibility of "partial truths,"[46] that is, truths that appear as such only to those in particular states or from particular backgrounds.

The third key element of Stone's sociological approach is his focus on *justice*. For Stone, the aim of sociological analysis is always to reveal how law, as a social – and therefore changeable – construction could be improved to achieve greater justice.[47] Stone "stressed that empirical social inquiry and even "scientific" generalizations about facts were but foundations for central questions concerned with what should be done – questions of ethics, social policy, and justice."[48] He was concerned with understanding how international law could be made to work in the interests of global justice, and considered issues such as human rights, equality, the fair distribution of

---

[43] *Id.* at 84.

[44] *Id.* at 129.

[45] *Id.* at 137.

[46] *Id.* at 169. Stone's awareness of the differences among states, the existence of competing national versions of "truth" and the absence of a unified "international community" are nicely illustrated in an anecdote he tells in one of his radio broadcasts, the transcripts of which have recently been published. Stone tells the story of Garry Davis, who camped out before the opening of the UN General Assembly in Paris and declared himself "the world's first world citizen." Stone asks: "Who is it then that is mad? Garry with his one world, one truth, sitting there under the banner of the United Nations, or the rest of us, scattered among the sovereign states? Of that none of us can yet be too sure. But what, alas, we do know is this. That as soon as the many national versions of truth reached Paris, a week later, in the form of the governmental delegations to the General Assembly, young Garry Davis and his one-world truth were arrested by the French police, packed into a van with his belongings, and translated back into the French national version of truth." STONE, *supra* note 17, at 279–81. *See* the further discussion of this actual historical episode in CHRISTOPHER N. J. ROBERTS, THE CONTENTIOUS HISTORY OF THE INTERNATIONAL BILL OF HUMAN RIGHTS (2014).

[47] The purpose of his sociological jurisprudence was "to state in orderly fashion the contexts and the range of tasks confronting modern democratic governments in using law as an instrument of social control, and as a means towards justice": STONE, *supra* note 26, at 1.

[48] Harding, *supra* note 39, at 139.

resources between developed and developing states, and self-determination, as well as theoretical questions of how to understand "international justice." Critically, Stone differed from other international lawyers of his time in refusing to see international justice purely in terms of justice between states. In *Approaches to the Notion of International Justice*, he specifically rejects this "facile" and "unacceptable" view, which leaves "outside the ambit of *international* justice the relation of ... human beings."[49] While not offering a comprehensive account of justice as involving the rights of individuals, Stone nonetheless concludes that neither a focus on states nor a focus on individuals "can serve as an *exclusive* basis of present thinking about international justice."[50]

Stone's thinking about justice was also distinctive in that he refused to start from the idea of absolute or universal principles, the way natural law thinkers did. His emphasis was not on grand visions and abstract theories of justice, but on justice as a social phenomenon. As a result, he was sensitive to the fact that different people and societies understand justice in different ways: "[S]uch meaning as is confidently offered by some seems always no less confidently unacceptable to others."[51] According to Stone, this finding

> need not preclude the search for unchanging principles of justice valid for all times and places ... It is to be expected, however, at the present stage of history, that judgment will be deeply sensitive to the actual conditions of man's social, economic, and political life at the particular time and place of judgment.[52]

Stone thus adopted an interesting position in between absolute and relative notions of justice: he acknowledged that ideas of justice may differ in different times and places, but he did not dismiss the search for absolute or "quasi-absolute precepts of justice."[53] This idea finds particular expression in Stone's key concept of "enclaves of justice."[54] His idea here is that, in particular societies at particular times, there emerges consensus on certain principles of justice, this consensus being reflected in shared social values and their institutionalization. For Stone, international justice requires "holding" these national enclaves of justice against "forces which threaten" them,[55] extending

---

[49]   JULIUS STONE, APPROACHES TO THE NOTION OF INTERNATIONAL JUSTICE 61 (1970).
[50]   *Id.* at 66.
[51]   *Id.* at 4.
[52]   *Id.* at 7.
[53]   JULIUS STONE, HUMAN LAW AND HUMAN JUSTICE 341 (1965).
[54]   *Id.* at 344–45.
[55]   STONE, *supra* note 48, at 55.

these to the international sphere, and developing "international enclaves of justice."[56]

Taken together, these three elements of Stone's sociological approach – his focus on extralegal, objective analysis of law; his adoption of an intercultural, inter-systemic approach; and his attention to the demands of justice – provide the basis for Stone's distinctive contribution to the field of international law. Let me turn now to consider how the development of each of these three key elements of his approach can be seen as enabled or encouraged by his Jewish identity.

THE ROLE OF STONE'S JEWISH IDENTITY: ENABLING AND SHAPING

I Extralegal, Objective Approach

It is easy to see how Stone's awareness of Jewish history, and the way in which law had been used to affect the interests of Jews, would incline him toward an interest in the social effect of law. In more concrete terms, this influence can be seen in his earliest publication, on the numerus clausus provisions restricting the entry of Jews to universities. In preparing this publication, it was clear that Stone was concerned not just with the validity of these laws, but with establishing the facts concerning their application. So, for example, Stone "wrote repeatedly to the Secretary of the Board of Deputies of British Jews ... asking for statistics, [and] information about social conditions in the affected countries."[57] From the outset, then, Stone's interest in Jewish affairs drove him to consider not just law, but its social context, and to obtain empirical evidence of the social impact of law. This outlook continued to shape Stone's approach to international law in his more detailed work on the position of minorities under the international system. His work *Regional Guarantees of Minority Rights*,[58] for example, was informed by a visit to Upper Silesia to gather information on how this particular regional system for addressing minority issues was working in practice.[59] Thus while Stone's interest in, and development of, a sociological approach to international law are often attributed, almost exclusively, to the influence of Pound while Stone was at Harvard, in

---

[56]   *Id.* at 81–89. Stone himself argues, in particular, for the emergence of a principle of international justice that would require developed states to assist developing states to ensure a minimum standard of human subsistence for all.

[57]   Star, *supra* note 1, at 20–21.

[58]   Julius Stone, Regional Guarantees of Minority Rights: A Study of Minorities Procedure in Upper Silesia (1933).

[59]   *See* Star, *supra* note 1, at 34; Jessup, *supra* note 27, at 1292.

fact his disposition toward this approach predated his encounter with Pound and was driven, at least in part, by factors much more intrinsic to Stone himself – namely, his Jewish identity and consciousness of Jewish history.

Stone's Jewish identity also drove him to focus on extralegal factors and social context in other ways. In particular, his Zionist beliefs and deep sympathy for the position of Israel heavily shaped his analysis of international law, in ways that required him to focus not only on the relevant rules, but also on the social and historical context in which they were applied. This can be seen clearly in his 1958 work *Aggression and World Order*, written against the background of the Suez Crisis of 1956–57.[60] Stone felt strongly that the dominant view, that Israel's actions in Egypt constituted unlawful aggression under international law, failed to take into account the broader context within which those actions should be understood. While Stone refers to aspects of this context in *Aggression* itself,[61] it is perhaps put best, as Star has noted,[62] in one of his non-academic pieces:

> To decide which State was an aggressor, the Security Council would have to consider ... the lamentable record of Egyptian operations against Israel, including four hundred and more armed invasions, the violation of Israel's right of access through Suez and Elath, the waging for years of a curious unilateral war against Israel, the organization of alliances openly aimed at destroying Israel, and her build-up of Soviet arms and influence mortally threatening Israel's survival.[63]

This view of the context within which the Israeli incursions into Egypt occurred led Stone to characterize the common view that the UN Charter prohibited force except in the case of self-defense or collective action by the UN as "extreme."[64] According to Stone, this view was contrary to principles of justice, for it could "require law-abiding Members of the Organization [the UN] to submit indefinitely to admitted and persistent violations of rights."[65] Stone argued that it could not be the case that "military initiative is always the grave crime of aggression, and military passivity is always righteous,"[66] and rather use of force should be permitted to achieve justice. And this assessment cannot be based on precise legal definitions of aggression, but requires

---

[60]   See STONE, *supra* note 16, *Preface* vii.
[61]   *See, e.g., id.* 1–2, 102–03, esp. footnote 22.
[62]   STAR, *supra* note 1, at 143–44.
[63]   Julius Stone, *Aggression and International Law*, ABC WEEKLY, Feb. 2, 1957, quoted in STAR, *supra* note 1, at 144.
[64]   STONE, *supra* note 16, at 98.
[65]   *Id.* at 97.
[66]   *Id.* at 101.

consideration of the broader social context within which supposed acts of aggression take place.[67] This explicitly sociological approach to questions of use of force was then developed further in his other international law works.[68]

One further point is worth mentioning here: the need to study international law through the empirical and objective analysis of extralegal factors implies the need to study law "from the outside." As a Jew, Stone was an "outsider" from the very beginning. Particularly in his early career, Stone's Jewish identity meant that he never really belonged to the legal "establishment," but instead was always on its margins. As a Jewish student at Oxford he felt isolated and alienated from his fellow students. Antisemitism then frustrated his efforts to find an academic legal position in the United States and the United Kingdom, leading to his "effective banishment to the Antipodes."[69] Even there, his appointment to the University of Sydney was strenuously opposed by a legal profession that "could not countenance the fact that a professor of law at the University of Sydney could be a Jew."[70] From this perspective, Stone's personal experiences reflected, and perhaps contributed to, his professional inclination to work with law not from the "inside" but from the "outside," that is, in terms of its social context. Certainly his position as an outsider enabled him to develop, to a greater extent than most, the objectivity necessary for empirical analysis of extralegal factors. And Stone himself came to embrace his position as an outsider as critical to his scholarly work:

> Having the concrete temptations offered to him, from time to time, to return permanently to the United States, or to move to other postulated *World* legal centres, ... he always counselled [*sic*] the merits of operating as a world jurist, from a base in a lesser or "middle" state.[71]

This was because it left him free to analyze objectively the claims and interests of "superpowers" in relation to international law and relations. Stone developed this objectivity further by not acting for the Australian government in relation to foreign affairs matters.[72] This enhanced the status and influence of Stone's work. As Edward McWhinney noted in 1986, *Legal*

---

[67]   *Id.*, esp. at 92–103.

[68]   *See, e.g.,* JULIUS STONE, CONFLICT THROUGH CONSENSUS: UNITED NATIONS APPROACHES TO AGGRESSION (1977).

[69]   Kirby, *supra* note 9, at 333.

[70]   STAR, *supra* note 1, at 72.

[71]   McWhinney, *supra* note 15, at 15.

[72]   This approach was questioned by other members of the international law academy, who saw obtaining briefs for such advice as signs of a "very successful" legal career: J. R. Crawford, *Teaching and Research in International Law in Australia*, 10 AUSTR. Y.B. INT'L. L. 176, 194 (1981).

Controls,[73] published in 1954,"remains, today, the standard international reference work, free as it is from the Cold War affiliations, one way or another, that too often tinge other works written by other jurists who have held their own national Foreign Ministry legal briefs."[74] Stone's position as an outsider, a consequence of his Jewish identity, thus became an asset for his work in general, and for his development of a sociological approach to international law in particular.

II Inter-systemic, Intercultural Approach

In very general terms, it seems possible to argue that there is something inherently Jewish in Stone's adoption of an inter-systemic, intercultural approach. The history of the Jewish diaspora is a history of intercultural encounters: encounters between Jewish cultural identity and the culture of the nations in which Jews came to live; and encounters between the different national cultures to which the Jewish diaspora was exposed over the course of centuries seeking freedom from persecution. Modern Jewish identity can be seen as characterized by hybridity and diversity.

In more concrete terms, it is clear that Stone's experiences as a Jewish man living in a non-Jewish world made him more aware than most of social and cultural difference, and the possibilities of intercultural experience. Throughout his life, Stone was forced to juggle the competing demands of commitment to his Jewish faith and culture, and his desire to be respected in the communities in which he lived and worked.[75] Stone also shared the Jewish experience of being forced to relocate to different countries in response to antisemitism, as a result of which he had direct exposure to different cultures to a far greater extent than other legal academics at the time. This meant that he was exposed to many different traditions of thought, which he synthesized into his own. He was unusual, for example, for his synthesis of American and Anglo-Australian jurisprudential thinking. And as Upendra Baxi has noted, he was "remarkable for his time in respecting the potential that the diversity of the non-European perspective could bring to the social theory of law."[76] The

---

[73] STONE, *supra* note 13.

[74] McWhinney, *supra* note 34, at 152.

[75] This came to a head, for example, when he publicly opposed Sir Isaac Isaacs, a prominent Australian Jewish lawyer and first Australian-born governor-general, over proposed British restrictions on Jewish immigration to Palestine in the early 1940s. See STAR, *supra* note 1, at 190–93.

[76] Upendra Baxi, *Revisiting Social Dimensions of Law and Justice in a Post-Human Era*, in JULIUS STONE: A STUDY IN INFLUENCE 69, 74 (Helen Irving, Jacqueline Mowbray, & Kevin Walton, eds., 2010).

intercultural was therefore part of his jurisprudential thinking from the start, and his experience of different societies and cultures meant that he was better equipped than most to carry out this inter-systemic analysis.

Stone's Jewish identity also led him to develop his intercultural approach in another way, in that it sparked his initial interest in the question of the treatment of minorities under international law. This led Stone, almost inevitably, toward consideration of the role of culture in international law and relations, because culture lies at the very heart of the "minority issue": special schemes of minority protection are necessary to protect cultural difference and to prevent discrimination against groups whose social and cultural identities differ from that of the majority population.

In considering how these minority protection regimes functioned, both in law and in practice, Stone was forced to confront the realities of intercultural difference and the difficulties it created for international law. Stone realized that international law could not contribute to international justice in this field unless it engaged with these issues of cultural difference, and specifically considered the particularities of the social and cultural situation of the groups concerned. Thus he found that particular, sui generis regional systems for the protection of minorities, with dispute resolution organs based in the territory concerned and presided over by those with knowledge of the particular local conditions, were more effective instruments of minority protection than general, international organs.[77] This can be seen, in many ways, as a precursor to his later interest in, and attention to, "partial international legal orders."[78] In this sense, Stone's Jewish identity was significant both in terms of attracting his interest to questions of intercultural and inter-systemic analysis and providing him with the personal experience to conduct such analysis effectively.

III Justice

The fact that Stone's interest in the question of justice can be traced to his concern for the plight of the Jewish people has been noted by many commentators.[79] Indeed, Stone himself has suggested that his "bias towards justice" "grew out of his own experiences of anti-Semitism, his witness to Jewish people's sufferings in the Holocaust and his belief that the creation of a homeland for the Jewish people was both timely and necessary."[80] However,

[77] See STONE, *supra* note 57.
[78] Stone, *supra* note 30, at 137.
[79] See, e.g., BRASCH, *supra* note 1, at 223; STAR, *supra* note 1, at 19.
[80] Kirby, *supra* note 9, at 332.

I think there is also evidence that Stone's Jewish identity influenced his engagement with questions of justice in more substantive ways, in that it shaped both the issues of justice with which he was concerned in his work and the intellectual approach that he took to this key concept.

To start with, Stone specifically acknowledged the significance of the Jewish idea of justice for his thinking. In his major work on the concept of justice, *Human Law and Human Justice*, Stone starts his analysis with a study of historical approaches, stressing in particular the Jewish concept of justice according to law: "It was in the land of Israel that, for the first time, the ideas of justice and law were inextricably interwoven with each other."[81] This sense of the interconnectedness of law and justice can be seen to underpin his entire body of work, and to form the basis for the intellectual approach he adopted throughout his life.

In this way, Stone's thinking on the issue of justice and its relationship with law was always influenced by Jewish thought. His ideas, of course, developed substantially over the course of his long career. However, this intellectual development, too, seems to have been shaped by the issues on which he chose to focus, which were often matters of particular concern to the Jewish people: minority rights; the Nuremburg trials; the Eichmann trial; the justice and legality of Israel's actions in the Middle East; and so on. So, for example, Stone's insistence that international justice includes justice not only for states but also for individuals can be partly traced, I think, to his consideration of the injustices suffered by the Jewish people during the Holocaust, and the subsequent international legal measures to bring the perpetrators to justice. Certainly, examination of these issues drew him onto the terrain of international human rights law and international criminal law, the two areas of postwar international law that directly engaged issues of "justice" and, critically, made individuals subjects of international law in their own right. Writing on Eichmann, Stone explicitly tied the concept of justice to the rights of individuals, noting that "[l]egality is ever to be checked and enriched by the sense of justice and awareness of the inviolable dignity of every human being."[82] This focus on the rights and "justice claims" of individuals follows also from Stone's interest in minority rights regimes.

Similarly, Stone's refusal to adopt either a purely absolute or a purely relative notion of justice can be seen to have developed, at least in part, through his interest in the status of laws and justice in Nazi Germany.[83]

---

[81] STONE, *supra* note 52, at 22.
[82] JULIUS STONE, THE EICHMANN TRIAL AND THE RULE OF LAW 21 (1961).
[83] This issue underlies much of the discussion in STONE, *supra* note 52.

Debates among scholars concerning how to classify antisemitic Nazi laws (as, for example, not-law or unjust law), and the associated issue of whether relativism or absolutism provided a better basis for the idea of justice, attracted considerable attention at the time. Stone's interest in this issue, driven by his concern for justice for the Jewish people, led him to this debate and also, perhaps, to his distinctive solution to it: "whether relativism or absolutism provided a sounder basis for the justice idea" depended "largely on which view was more likely to provide a better defense against tyrannical political power."[84] In other words, his position was a pragmatic one, in favor neither of relativism nor of absolutism, but requiring a detailed consideration of the social context in which the idea of justice would be deployed. In a similar way, Stone's view that justice cannot be seen in abstract terms, but needs to take account of social context, including factors such as history, was developed through his analysis of Israel's intervention in Egypt in *Aggression*, as discussed above.

The ultimate development of Stone's particular approach to justice was, of course, his concept of enclaves of justice. Without wanting to overstate it, it seems possible to see something rather Jewish about this idea of hard-won enclaves of justice. There is no doubt that it can be seen to flow from Stone's inter-systemic and intercultural approach which, as discussed above, was influenced by his Jewish identity. More tentatively, and at a more abstract level, the idea that situations of safety and justice are continually under threat from prejudice and change reflects, in many ways, the Jewish experience of history. Against this background, the idea of an "enclave of justice" seems rather like a metaphor for Israel, imagined as a state of safety and justice and democracy surrounded by hostile Arab nations. Certainly, Stone himself tied his concept of enclaves of justice to biblical ideas of bringing justice to the wilderness, noting:

> [I]t would be wrong for those who hold these enclaves to surrender them again to the wilderness ... Rather (we would declare) should men still press forward with courage to realize the vision of Isaiah – that, in the day of human redemption, Justice shall dwell even in the wilderness.[85]

THE ROLE OF STONE'S JEWISH IDENTITY: LIMITING AND CONSTRAINING

Thus far, I have argued that Stone's Jewish identity encouraged and enabled the development of his sociological approach to international law. It drove

---

[84] STAR, *supra* note 1, at 177.
[85] STONE, *supra* note 26, at 798.

him to focus on issues that were critical to developing his sociological under-standing of international law, it shaped his approach to those issues, and it gave him the tools to develop and implement his sociological approach in a way that commanded respect and influence. And yet, for all of Stone's impact on international relations, and all the accolades he received from the interna-tional legal academy, his sociological approach has not been taken up to the extent that might have been expected within international legal scholarship.[86] More significantly, Stone himself never fully developed his approach into a complete and comprehensive legal theory. As a result, Stone's "contribution to the evolution of a new general theory of International Law ... remain[s] inchoate or somewhat unfulfilled."[87] In what follows, I suggest that these limitations on Stone's sociological approach can, paradoxically, be attributed in part to the same factors that drove and enabled its development, particularly Stone's Jewish identity.

At the most basic level, it is clear that throughout his life antisemitism constrained Stone's personal opportunities and positioned him as an outsider in ways that limited the influence of his work. While this position facilitated and enhanced his work in important ways, it also meant that he was "cut off to some extent from the intellectual mainstream of his discipline"[88] in the United States and the United Kingdom. As a result, Stone and his work tended to be "sidelined."[89] This was exacerbated by the fact that, as an outsider, Stone's thinking developed in ways that were in marked contrast to those within the "mainstream" of international law scholarship at the time. Thus Stone has been discounted for being too academic,[90] for dealing with periph-eral issues of only marginal relevance to the mainstream of international law,[91] and for adopting a position of "articulate dissenter from positions taken by many colleagues."[92]

Above all, however, it was Stone's work on Israel, and the impact (real or perceived) of his sympathy for the Zionist cause on his analysis, which affected his development of a sociological approach to international law and its

---

[86] *See* Fleur Johns, *The Gift of Realism: Julius Stone and the International Law Academy in Australia, in* JULIUS STONE: A STUDY IN INFLUENCE 21, 22–29 (Helen Irving, Jacqueline Mowbray, & Kevin Walton, eds., 2010).

[87] McWhinney, *supra* note 34, at 151.

[88] Kirby, *supra* note 9, at 333.

[89] *Id.*

[90] James Crawford, *Realism, Scepticism and the Future World Order: Some Thoughts on Julius Stone's Contribution to International Law,* 13 SYDNEY L. REV. 475, esp. at 476–78 (1991).

[91] *Id.* at 481–82.

[92] *Id.* at 477, quoting JULIUS STONE, OF LAW AND NATIONS: BETWEEN POWER POLITICS AND HUMAN HOPES xi (1974).

reception within the international legal community. Stone's writing on matters concerning Israel is vast, encompassing numerous articles, book chapters, opinions, and nonacademic works, as well as his major book, *Israel and Palestine: Assault on the Law of Nations*.[93] In purely practical terms, then, Stone's preoccupation with Israel took away significant time and intellectual energy that he might otherwise have spent developing a more coherent and complete sociological theory of international law. It also affected the reception of his work, for it is his writings on Israel for which he is perhaps best remembered: "[I]t is the one area where his work is constantly cited, where his articles are invariably listed in conference readings and are reprinted in relevant collections."[94] As a result, when considering the overall influence of Stone's oeuvre, his work on a sociological approach to international law is often sidelined in favor of more legalistic and pragmatic aspects of his work on Israel.

Further, there has been a general perception that, on the question of Israel, Stone's personal feelings influenced his analysis. So, for example, one reviewer of *Aggression* described the book as "[t]o some extent ... an essay in special pleading by a man with a profound interest in the fortunes of Israel."[95] Similarly, one reviewer of *Israel and Palestine* complained that "[w]hen one picks up a book by a scholar who has been an authority on international law since 1930, one is entitled to expect something more than a partisan plea,"[96] while another noted that "[r]eaders in search of a balanced treatment of the legal issues in the Middle East will not find it in this book."[97] Among contemporary scholars of international law, Ben Saul observes that Stone's views "are often more like those of an impassioned advocate than those of a somewhat drier, but more faithful, international legal scholar."[98] Whether these judgments are entirely accurate is open to debate. But regardless of whether his work did, in fact, show bias toward the state of Israel, it is certainly true that Stone's Zionist sympathies enabled critics to cast doubt on his analysis of this issue and, by extension,

---

[93] STONE, *supra* note 21.

[94] STAR, *supra* note 1, at 213.

[95] Geoffrey Sawer, *Review of Julius Stone*, Aggression and World Order, 12 AUSTRALIAN OUTLOOK 64 (1958).

[96] Anthony D'Amato, *Israel and Palestine: Assault on the Law of Nations?* 91 YALE L. J. 1725, 1733 (1982).

[97] Frederic L. Kirgis, *Review of* Israel and Palestine: Assault on the Law of Nations *by Julius Stone* 76 AM. J. INTL'L. L. 875 (1982).

[98] Ben Saul, *Julius Stone and the Question of Palestine in International Law*, in JULIUS STONE: A STUDY IN INFLUENCE 238, 261 (Helen Irving, Jacqueline Mowbray, & Kevin Walton, eds., 2010).

on his broader body of work, including his sociological approach. According to Star:

> There is no doubt that Stone's passionate defenses of Israel, and his continued approval of the state's actions, argued from a legal perspective, caused his general reputation as an international lawyer to suffer. He was seen as a committed apologist for Israel, but one who was lacking in discrimination: this judgment was then attributed to his other, less polemical works.[99]

More fundamentally, however, I think a close reading of Stone's work demonstrates that, at key points, his position on Israel undermines the coherent development and implementation of his sociological approach to international law. In particular, I think it impacts adversely on the realization of each of the three key elements of his sociological approach. I turn now to consider how this occurs in relation to each of these elements, through a close reading of one of Stone's representative pieces on Israel, "Peace and the Palestinians."[100]

I Extralegal, Objective Approach

While Stone occupied the position of an objective "outsider" in relation to his general international law work, with respect to Israel he was, in several ways, no longer outside the "establishment." As a Jew and a Zionist, he was clearly invested in the cause of Israel, with a personal and emotional commitment to its creation and preservation. And he took this commitment further by acting, contrary to his own warnings against such a course,[101] as a legal adviser for this cause: first to the Jewish Agency in Palestine[102] and later to the Israeli government itself.[103] On Stone's own account, this had the potential, at least, to jeopardize or undermine his implementation of a sociological approach to international law, for "this kind of commitment is a fertile source of error and distortion."[104] Certainly it has been noted, even by sympathetic reviewers such as Star, that Stone's work "always pictured the Israeli side as the legally correct side."[105]

However, it is not only in this potential loss of objectivity that Stone's commitment to Israel undermines his empirical analysis of the social context

---

[99] STAR, *supra* note 1, at 258.
[100] Julius Stone, *Peace and the Palestinians*, 3 N.Y.U. J. INT'L. L. AND POL. 247 (1970). This article presents an overview of many of the ideas that are developed in greater detail in Stone, *supra* note 21.
[101] *See, e.g.*, Stone, *supra* note 30, at 159.
[102] STAR, *supra* note 1, at 194–95.
[103] *Id.* at 208–11.
[104] Stone, *supra* note 30, at 159.
[105] STAR, *supra* note 9, at 74.

of law. More fundamentally, Stone tends, at key points in his examination of issues concerning Israel, to lapse back into pure legal-technical analysis. And this involves a corresponding shift away from consideration of the broader, social context within which the law operates. I do not wish to overstate the significance of this "return to legal analysis" in Stone's writings on Israel. After all, it was Stone's sensitivity to the position of Israel that drove him, in general works such as *Aggression*, to focus on extralegal factors and thus develop his sociological approach. And this approach remains evident in works such as "Peace and the Palestinians," which examines the claims of the Palestinian people in broad historical and social terms, considering the practical impact of these claims on the prospects of peace in the Middle East. Nonetheless, this work does reveal a certain emphasis on legal analysis as conclusive of key issues. Let me cite two examples.

First, Stone argues that the Palestinians have no claim in relation to territory currently held by Israel, because there was no "identifiable *Palestinian* Arab people,"[106] for the purposes of international law, at the time Israel was created. As a result, the relevant legal "claimants," which Stone argues must be carefully identified for the purposes of "[m]odern concepts of national self-determination,"[107] are not Palestinian Arabs, but "Arabs throughout the entire area"[108] of the Middle East. The claims of this group were satisfied, in Stone's view, with the creation of the state of Jordan, and the current claims of the Palestinians cannot affect the established, *legal* position of Israel.[109] As Anthony D'Amato puts it, in relation to the equivalent argument in *Israel and Palestine*, for Stone,"[l]egally speaking, the Palestinians do not exist."[110] This focus on the formal, legal position as conclusive of the issue undermines Stone's sociological approach of considering the contemporary social context within which the law takes effect. It shuts down further consideration of the issues, including the contemporary and practical interests of the Palestinian Arabs today, and whether international law may be developing toward taking account of such interests. This approach is surprising in light of Stone's long-standing interest in the rights of minorities and the possibilities of drawing on both established and novel mechanisms of international law for their protection.

---

[106]   Stone, *supra* note 99, at 251.
[107]   *Id.* at 250.
[108]   *Id.*
[109]   "An emergent nationalism cannot be treated as if it had developed decades before for purposes of facilely ignoring entitlements previously fixed and acted upon": Stone, *supra* note 99, at 249.
[110]   D'Amato, *supra* note 95, at 1729.

Secondly, Stone dismisses Arab arguments against Israel's title to disputed territory by referring to "Israel's possession, based on rightful entry under international law."[111] Here, again, formal legal analysis functions as a sort of "trump card," which shuts down consideration of the broader historical and social context of Arab claims, which Stone considered in the preceding paragraphs. This seems almost a reversal of Stone's characteristic sociological approach, which requires the legality or otherwise of a position to be examined in light of the broader social context and analysis of extralegal factors. Here Stone uses his findings on the legal position to render his analysis of the extra-legal factors irrelevant. Interestingly, Stone relies in this passage, in support of his conclusion that Israel's position is based on "lawful entry under international law," on the relevant General Assembly resolution.[112] This is in spite of the fact that he has, elsewhere in his work, spent considerable time and intellectual resources questioning the legal validity of such resolutions.[113]

This focus on law as conclusive of certain issues is accompanied, in this article, by a move away from detailed, empirical analysis of extralegal factors and toward generalizations and assumptions concerning the social context within which the law operates. Thus Stone argues that younger generations of Palestinians "probably do not share feelings of nostalgia for a lost homeland,"[114] but gives no analysis to support this sweeping statement. Similarly, after a brief, one-paragraph overview of the history of Palestinian nationalism, Stone concludes that "these facts seem to point to a movement merely stirred and manipulated, and then only sporadically, by forces outside Palestine."[115] This analysis appears to fall significantly short of the rigorous standards demanded by Stone in his Hague Academy lectures.[116] Taken together with Stone's privileging of law in this piece, and his potential loss of objectivity in matters relating to Israel, it suggests that Stone's work on Israel may, in substantive terms, undermine this key element of his sociological approach.

II Intercultural, Inter-systemic Analysis

Stone's inter-systemic, intercultural analysis and his acceptance and embrace of diversity are key strengths of his work when compared with those of his

---

[111]   Stone, *supra* note 99, at 254.
[112]   *Id.* at 254, footnote 33.
[113]   Saul, see *supra* note 97, at 242.
[114]   Stone, *supra* note 99, at 258.
[115]   *Id.*
[116]   Stone, *supra* note 30.

peers. However, this sensitivity to diversity and willingness to adopt an intercultural perspective seems to break down, to a certain degree, in Stone's
writings on Israel. In the context of "Peace and the Palestinians," this manifests
itself in three ways.

First, it is difficult to escape the conclusion that Stone focuses heavily on
the Jewish perspective at the expense of the Palestinian. He considers the
history of the region and the peoples within it primarily from the Jewish
point of view, placing claims to the relevant territory within the context of
Jews being persecuted and "driven from Palestine by invading
conquerors."[117] Stone notes that "for Jews everywhere Palestine continued
into the modern era to be the focus of religious and national life."[118] In
contrast, he never once considers the significance of Palestine for the
Palestinian Arabs. The question of what cultural and religious connections
they may have to the land is obscured in the face of his historical and legal
analysis and general rhetoric, as when he questions whether an Arab "who
in 1948 deliberately chose to leave his home and his Jewish fellow citizens
in obedience to the call of Arab armies, now manifests painful personal
nostalgia or real feelings of 'national' resurgence."[119] Overall, what is striking
about this article is Stone's conviction that there is a "truth" concerning the
history of the region and the justice claims arising from it. This is
a conclusion that even casual observers of the Israeli–Palestinian conflict
might find surprising.[120] It is even more surprising from a scholar like Stone,
who emphasized the indeterminacy and "nationalization" of truth,[121] and
the need to acknowledge "partial truths."[122] In this way, Stone's practice
here contradicts, to some degree, the theoretical approach that he so carefully developed in his other work.

Secondly, Stone appears to undermine his intercultural approach by
failing to acknowledge diversity within Arab and Palestinian group identity.
In making his claim that there is no distinct Palestinian people entitled to
be taken into account for the purposes of international law, Stone obscures
or denies the possibility of diversity within the group he identifies as "Arab
claimants" in the Middle East. He treats the two groups making claims in
the conflict as, quite simply, the Arabs and the Jews. He then proceeds to

---

[117] Stone, *supra* note 99, at 250.
[118] *Id.*
[119] *Id.* at 257.
[120] This was the case even at the time this article appeared, in 1970, although arguably even more
so today.
[121] Stone, *supra* note 30, at 167.
[122] *Id.* at 169.

apply notions of law and justice to the respective claims of these groups by treating each as if they were a homogenous, monolithic group whose members can be treated as sharing common interests. Thus he argues that the struggle should not be seen as one "between the Jews of the world on one hand and the Arabs of *Palestine* on the other," but rather as one "between the Arabs of the Middle East region ... and the Jews of the world."[123] Stone repeatedly treats the Arab states as a unified bloc, referring, for example, to "the Arab position"[124] or the position of "the Arab States."[125] In this way, Stone elides differences and diversity among the Arabs in the Middle East, and the complex ways in which group identities in the region have been constituted and evolved. In doing so, he seems to ignore the insights of his own sociological approach, and its emphasis on "the recognition of present diversities and incongruities"[126] through careful observation of actual social conditions.

Stone not only fails to consider diversity and difference within cultures in the region; he also fails to consider diversity and difference over time. Stone's theoretical work emphasizes that intertemporal analysis is an aspect of intercultural analysis. His sociological approach requires consideration of the "full individuality of the facts of the time and place."[127] This is because extralegal factors that influence the operation of law are "liable to constant transformation and change,"[128] as indeed is international law itself. However, when it comes to his consideration of Palestinian identity, and its relevance for international law, Stone seeks to "fix" facts and law at a particular moment in time. He argues that there was no Palestinian "people," for the purposes of international law, at the time Israel was created, and that any subsequent emergence of a Palestinian people cannot alter the established international legal position. This seems to undermine his idea of international law as open to transformation and change in response to shifting social conditions, seeking instead to fix legal entitlements "once and for all." This failure to acknowledge what Stone himself has termed the "changefulness of the modern State system"[129] seems to undermine further the dynamic and intersystemic perspective that characterizes his sociological approach to international law.

---

[123] Stone, *supra* note 99, at 251.
[124] *See, e.g., id.* at 253.
[125] *See, e.g., id.* at 247, 262.
[126] Stone, *supra* note 30, at 84.
[127] *Id.* at 88.
[128] *Id.* at 89.
[129] *Id.* at 88.

III Justice

I am not the first to suggest that Stone's approach to the question of justice, so central to his sociological approach and to his work generally, is challenged by his work on Israel. This is the one area where Star, his otherwise sympathetic biographer, felt that his approach lacked "balance":[130]

> Stone seemed unaware of the practical injustice under which many Palestinian Arabs, including women and children, labored, regardless of the source of that injustice. One alternative to basing Israel's position on its legal status is to look at the problems in the region as they now exist and try to bring justice to the aid of solving them. Stone was better equipped than most international lawyers to address questions of justice between peoples but chose not to deal with the question in these terms.[131]

In fact, the complex issue of justice in the Middle East offers a perfect vehicle for the application of Stone's sociological approach. It is an issue that cannot be resolved by technical application of the law, and the competing interests at stake are complex, with deep roots in the cultural and social fabric of diverse societies. Yet on this issue Stone seems to step back from his nuanced and sophisticated approach to questions of justice, and reverts to general, absolute, and abstract approaches to the concept.

A key feature of Stone's approach to justice is his refusal to consider the concept exclusively in either absolute or relative terms. On questions touching the interests of Israel, however, Stone tends to fall back onto absolute, almost natural law notions of justice.[132] Thus in "Peace and the Palestinians," he asserts the principle that "marginal wrongs occurring in the course of a distribution should be righted by those who benefited from the distribution in proportion to that benefit,"[133] a principle he then applies to minimize Israel's responsibility toward Palestinian refugees on the basis that "[c]orrectly seen, any injustice which the Arabs of Palestine suffered was as much a function of the creation of the present Arab States as it was a direct result

---

[130]   STAR, *supra* note 9, at 72.

[131]   STAR, *supra* note 1, at 213.

[132]   This was evident in his work on the Nuremburg trials, where, as McWhinney has noted, Stone ultimately adopted a "pure natural law position," arguing that while the rules applied at Nuremburg were not positive rules of international law, they were "at least rules of positive ethics accepted by civilized men everywhere, to which the accused could properly be held": Edward McWhinney, *Review of* Julius Stone, Legal Controls of International Conflict, 64 YALE L. J. 959, 962 (1955). A similar, absolute idea of justice seems to be at work in Stone's writings on the Eichmann trial: *See* STONE, *supra* note 81.

[133]   Stone, *supra* note 99, at 252–53.

of the establishment of Israel."[134] Since Israel had already assumed responsibility for some 500,000 Jewish refugees displaced in this process, the Arab states, according to Stone, should accept responsibility for the Palestinian refugees. The phrase "correctly seen" is telling here, for it suggests that there is a "correct" view, thus seeming to deny the possibility of diverse and relative perspectives on issues of justice.[135] In suggesting such an absolute concept of justice, Stone seems to undermine the rich insights of his theoretical work on complex and relative aspects of justice.

Overall, the ideas of justice invoked in "Peace and the Palestinians" are not the carefully analyzed and empirically evaluated ones called for in Stone's theoretical work. His analysis of justice in this piece operates instead at a rather abstract level, in terms of broad narratives of history and undifferentiated assessments of the general claims of "the Jews" and "the Arabs." While Stone's sociological approach is based on the rejection of abstract, "grand visions" of justice, requiring instead careful attention to the particular social facts and circumstances of individual cases, there is very little of such analysis in this article. The "justice" or "injustice" of the present situation is considered in global terms, rather than on an issue-by-issue basis, and with no consideration of the practical, social conditions of everyday life for Israelis and Palestinians. Contrary to Stone's sociological approach, the overwhelming impression here is of justice as an abstract concept, rather than a social phenomenon.

Associated with this move toward a more general and abstract assessment of issues of justice is a marked tendency, in this article, for Stone to treat questions of international justice instead as questions of justice between states. In delegitimizing the claims of the Palestinian people, on the basis that they did not qualify for legal recognition at the relevant time, Stone suggests that the only entities entitled to justice in the international arena are states. His analysis proceeds to consider the relative rights and responsibilities of Israel and the other Arab states, particularly Jordan, with almost no consideration of injustice faced by *individual* Palestinians. To the extent that injustices faced by Palestinians are considered at all, they are considered in relation to *the group*, and in the context of the past actions and history of that group, rather

---

[134] *Id.* at 252.
[135] A similar "correct" framing of the issue can be found at *id.* at 251: "[I]t twists and parodies both history and justice to present the Palestine issue as a struggle between the Jews of the world on one hand and the Arabs of *Palestine* on the other in which the Jews seized the major share. The struggle was rather between the Arabs of the Middle East region, including some hundreds of thousands living in Palestine, and the Jews of the world in which the Arabs took a lion's share and from which more than a dozen Arab States emerged."

than from the perspective of individuals, such as children who have no association with the historical facts on which Stone draws to deny their claims. In this way, Stone undermines the expansive vision of justice developed in his other work as including, at least to some extent, justice among individuals. Taken together with the other limitations on his approach to justice in this piece, it suggests that Stone not only failed to take up the challenge of applying his sophisticated concept of justice to questions of Israel and Palestine, but that his work on Israel in fact undermined, to a certain degree, his brilliant and nuanced theoretical work on this concept.

Overall, this analysis suggests that the question of Israel represents something of a limit for Stone's sociological approach to international law. Stone's strong feelings about Israel challenged his ability to maintain the level of objectivity and commitment to extralegal, intercultural, and relativist analysis that he himself demanded of his approach. Ultimately, then, while Stone's Jewish identity and Zionist sympathies made his development of a sociological approach to international law possible, in other ways, and at the same time, they constrained his ability to develop that approach fully.

CONCLUSION

Julius Stone rose from humble beginnings as the son of poor, Jewish immigrants to become one of the great international lawyers of the twentieth century. Throughout this journey, he retained a strong and public sense of Jewish identity, even in the face of prejudice and discrimination. I have argued that this Jewish identity exercised a profound, if contradictory, influence on Stone's development of a sociological approach to international law. On the one hand, the three key elements of Stone's sociological approach – his focus on extralegal, objective analysis of law; his adoption of an intercultural, intersystemic approach; and his attention to the demands of justice – can be attributed to his Jewish consciousness and experiences as a Jewish man in a non-Jewish world. On the other hand, Stone's work on Israel challenged his ability to develop and implement a complete sociological theory of international law, and the real or perceived bias of his work on this topic affected the reception of his scholarship more generally. In this way, Stone's Jewish consciousness both enabled *and* constrained the development of his sociological approach to international law. The contours of Stone's distinctive contribution to the quest for international justice will be forever marked by his Jewish identity.

14

An Axionormative Dissenter

Reflections on Julius Stone

David N. Myers

The opportunity to comment on Jacqueline Mowbray's discussion of Julius Stone is doubly welcome. Not only does it afford me the opportunity to engage in a set of scholarly issues that have long interested me at the intersection of law and history, but it has also exposed me to a fascinating figure, Stone, about whom I knew precious little. Stone's life story is, on my very basic reading, one of intriguing tensions: exclusion and high attainment, a sweeping catholicity of mind and a certain rigidity of disposition, and a keen concern for the fate of minorities alongside a surprising tone-deafness to the plight of one in particular. Mowbray skillfully teases out another defining tension: Stone's commitment to the ideal of objectivity, borne of the outsider's perspective, and his recognition, resulting from his commitment to cross-cultural analysis, of the inescapability of a measure of relativism in scholarly inquiry.[1]

Mowbray's basic premise is that Stone's Jewishness played a central role in the formation of a new approach to international law, a more dynamic, sociological method than the staid views of jurisprudence to which he was first exposed at Oxford. She also suggests that his Jewishness placed serious constraints on this approach – and contributed to the tensions noted above. I am in agreement with this basic premise and was persuaded by Mowbray's analysis of the three Jewishly inflected themes in his work on international law.

What I propose to do is offer a slight recasting of the portrait of Stone from my vantage point as a Jewish historian. There are significant areas of overlap between this and Mowbray's approach, but my account will seek to situate

---

[1] In his attempt to overcome a similar tension, the eminent Oxford philosopher R. G. Collingwood spoke of the quest for "relative truth" in his "Lectures on the Philosophy of History" from 1926: "It may seem paradoxical to say that one account is nearer to the truth than another while yet confessing that we do not know what the truth is; but we must face this paradox ... " R. G. COLLINGWOOD, THE IDEA OF HISTORY 391 (rev. with Jan van Der Dussen, 1993).

Stone more squarely within the frame of modern Jewish intellectual history than legal studies. This modest alteration of perspective will, I hope, yield new areas of juxtaposition that may provide a deeper understanding of the sources and impact of Stone's work.

By way of introduction and reorientation, I suggest that we draw on a number of insights embedded in the pioneering article by Paul Mendes-Flohr from 1982, "The Study of the Jewish Intellectual: A Methodological Prolegomenon." In the course of his exhaustive review of sociological litera-ture on the intellectual, Mendes-Flohr recalls that it was likely Georges Clemenceau who coined the term "intellectuals" in 1898, referring to the Dreyfusards who "defended Dreyfus's innocence and the democratic princi-ples of the French Republic."[2] The Dreyfus-era setting and connotation for the term point us to the realization that intellectuals, among whom we can count Stone, were and are not mere disinterested observers. We often add the qualifier "public" to distinguish those intellectuals who comfortably and will-ingly announce their views to wide audiences from those who prefer the cloistered archive or study. But in fact, a wider public role – and the task of advocacy – belonged to the core and original mission of the intellectual. Especially when we recall his views on Israel and the Palestinians, we can see the extent to which Stone satisfies this early understanding: his intellectual project included a healthy dose of advocacy on an issue of utmost importance to him that extended beyond the narrow strictures of scholarship.

Mendes-Flohr makes a second key point about Jewish intellectuals that is apposite to Stone. One of the characteristic features of the intellectual in general is the tendency to challenge convention and assume a position of what Mendes-Flohr calls "axionormative dissent," all the while achieving fluency in the linguistic and cognitive world of mainstream society. The modern Jewish intellectual, who acquired this fluency through university attendance, has been further shaped by the phenomenon of social exclusion, especially in Europe, which created its own feedback loop in the direction of axionormative dissent. Mendes-Flohr explored this combination of properties in his main area of expertise, German Jewish intellectual history. He noted that German Jewish intellectuals, facing barriers to advancement in academia and the civil service, could pursue several paths, including conversion to Christianity. But the intellectual could also opt out of the cognitive world in which he was educated either through "escapism" or "rebellion." Those forms of

[2]   Paul Mendes-Flohr, *The Study of the Jewish Intellectual: A Methodological Prolegomenon, in* PAUL MENDES-FLOHR, DIVIDED PASSIONS: JEWISH INTELLECTUALS AND THE EXPERIENCE OF MODERNITY 28 (1991).

axionormative dissent were not unique to Jewish intellectuals in Germany. They were found in other contexts in which Jews confronted ongoing discrimination even as they gained entry to universities as students. Indeed, the formative milieux in which Stone found himself – Leeds, Oxford, and later Cambridge, Massachusetts – allowed for a good deal of intellectual integration, but still manifested traces of social exclusion. In light of this, we might consider the development of his distinctive approach to international law as a form of axionormative dissent.

BETWEEN LAW AND JEWISH LAW IN STONE'S THOUGHT

To get a bit more clarity on this process, it might make sense to retrace some of the steps followed by Mowbray, as well as by Leonie Star in her biography *Julius Stone: An Intellectual Life*. Stone was born to immigrant parents in a poor neighborhood in Leeds in 1907. He was raised in an ambience in which deep suspicion toward and dislike of immigrant Jews were common, which may have implanted in young Julius the imperative to work hard and succeed in the Gentile world. This was an experience familiar to Jewish children of immigrants of his generation across Europe and in North America. As they experienced varying degrees of nativist antisemitism in the early twentieth century, this generation of Jews labored to excel in educational and professional pursuits and thereby prove the folly of their detractors. For some of this generation, the pressures of external enmity and the need for success necessitated flight from their Jewish origins. In the most extreme cases, it was only baptism that offered, as Heinrich Heine famously declared, the requisite "ticket of admission" to Gentile society. For others, removing lingering traces of Jewish roots – linguistic affects, ritual norms, dietary habits – provided sufficient distance from the old world to gain leverage in the new.

Stone did not belong to these subsets of Jews. He was brought up in an observant home with a strong sense of Jewish affiliation, and remained deeply connected to synagogue and Jewish community throughout his life. The anti-Jewish slights and cold shoulders he absorbed throughout his long academic career did not make him more deferential or intent on full assimilation. Rather, they seem to have fortified his resolve to work exceptionally hard in order to reach lofty goals, as well as his impulse to depart from convention, which surfaced early on. For example, as a Jew of his economic status and means, he was supposed to go to the University of Leeds, but instead he defied those who advised him, including the eminent Jewish mathematician Selig

Brodetsky, by reaching beyond his milieu to attend Oxford.[3] Once there, as Mowbray notes, he felt himself an outlier, both socially and intellectually. Constantly impoverished, he was not able to participate in the full range of student activities. And intellectually, he found that the field of jurisprudence in which he had developed an incipient interest was under the sway of a certain Austinian analytic aridity. The seeds of his "axionormative dissent" were sown here and animated his search for an alternative that would even-tuate in his externalist, contextualizing sociological method.

The mix of Stone's rapid rate of scholarly productivity, methodological iconoclasm, and difficulty in finding a permanent academic post reinforced his sense of being a Jewish outsider. That vantage point was a haven of retreat from hostile forces, but also a platform for the articulation of his distinctive views. His outsider status informed, as Mowbray has chronicled, Stone's unrelenting defense of Israeli government policy, which he felt called upon to provide due to the bias he perceived in international forums. Mowbray has also noted that Stone's Jewishness, and particularly "his own experiences of anti-Semitism,"[4] was a catalyzing force in his effort to formulate a theory of the origins, varieties, and endpoints of *justice.*

I would like to probe a bit deeper into Stone's Jewish intellectual formation and motivations. As a synagogue-attending Jew, he was well aware of the oft invoked injunction that he would have read in Chief Rabbi Joseph Hertz's edition of the Pentateuch: "*tsedek, tsedek tirdof,*" or "justice, justice shalt thou follow."[5] But a cursory reading of Stone's major works on the idea of justice reveals a number of interesting additional features of his understanding of justice. First, the Jewish sources upon which Stone draws in the sweeping *Human Law and Human Justice* (1965) move well beyond what an interested layperson would be capable of drawing on. He was intimately familiar with the work of a range of notable twentieth-century scholars including Salo Baron, Boaz Cohen, Louis Finkelstein, Solomon Freehof, Abraham Joshua Heschel, and George Mendenhall. More impressively, he melded his solid knowledge of the Bible with a competent understanding of Talmudic and medieval rabbinic sources, often mediated through the research of Israeli scholar and supreme court justice Haim Cohn.[6]

This sense of the arc of Jewish legal development gave Stone a unique angle on the differing regimes of justice he surveyed in *Human Law and Human*

---

3   LEONIE STAR, JULIUS STONE: AN INTELLECTUAL LIFE 11 (1992).
4   This and other quotations, unless otherwise attributed, refer to Jacqueline Mowbray, *Enabling and Constraining: Julius Stone and the Contradictions of the Sociological Path to International Law,* Chapter 13 in this volume.
5   *Deuteronomy* 16:20 (Joseph Hertz, *The Pentateuch and Haftorahs*).
6   JULIUS STONE, HUMAN LAW AND HUMAN JUSTICE, 22ff (1965).

Justice. At the outset of his chapter "Early Horizons of Justice in the West," he invoked Matthew Arnold's renowned view that "Hebraism and Hellenism are the main source waters which fed the Western cultural stream."[7] Reverting to his outlier perspective, he aimed to correct the historical record that, to his mind, had cast upon Jewish law an undeserved reputation for vengefulness. In fact, Mosaic law, more than Greek law, bestowed on the world what he regarded as a worthy ideal, "justice-according-to-law," as opposed to an abstract and utopian ideal of justice detached from the real world. It was the Hebrews who invented this grounded view of justice, which was then passed on to the Christians who carried it forward.

What is striking, though not surprising, is Stone's role as an advocate for Jewish primogeniture, particularly in asserting Judaism's role in giving birth to a sustainable notion of justice. This tendency to assert Jewish primacy or ethical virtue, in fact, was a common feature in the founding generations of modern Jewish scholars who operated under the banner of *Wissenschaft des Judentums* in Germany. They sought to fight a defensive battle against Christian scholars who depicted Second Temple Judaism as the dying embers of a spiritual flame that was rekindled in early Christianity. The greatest of nineteenth-century Jewish historians, Heinrich Graetz, characteristically turned the tables on his Christian scholarly contemporaries when he asserted: "The farther Christianity moved from its origins, the more it forgot or made itself forget not only where it had come from, but also from whom it had taken the largest part of its doctrines that won people's hearts."[8]

This project of scholarship as advocacy, which recalls Georges Clemenceau's definition of the intellectual, neither ended with Graetz nor invalidated the results of the research undertakings of Jewish historians. Acknowledging this feature of academic scholarship widens our understanding of the context in which German Jewish historians wrote and allows us a better handle on the importance and relevance of their work. In light of this, it seems reasonable to read Stone's discussion of the origins of a grounded notion of justice in a similar vein. Like the earlier Jewish scholars, he preached the need for objectivity in scholarly labor. And like them, his enduring warmth for and defense of Judaism likely figured in his granting it pride of place in shaping regimes of justice in the world.

---

[7] *Id.* at 9.
[8] Heinrich Graetz, Geschichte der Juden 97 (vol. 4, 1900), quoted in Michael Brenner, Prophets of the Past: Interpreters of Jewish History 67 (2010).

THE PLACE OF MINORITY RIGHTS IN STONE'S THOUGHT

Stone's fierce Jewish ethos was a constant, if not always declared, presence in his work. Mowbray is well aware of this and suggests that Stone's interest in minority rights as a component of international law "was driven, at least in part, by factors much more intrinsic to Stone himself – namely his Jewish identity and consciousness of Jewish history." I couldn't agree more, and would like to elaborate on Stone's interest in minority rights, which was a central preoccupation of Jewish scholars and activists both before and after World War I. Jewish nationalists of different stripes, both Diasporists who favored national cultural autonomy in Europe and Zionists who favored a return to Palestine, agreed on the importance of achieving legal guarantees for Jews who lived under non-Jewish regimes.[9] In most cases, they believed that such guarantees of the right to maintain their own religious, cultural, and linguistic norms rested on recognition of their status as a cultural nation. Their support for this proposition had its most important hearing at the Paris Peace Conference that followed World War I. Among other tasks, the conference set out to redraw the map of Europe and the world, allowing for new nation-states to emerge out of the husks of crumbled empires. In the process of carving out these new entities, the League of Nations sought to write into the foundational treaties and other documents relating to the new states protections for minorities living within their midst.

Interested Jewish parties, especially the Comité des Délégations Juives, followed the deliberations in Paris with great concern. The war had exposed the physical vulnerability of Jews, millions of whom were caught at the ever-shifting boundaries that were contested by warring parties in Eastern Europe. And in the immediate post-war chaos, tens of thousands of Jews were murdered by nationalists in Ukraine. The central question Jewish activists posed of the new minority rights system that was taking form out of the Treaty of Versailles was: What mechanism could assure that the new nation-states of Europe would uphold the guarantees made to Jews, circumscribed as they may have been? This was especially relevant given the peculiar fact that minorities themselves did not have the standing to pursue claims against states

---

[9] *See, e.g.* JEWS & DIASPORA NATIONALISM: WRITINGS ON JEWISH PEOPLEHOOD IN EUROPE & THE UNITED STATES (Simon Rabinovich, ed., 2012); JOSHUA SHANES, DIASPORA NATIONALISM AND JEWISH IDENTITY IN HABSBURG GALICIA (2012); Dimitry Shumsky, *Tsiyonut u-medinat le'om: ha-'arakhah mi-ḥadash*, 77 ZION 223 (2012). For a review of recent literature that explores the intersection between Zionists and Diasporists, *see* David N. Myers, *Rethinking Sovereignty and Autonomy: New Currents in the History of Jewish Nationalism*, 13 TRANSVERSAL 44 (2015).

for violation of their articulated rights. Who, then, was to defend their interests? Indeed, who had the right to raise claims against member states of the
League of Nations?

It was these questions that engaged Jewish activists such as Louis Marshall,
Leo Motzkin, and Lucien Wolf at Paris – and for the next decade and a half.[10]
Jewish scholars also weighed in, such as historian Oscar Janowsky in his 1933
book *Jews and Minority Rights, 1898–1919* and *Nations and National
Minorities* (1945). Janowsky used his historical examination to call for a new
system of "national federalism" that extended existing rights for minorities
with more stringent means of enforcement. In the same vein, scholar and
activist Jacob Robinson joined together with a group of colleagues to provide
a book-length response to the question, *Were the Minorities Treaties a Failure?*
After a detailed evaluation, Robinson and his colleagues concluded in 1943
that "[d]espite all the faults and shortcomings, some inherent and others
external, the experience of twenty years does not justify the condemnation of
a most remarkable experiment; an experiment that could not but share the fate
of the political organism in which it lived – the League of Nations itself."[11]

It was on the ground trodden by the likes of Wolf and Janofsky that Stone
engaged in his own study of the minority rights enforcement process in a pair
of books published in successive years while he was at Harvard Law School:
International Guarantees of Minority Rights (1932) and *Regional Guarantees
of Minority Rights* (1933). Although the Jews of Europe made infrequent
appearances in these two books, it is reasonable to assume that they were
uppermost in his mind. The first of the books, which was dedicated to his
father, spelled out the existing mechanisms for addressing violations of the
minority guarantees in the post–World War I treaties within the
existing League of Nations structure. Stone's careful analysis identified imperfections in the structure, while also generating recommendations about how to
maximize positive results within the prevailing order.[12] The second book
examined a more specific case study in the law of minority rights – the 1922
German-Polish Convention over the status of Upper Silesia. Here again, Jews
were mentioned on but a few occasions. But Stone was surely mindful of the
importance of the minority rights question in Jewish political and legal

---

[10] For a detailed description of Jewish efforts at Paris, *see* CAROLE FINK, DEFENDING THE
      RIGHTS OF OTHERS: THE GREAT POWERS, THE JEWS, AND INTERNATIONAL MINORITIES
      PROTECTION, 1878–1938 (2004).
[11] JACOB ROBINSON, O. KARBACH, M. LASERSON, N. ROBINSON, AND M. VICHNIAK, WERE
      THE MINORITIES TREATIES A FAILURE? 265 (1943).
[12] JULIUS STONE, INTERNATIONAL GUARANTEES OF MINORITY RIGHTS: PROCEDURE OF
      THE COUNCIL OF THE LEAGUE OF NATIONS IN THEORY AND PRACTICE 246–67 (1932).

discourse since 1919. He also was aware of the fact that in 1933, the year in which his book appeared, Jews in Germany fell under the shadow of "the anti-Jewish policy of the National-Socialist Government," a development that prompted the League of Nations to bestow formal minority status on Jews in Upper Silesia. As in his previous book, Stone adopted here a contextually nuanced stance that eschewed utopian fantasy. He remained hopeful that the regional 1922 Convention, imperfections notwithstanding, would be renewed. In it inhered an opportunity for stability and security for minorities even more likely to succeed than a system of international guarantees. And yet, failure to renew the convention would be "an event of most grave import to Europe."[13]

In these two works, Stone evinced strong support for minority rights, as well as for better enforcement of them in international and state-based law. His support grew out of a larger concern and debate over Jews as a national minority that operated at two levels: first, as a manifestation of Stone's visceral anxiety over the physical well-being of Jews in a time of upheaval; and second, as a reflection of his realist sense of "justice-in-the-law," that is, a bottom-up system of justice rooted not in abstract principle, but in concrete norms whose origins lay in "the Mosaic law" and "in the land of Israel."

FROM MINORITY RIGHTS TO THE RIGHTS OF THE MAJORITY

Stone's fervent defense of minority rights was animated, as Mowbray suggests, by his Jewish commitments and experience. We might suggest further that his was a form of "axionormative dissent" from mainstream strands of international law concerned largely, if not exclusively, with nation-states.

It is curious to juxtapose this stance with Stone's views on Zionism and the State of Israel, which developed over time into a full-blown majoritarianism. On this point as well, Mowbray offers perceptive and detailed insights. As a general matter, she argues that "his position on Israel undermines the coherent development and implementation of his sociological approach to international law." I'd like to continue in this vein by suggesting that Stone's position on Israel – and more specifically, on the Palestinians – represents a moral and logical lapse on his part insofar as it ignores both his previous advocacy of minority rights and important lessons from the historical experience of the Jews. The unyielding nature of his support for Israeli government policy resonates with the stance of some pro-Israel advocacy groups today. But

---

[13] JULIUS STONE, REGIONAL GUARANTEES OF MINORITY RIGHTS: A STUDY OF MINORITIES PROCEDURE IN UPPER SILESIA 35, 202–10 (1933).

alternative positions were available to Stone that may have fitted his overall worldview more consistently.

To be sure, the establishment of the State of Israel in 1948 had a dramatic effect on world Jewry. Coming a few short years after the Holocaust, it generated pride, joy, relief, and a sense of messianic fulfillment. Even among Jews who previously had expressed opposition to Zionism, the creation of the state was a moment of reckoning marked by an irreversible fait accompli.

Stone's own Zionist commitments well preceded 1948, as Mowbray and Star note. He subscribed to Zionism as a solution to the stateless condition of Jews, growing more committed as the threat of Nazism became direr. Once in Australia, he became a vocal and visible supporter of Zionism, challenging fellow Jews who failed to see its virtue. And he signed on as a legal adviser to the Jewish Agency in 1947, authoring a brief for the United Nations as it contemplated the end of the British Mandate in Palestine.[14] Stone's profound identification with his fellow Jews and desire to improve their lot anchored his belief that they deserved a legally recognized homeland of their own.

This concern is consistent with Stone's prior interest in minority rights. What is not is his seeming disregard for the historical experience and legal status of the Palestinians. Three claims in particular stand out, all of which are advanced in Stone's 1981 book *Israel and Palestine*. Mowbray has identified and discussed these claims; I would like to elaborate on them with reference to personalities and themes in twentieth-century Jewish history.

First, Stone followed a common trope of Israeli public diplomacy of the day, made famous by Golda Meir in 1969, by denying that there was a Palestinian people worthy of legal recognition. As he wrote:

> To present, in 1980 a "Palestinian nation" as having been displaced by Israel in Palestine, when no such distinctive entity recognized itself or existed at the time of the allocation between the Jewish and Arab peoples after World War I, is an impermissible game with both history and justice.[15]

Second, Stone did not only place the onus or responsibility for the conflict between Israelis and Palestinians on the latter. He seemed to discount the impact of the hostilities of 1948 – and the dispossession of hundreds of thousands of Palestinian Arabs – by asserting that "any wrong to the Palestinians flowed ... far more from the creation of so many Arab states in so vast an area than it did from the creation of the tiny state of Israel."

---

[14] Star, *supra* note 3, at 193–94.
[15] Julius Stone, Israel and Palestine: Assault on the Law of Nations 16 (1981).

Third, Israeli settlements in the West Bank, he maintained, should not be deemed illegal under Article 49 of the Fourth Geneva Convention, which states that an "Occupying Power shall not deport or transfer parts of its own civilian population into the territory it occupies."[16] That article was crafted, he argued, to prevent the kinds of excesses committed by Nazis during World War II, and thus does not apply to the case of Israeli settlements in the West Bank.

This last point has been hotly contested. The Israeli government continues to hold to the view articulated by Stone, while much of the world regards Israeli settlements as illegal under international law. Against that backdrop, it is interesting to compare Stone's strong view to another eminent Jewish international lawyer, Theodor Meron, who has had a long and diverse career as scholar, diplomat, and presiding judge of a number of international criminal tribunals (e.g., the former Yugoslavia and Rwanda). Meron was born in Poland in 1930, and spent time in a Nazi labor camp before arriving in pre-state Palestine in 1945. After training in law in Jerusalem and at Harvard and Cambridge, he joined the Israeli Foreign Service. In the late 1960s, Meron served as the legal adviser to the Israeli foreign minister. In that capacity, he was asked by Prime Minister Levi Eshkol in September 1967, a few short months after the Six Day War, to advise him on whether Israel was permitted to settle civilians in the newly conquered territories. Meron's answer was unequivocal and at stark odds with Stone's. On the basis of his reading of Article 49, Israel, as an occupying power, was not at liberty to "deport or transfer parts of its own civilian population into the territory it occupies." Meron continued by insisting that "[t]he prohibition therefore is categorical and not conditional upon the motives for the transfer or its objectives." Should Israel decide to place settlements in the newly acquired territories, it must do so through military units and on a temporary, not permanent, basis.[17]

This opinion, which Meron described nearly a half-century later as "my best reading of international law," was based on the author's intricate familiarity with international law.[18] Whether Meron brought his own experience as a victim of Nazi persecution into this opinion remains an open question.

---

[16] *Id.* at 17, 25, 177–78.
[17] Theodor Meron, Memorandum, Sept. 18, 1967 (www.southjerusalem.com/wp-content/uplo ads/2008/09/theodor-meron-legal-opinion-on-civilian-settlement-in-the-occupied-territories-s eptember-1967.pdf). An English translation can be seen at www.soas.ac.uk/lawpeacemideast/ resources/file48485.pdf.
[18] *See* Samantha Lachman, *How Palestinians Could Use Israel's Own Legal Analysis Before the ICC*, HUFFINGTON POST, Jan. 16 2015, at www.huffingtonpost.com/2015/01/16/palestinians-international-criminal-court-_n_6472398.html.

But his words do point to an alternative position on Israel's occupation of the West Bank, articulated by a figure no less connected to the Jewish people and Israel than Stone.

It is not the case that anyone who adopts a position on Article 49 similar to Stone's is ipso facto insensitive. But it is surprising, at least to this reader, that Stone did not evince more nuance and sensitivity in his analysis, opting to promote a rather Manichean divide between good Israelis and bad Arabs. It is indeed surprising, as Mowbray observes, that he did not have a more sophisticated grasp of history when he denied, in 1981, that there was a Palestinian people or claimed that the creation of the State of Israel caused less harm to the Palestinians than the emergence of Arab states.[19]

Maintaining those positions is not a necessary requirement of support or even love for the State of Israel. I am reminded of the wide-ranging Jewish scholar, Simon Rawidowicz, who, like Stone, was keenly attuned to the experience of the Jewish minority in Europe and believed passionately in their national minority rights. He also believed that Israel was a central axis of Jewish life that could not be ignored or dismissed. And yet, Rawidowicz held to the view, as he expressed in an essay in the early 1950s, that the historical experience of the Jews as an oft oppressed minority must inculcate in them a sensitivity to the plight of other beleaguered minority groups, especially the Palestinians. Rawidowicz's evocative image of the recently concluded battle in Palestine, drawn from the Talmud, was of "'two people holding on to a garment,' both of whom claim to the master watching over them that the garment is all theirs." As of 1948, Rawidowicz continued, one side has grabbed hold of the garment and now "rules as a decisive majority, as a nation-state." The other side, he continued, "is dominated as a minority."[20] The cause of the malaise in which the Israelis and Palestinians now found themselves was, to a great measure, the historical amnesia of the Jews, who failed to remember their own experiences of persecution and yet acted like a "servant when he reigneth."[21] The effect, he warned, would be a very heavy moral and political cost to Israel, whose claim to an exalted democratic standing would be compromised.

Rawidowicz went as far as to call for the repatriation of hundreds of thousands of Palestinian refugees, a claim so violative of Jewish communal discourse at the time that he decided never to publish his essay.[22] Rereading

---

[19] Stone, *supra* note 17, at 25.
[20] Baba Metzia 1:1, quoted in Rawidowicz's unpublished essay from the early 1950s *in* DAVID N. MYERS, BETWEEN JEW AND ARAB: THE LOST VOICE OF SIMON RAWIDOWICZ 136 (2008).
[21] *Proverbs* 30:22 (Jewish Publication Society, 1917).
[22] It is translated and published for the first time in MYERS, *supra* note 22, at 135–80.

this provocative piece today reminds one of a rather simple but easily forgotten point, namely, that abiding identification with one's own group need not be exclusive of empathy for another group, even and especially one's putative enemy. This seemed to be a lesson that Stone, for all of his erudition, innovation, and concern for justice, did not fully absorb in the case of Israel and the Palestinians. Indeed, on this issue, Rawidowicz, with his impassioned call for empathy, followed the intellectual's path of "axionormative dissent" more than Stone.

In conclusion, the task of this commentary has been less to challenge than to amplify Mowbray's finely grained treatment of Stone. While she has identified a number of key spots in which his Jewish background stimulated and limited the reach of his sociological method, this commentary has sought to wrap his life and thought in an added layer of contextual swathing by drawing, first, on the profile of the modern Jewish intellectual and then on specific themes and personalities from Jewish history that present suitable sources of comparison. When read together with Mowbray, it is hoped that this layer provides a richer understanding of Stone.

Index

ABC. *See* Australian Broadcasting Corporation
African-American civil rights, 111–12, 123, 126–27, 154
The Age of Rights (Henkin, L.), 98, 108
Aggression and World Order (Stone), 268, 273, 275, 277
AIU. *See* Alliance Israélite Universelle
AJC. *See* American Jewish Committee
Akzin, Benjamin, 64, 65
Algemeine Staatslehre (Kelsen), 84
Alliance Israélite Universelle (AIU), 191–93, 195, 213–14
Altneuland (Herzl), 67
American Bar Association, 101
American Civil Liberties Union, 138
American Jewish Committee (AJC), 107, 231
    Henkin, L., and, 103–4, 110–11, 121, 132, 138–40
    human rights and, 136, 137–38
    Israel and, 137–38
    Kohler, M., and, 126–27, 133, 136
    Marshall and, 126–27, 133
    Reform Jewry and, 131, 132, 135, 137, 138–39
    UN and, 137
    Zionism and, 131, 132, 133–34, 135, 136, 137–38
American Jewish Congress, 103–4, 123
Anglo-American Committee of Inquiry, 68
Animal Farm (Orwell), 162
anti-colonialism, 104
antiquarian approach, in Jewish history, 9–12
anti-Semitism
    Lauterpacht, H., and, 35–36
    Stone facing, 258, 259–60, 269, 270, 271, 274, 287
anti-utopianism, postwar, 145–46

Approaches to the Notion of International Justice (Stone), 266
Arendt, Hannah, 59, 72
Arnold, Matthew, 288
Article 6. *See* Nuremberg Charter, Article 6 of
Article 49. *See* Fourth Geneva Convention, Article 49 of
Aspen Institute, 108
assimilationism, 73
    antinomies of, 71–74
    Arendt on radical, 72
    in Austria, 58–60, 72
    Kelsen and, 57–63, 65, 66–67, 69–73, 80
    through law, 57–58, 72
    private property rights and, 70–71
    progressivism and, 75, 78–79
    public/private divide and, 72–73
    universal rights and, 69–70
    into world community, 73–74
Association for Civil Rights in Israel, 137–38
Auerbach, Jerold, 124
Australia, 270, 292
    anti-Semitism in, 259–60
    University of Sydney, 257, 259–60, 269
Australian Broadcasting Corporation (ABC), 261
Austria
    assimilation in, 58–60, 72
    Constitutional Court in, Kelsen introducing, 79
    fascism in, 52, 62
    Jews of, 51, 57, 58–60, 72
    Kelsen and, 51, 52–53, 57–63, 64, 65, 68, 79, 80
    Social-Democrats of, 62

autonomism, 233–34, 235, 236
axionormative dissent, 285–86, 291, 295

Basle Program, 233, 246–47
Baxi, Upendra, 270
Beatson, Jack, 10–12
Belarus, 95
Bell, Duncan, 168–69
Beller, Steven, 59, 72
Benes, Eduard, 148–50, 153
Berlin, Isaiah, 30–31
Bernheim, Franz, 191
Bernheim Petition, 191
Bethlehem, Daniel, 16
Bialik, Haim Nachman, 28
biographical approach, in Jewish history, 12–13
Black Sabbath (Operation Agatha), 221–22
Bodin, Jean, 6
Borchard, Edwin, 9
Bosnia and Herzegovina, 250, 251, 252
Boudin, Leonard, 157–58
Brandeis, Louis, 126, 136
    pluralism of, 135–36
    Zionism and, 134, 135–36
Bricker, John, 114
Bundists, 33
Burke, Edmund, 99

Cabranes, José A., 164–65
Carr, E. H., 44
Carter, Jimmy, 107–8, 113, 114
Cassin, René
    in AIU, 191–93, 195, 213–14
    domicile right and, 182–86, 189, 200–01, 204, 206–10, 211, 213, 214–16
    on entry, 184, 185–86, 189
    exit and, 184–85, 186, 189–90, 196–97
    France and, 187–88, 191, 193–94, 210, 213
    Henkin, L., and, 16–17, 105
    Holocaust and, 193, 194, 195, 202
    International Colloquium of, on return, 195–96, 201
    International Institute for Human Rights founded by, 105
    Jews and, 178, 190–95, 196, 201, 212–14
    League of Nations and, 183, 187, 206, 211–12
    on Leviathan State, 187–88, 212
    mobility and, 177–78, 195, 196, 201
    on nationality, law of, 207–10
    on nation-state, 186–90, 214
    to Nazism, reaction of, 186–88, 191, 211–12
    1930 Hague Academy lectures of, 206–10, 211, 214–15
    1968 Nobel Peace Prize Lecture of, 210–11
    non-Jewish influences on, 16–17
    Palestinians and, 178, 192, 194–96, 197–202, 213, 215–17
    return, right of, and, 195–96, 197–201, 214–15
    Soviet Jews and, 195–97, 202
    UDHR and, 177, 195, 214
    at UN, 177
    veterans and, 184–85, 190, 205–6
    Zionism and, 191–93, 195, 212–14
Central European legalism, 160–61
Christian Human Rights (Moyn), 119
Christianity, 288
Christian-Social Party (CSP), Austrian, 62
Churchill, Winston, 226
Civil War, American, 125
Clemenceau, Georges, 285, 288
Cleveland, Grover, 128
Cohen, Albert, 143
Cohen, Hermann
    on God, 87–90
    hypothesis, method of, and, 86–88
    on Judaism, philosophical account of, 87–90
    Kelsen and, 83, 84–90
    Maimonides and, 88–89
    natural law rejected by, 87
    neo-Kantianism of, 86–87, 88, 89
    Strauss and, 84–85
Cohn, Haim, 287
Collingwood, R. G., 284
Cologne, Germany, 63
Constitution, American
    Henkin, L., and, 101, 114, 115, 116, 127
    Jews and, 112, 124–26, 127–28, 129, 135–36
    Reform Jewry and, 129–30, 138, 139
Constitutional Court, Austrian, 79
continuity
    domicile right as, 183–84
    of Israel, political, 198–200, 201
    Palestinians and, 199, 201, 201
    political, 198–200, 201, 204
Convention on Marriage and Human Rights, 158
cosmopolitanism, legal
    Kelsen and, 69–70, 78
    of Lauterpacht, H., 26–28, 29, 34, 40–41, 43, 44, 46–47, 73

cosmopolitanism, legal (cont.)
  national sovereignty and, 43–44
  post-World War II disappointment of, 146
Crawford, James, 16, 198–99
crimes against humanity
  in Nuremberg trials, concept of, 26
  Schwelb on, 150–53
Croatia, 252–53
CSP. *See* Christian-Social Party
Cuban Missile crisis, 260
Czechoslovakia
  Kelsen and, 63, 68
  Prague, 52–53, 63
  Schwelb and, 148–50, 153, 160–61

D'Amato, Anthony, 277
Davis, Garry, 265
de Gaulle, Charles, 188, 191, 213, 216
Dicey, A. V., 150
Le Différend (Lyotard), 44
domicile, right of, 179–80, 181
  Cassin and, 182–86, 189, 200–01, 204, 206–10,
    211, 213, 214–16
  as continuity, 183–84
  entry and, 184, 185–86, 189, 214–15
  exit and, 184–85, 186, 189–90
  nationality, law of, and, 207–10
  Palestinian, 200–01, 214–16
Dreyfusards, 285
Du Bois, W. E. B., 154
Dubnow, Simon
  autonomism of, 233–34, 235, 236
  Diasporic Jewish nationalism of, 232–34,
    235–37, 244
  Rosenne and, 232, 235–37, 244
  Versailles Conference and autonomism
    of, 234
  Zionism and, 232–33, 234–37

Eban, Abba, 37
Edel, Geert, 86, 88, 89
Egypt, 230, 268–69, 273
Eichmann, Adolf, 272, 281
Englard, Izhak, 64
entry, right of, 178–82
  Cassin on, 184, 185–86, 189
  domicile right and, 184, 185–86, 189, 214–15
  host country deciding, 180–81
  in ICCPR, 214, 215, 216
  Palestinian, 200, 214–15
  under refugee status, 180

under return, right of, 179–80, 181
  for Soviet Jews, 196–97
Eshkol, Levi, 293
Ethik des reinen Willen (Cohen, H.), 87–88
Evatt, H. V., 261
exit, right of, 181–82
  Cassin and, 184–85, 186, 189–90, 196–97
  domicile right and, 184–85, 186, 189–90
  in ICCPR, 178–79
  for Moroccan Jews, 196
  for Soviet Jews, 196–97
  in UDHR, 178

Falk, Richard, 159, 263
fascism, Austrian, 52, 62
Federal Republic of Yugoslavia (FRY), 250–53
Federation of Zionist Youth (FZY), 231
Feinberg, Nathan, 41
  on genocide, legal concept of, 16
  Kelsen and, 64–66, 67–68, 72
Florence Nightingale, 227
Forbath, William, 112
formalism, legal, 160–66, 169–72, 174
Fourth Geneva Convention, Article 49 of,
    293–94
France
  Cassin and, 187–88, 191, 193–94, 210, 213
  Jewish emancipation in, 99
  UN General Assembly in, Davis at, 265
Frankenstein, Ernst, 244
Frankfurter, Felix, 96, 112, 123, 135,
    139
Fraser, Donald, 105
Freud, Sigmund, 53
Fried, John, 152
FRY. *See* Federal Republic of Yugoslavia
*Function of Law in the International
    Community* (Lauterpacht, H.), 45, 46
FZY. *See* Federation of Zionist Youth

Garcia-Salmones Rovira, Monica, 61, 78
*A Gateway between a Distant God & a Cruel
    World* (Paz, R.), 12–13
Gaza Strip, 195, 198
General Theory of Law and State (Kelsen), 84
genocide
  legal concept of, 16
  Lemkin and, 16, 146, 152–53, 173
Genocide Convention, 146
  Rosenne and, 245, 250
  Schwelb and, 152–53

The Gentle Civilizer of Nations (Koskenniemi), 12–13, 159
German National Union of Students, 36
Germans, 290–91
   Lauterpacht, H., as, 11
   national paradigm of, Jews under, 11–12
Ginsburg, Ruth Bader, 116
God, 87–90
Goebbels, Joseph, 191
Gordon, Judah Leib, 73
Graetz, Heinrich, 288
Greek law, 287–88
Grotius, Hugo, 6, 38, 45, 46
group equality, 135–36
Guide of the Perplexed (Maimonides), 89

Hague Academy
   Cassin lectures to, 206–10, 211, 214–15
   Stone lectures to, 264, 278
Hammarskjöld, Dag, 159
Hand, Learned, 96
Harding, Don, 264
Harvard University, 162, 259, 262, 267–68
Hathaway, Oona, 26–27
Hazzard, Shirley, 143
Hebraic Political Studies field, 7
Hebrew University
   Kelsen and, 64, 67
   Lauterpacht, H., and, 28, 41
   Law Faculty of, 41, 64, 65–66, 67
Heine, Heinrich, 286
Henkin, Alice, 108
Henkin, Joshua, 96
Henkin, Louis, 94, 95–96, 100, 108, 112
   The Age of Rights, 98, 108
   AJC and, 103–4, 110–11, 121, 132, 138–40
   American Constitution and, 101, 114, 115, 116, 127
   American liberalism of, 111–17, 121–24, 138, 139–40
   on anti-colonialism, human rights and, 104
   Cassin and, 16–17, 105
   early career of, 100–2
   Frankfurter compared with, 139
   on human rights, first writings of, 102–3, 104
   with human rights, early engagement of, 102–6
   as human rights advocate, self-reinvention of, 106–9, 118
   as human rights leader, 93, 103, 121, 138
   on ICCPR, 113, 122, 189

Israel and, 109–12, 114–15, 120–21, 133–34
Jewish internationalism and, 106–9, 111, 119–21, 126, 132, 133
   on Jewish political experience, human rights and, 98–100, 102–3, 108–11, 119–21, 122
   on Jim Crow, 111–12, 123, 127
   Judaism, observant, of, 13–14, 95–96, 116, 121, 138–40
   on Judaism, human rights and, 16–17, 93–95, 96–98, 105–6, 116, 118–19, 122
   "Judaism and Human Rights," 94–95
   Lauterpacht, H., and, 113
   McGill University colloquium of, 105–6, 108–9
   on religion, human rights alternative to, 98
   The Rights of Man Today, 108–9, 113–14, 122
   Soviet Jews and, 107, 110
   on UN, 100–01, 104, 105, 110
   at Uppsala conference, 107, 108
   Zionism and, 109–12, 114, 115, 121, 122–23, 133–34, 138, 139
Hertz, Joseph, 287
Herzl, Theodor, 29, 58–59
   Altneuland, 67
   Dubnow and Zionism of, 232, 233
   Das Neue Ghetto, 65
Hitler, Adolf, 52, 63, 186–87
Hoffman, Stanley, 162
Holocaust
   Cassin and, 193, 194, 195, 202
   genocide as term and, 16
   international law after, 2, 15–16, 99
   Lauterpacht, H., and influence of, 26–27
   Rosenne on, 252
How Nations Behave (Henkin, L.), 102
Hula, Erich, 154
Human Law and Human Justice (Stone), 287–88
human rights. *See also* Henkin, Louis; Schwelb, Egon
   AJC and, 136, 137–38
   American liberalism and, 111–17, 121–24, 136
   anti-colonialism and, Henkin, L., on, 104
   International Institute for, 105
   Israel and, 94, 104, 107, 109–12, 120–21, 137–38
   Jewish historical experience and, 98–100, 106–7, 118–21, 122
   Judaism and, 93–95, 96–98, 105–6, 116, 118–19, 122
   law school courses in international, 144, 162–65

human rights (cont.)
  on mobility, myopia in, 177–78
  modern Jewish politics and, 94, 99–100,
    108–9
  natural law and, 97
  Protestant theology and, 119
  UN and, 143–44, 146–47, 152–59, 173, 179–80,
    201, 216
  Universal Declaration of, 137, 146–47,
    154–57, 161, 177, 178, 195, 198, 214
  Uppsala conference and, 107, 108
  after World War II, 146
Human Rights and International Law
  (Lauterpacht, H.), 44
*Human Rights and the International
  Community* (Schwelb), 146–47
humanism, 173–74
Humphrey, John, 152, 153–54, 155, 159
Hyderabad, 23–25, 39–40
hyphenated Americans, Jews as, 135–36, 139
hypothesis, method of, 86–88

ICCPR. *See* International Covenant on Civil
  and Political Rights
ICJ. *See* International Court of Justice
Ideal Film Renting Company, 227
idealism
  of Lauterpacht, H., liberal, 26–27
  realism and, 43, 145
  Zionism and, 25
Ignatieff, Michael, 27
immigrants, Jewish
  Kohler, M., and Marshall, L. defending, 127,
    129, 130–31
  racism against, 127
  Reform Jewry and, 129
India, 23–24, 39–40
individual and community, antinomy of,
  70–73, 74
individual rights, justice and, 272, 282–83
An International Bill of the Rights of Man
  (Lauterpacht, H.), 27–28
International Court of Justice (ICJ), 23–24,
  222
  Lauterpacht, H., on, 41
  Rosenne advising FRY at, 250–52
International Covenant on Civil and Political
  Rights (ICCPR), 198
  entry right in, 214, 215, 216
  exit right in, 178–79
  Henkin, L., on, 113, 122, 189

International Guarantees of Minority Rights
  (Stone), 290–91
International Institute for Human Rights, 105
International Law and Human Rights
  (Lauterpacht, H.), 155
internationalism, Jewish
  of AJC, human rights and, 137–38
  Henkin, L., and, 106–9, 111, 119–21, 126,
    132, 133
  Kohler, M., Marshall, L. and, 126, 132
  Zionism and, 34, 132, 133–34, 136
Inter-University Federation of Jewish Students
  of Britain and Ireland, 32–33
Introduction to the Problems of Legal Theory
  (Kelsen). *See Pure Theory of Law*
inventorying, Jewish practice of, 4
Iraq, 68
Isaacs, Isaac, 270
isolationism, 9
Israel
  AJC, Jewish liberalism and, 137–38
  Henkin, L., and, 109–12, 114–15, 120–21,
    133–34
  human rights and, 94, 104, 107, 109–12,
    120–21, 137–38
  Kelsen and institutions of, 67
  Lauterpacht, H., and independence of,
    23–25, 28, 37, 39–40
  Lauterpacht, H., identifying with, 40–41
  Law of Return in, 196–97
  MFA of, 222, 225, 245
  in occupied territories, settlements of,
    114–15, 293–94
  political continuity of, 198–200, 201
  post-1967 occupation by, 114–15, 195, 197–98,
    293–94
  Rosenne as legal adviser for, 222, 225, 245–46,
    249, 254
  Soviet Jews and, 196–97
  Stone and, 261, 268–69, 273, 274–80, 281–83,
    285, 287, 291–94, 295
  in Suez Crisis, 268–69, 273
  UN and independence of, 24, 37
Israel and Palestine (Stone), 275, 277, 292–93

Jabloner, Clemens, 61
Jackson, Robert, 1–2
Janowsky, Oscar, 290
Jenks, Wilfred, 155
Jessup, Philip, 101, 158
Jewish Agency

Lauterpacht, H., advising, 28, 35
  Rosenne at, 221–22, 239–41
  Stone advising, 276, 292
Jewish Congress Movement, 134, 135, 136
Jewish history, international law in, 5
  antiquarian approach to, 9–12
  biographical approach to, 12–13
  modernist approach to, 8–9, 12
  multidisciplinary approach to, 13
  primordialist approach to, 5–7, 12
Jewish Law, influence of, 64
Jewish primogeniture, 288
Jim Crow
  Henkin, L., on, 111–12, 123, 127
  Kohler, M., opposing, 126–27
Jordan, 277, 282
Joseph, Dov, 240–41
"Judaism and Human Rights" (Henkin, L.),
    94–95
Julius Stone (Star), 286
Jurists Uprooted (Beatson and
    Zimmermann), 10
justice
  enclaves of, 266–67, 273
  individual rights and, 272, 282–83
  Stone and, 265–67, 271–73, 281–83,
    287–88, 291
Justice for My People (Frankenstein), 244

Kant, Immanuel, 45, 187
Kelsen, Hans, 52–53
  assimilationism and, 57–63, 65, 66–67,
    69–73, 80
  from Austria, departure of, 52, 62
  Austrian Constitutional Court introduced
    by, 79
  Austrian identity of, 51, 52–53, 57–63, 64, 65,
    68, 80
  autobiography of, 61–62
  basic norm and, 85–87, 89–90
  on Christian civilization, 59–60
  Christian conversions of, 13–14, 59
  Cohen, H., and, 83, 84–90
  in Cologne, 63
  cosmopolitanism and, 69–70, 78
  descriptive period of, 53–54, 75–78, 80–81
  dualisms rejected by, 70–71, 72–73, 74,
    77
  Feinberg and, 64–66, 67–68, 72
  followers of, 54–56
  Hebrew University and, 64, 67

  on individual and community, antinomy of,
    70–73, 74
  Israeli institutions and, 67
  Jewish and Austrian identity of, 58–63, 64,
    65, 80
  Jewish identity of, 13–14, 56–57, 62, 63–69,
    80, 82–83, 84–85, 90
  on Jewish Law, influence of, 64
  Koskenniemi on, 76, 78
  Lauterpacht, H., and, 26
  on legal person, 71–73
  monism of, 53, 64, 70, 73, 77, 82
  Nazi condemnation of, 60
  normative thought of, 54, 78–81, 83
  on Nuremberg trials, 151–52
  Peace through Law, 59–60, 78
  positivism of, 52, 54–56, 57–58
  as pragmatist, 79
  in Prague, 52–53, 63
  on primitive, 75–77
  on private property, 70–71
  Prochazka and, 160–61
  progressivism of, 58, 74–80, 83, 84–85
  Pure Theory of, 52, 54–56, 57, 58, 60, 64,
    69–70, 74, 76, 77–78, 82–83, 84, 85–87, 88,
    89–90
  Pure Theory of Law, 56, 57, 58, 77–78, 79, 80
  Schmitt and, 53, 60
  on sovereignty, 73–74, 77–78, 85–86, 89
  Strauss and, 83–85, 90
  on UN Charter, 79–80
  on world community, state sovereignty and,
    73–74, 77–78
  on world peace, 79
  on world state, 77
  writing of, periods in, 53–54
  Zionism and, 17, 63–69
Kennedy, David, 76, 79, 165
Kirby, Michael, 259
Kita, Yasuo, 27
Koh, Howard, 93
Kohler, Kaufmann, 128, 129–30, 131, 138, 139
Kohler, Max, 138, 139
  AJC and, 126–27, 133, 136
  Jewish immigrants defended by, 127, 129,
    130–31
  Jewish internationalism and, 126, 132
  Jim Crow opposed by, 126–27
  Marshall and, 126–27, 129, 134, 135, 136
  Zionism and, 132, 134, 135, 136
Koskenniemi, Martti

Koskenniemi, Martti (cont.)
  The Gentle Civilizer of Nations, 12–13, 159
  on Kelsen, 76, 78
  on Lauterpacht, H., 27, 29, 30–31, 38
Kuhn, Arthur, 5–6, 12
Kunz, Josef, 54, 147, 163, 225–26

Lahav, Pnina, 8, 12
Lasson, Adolf, 71
The Last Utopia (Moyn), 100, 144
Lauterpacht, Elihu, 28–29, 31, 45, 249
Lauterpacht, Hersch Zvi, 38–39, 145
  anti-Semitism work of, 35–36
  Article 6 crafted by, 15–16
  British ideals of, 30–31
  Bundists conflict with, 33
  Carr and, 44
  *Function of Law in the International
    Community*, 45, 46
  as German, 11
  on Grotius, 45, 46
  Hebrew University and, 28, 41
  Henkin, L., and, 113
  historical method of, 38–39, 45–46
  Holocaust influencing, 26–27
  Human Rights and International Law, 44
  Hyderabad independence claims and,
    23–25, 39–40
  on ICJ, 41
  idealist legal liberalism of, 26–27
  An International Bill of the Rights of Man,
    27–28
  Inter-University Federation of Jewish
    Students addressed by, 32–33
  with Israel, identification of, 40–41
  Israeli independence and, 23–25, 28, 37,
    39–40
  Kelsen and, 26
  Koskenniemi on, 27, 29, 30–31, 38
  legal cosmopolitanism of, 26–28, 29, 34,
    40–41, 43, 44, 46–47, 73
  Lemkin and, 9, 26, 27
  natural law and, 27–28, 38, 46, 69, 76
  numerus clausus policies opposed by, 35–36
  Nuremberg trials and, 26, 47, 253–54
  Paz, R., on, 29, 73
  positivism of, 45–46
  positivism rejected by, 26–28
  Private Law Analogies, 45
  progressivism and, 75, 76
  Rosenne and, 226, 240–41, 249, 253

Schwelb and, 155
sovereignty and, 27–28, 35–36, 37–38, 46–47
Stone compared with, 262–63
territorial sovereignty and, 35–36, 37–38
on UDHR, 146, 155
at Warsaw Congress on International
  Education, 35–36
World Union of Jewish Students and, 28, 32,
  33, 34–36
Zionism of, 28–30, 31–37, 39, 41, 43, 44,
  46–47
Law of Nations, 5, 6
Law of Return, Israeli, 196–97
Lawyers Committee for Human Rights, 108
League of Nations, 99, 289–91
  Bernheim Petition to, 191
  Cassin and, 183, 187, 206, 211–12
  Cohen, A., on, 143
  sovereignty in, Jews and, 35
Legal Controls (Stone), 269–70
legalism, 160–66, 169–72, 174
Lemberg pogrom, 35
Lemkin, Raphael
  genocide and, 16, 146, 152–53,
    173
  Lauterpacht, H., and, 9, 26, 27
  Schwelb and, 152–53
Letters on Ancient and Modern Judaism
  (Dubnow), 235
Leviathan state, 187–88, 212
Levontin, Avigdor, 64
Lewis, David Levering, 127
liberalism
  American Jews and, 111–17, 123–27
  Bell on, 168–69
  of Henkin, L., American, 111–17, 121–24, 138,
    139–40
  human rights and American, 111–17,
    121–24, 136
  idealist, of Lauterpacht, H., 26–27
  Jewish, Israel and, 137–38
  progress in, Strauss on, 75, 83–84
  Reform Jewry and, 128, 130,
    138
  Zionism and, 9, 83–84
Lieblich, Eliav, 40
Liskofsky, Sidney, 103–04
Lloyd George, David, 227
Loveday (reverend), 228, 230–31
Lueger, Karl, 58–59
Lyotard, Jean-François, 44

Machiavelli, Niccolò, 84
Maimonides, 88–89
The Man Who Saved the Empire, 227
Mancini, Pasquale Stanislao, 207–08
Marshall, Louis
  AJC and, 126–27, 133
  Jewish immigrants defended by, 127, 129
  Jewish internationalism and, 126, 132
  Kohler, M., and, 126–27, 129, 134, 135, 136
  Zionism and, 132, 134, 135, 136
Masaryk, Thomas, 148–49
Mazower, Mark, 153, 173
Mazzawi, Musa, 108, 201, 216
McDougal, Myres, 159, 162
McGill University, 105–6, 108–9
McWhinney, Edward, 269–70, 281
Meir, Golda, 292
Mendes-Flohr, Paul, 285–86
Meron, Theodor, 293–94
Métall, Rudolf Aladár, 51, 54, 62
Ministry of Foreign Affairs (MFA), Israeli, 222, 225, 245
minority rights
  Jewish scholars on, 290
  Palestinian, Rawidowicz on, 294–95
  Rosenne on, 237, 243
  Stone on, 262, 271, 272, 289, 290–92
  after World War I, Jews and, 289–90
mobility, 178, 204. *See also* domicile, right of; return, right of
  Cassin and, 177–78, 195, 196, 201
  entry right in, 178–82, 184, 185–86, 189, 196–97, 200, 214–15, 216
  exit right in, 178, 181–82, 184–85, 186, 189–90, 196–97
  myopia on, in human rights law, 177–78
  Palestinian, 200, 201, 214–15
  of Soviet Jews, 195–97, 202
modernist approach, in Jewish history, 8–9, 12
monism, 53, 64, 70, 73, 77, 82
Morgenthau, Hans, 169, 262–63
Moroccan Jews, 196
Mosaic law, 6, 287–88, 291
Moskowitz, Moses, 156–57, 158
Moyn, Samuel, 173
  Christian Human Rights, 119
  The Last Utopia, 100, 144
multidisciplinary approach, in Jewish history, 13

National Association for the Advancement of Colored People (NAACP), 126
nationality, law of, 207–10
nation-state, 186–90, 214
natural law
  Cohen, H., rejecting, 87
  human rights and, 97
  Lauterpacht, H., and, 27–28, 38, 46, 69, 76
  positivism and, 46
  revival of, 25
Natural Right and History (Strauss), 84
Nazism. *See also* fascism, Austrian
  Cassin reaction to, 186–88, 191, 211–12
  Kelsen condemned under, 60
  Stone and, 272–73, 291
neo-Kantianism, 86–87, 88, 89. *See also* Kant, Immanuel
Das Neue Ghetto (Herzl), 65
Nobel Peace Prize Lecture (1968), 210–11
norm, basic, 85–86, 87, 89–90
numerus clausus policies, 35–36, 258–59, 267
Nuremberg Charter, Article 6 of, 15–16
Nuremberg Principles, 150–52
Nuremberg trials
  European-born Jewish lawyers in, 3–4
  failures of, 146
  Jackson and, 1–2
  Kelsen on, 151–52
  Lauterpacht, H., and, 3–4, 26, 47, 253–54
  Schwelb and, 150–52, 153
  Stone on, 281

occupied territories, 114–15, 195, 197–98, 293–94
Operation Agatha (Black Sabbath), 221–22
optimism, 146, 163
The Organization Man (Whyte), 143
Orwell, George, 162
Ottoman Empire, 251
Oven of Akhnai, Talmudic story of, 97
Oxford University, 258–59, 262, 269, 286–87

Paine, Thomas, 113, 114, 122
Pakistan, 23–24, 39–40
Palestine, British
  Black Sabbath in, 221–22
  Rosenne in, 238–41
  Stone and immigration to, 270

Palestine question
  Kelsen on, 67–68
  in Zionism, different opinions on, 67–68
Palestine Special Session, 241
Palestinians
  Cassin and, 178, 192, 194–96, 197–202, 213,
    215–17
  continuity and, 199, 201
  domicile right of, 200–01, 214–16
  entry right of, 200, 214–15
  minority rights of, Rawidowicz on,
    294–95
  mobility and, 178, 200, 201, 214–15
  post-1967 occupation of, 114–15, 195, 197–98,
    293–94
  return right for, 197–201, 214–16
  settlements and, 114–15, 293–94
  Stone and, 261, 277–80, 281–83, 285,
    291–94, 295
  Uppsala conference and, 108, 215–16
Paris Peace Conference, 289–90
Paz, Reut, 12–13
  on Kelsen, 77
  on Lauterpacht, H., 29, 40, 73
Peace through Law (Kelsen), 59–60, 78
Pella, Vespasian, 154
Pentateuch, 287
People in Glass Houses (Hazzard), 143
Permanent Court of International Justice,
    23, 26
person, legal, 71–73
Pettiti, Louis E., 196
pluralism, 135–36
Poland, 290–91
  Galician region of, Jews in, 34
  Lemberg pogrom in, 35
Politis, Nicolas, 172–73
positivism
  of Kelsen, 52, 54–56, 57–58
  Lauterpacht, H., and, 26–28, 45–46
  naturalism and, 46
  rejection of, 25, 26–28, 39
postcolonial states, 161
Pound, Roscoe, 259, 267–68
Prague, 52–53, 63
primitiveness, 75–77
primogeniture, Jewish, 288
primordialist approach, in Jewish history,
    5–7, 12
Prinz, Joachim, 123
private affair, Judaism as, 124, 140

Private Law Analogies (Lauterpacht, H.), 45
private property rights, 70–71
*Das Problem der Souveränität und die Theorie
    des Völkerrechts* (Kelsen), 85
Prochazka, Adolf, 160–61
progressivism, 76
  assimilationist Jews and, 75, 78–79
  descriptive, Kelsen and, 75–78, 80
  of Kelsen, 58, 74–80, 83, 84–85
  Lauterpacht, H., and, 75, 76
  normative, of Kelsen, 78–80
  primitive and, 75–77
  Strauss and, 75, 83–84
Protestant theology, 119
public/private divide, 72–73
Pure Theory. *See* Kelsen, Hans
Pure Theory of Law (Kelsen), 56, 79, 80
  assimilationist reading of, 58
  preface to, 57
  progress in, 77–78

Rabbis and Lawyers (Auerbach), 124
Rawidowicz, Simon, 294–95
realism
  idealism and, 43, 145
  Schwelb and legal, 159–60, 162–63
  Stone and, 262–63
  at Yale Law School, 159
Reconstruction Era constitutionalism, 125
Reform Jewry, 125, 127
  AJC and, 131, 132, 135, 137, 138–39
  American Constitution and, 129–30, 138,
    139
  Jewish immigrants and, 129
  liberalism and, 128, 130, 138
  Pittsburgh Platform of, 128
  Zionism and, 128, 131–32
Refugee Convention, 245
refugees. *See* mobility
Regional Guarantees of Minority Rights
    (Stone), 290–91
*Religion of Reason Out of the Sources of
    Judaism* (Cohen, H.), 84–85
return, right of
  Cassin and, 197–201, 214–15
  Cassin and International Colloquium on,
    195–96, 201
  domicile right and, 215–16
  entry right under, 179–80, 181
  Israeli, 196–97
  mobility and, 178

for Palestinians, 197–201, 214–16
UNHRC and, 179–80, 201, 216
The Rights of Man Today (Henkin, L.), 108–09, 113–14, 122
Robinson, Jacob, 225–26, 290
Roman Empire, 51
Roosevelt, Eleanor, 153
Rosenne, Shabtai, 222, 246, 250
  Black Sabbath and, 221–22
  in British Palestine, 238–41
  Dubnow and, 232, 235–37, 244
  early life of, 227–29, 230–31, 249–50, 253
  in Egypt, 230
  family of, 226–29, 230, 249–50
  Genocide Convention and, 245, 250
  on Holocaust, 252
  at ICJ, advising FRY, 250–52
  on international law, Jews and, 6–7, 12, 241–44, 245–48
  with international law, early engagement of, 223–26
  as Israeli legal adviser, 222, 225, 245–46, 249, 254
  with Jewish affairs, engagement of, 222, 224–26, 230–37
  with Jewish Agency, 221–22, 239–41
  Jewish identity of, international law and, 251–53, 254
  Lauterpacht, H., and, 226, 240–41, 249, 253
  on minority treaties, 237, 243
  obituaries for, 222
  Sephardic descent of, 251
  Suriname case of, 254
  during World War II, 229–30, 254
  Zionism of, 231–32, 235–37, 238–39, 242–43, 244, 245, 246–47
Rowson, Harry, 226–28, 229
Rowson, Sefton. *See* Rosenne, Shabtai
Rowson, Vera, 227–28, 229

Sands, Philippe, 26, 29
Sasson, Elihu, 240–41
Saul, Ben, 275
Schabas, William, 252–53
Schechtman, Joseph, 173
Schmitt, Carl, 53, 60
Schwarzenberger, Georg, 156
Schwebel, Stephen, 41
Schwelb, Egon, 144–45, 157, 167
  Cabranes on, 164–65
  Central European legalism and, 160–61

class affiliation of, 172–74
Czechoslovakia and, 148–50, 153, 160–61
emotional restraint emphasized by, 145, 158, 168, 170, 174
formalism, legalism of, 160–66, 169–72, 174
Genocide Convention and, 152–53
humanism of, 173–74
on humanity, crimes against, 150–53
international human rights course of, 144, 162–65, 171
on jurist, character of, 147–48
Kunz cited by, 147, 163
Lauterpacht, H., and, 155
legal realism and, 159–60, 162–63
Lemkin and, 152–53
Moskowitz and, 156–57, 158
Nuremberg trials and, 150–52, 153
on optimism, 146, 163
peers of, 172–73
postwar anti-utopianism and, 145–46
on professional conduct, role of, 163–64
Stoicism and, 158, 170
UDHR and, 146–47, 154–57, 161
UN, state sovereignty and, 156–58
at UN, 106, 143–44, 145, 146–47, 150–59, 167–68
at UN, postcolonial states and, 161
on UN War Crimes Commission, 150–52
World War I and, 148
during World War II, 148–50
at Yale, 159, 162–65, 171
Selden, John, 6
Sephardic Jews, 251
Serbia. *See* Federal Republic of Yugoslavia
Shachar, Yoram, 40
Shandler, Jeffrey, 4
Shapiro, Scott, 26–27
Sharett, Moshe, 221, 241, 243
Shawcross, Hartley, 47, 253–54
Shelley v. Kraemer, 101
Sidorsky, David, 110
Siehr, Kurt, 10
Simmons, Beth, 155
Simon, Leon, 237
Six-Day War, 120–21, 293
Social-Democrats, Austrian, 62
Sohn, Louis, 100, 105, 145, 157, 162, 165
sovereignty. *See also* states
  Cassin and, 186–90
  cosmopolitanism and national, 43–44
  Kelsen on, 73–74, 77–78, 85–86, 89

sovereignty (cont.)
  Lauterpacht, H., and, 27–28, 35–36, 37–38,
    46–47
  in League of Nations, Jews and, 35
  territorial, 35–36, 37–38
  UN, Schwelb, and state, 156–58
  world community and, Kelsen on, 73–74,
    77–78
  Zionism and, 25
Soviet Jews, 108
  Cassin and, 195–97, 202
  Henkin, L., and, 107, 110
  Israel and, 196–97
  mobility of, 195–97, 202
Spinoza, Benedict, 7, 45–46
Spinoza's Critique of Religion (Strauss), 83–84
Stalin, Joseph, 231
Star, Leonie, 286
  on anti-Semitism, Stone facing, 259
  on Israel, Stone and, 276, 281, 292
states
  Cassin on, 186–90, 214
  dissociation from, 204–5, 216–17
  Leviathan, 187–88, 212
  postcolonial, Schwelb and, 161
  world, 77
Steinberg, Michael, 11
Stoicism, 158, 170
Stone, Julius
  Aggression and World Order, 268, 273,
    275, 277
  anti-Semitism faced by, 258, 259–60, 269,
    270, 271, 274, 287
  *Approaches to the Notion of International
    Justice*, 266
  axionormative dissent of, 285–86, 291, 295
  background and achievements of, 257,
    258–62, 286–87
  Cuban Missile crisis and, 260
  on Eichmann, 272, 281
  extralegal, objective focus of, 264, 267–70,
    276–78, 283, 284
  Hague Academy lectures of, 264, 278
  Harvard and, 259, 262, 267–68
  Human Law and Human Justice, 287–88
  on individual rights, justice and, 272, 282–83
  international policy shaped by, 257
  inter-systemic, intercultural analysis of,
    264–65, 267, 270–71, 278–80, 283
  Israel and, 261, 268–69, 273, 274–80, 281–83,
    285, 287, 291–94, 295

Israel and Palestine, 275, 277, 292–93
  Jewish Agency advised by, 276, 292
  Jewish identity of, 273–76, 284–86,
    295
  Jewish identity of, justice and, 271–73,
    281–83, 287–88, 291
  Jewish identity of, sociological approach
    and, 257–58, 261–62, 267–83, 284, 286–87,
    289–91, 295
  Jewish primogeniture advocated by, 288
  on justice, 265–67, 271–73, 281–83,
    287–88, 291
  on justice, enclaves of, 266–67, 273
  Lauterpacht, H., compared with, 262–63
  as majoritarian, 291–94
  on minority rights, 262, 271, 272, 289,
    290–92
  Nazism and, 272–73, 291
  numerus clausus policies opposed by,
    258–59, 267
  on Nuremberg trials, 281
  as outsider, 269–70, 274, 287
  Oxford study of, 258–59, 262, 269, 286–87
  Palestinians and, 261, 277–80, 281–83, 285,
    291–94, 295
  pragmatism of, 260–61, 262
  realism and, 262–63
  sociological approach of, 257, 259, 260–61,
    262–67
  Suez Crisis and, 268–69, 273
  on UN Charter, 268–69
  at University of Sydney, 257, 259–60,
    269
  White House–Kremlin hotline and, 257,
    260–61
  Zionism of, 291–94
Strauss, Leo
  Cohen, H., and, 84–85
  Kelsen and, 83–85, 90
  Natural Right and History, 84
  on progress, 75, 83–84
  Spinoza's Critique of Religion, 83–84
  on Zionism, 83–84
Suez Crisis, 268–69, 273
Suriname, 254
sutler, 51
Syria, 23–24

Talmud, 97, 294
Taylor, Telford, 114
Torah, 64

UDHR. *See* Universal Declaration of Human
Rights
UN. *See* United Nations
UN Palestine Partition Plan, 68
UNHRC. *See* United Nations Human Rights
Committee
United Nations (UN)
African-American civil rights and, 154
AJC and creation of, 137
Cassin at, 177
Davis at, 265
Hazzard and, 143
Henkin, L., on, 100–01, 104, 105, 110
human rights and, 143–44, 146–47, 152–59,
173, 179–80, 201, 216
Israel, Stone, and, 261
Israeli independence and, 24, 37
Kelsen on Charter of, 79–80
Palestine Partition Plan of, 68
Palestine Special Session of, 241
postcolonial states and, 161
return right and, 179–80, 201, 216
Schwelb at, 106, 143–44, 145, 146–47, 150–59,
161, 167–68
state sovereignty and, 156–58
Stone on Charter of, 268–69
War Crimes Commission of, Schwelb on,
150–52
United Nations Conference on International
Organization, 1
United Nations Human Rights
Commission, 155
United Nations Human Rights Committee
(UNHRC), 179–80, 201, 216
Universal Declaration of Human Rights
(UDHR), 137, 198
Cassin and, 177, 195, 214
exit right in, 178
Lauterpacht, H., on, 146, 155
pessimistic reaction to, 146–47
Schwelb and, 146–47, 154–57, 161
universal rights, 69–70
University of Sydney, 257, 259–60, 269
Upper Silesia, German-Polish Convention on,
290–91
Uppsala conference, 107, 108, 215–16

Verdross, Alfred, 54
Versailles, Treaty of, 289–90
Versailles Conference, 234
Vienna School, of international law, 54–56

Vietnam war, 113, 114, 117
Von Bernstorff, 78, 159

Warsaw Congress on International Education,
35–36
Weber, Max, 159
Weis, Paul, 144, 197–98, 215–16, 245
Were the Minorities Treaties a Failure?
(Robinson), 290
West Bank, 195, 293–94
Westlake, John, 41
Weyl, Joseph, 149
White House-Kremlin hotline, 257, 260–61
Whyte, William, 143
Wilson, Woodrow, 1–2, 136, 148–49
Winter, Jay, 177
Wise, Stephen, 123
Wittgenstein, Ludwig, 18
Wolf, Lucien, 290
world community, 73–74, 77–78
world peace, 79
world state, 77
World Union of Jewish Students
Lauterpacht, H., and, 28, 32, 33, 34–36
numerus clausus policies opposed by, 35–36
World War I
Cassin and, 184–85, 190, 205–6
minority rights after, Jews and, 289–90
Paris Peace Conference following, 289–90
Schwelb and, 148
Zionism and, 134, 136
World War II
human rights after, 146
Rosenne during, 229–30, 254
Schwelb during, 148–50

Yale Law School
legal realists of, 159
Schwelb at, 159, 162–65, 171
Yerushalmi, Yosef, 93
Yugoslavia, former, 250–53

Zangwill, Israel, 228
Zimmermann, Reinhard, 10–12
Zionism, 25, 228
AJC and, 131, 132, 133–34, 135, 136, 137–38
Basle Program of, 233, 246–47
Brandeis and, 134, 135–36
Cassin and, 191–93, 195, 212–14
Dubnow and, 232–33, 234–37
on Europe, dualism in, 67

Zionism (cont.)
FZY, 231
group equality and, 135–36
Henkin, L., and, 109–12, 114, 115, 121, 122–23,
133–34, 138, 139
Herzlian, 29, 58–59, 65, 67, 232, 233
internationalist, 34
Jewish internationalism and, 34, 132,
133–34, 136
Kelsen and, 17, 63–69
Kohler, M., and, 132, 134, 135, 136
of Lauterpacht, H., 28–30, 31–37, 39, 41, 43,
44, 46–47

liberal model and, 9
Marshall and, 132, 134, 135,
136
on Palestine question, different opinions in,
67–68
pluralism and, 135–36
Reform Jewry and, 128, 131–32
of Rosenne, 231–32, 235–37, 238–39, 242–43,
244, 245, 246–47
of Stone, 291–94
Strauss on, 83–84
World War I and, 134, 136
Zweig, Stefan, 52, 78–79

For EU product safety concerns, contact us at Calle de José Abascal, 56–1°,
28003 Madrid, Spain or eugpsr@cambridge.org.

www.ingramcontent.com/pod-product-compliance
Ingram Content Group UK Ltd.
Pitfield, Milton Keynes, MK11 3LW, UK
UKHW020942270426
470322UK00029B/348